FLASHBACKS
IN FILM

FLASHBACKS IN FILM

MEMORY & HISTORY

MAUREEN TURIM

Routledge   New York & London

Published in 1989 by

Routledge
An imprint of Routledge, Chapman and Hall, Inc.
29 West 35 Street
New York, NY 10001

Published in Great Britain by

Routledge
11 New Fetter Lane
London EC4P 4EE

Library of Congress Cataloging in Publication Data

Turim, Maureen Cheryn, 1951–
    Flashbacks in film: memory and history / Maureen Turim.
        p.   cm.
    Includes index.
    ISBN 0-415-90005-0; ISBN 0-415-90006-9 (pbk.)
    1. Flashbacks.   2. Memory in motion pictures.   3. Motion pictures—History.
    I. Title.
PN1995.9.F56T87   1989
791.43′015—dc20   89-6343
                                                                                    CIP

British library cataloguing in publication data also available.

In memory of my father, Sol Turim,
a generous and loving man.

Contents

Acknowledgments

I wish to gratefully acknowledge the help of many individuals and institutions in the writing of this book. A semester fellowship from the State University of New York-Binghamton allowed for important research at archives and time to devote to the early stages of its writing. Several archives provided access to films that is so essential to such research: the Wisconsin Center for Film and Theater Research, the Library of Congress Motion Picture Division, the British Film Institute, the UCLA Film Archive, and the film collection at l'Université de Paris III. These archives are a treasure and their staffs' encouragement of scholarly research vital to this endeavor.

A number of friends and colleagues deserve special thanks for their suggestions of films to include in this study and for their help in access to prints or tapes; let me single out especially the generosity of Kristin Thompson, Dana Polan, David Bordwell, Richard Abel, Michael Renov, Frank Tomasulo, Mike Walsh, Paulo Cherchi Usai, Michel Marie, Sylvie Pliskin, Michèle Lagny, and Scott Nygren. Dana Polan and Richard Abel deserve an additional thanks for their careful readings of my manuscript; I am grateful to have had readers who appreciated what I was trying to do while making expert suggestions. I wish to thank all my students who have challenged and delighted me through their mutual interest in cinema and in particular two students helped in the initial stages of filmography and review gathering, Lisa Dickerson and Jim Fanning. My thanks to Herman Paikoff, formerly of Pathé News and currently photographer at SUNY-Binghamton, for his help with photo reproductions.

To Diane Gibbons whose expert copyediting comes with the added plus of a fine background in film history and to Bill Germano who has been a most supportive editor throughout the entire process, my sincere thanks.

Personal support is also a most crucial factor, especially when it comes with intellectual stimulation, so let me also thank my friends, particularly Diane Waldman, Fina Bathrick, Elly Spiegel, David Tafler, Donna Devoist, Sidonie Smith, Don Preziosi, Fred Garber, Jane Collins, Deborah Hertz, Larry Gottheim, and Josephine Gear. To my mother Ruthanne and my sisters Shereen and Dona, love and thanks. To Scott whose love and intelligence are equally invaluable to me, and to Mika, whose babyhood is a constant flashback memory to my own as well as a discovery of her unique personality, you are special indeed.

1

Definition and Theory of the Flashback

Why a study devoted to the flashback in film? Why single out one narrative device and trace its use over eighty years of cinematic expression? The selective focus on the trope of the flashback is a way of slicing through the enormity of film history, a method for considering the aesthetic history of film as just such a diverse composite of the history of filmic forms. We will ask what role the flashback played in the history of film, in the life of various film aesthetics and particularly in the development in cinematic modernism. As complex as these issues are, the goal of this book is not simply that of a focused aesthetic history.

The flashback is particularly interesting to theoretical conceptualization of film. The flashback is a privileged moment in unfolding that juxtaposes different moments of temporal reference. A juncture is wrought between present and past and two concepts are implied in this juncture: memory and history. Studying the flashback is not only a way of studying the development of filmic form, it is a way of seeing how filmic forms engage concepts and represent ideas.

Most readers are probably familiar with what we mean by a flashback in film. For many, Hollywood classics have defined this familiarity with the flashback technique including such famous examples in Orson Welles's *Citizen Kane*, (1941), cited in virtually every dictionary of film that attempts a definition of the flashback.[1] A body of literature discussing the flashback exists, ranging from scriptwriting manuals to introductory books on film study.[2] In its classic form, the flashback is introduced when the image in the present dissolves to an image in the past, understood either as a story-being-told or a subjective memory. Dialogue, voice-over, or intertitles that mark anteriority through language often reinforce the visual cues representing a return to the past. Both earlier and later in film history, other forms of flashbacks occur that are less obviously marked. We therefore need a more general definition for the flashback that includes all types of flashbacks. In its most general sense, a flashback is simply an image or a filmic segment that is understood as representing temporal occurrences anterior to those in the images that preceded it. The flashback concerns a representation of the past that intervenes within the present flow of film narrative. As we shall see shortly, there is a great deal more to be said about the definition of the flashback and the implications of this term.

Memory, in its psychoanalytic and philosophical dimensions, is one of the concepts inscribed in flashbacks. Memory surges forth, it strengthens or protects or it repeats and haunts. A plethora of depicted memories are offered across the history of flashback use, each slightly different in form, ideology, tone. Some are subjective, interiorized; others represent a telling-in-language whose degree of subjectivity might be considerably less. To analyze this constant play of difference, the films need be examined as fragments of a cinematic discourse on the mind's relationship to the past and on the subject's relationship to telling his or her past.

The cinematic presentation of memory in these films can be compared with the knowledge proposed by various disciplines that research and speculation on memory processes. We shall find that this comparison shows some mirroring and some fascinating discrepancies, some anticipations of the future of science by art and some anachronisms used blithely because they correspond to some dramatic imperative of a given mode of fiction.

If flashbacks give us images of memory, the personal archives of the past, they also give us images of history, the shared and recorded past. In fact, flashbacks in film often merge the two levels of remembering the past, giving large-scale social and political history the subjective mode of a single, fictional individual's remembered experience. This process can be called the "subjective memory," which here has the double sense of the rendering of history as a subjective experience of a character in the fiction, and the formation of the Subject in history as the viewer of the film identifying with fictional character's positioned in a fictive social reality. The play of different voices within film narration, however, implies certain departures or divisions within this formation of subjectivity. Even flashbacks that are themselves marked by subjectivity or the single focalization of a character may engender a representation of history not so subjectively circumscribed, or so unified. The telling or remembering of the past within a film can be self-conscious, contradictory, or ironic. Some flashback narratives actually take as their project the questioning of the reconstruction of the historical. A close study of the variations in flashbacks is actually a means of questioning the conceptual foundations of history in its relationship to narrative and narrative in its relationship to history.

The goal of this study is to produce a multidimensional overview of the functioning of flashback. Multidimensional because film history, film theory, film analysis merge in the investigation of the flashback and open to the issues of social history and philosophy. Multidimensional also due to the manner in which the analysis of the films themselves is considered a project of multiple perspectives. This first chapter aims to define these goals, as emblemized by five words— form, image, voice, memory, and history.

Etymology of the term "Flashback"

One aspect of a definition and theory of the flashback as a cinematic device is the etymology of the term itself. The term "flashback" is a marvelously appropriate turn-of-the-century coinage, sparked with the modern notions of speed, movement, energy, of the relativity of spatio-temporal relationships and the vicissitudes of mental processes. How did these connotations come to reside in this particular word, and how did it come to be used as a cinematic term?

We know for certain that the term flashback is highly derivative of certain uses of the verbal and nominative form of "flash," but other aspects of the etymology are more speculative and arbitrary. The term "flashback," probably came to its cinematic context in a migration from mechanics and physics, where the term "flash" and the phrase "to flash back" were in general usage at the turn of the twentieth century. "Flash," long used to describe a brief interval of light, as in "lightning flashes," had come to be used to describe the brief and violent consequences of combustion. Flash was therefore applied to explosions and the firing of engines. "To flash back" evolved to indicate a kind of misfiring, as in the example from the *Encylopaedia Britanica* of 1902 cited in the *O.E.D.*: "A still further addition of air causes the mixture to become so highly charged that it flashes back into the tube of the burner."[3] This evolved, according to the *O.E.D.*, into the nominative form, at first hyphenated: "the highly flammable vapor of petrol and a 'flash-back' resulted in the total destruction of the car" *(Motoring Annual)*.[4]

Beginning around the mid-nineteenth century, "flash" comes to mean a quick glance, as in the following examples the O.E.D. cites from literature: "Cyril flashed upon him one of his droll glances, and laughed" (M. Gray, *Silence of Dean Maitland*, 1844); "The young man flashed his insolent eyes at her," (R. Langbridge, *Flame & Flood*, 1903). "Flash" becomes connected to vision, paving the way for the figuration of memory inherent in the cinematic flashback.

This combination of brief instances of light, of explosive power, and of the change in direction and quality of a glance, are appropriate antecedents to the term flashback in its cinematic sense. The O.E.D. gives the cinematic definition as follows:

flashback, *sb.* [f. the verbal phr. * *to flash back*], . . . **2.** *Cinema:* A scene which is a return to a previous action in the film, a * CUT-BACK; hence a revival of the memory of past events, as in a pictorial or written presentation, . . .

    1916 *Variety,* 13 Oct. 28/4 In other words the whole thing is a flash-back of the episodes leading up to her marriage. **1928** J. Gallishaw *Only two ways to write a story* I. vii. 177 With *Sunk* the method of presentation was chronological . . . In the case of *Paradise Island* the method is reversed. The order instead of being chronological is anti-chronological: It is the flash-back method. **1934** H.G. Wells *Exper. Autobiogr.* II. vii. 486 When goddesses and Sea Ladies vanish and a flash back to the ancestral chimpanzee abolishes the magic caverns of Venus, human beings arrive. **1947** *Times* I Nov. 6/4 The film relates, in a prolonged flash-back how the innocent Indian became corrupted by bewildering contact with those supposed to be his superiors in civilization. **1957** *Times Lit. Suppl.* 26 July 453/2 In his new novel . . . [he] uses with enviable ease a complicated system of flash-backs (p. 1099).

The *O.E.D.* definition seems to confirm the hypothesis that the term flashback was first used in its sense of narrative returns to the past in reference to film, rather than other forms of storytelling. Literature and theater certainly used techniques similar to the flashback before cinema, but the etymology of this term for a return to a narrative past inserted in a narrative present is apparently derived from the speed with which cinematic editing was able to cut decisively to another space and time. Flash—the audience was transported in the movie's time machine—back in time. It is my sense that only after the term "flashback" was accepted in film criticism and screenwriting did it attain a more general application to literature and theater, both to describe contemporaneous works, and to be retrospectively applied to similar techniques of narration in earlier poems, novels, and plays.

Eventually "flashback" becomes incorporated into literary terminology, and its probable etymology as a cinematic term is not necessarily noted, as is indicated by the "plot" entry in M.H. Abrams's *A Glossary of Literary Terms*:

> In the novel, the modern drama, and especially the motion picture, exposition is sometimes managed by flashbacks: interpolated narratives or scenes (which may be justified as a memory or a revery, or as a confession by one of the characters) which represent events that happened before the point at which the work opened. Arthur Miller's play *Death of a Salesman* and Ingmar Bergman's film *Wild Strawberries* make persistent and skillful use of this device.[5]

Abrams's definition, in merely describing the "flashback" as occurring in the novel, the modern drama, and the motion picture gives us no sense that whatever literary and theatrical precedents there were for the concept, the term "flashback" was not apparently used until the advent of cinema and then only ten or fifteen years after the first filmic flashbacks appeared.

A more detailed look at the filmmakers' introduction of the technique and the critics' introduction of the term "flashback" will occur in chapter two, where it will be treated as a part of the historical development of the technique rather than as the specific etymology of the term. We will also examine the interplay between film and literature later in this chapter, as well as the next one. Suffice it to say for now that except for the earliest period of flashback films (before 1915), films of the avant-garde, and more recent modernist films, the "flash" presented in films is often a rather slow dissolve and that the audience is offered explanatory intertitles or verbal support to smooth the time travel. Still, the term "flashback" that gained currency in the late teens and early twenties marks a recognition that something particularly transformative and jarring occurred in cinema's montage of disparate temporalities in disjunct order.

The etymology of the term "flashback" includes a fascinating migration into our language beyond its original reference to narrative technique. It has now been adopted by psychology to refer to the spontaneous recall of a memory image, especially in the context of a war trauma, in which former soldiers are said to have "battlefield flashbacks." "Drug flashback" may have started as a counter-culture slang term, but it is now used by the medical profession to describe recurring effects of drug experiences. The phrase even has a more general colloquial use to describe an individual's personal memories, often shortened as the phrase "I just flashed on" (". . . what we were doing last year at this time" or ". . . the last time I was in Y's house," etc.). This colloquial use of the term indicates how movies as popular culture begin to affect the way people think about their own experience. Cinematic renderings of storytelling and memory processes may have borrowed from literature and sought to reproduce human memory mimetically, but ironically, the cinematic presentation of the flashback affects not only how modern literature is organized and how plays are staged, but perhaps also how audiences remember and how we describe those memories.

The Question of Formalism and the Device

The analysis of flashbacks in film is first of all a history of formal changes in storytelling techniques. As such, this study owes much to Russian formalist methodology in establishing a theory and method for analyzing the permutations of form found in flashback films. The formalists introduced the basic distinction in terminology between story and plot.[6] The term "story" refers to narrative events as understood in a "real" temporality, a logic of linearity and causality that refers to the ordering of time in the "natural" world. Plot is the inscription of events in their actual presentation in the narrative (the book as read or film as viewed). Thus plot order can vary from story order to various effects, and story order is often left for the reader/viewer to conceptualize according to different cues of dating and reference.

Another concept Russian formalism introduced was the notion of a "device," a construct within form that complicates the formal patterning of the textual object, providing form with variations. The flashback can be seen as one such device, as it rearranges plot order. In some ways the device is similar to the notion of the figure within earlier rhetorical theory, but it is at once a larger category and one which has a different status. Rhetoric in the earlier tradition saw figures as creating meanings that the reader/analyst's job was to explicate and evaluate. The formalists inverted the device/signification relationship previously assumed in explanations of how texts functioned. Content exists to naturalize or justify the device, except in cases where the device is bared in displays of narrative reflexivity.[7] The great contribution of early formalism was to accentuate *another* history of textual development by inverting the value assigned to content over form.

Recently, a "neo-formalism" has been introduced into American film theory by David Bordwell and Kristin Thompson which makes much use of this story/plot

distinction and its theoretical consequences, as well as the theory of fictional devices.[8] Their work demonstrates the continued significance of these principles as
fundamental to the theory of narration.

Returning to Abrams's gloss of the term "flashback," we can see how his treatment
of flashbacks as a device of narrative exposition subscribes to the formalist inversion.
According to his view of narrative construction, such expository devices must be
naturalized or as he says, "justified" somehow.[9] Flashbacks typically hide their
formal function, he says, by being presented as memories, dreams, or confessions.
This formalist explanation only begins to suggest the complex weave of factors that
are at play in the evolution of narrative structures.

While acknowledging the debt to formalist theory, let me also suggest that the
formalism that informs this study is not a formalism conceived of as separate from
or in opposition to a larger sense of historical development; quite the contrary. My
premise is rather that the history of the flashback from 1902 through 1985 is also a
complex fragment of more general developments within film history and social
history. By slicing through film history focusing on a single narrative technique we
can examine important changes in cinematic representation and ideology, not always
discussed in formalist studies as such.

We can easily suggest that the flashback developed as a means of mimetic
representation of memory, dreams, or confession, and in so doing we are not
necessarily returning to an outmoded thematic treatment of technique. We can
instead see flashbacks simultaneously as both devices to be covered with referential
and narrative justification and as a means of portraying thought processes or circuitous investigations of enigmas. We can see that it is this weave of motivation that
makes the inscription of flashbacks in fact so fascinating.

We might also extrapolate a complex pattern of evolution and influence among
novel, play, and film. Film influences the modern novel to duplicate a cinematic
sense of the flashback mimetically, while the traditional novel, especially the 19th-
century novel, can be seen as already containing the literary equivalent of a filmic
flashback, though "naturalized" in language.[10]

The history of the flashback device is not linear, however, and formalist method
can help overcome a tendency to make history into a linear or developmental
progression. The chronological organization of this study, in fact, serves to point
out the asynchronous and paradigmatic aspects of the history of this device. The
development of the flashback is not a linear progression from an awkward form to
an increasingly complex and sophisticated inscription. If we can apply terms to
periods of flashback uses like "primitive" "classical," and "modernist," we also find
that there are asynchronic developments that place some of the most modernist and
innovative uses of the flashbacks in films of the twenties. The modernist innovations
of flashbacks during the sixties are a reprise of the flashback concepts developed in
the twenties avant-garde. Further, the earliest flashbacks of silent American films
are, as we shall see, rich and suggestive images. Though they may appear more
simple in form (a single shot tableau or a reprise of shots already seen) this inherent

simplicity of imagery actually functions to create an expansion of meanings. These tableaux function as context-dependent signifiers and concentrated junctures in narrative coding. The flashbacks of the Hollywood sound period present a different kind of semiotic complexity, for the sound/image relationships weave between different temporalities and focalizations. The most recent Hollywood flashbacks, conversely, are often less sophisticated than those found in films of earlier periods; they are redundant in their internal coding and serve primarily to deliver missing narrative exposition. So this study poses the question of why and how certain forms appear at certain historical moments in different cultures. We will see that there are prevailing philosophies and ideologies that favor flashback narration in some periods and discourage it in others.

The link between the 19th-century novel and early film was astutely made by Sergei Eisenstein in his essay,"Dickens, Griffith and the Film Today."[11] Eisenstein cites passages from *A Tale of Two Cities*, *Nicholas Nickleby*, and *Hard Times* to show literary equivalents to cinematic montage. Parallel montage, the cutting from one series of actions in one space to another simultaneous series in another space, is the main object of Eisenstein's attention. He also discusses the use of "close-up" details in descriptive passages and the montage insert of an element of the action in a kind of "skipped" order. Eisenstein mentions Stefan Zweig's discussion of the masked autobiographical memory traces that give *David Copperfield* a richness of details as it describes the hero's reminiscences.[12] Flashback narration as such, however, is not one of the elements that Eisenstein discusses as a point of comparison between Dickens and Griffith, though it certainly is among their shared narrative techniques; temporal shifts are less Eisenstein's concern in this essay than are spatial shifts and metaphoric montage.

The literary equivalent to the flashback is often less distinct and abrupt than the cinematic flashback in its temporal shifts. Verbal storytelling can ease temporal shifts through the sustaining power of the narrative voice, whether that of authorial omniscience or of a character in first-person narration. An arsenal of verb tenses and qualifying clauses render these shifts as an invisible act of language. The concept "flashback" as developed by the cinema makes us more aware of these temporal shifts in literary narration. After cinema makes the flashback a common and distinctive narrative trait, audiences and critics were more likely to recognize flashbacks as crucial elements of narrative structure in other narrative forms. This may be particularly true for the popular conception of narrative temporality among a general audience, but it is perhaps also a factor in scholarly recognition of modes of narrative temporality, first in formalist literary theory and more recently in structuralist theory. Both the formalists of the early years of the 20th-century and the post-World War II structuralists developed their narrative theories with film as a common cross-reference to their usually primary focus on literary narration. As Gérard Genette acknowledges in the context of a discussion of the contribution of the Russian formalists, "Everyone knows that the birth of the cinema altered the status of literature: by depriving it of certain of its functions, but also by giving it some of its own means."[13] The flashback may well be one of the functions that cinema altered and gave back to literature. It seems likely that the manner in which the cinematic flashback manipulates narrative temporality highlights literature's differential treatment of temporal modalities.

Genette's Delineation of Narrative Temporality

Structuralist approaches to narrative owe much to the formalist tradition of narrative theory, but structuralism, coupled with semiotics, makes a new contribution to our understanding of the basic ways in which texts function. First, structure is for the most part not isolated within structuralism the way form is within formalism. Structures function, they generate meaning. The tendency to replace the notion of "structure" with that of "structuration" in more recent structuralist writing indicates a movement towards a more dynamic concept of textual processes, a more advanced semiotics. Two major figures in structuralist and semiotic theory, Gérard Genette and Roland Barthes, introduced a series of concepts concerning narrative textuality that provide a background against which a theory of the flashback can be constructed. I will therefore summarize briefly the relevant aspects of their approaches to the text. We should keep in mind, however, that their models are usually literary, especially significant in light of the preceding discussion of the difference, historically and semiotically, between literary and filmic texts.

In his essay "Discours du récit" in *Figures III*, Genette considers the ordering of narrative events one of the basic aspects of narrative construction.[14] He establishes a series of useful terms to describe variations in order. "Anachrony" is the general term he proposes for any temporal rearrangement, while "analepse" indicates a movement from a narrative present to the past (as in a flashback) and "prolepse" indicates a movement from a narrative present to a disjunct future (as in a flashforward) (pp. 79–82). Both the analepse and prolepse can be distinguished further by the opposition interior/exterior; an interior analepse is one that returns to a past of the fiction that remains within the temporal period of the rest of the narration. All flashbacks which repeat incidents narrated previously or referred to elliptically within the prior linear development of the narration are interior analepses. Exterior analepses jump back to a time period prior to and disjunct from the moment of the narrative's beginning.

The interior/exterior distinction is related to Genette's notion of the "portée" of the analepse, that is, how long ago the past event occurred. Flashbacks can skip back over years, decades, days, hours, or just a few moments. "Amplitude" is Genette's term for the duration of the event within the analepse, or to put it more simply, how much of the past is told in the flashback. A flashback can cover a period of time in the past understood as being several years long or conversely, just a few moments (pp. 89–92). The term "duration" then is freed to mean the actual length of the flashback as it is told. In literature this can be measured in lines or pages, while in film we speak of minutes. Each of these concepts, amplitude, portée, and duration, is significant in the analysis of the flashback as a narrative device; each not only contributes to the more precise description of differences between flashbacks, but the nature of the structural view implied in these terms allows us to conceive of the flashback in the context of the narrative structure as a whole.

Genette also develops the notion of ellipses (periods of time that are left out of narration) beyond its definition in standard literary analysis. We can combine these terms to formulate analytical statements about flashbacks; for example, we find that analepses sometimes retrospectively fill in ellipses. This combination of devices is one of the ways narratives build suspense by withholding the revelation of information until an efficacious moment, often the climax of the story. The combination of terms can also provide a description of another kind of flashback; we can say that in these cases analepses themselves contain ellipses. Sometimes flashbacks carry this to an extreme, bracketing several incidents together to relate the past paradigmatically. The incidents narrated within the analepse can themselves be organized achronologically.

Genette often diagrams passages from literature as part of his analysis of their structure, creating a visual description of order, portée, amplitude, and duration. I will use similar diagrams in this book to explain and amplify a point I wish to make about flashback structure.

Genette's purpose in *Figures III* seems divided between the illustration of types of temporal organization and the analysis of the function of specific types in Proust. This division in his theoretical purpose has two consequences, the first of which is that his terminology is cumbersome, especially in transliteration into English. While a passage from Proust can be used to explain the notion of amplitude, the converse is not so evident. In actual textual analysis, one can speak directly and perhaps more convincingly of the actual arrangement of temporality in the passage. It therefore seems unnecessary to use Genette's terms for the dimensions of flashbacks in all the actual analyses in this book—"amplitude" or "portée" can be discussed in simple language, by analyzing, for example, how a certain flashback inserts a reference to a day in time several years earlier, for example. This seems more direct than saying the amplitude of the flashback is restricted (one day) while its portée is fairly extensive (several years). The decision on my part to use more direct language may have the unfortunate consequence of making what are elements of the theoretical dimensions of temporal organization seem like mere description; it is therefore in reference to Genette's exposition of what is at stake for narrative in temporal organization that I hope such specific analyses of analepse structure can be read.[15]

The second drawback to Genette's project is its potential for remaining at the level of typology. Genette's major contribution in "Discours du récit" is not the typology itself, but his sensitive analysis of Proust's language in relationship to temporality, its rich comparison with a wide range of literature, and the theoretical speculations that occur over the course of the essay. Genette demonstrates how much the organization of events in narrative can vary and how significant this process of variation can be. Ultimately, this essay points out much of what is most innovative about Proust's writing. In abstracting the level of temporal organization from its naturalized embedding in the narrator's voice, Genette points to how Proust's work achieves its density in constructing time, language, and subjective experience. Though the distinctions Genette introduces are mostly applied to examples from literature, they allow us to develop a concept of a specifically filmic treatment of narrative time.[16]

This relevance to film analysis is suggested indirectly by Genette in the selection of a quote from Christian Metz at the very opening of "Discours du récit":

> [Narrative is] a doubly temporal sequence, ... There is the time of that which is told and the time of the plot (the time of the signified and the time of the signifier). This duality is not only that which makes possible all temporal distortions that are commonly found in narratives (three years in the life of the hero summarized in two lines of a novel, or in a few shots of a montage sequence in cinema, etc.); more fundamentally it invites us to remark that one of the functions of narrative is to create one time in another time.[17]

While Genette goes on from here to discuss that filmic unfolding is perhaps more fixed than reading time, he accepts the basic parallel between the two narrative processes. Is the figure of duality in itself adequate to describe narrative temporality? Has the binary opposition of the formalist story-plot distinction reemerged as the image of a dual narrative temporality? Similarly, Gilles Deleuze introduces the term "bifurcation" in his *Cinéma 1: L'Image-Temps* to discuss the temporality of the flashback, though he means for the term to indicate a multiple splitting beyond the pair of temporalities bifurcation implies.[18] While this duality may be a basic structuring principle of film that the flashback makes particularly evident, temporality in the filmic narrative may not be so simply double. Analysis of focalization, as proposed by Marc Vernet, is one way of modifying the notion of dual temporality in film: this concept becomes extremely useful in his analysis of the function of voice-off narration in the flashback sequences of film noir.[19] In a more general sense, when we consider narrative as a weave of voices and as a construction of narrative codes as introduced by Roland Barthes, we can see how temporality is multiply inscribed.

Barthes's Narrative Codes and Temporality

Roland Barthes's work on narrative coding, first in a series of articles, then in his book *S/Z,* is another structural view of the ordering of narrative exposition.[20] Less concerned with temporality per se than is Genette, Barthes nonetheless provides important constituents of our theory of the flashback by defining narrative as organized by five different codes, or sets of information. Barthes's analysis in *S/Z* strives in his reading of Balzac's "Sarrasine," to counteract the linearity he sees as recapitulated in the traditional *"explication des textes"* as well as in prior structural studies that stop at "the major structures" (pp. 3–21, 90). This goal becomes all the more difficult since the analysis itself proceeds through the short story from phrase to phrase in order to comment upon the "lexias" of the text, small units of coded significations. Yet Barthes insists he wants to disperse the text. His phrase is *"étoilé,"* which is rendered in the English translation as "starred"; this unfortunately suggests "marking" rather than the French connotation of a systematically spread out universe of stars (pp. 13–14). His goal is to avoid "assembling" the text, which leads him to statements like the following when speaking of sequential actions: "we shall not attempt to put them in any order." Barthes wishes to highlight "the plural meaning entangled" in actions (pp. 14–15). He contributes to a theory of the flashback precisely because in delineating five narrative codes he breaks with a simple story/plot polarity and provides a more multi-faceted view of narrative inscription, reference, and signification. Barthes's analysis highlights other functions that we might consider for the flashback besides that of affecting order, and allows us to consider temporality itself as more multiple.

A linear, causal temporality is implicit in the proairetic code, or the code of actions as it can be called. This linear sequence of cause and effect forms a hypothetical logic, a kind of assumed background against which narrative events unfold. It is based on a sense of the "way things work in the real world," from the way a street is crossed to what happens when an engine fails on a plane. It borrows heavily from the physical properties of existence and movement in time and space, what might be called the "laws of nature." This logic of time and space is ultimately what helps the viewer to distinguish a flashback from a purely imaginary sequence or an arbitrary narrative disruption. The abstract logic of a hypothetical time-line of events is a necessary prerequisite to understanding a narrative in which any elements are left out or told in an altered chronology. We acquire this abstract logic initially by experiencing chronologies both as observers of the world and as consumers of chronologically narrated tales. This learned expectation which develops as our abstract logic for understanding stories can be referred to indirectly and differentially by the achronological tale, the fantastic or the absurd story. If the logic of narrative is set up against the physical properties of the world as we know it, the play of narrative is as departure and deviation.

Many kinds of flashbacks are, in addition, hermeneutically determined. The hermeneutic code, or code of enigmas, is one way in which narrative organizes the exposition of events so as to keep interest invested in a posed question, the answer to which is delayed. Barthes sees it as the code most intimately entwined with the proairetic code; in his section called, "The Full Score," he develops an analogy to musical composition that implies a hierarchy of relations amongst the codes, with the proairetic and the hermeneutic forming a combined flow that sustains the more flashy and disjunct flourishes of the other three codes (pp. 28–30).

Some flashbacks directly involve a quest for the answer to an enigma posed in the beginning of a narrative through a return to the past. The frame-tale which opens with a consequence, such as murder, the erection of a monument, etc., and then flashes back to tell how or why this event came to be, is one example. Another is the narrative which employs a flashback just prior to the climatic revelation of the enigma, to provide a missing aspect of the enigma. Other narratives use a series of flashbacks to develop an enigma and delay its resolution before reaching the final flashback of revelation, or conversely, revealing the solution to the enigma by other means.

Flashbacks can also be important sources of association of a character or place with certain connotations, a process Barthes calls the semic code. By suddenly presenting the past, flashbacks can abruptly offer new meanings connected to any person, place, or object. Flashbacks then gain a particularly rich dimension in the coding of the psychology of character, and because their evidence is the past, they immediately imply a psychoanalytic dimension of personality.

Flashbacks can be devoted to citing historical and scientific knowledge of the culture within fiction, Barthes's referential code. As we shall see in the course of the analyses of specific films, flashbacks sometimes are the primary sites for fixing referential meaning in texts which otherwise evade direct references to history. They become a means for developing an ideology of history that colors the "eternal" or "timeless" connotations evoked by certain types of stories. This is why I have chosen the phrase "subjectivizing of history" to explore the function of flashbacks in creating specific ideologies of history.

Every flashback draws an antithesis between past and present, but there are various ways this antithesis can be animated within what Barthes calls the symbolic coding of the narrative, the code that constructs the textual play of power and desire. Subjective truths and the emotional charge of memory are often values associated with flashbacks. These charged sequences are inserted into the less individuated, more "objective" present unfolding of events, often combating and overturning a certain view of the law. Knowledge of the past is often presented as a privilege afforded by the fiction, access to which is transformative, but temporary and didactic. Nostalgia is a figure ambiguosly attached to the flashback; the past is an object of desire, due to its personal, intense, and even liberating attributes, but it is also dangerous and frightening. Flashbacks in most cases terminate at precisely the point at which they must be sealed off, in which the imperatives of fixing interpretations and reaching judgments in the present must be imposed. Made aware of the past, the spectator is freed to forget it once again. This symbolic order vacillates between knowing and forgetting, the shifts determined by the positioning of the spectator within the structured operations of narrative temporality. The psychoanalytic dimensions of these symbolic narrative operations are indeed rich, and one of the goals of my analysis of flashbacks is to highlight these unconscious and disguised operations of films.

The Deconstruction of Fiction

The question of the psychoanalytic dimensions of textuality brings us to the theoretical limits of the formalist and structuralist methodologies I've examined. Though they will prove extremely useful in developing a theory of the functioning of the flashback, they remain fixed on an analysis of how the structuration of a text functions rather than the transformative implications of its process of structuring meanings. Another type of textual investigation termed "deconstruction," by Jacques Derrida (but practiced by others as well who do not necessarily employ this term), goes against the grain of the text's own weave of representation.[21] Rather than just analyzing elements or even the structures of a text, deconstruction allows us to see the structuring of the text as itself a configuration. In a sense, deconstruction follows from the structural perspective, but also follows through, beyond its points of departure and its goals, into the realm of an analysis of philosophical configurations.

For example, consider the way in which Barthes analyses in *S/Z* the "truth" of the fiction molded by hermeneutic code, the "truths" the text cites in its referential code, and the "natural" logic of the proairetic code. Deconstruction puts a sharper edge on these various ways of slicing through the truth values assigned by a text to itself and its implicit philosophical discourse. Deconstruction's debt in regard to the decentering of truth to the writings of Nietzsche is another reason why it is particularly useful for this study—specifically in chapter five—as Nietzsche's writings discuss the figures of repetition and fate that the flashback, particularly during the forties, presents.

The quotes surrounding the "true" and the "natural" are one way of granting a questioning force to the inscription of these terms that will not allow their use to conform with an ideal reality. Derrida substitutes another mark, that indicates an erasure that retains the trace, an X crossing out the representation of truth to indicate the double energy of a deconstructive mode that allows one never to fix on what is present nor on what is absent, but inscribes the conflict between the opposition present/absent in the realm of representation. This conflict is deeply embedded in the functioning of language itself. Psychoanalysis was able to indicate certain figures in dream representation and in parapraxis that presented a limited model for a deconstructive reading. Marxist analysis of ideology also contributed to an understanding of significant absences and figural representations within discourse.[22] However, both psychoanalysis and Marxism have their own borders through which they frame truths. Deconstruction attempts, in its shifting energies to show frames rather than to construct them, and in showing them to permeate these structures of thought.

Deconstruction, for this reason is complex and threatening. Some dismiss it, some simplify or deform it to their own ends; unfortunately its proposals can easily be downshifted to a return to absolute formalism, a mechanical description of the form of representational tropes. However, in the writings of the most vibrant deconstructive analysts, there is always more at stake. Form is not reinforced, but divided and multiplied in an investigation that allows this division and multiplication to affect the process of textual analysis.

For an investigation of the flashback, this has significant consequences: inherent in the flashback as trope is a certain assumption of temporality and order. The very term "chronological" implies an implicit clockwork logic to events. Our notion of duration is in this context something measurable and absolute. Yet, we know that it is also possible for events to cease to be discrete and for duration to be differentially measured or entirely called into question. In these instances we begin to see how the notion of chronology is marked as a culturally determined means of representation. The camera and projector, like the printed pages of a book before it, imply a certain temporality, an unfolding that other representational apparati do not. Perhaps the film does so even more than the book, whose pages can more easily be turned in various orders against the flow of the printing; but this is more of a physical difference than a theoretical one, for all it takes is a multiple video display bank to project a film as the disordered sum of its temporal units. The point is that in traditional practice, we have a very fixed frame through which we read and watch films. All inversions of temporality that occur within their representations are framed by this assumed clockwork mechanism and measured against it. If structuralism maps the ordering of texts, deconstruction allows us to see the view of the world implicit in the design of the map itself.

The aim of this book is to perform both types of analysis in an interactive relation. From moment to moment, chapter to chapter, shifts of focus will necessarily occur. It is at these junctures that one can see the importance of several different types of analysis, as one perspective lays the groundwork for another or opens inquiries outside the frame of the other methods.

"Tense" of the Image and Cinematic Temporality

So far in developing a theory of the flashback, I have been reviewing relevant theories of narrative structuring whose reference is literature. Equally relevant is the concept of temporality as expressed in images and the way in which verbal commentary that may accompany them affects this image temporality.

Many theorists of photography have remarked on the evidential quality of photography, the manner in which it appears to bear witness to the scenes it depicts. The viewer often interprets a photo as documenting fragments of the real world. André Bazin, for one, championed this indexical aspect of the photographic sign, assigning an ontological status to photography's ability to imprint a mimetic image of a perceived reality. Bazin extended this ability to "mummify" the world, to capture and preserve it as "it really was" to the cinematic image.[23] Roland Barthes borrows from Bazin's phenomenological approach to the photograph, contending that photos provide evidence that what we see imaged within them once existed. Barthes says the photo implies the "having been there" of the scene or objects depicted; according to Barthes, its assumed tense is the past.[24]

Cinema's ability to display motion in time is seen by Bazin, as it was by many earlier film theorists, as in addition to the realist vocation of photography. This establishes film as an even more powerful medium of realism than photography. Bazin championed putting this realist capacity to the service of filmic fiction as a means of creating stories that closely described a perceived reality. According to Barthes, however, cinema partakes of a different implied temporality; on one level, the cinema implies the same past tense as the photograph, presenting "the having been there" of the actors. However, the fictional functioning of film presents what Barthes calls another "pose," effacing this indication of the past existence of the referent in favor of a presence of a character within the ongoing present of the story, that is, the impression of an imaginary reality (pp. 122–26). Of course, the cinema that Barthes is considering is the fiction film rather than other types of film, such as archival documentary footage and home movies.

Some documentary footage is understood by its spectators in much the same way as is archival photography, as a document of a reality that once existed at the moment the images were taken. However, when incorporated into a documentary film such archival footage can be introduced into a narration that incorporates a nearly fictional presentation, as it strives to transport the spectator to another scene, another time. The "nearly present" is an important mode for documentary films that chronicle current events, with the simultaneous broadcast capacity of television striving to make the image "live" and therefore a present reality. Home movies have much the same status as family photographs as regards this question of temporal reference; they offer an image of the past of the individuals and places depicted and are understood as records of this past in much the same way as the photo album has become the archive of the family. The response to such images can vary from one which understands their pastness, to one that relives the past as part of an ongoing present, positions marked respectively by such verbal responses as "there was X when he was a baby," and "there is X swimming."

If documentary modes of filmic representation can indicate a definitive past, even if in some instances they edge towards the present, what of the temporality of the image within the fiction film? Barthes's formulation of the different temporal understanding of photographic and cinematic images coincides with a certain widely held belief that cinema is understood in the present tense. One supporting argument for this belief, in fact, involves flashbacks. The argument claims that within a given flashback segment, the spectator experiences the film in exactly the same way that one experiences any other segment of a fiction film, as an ongoing series of events happening to the characters in their immediate temporal experience, that is their "present." As this type of statement is most often made in the context of a comparison of literary and filmic modes of narration, the contrast is drawn between the variety of tenses available to the writer of literature and the singularity of tense available in cinema. Literature can qualify its mode of narration, while cinema simply presents actions. This position holds that beyond the initial entrance into and exit from a flashback, the spectator has no temporal markings of anteriority for the events depicted, and should a spectator begin watching the film in the middle of the flashback, he or she would never know that the flashback segments were actually meant to depict the past.

Such arguments ignore the way a filmic text codes its temporality. First it does so as a product of its diachronic unfolding; segments are defined temporally in relation to what preceded or what will follow them. Secondly, the temporal reference of a filmic segment is defined by a complex combination of visual and auditory indications, which can include: voice-over narration, filmic punctuations such as dissolves, changes in image qualities such as color to black and white, changes in elements of mise-en-scene such as costumes indicating an earlier time period or make-up differences that indicate younger periods in a character's life, and changes in non-diegetic music. This does not mean that the filmic image has the semantic fluidity and precision of verbal expression when it comes to articulating temporal references; language provides a subtle delineation of different modalities of temporal reference that are only available to film through the use of language either in the form of voice-over or written intertitles or subtitles. The history of the flashback in film, however, constitutes just this struggle to code a cinematic past.

Finally, a remark on the assumption that it is the equivalent of a present-tense narration that is created by filmic fictions as part of the impression of an imaginary reality; even films whose fiction creates an ongoing present for its characters are not necessarily received by its viewers entirely within this imaginary frame. Sometimes spectators maintain their distance and experience the narrative as a story that is being narrated, as a story from a past or from another scene to which they do not have an unmediated access. This distance may be encouraged by the film by internal distancing devices of several kinds, such as voice-over narration, stylized mise-en-scene, or the foregrounding of historical references. Some film narratives acquire through these means a sense of a past-tense narration which is somewhat analogous to the distancing modalities of the past-tense in literary discourse. Similarly, a "painterly" or "theatrical" mise-en-scene operates differently from images whose mise-en-scene is in a realistic mode. Bazin and Barthes tend to assume a style of photographic image that utilizes codes of analogy that have come to be phenomenologically invisible. It is for this reason that Barthes makes such a strong distinction between looking at a photograph and looking at a drawing, a distinction that is no longer appropriate for pictorial photography, for example, any more than it is appropriate for German expressionist film.

Fiction film, then, has many ways to develop temporalities through which the cinematic image can be understood. More complicated flashback structures tend to emphasize the means by which film presents its fiction. The imaginary entrance into a present reality is provided, but the spectator is made aware of the threshold and the process of transversing it. The spectator in this case is acutely aware of the filmic fiction as a story-being-told. Multiple flashbacks, embedded flashbacks, abrupt modernist flashbacks can make spectators more aware of the modalities of filmic fiction, of the processes of narrative itself. These manipulations of narrative temporality can serve to self-consciously expose the mechanisms of filmic narration, the artifice through which time becomes an expressive element of narrative form. However, various techniques simultaneously can be used to naturalize these temporal manipulations, such as locating them in the psyche or the storytelling capacity of a character within the fiction. A spectator then is suspended between two different ways of looking at temporal manipulations within filmic imagery, one that is aware of the formal operations of narrative and one that forgets these elements due to naturalizing processes within th fiction.

Ideologies of Narration, Temporality, and History

This split between knowledge and forgetfulness through which the flashback operates within filmic fiction is similar to the more general split belief system that operates in fiction's formulation of the "impression of reality" as it has been described by Christian Metz.[25] One knows that one is watching a film, but one believes, even so, that it is an imaginary reality. The difference I am pointing out here is that the flashback structure tends to override this split constituting the impression of reality with a second level rearticulating a similar conflict of beliefs. On this level, the spectator is again presented with a duality, and this time the balance often tilts towards a knowledge of structure, an awareness of the process of telling stories about the past. This may be a reason flashback structures are negatively received as too artificial and as slowing the action by many critics, some filmmakers, and undoubtedly other people as well.[26] They have a potential for disturbing a participatory viewing of a film and encouraging a greater intellectual distance, although, again, the countervailing forces that naturalize the flashbacks as personal memories can produce just the opposite effect—no emotional distance, extreme identification.

It is in this context that we can explore the ideological implications of the flashback as a framing device for stories and for representation of history within these stories. For if the flashback presents a narrative past, this past often refers to an historical past. The rendering of this historical past is colored by both the general processes of fictional transformation, and by the specific framing and focalization of this fictional version of the historical past as a flashback. In chapter four, I will explore this process of framing and focalization as it was used in Hollywood sound films through the mid-fifties, for this is a period in which several genres of American films specifically address history, the individual as a part of a social group, the relationships between historical periods and between biography and history. However, virtually all the films discussed in this book engage in framing and focalizing historical elements through the flashback, so that the manner in which the flashback subjectivates history will be a concern throughout.

One of the ideological implications of this narration of history through a subjective focalization is to create history as an essentially individual and emotional experience. Another is to establish a certain view of historical causality and linkage. By presenting the result before the cause, a logic of inevitability is implied; certain types of events are shown to have certain types of results without ever allowing for other outcomes than the one given in advance. Many flashback narrations contain an element of philosophical fatalism, coupled with a psychoanalytic fatalism I will discuss shortly. This fatalism presents a cynical view of history cyclical, guaranteed to repeat that which we have already seen; the release from the repetitions inherent in history is then forged in a singular solution that serves a prevailing ideology, such as patriotic identification or a retreat into the "personal" as a microcosmic, idealized world. Further, the history narrated in flashback is often a didactic history, containing moral lessons. The lessons vary from one historical period or location to another, which is one of the reasons it is useful to organize this study in historical periods. Considering the nationality of production is another means of analyzing differences in the lessons about history that flashbacks try to teach.

However, it is possible in a more modernist and experimental reinscription of history in the flashback to call all these ideological implications into question. In these cases, changes in the form of the flashback and the voice-over narration can not only reorient the stated ideology but question the ideological processes of making and telling histories.

Psychoanalytic Implications of the Flashback

In psychoanalysis, the case history and the "cure" is a process through which the patient retells the past and deciphers dreams that are in many ways reworkings of this personal past history. The analyst hears the many versions and symbolic representations of this story and in a sense becomes an accomplice in determining the form of its unfolding.

Flashbacks in film often parallel this operation as they present a past, like a dream, waiting to be interpreted. Sometimes the psychoanalytic analogy is directly taken up by the fiction with the flashback narrative becoming the story of the patient in analysis, as is the case in the twenties with G.W. Pabst's *Secrets of the Soul* (1926) and in the forties with Curtis Bernhardt's *Possessed* (1947), two examples among others I will not discuss in this book. More often, the psychoanalytic analogy is indirect; there is no analyst within fiction listening to the flashback narration. Even so the spectator can "hear" the flashback from the position of the analyst, which includes the possibilty of identification with the narrator of the flashback. The flashback invites this analytic reception, as it is offered as an explanation from the past for the situation in the present. However, when the texts themselves indicate a Freudian reading of the flashback material, they often utilize a simplified and determinist version of psychoanalysis, for example, the "popularized Freud" that combines interpretations by both American psychoanalysts and the mass media. This version of Freud often manifests a dark, fatalistic view of the human psyche when given expression in fiction. In flashback film, as we shall see in chapter five, implicitly psychoanalytic character portraits abound in American films of the forties and fifties. The pseudo-scientific principles of popular Freudianism can serve this tendency in genres such as the form of melodrama known as the women's film and the *film noir* . Part of our concern will be with examining how psychoanalysis is inscribed in these flashback narratives both directly and implicitly.

We need to consider the psychoanalytic theory on another level as well in building a theory of the functioning of flashbacks. Flashbacks often present images which are to be understood as memories. These films portray their own versions of how memories are stored, how they are repressed, how they return from the repressed. These representations can be compared to Freud's representations of the memory system, the unconsciousness, and his theory of the return of the repressed.[27] Then we can also look at how psychoanalytic theory and psycho-perceptual theory after Freud produced modifications and changes in his model. The comparison between representations of memory within the fiction of the films and representations of memory in scientific theory has as its goal not just the critique of the fictional representation by an application of the scientific, but also a critique of applied psychoanalysis as a tool for reading texts. If the films deviate from scientific knowledge, they do so for their own purpose and create their own effects. The kind of psychoanalytic methodology one needs to confront such textual strategies is of another order. For example, flashback films make specific use of the theory of associative memory, the way an event or sensation in the present brings forth a memory trace that was since forgotten. The elements placed into association in this way become linked in the text's symbolic code. The analyst, in playing with the association of these elements, can work against the grain of a habitual reading of what the film is supposed to mean, and find that the film is saying other things quite "unconsciously." Thus the way psychoanalysis figures into our analysis of the functioning of flashback is as both a reference and a tool in understanding the manifest representation of memory in the film and as a part of a deconstructive reading of the structure of the symbolic order of the film, in which the flashbacks play a key function.

In chapter six, the discussion of the modernist flashback films will analyze how many of these films pose theoretical questions implicitly in their images and structuration. These films sometimes posit an image theory of memory, one that locates the recovery of memories as the resurging of images, a theory that has its obvious correspondence to the flashes of cinematic montage. Did cinematic style itself influence scientific postulates on memory, give more credence to an image theory of memory than it might have gained otherwise? Perhaps, but even though scientists no longer believe that we store memories as images in most circumstances, they hold that eidetic memory (memory of images or through images) is an important factor in memory reconstitution from the complex traces of information that the brain does store.[28]

The discussion of memory by such philosophers as Nietzsche, Sartre, and Bergson will also be implicitly and occasionally explicitly referred to by these films. Nietzsche's concepts of *ressentiment* and the eternal return, for example, create a fascinating weave with Freudian theories of memory in certain modernist flashbacks (as they do with a reading of *film noir,* as discussed earlier). The modernist flashback inscribes and sometimes comments on prevailing philosophies, particularly romantic, phenomenological, existential philosophies. A deconstructive approach which examines the structures of these philosophies will be useful for analyzing the ways in which texts inscribe, echo, and divert philosophies. The flashback can indeed become a selected site for a study of the way philosophies and textuality interact.

A Summary of the Theoretical Issues

In this chapter I've defined the flashback as a technique of film narrative, and presented some reasons for a study that traces the functioning of this technique. The methodology I am using in this study and the theories that serve as reference have been explained as multiple; the formulation of a theory of the flashback needs to borrow from narrative theories of formalism and structuralism, from image theory and semiotics, from psychoanalysis and psycho-perceptual theory, from ideology theory and philosophies of memory and consciousness, all of which explain aspects of flashback functioning. In this chapter I've found it useful to discuss each of these theories and methods in turn, but in the chapters that follow, they will sometimes interact and coalesce, sometimes be at odds turning on each other and in their conflict give way to multiple readings. At other times one theory will come to the foreground temporarily, while another recedes. This ebb and flow of points is in part a response to the historical shifts that the flashback undergoes, but it is also a product of my desire not to fix on a single theoretical vantage point that ignores others. Rather than seek to hold on to all perspectives simultaneously throughout this analysis, an impossible and immobilizing task, it is better, I believe, to allow the vantages to shift and comment on one another self-consciously.

Finally a word about the organization of the study. I have chosen to follow an historical trajectory that also considers groupings of films through genres, national origin, formal, and thematic similarities. The historical structure of my investigation provides a coherent organization to this extended analysis of a rather large and diverse group of films. Further, I feel a work about cinematic ways of representing memory and the past is aided by an historical perspective. It allows me to highlight formal and ideological comparisons. I have tried to do so without assuming a purely developmental thesis. One of my strongest concerns has been to integrate theory and history. I have sought to overcome historicism as a reductive view of the linear and causal occurrence of all events, while still appreciating how filmic expression occurs in historical contexts as one of our most important forms of cultural expression.

2

Flashbacks in American Silent Cinema

When did the use of flashback in film begin? This apparently straightforward question is, in fact, very difficult to answer, for a variety of reasons. It is basically a question of origin, and therefore shares the difficulties of all questions of origin.

One set of problems in questioning the origins of cinematic techniques or devices is practical. How does one ever know one has found the historically accurate starting point, given the rarity of surviving prints from the early years of cinema? Of the hundreds of films shot and exhibited every week in the United States, France, Germany, Italy, and elsewhere, relatively few examples remain. Since more of the early films of D.W. Griffith were preserved than those directed by others, many historians have assumed that the flashbacks used in Griffith's films were the first. This assumption was spurred by the claim Griffith himself made in a bulletin advertisement in *The New York Dramatic Mirror* (Dec. 3, 1911) at the time of his departure from Biograph, wherein he claimed to have invented the "switchback" among other filmic devices.[1] Some historians have taken Griffith's term "switchback" to mean flashback, although the terms "switchback" and "cutback" also refer to "parallel" or "alternating" editing (a sequence composed of two or more strands of simultaneous action occurring in different spaces cross-cut with each other). Given the actual nature of Griffith's Biograph films, it is most certainly parallel editing that he is claiming as his invention.

A similar confusion occurs when historians find examples of "flashbacks" in early Griffith films. The supposed flashbacks are either cutaways (a cut to a space outside the main action) or alternating editing. One source cites *After Many Years* (1908), the first Griffith adaptation of Tennyson's *Enoch Arden,* as containing the first flashback.[2] The sequence in question alternates images of Enoch's wife Annie, waiting for her husband's return, with images of Enoch stranded on a desert island. There is no reason, however, to understand the image of Enoch on the island as temporally prior to the one of Annie waiting for him at home. It is far more plausible that the trope is one of simultaneity to be understood as: "While Annie waited at home, Enoch was shipwrecked on an island, far away." If historians have so firmly located the first flashbacks in Griffith's films, it is due not only to the unavailability of prints from the period, but also to an ideological bias. As Jean-Louis Comolli has pointed out, the search for origins by film historians, as indicated in the frequent use of the phrase "for the first time," can be seen as a symptom of a misplaced focus and a misconstrued system of values.[3] According to Comolli, film histories center on questions of origin, influences, and development as part of an erroneous view of a linear, autonomous, and progressive growth of cinematic technique. Historians have tended to champion the development of a technology or the contributions of individuals rather than to speak of the function of narrative forms within the early period of film history. Rather than searching for the first appearance of the flashback, our sense of history will be one forged through a combination of close analysis of films and theoretical principles of the life of cultural forms.

We cannot assume that cinema has an autonomous history. As I began to discuss in the last chapter, the distinctly filmic device of the flashback is tied to other devices in other narrative arts, as well as psychological and philosophical speculation on how memory and associative thought function. In the American silent period, these junctures of cultural forms and intellectual developments can be seen shaping the flashback into a narrative device that gathers a specific array of uses and meanings. The flashback will replace a character's verbally told story by a series of images, substituting dynamic visual expression for cumbersome verbal titles, and will provide emotional symbolic representation of a character's motivations or traits as determined by formative past experience. We will examine how this happens by first looking at film's relationship to the other narrative arts, then at its relationship to psychological theory of this period, and then how the films from this period use the flashback.[4]

Film and the Other Narrative Arts

Much early theoretical writing on film traces film's debt to other narrative arts, particularly the novel and theater, or traces film's need to distinguish itself from them.[5] The flashback is one response cinema itself made to the question of its heritage and specificity as a narrative art form. Though the pantomime, ballet, and early melodrama also made minimal use of verbal language to present narratives, the silent cinema's comparatively restricted verbal narration necessitated visual means of compensation for the eloquent narrative alternatives offered by the word in the novel and verbal theatrical forms. The flashback became one of these means of specifically cinematic storytelling. As the immediate visual drifting of one image into another image from the "past" through a cut, a dissolve or a fade-in and -out, or as a fade-in superimposition of an image from the past within a part of the early cinematic frame, the flashback in film is a cinematic device that fully exploits the properties of successive moving images.

In literature, the movement of narration from the present to the past is a common, traditional device of storytelling. It can be accomplished by first person, third person, or omniscient narration; by descriptions of a character's memories, or inserted passages describing or acting out events from the past, or even by changes of tense within the same sentence or paragraph. As was discussed in the last chapter, Gérard Genette has analyzed this long tradition of temporal fluidity in literature.[6] Genette reminds us that Homer employed the literary equivalent of the flashback near the beginning of the *Odyssey* and that such flashbacks are common in epics as a form. Novels employed this technique with considerable frequency, Genette finds, and he offers several examples from 19th-century literature as a prelude to his concern with the shift of temporal instances in the writing of Proust (p. 31). Yet there is often a difference between an analepse in literature and the filmic flashback, as the literary analepse, expressed in language, need not necessarily take on the same weight of recall or re-experiencing the past that is evident in flashbacks in film. In literature a moment of past history can be referred to in a past tense as an element of description or explication. When this occurs in film, through the voice of a character or narrator, unaccompanied by images from the past, we would not call it a flashback, not even an auditory flashback, which is a term we reserve for sounds, voices, or music whose diegetic occurrence is in the past but whose sound-image is inserted in the present as a subjective memory of a character of what was heard earlier. Monologues or dialogues that narrate the past but occur in the present are common in sound films, though, and often occur when we might expect a flashback. A notable example is the long verbal explanation of her past given by Lady Henrietta Flusky (Ingrid Bergman) in Hitchcock's *Under Capricorn* (1949). A single long take follows her movement around the bedroom as she delivers her extensive narration, the camera's panning emphasizing the character's telling, in the present. This scene would have been impossible to present in silent cinema; the telling could have been emblematically represented by a shot of a character talking, but the verbal intertitles would have had to abridge the story considerably, and the drama and fluidity of the process of telling would have been sacrificed.

Despite the differences between the literary analepse and the filmic flashback, it is important to appreciate the 19th-century literary antecedents to the uses of flashbacks in film. In chapter one, I noted that Sergei Eisenstein pointed out many elements of the link between the 19th-century novel and early film in his essay, "Dickens, Griffith and the Film Today."[7] As John Fell illustrates in his book, *Film and the Narrative Tradition,*[8] this comparison holds for the flashback as well. The popular romance adventure novels of the late 19th-century and the 20th-century psychological novel contribute to a narrative obsession with explaining what occurred before, with linking the present action to a fictional past. Though Proust certainly brought this pull of memory to the foreground of his literary expression, Thomas Mann, Joseph Conrad, and less well-known writers also manipulated such returns to past scenes.

On stage, thoughts of the past could occur as "vision" scenes, a technique which can be traced at least as far back as the Spanish "golden age" of theater and which becomes newly popular in the 19th-century melodrama. Fell quotes an example in a Charles Dickens-Wilkie Collins collaboration called *The Frozen Deep* (1837) "in which a tired traveler sees in his campfire at the north pole a glimpse of the girl he left behind" (p. 143). Such vision scenes were also common in lantern slide shows from the 1860s through the turn of the century. Photomontage techniques were used to connect an image of a character to a remembrance from his or her past.

In all probability the earliest flashbacks in film used this image-within-the-image technique rather than an edited cut to the past. This doubling of images could be achieved by a kind of double stage scenography which located the scene from the past in the background of the profilmic scene, by using slides or filmic rear projections, or by double exposing the image using mattes. These techniques were all common by 1902–03, as the recent restoration of the paper prints from the Library of Congress demonstrates.[9] Georges Méliès used these techniques before the turn of the century— although not to my knowledge for flashbacks proper, but for various types of fantasy or thought inserts.[10]

At the same time that many of the earliest films were greatly indebted to theatrical representation, theater at the turn of the century can be seen as prefiguring in its techniques the devices of vision scenes that would become easier to produce in filmic montage than they were on stage. We can find in what remains of early film production a few examples of flashbacks that illustrate this filmic use of the stage-inspired flashback.

Ferdinand Zecca, another French filmmaker, for example, uses a stage-inspired technique for a flashback in his film *Histoire d'un crime* (1901). The first three tableaux images depict a robbery and the arrest of the robber-murderer. The fourth takes place in the criminal's prison cell, where his subjective dream vision appears on a second stage set built into the wall prop so that it looks like a vision hovering above him. Though a dream, it constitutes a return to the time before the robbery. Three scenes, one of the man in his work as a carpenter joined by his wife and son, the second with his wife and son at a dinner table, and the third at a bar before he is arrested, appear in the shot. After this dream memory disappears, officials enter to take the man to his execution which comprises the final three shots of the film.

Though there doesn't appear to be any surviving print displaying a flashback this early in American film history, there may well have been examples that have not survived or have not yet been found. Certainly the inserted image was used in American films of this period, most notably in the opening of Edwin Porter's *Life of an American Fireman* (1903), one of the best known films from this period. A fireman is seen sleeping while a circular image representing his premonitory dream looms to the right of him. If such vision sequences were as common as they appear to be, based on surviving films and on accounts of films of this period, one suspects flashbacks as well as dreams were indicated by such techniques in the early cinema— particularly in British, French, and American films where we have evidence of these inserted images.

Recent research on early cinema has pointed to a number of early flashbacks, most of which seem to be variations of this type of vision scene; often the temporality of these early films is so ambiguous as to leave questionable whether these inserts are real flashbacks or a kind of imaginary image. For example, *The Old Chorister*, directed by James Williamson for his production company in Great Britain in 1904, opens with a shot in which an old man walking down a country road has a vision as he sits to rest on a bench on the right. The vision is a circular matte superimposition on the left of a boy singing in a choir. In the shots that follow, the old man enters a church and sings in the choir, comprised of boys and men, when an angelic vision appears in the center of the image. The old man walks towards it, faints, the angel disappears when the others surround him, and finally the angel reappears. It is possible that the first vision of the boy singing in the choir is a memory image that the man has of himself as a boy, as has been suggested in some sources.[11] This interpretation provides a certain narrative motivation, nostalgia, for the man returning to die in the church, but the internal evidence in the film is ambiguous.

The cross-fertilization of theater and film as regards temporal order can be gauged in a quite different way by the success of Elmer Rice's 1914 play, *On Trial*. The play has been described as one of the pivotal dramas of the American Theater, since a new technique in play construction was afterwards based on its adaptation of the then "new cinematic flashback scene."[12] The play begins with a prologue depicting the end of the jury selection and the opening addresses of the prosecuting and defense attorneys in a murder trial. Each act gives the testimony of a different witness, with curtains punctuating the shift from the scene in the courtroom to the flashback dramatization and back again. *On Trial* is seen by theater historians as borrowing its narrative structure from film. Films did not use the flashback format before 1914, though the first courtroom drama flashback I found, to be discussed shortly, is from 1916. Numerous other flashback films of the late twenties are adapted from similar plays based on trial testimony. The literary-theatrical-cinematic development of the flashback is best seen as a shared phenomenon, one that exemplifies the interdependence of these narrative arts.

Historical Development of Film Techniques: Empiricism and Theory

The discussion of the difficulty of pinpointing a real origin of the flashback has led us to an exploration of interrelated development of the arts that is perhaps more sound and certainly much richer theoretically. Now another question appears, that of tracing the historical development of the flashback, particularly problematic in this early period. Though some film historians have concentrated on the development of techniques during this period, most of the work on cinematic temporality in early film does not focus on the flashback, but rather on patterns of instantaneously repetitive camera angles and simultaneity of action, the most famous example being the shots showing the rescue in *Life of an American Fireman* from both the interior of the burning room and the exterior.[13] This work on repeated perspectives of action in early films has made a great contribution to the development of a theoretical frame for early film history and the manner in which one can investigate the surviving examples as historically meaningful. Though such pure repetition of an event might be taken as a flashback, the point that historians have made here is just the opposite.

According to their analyses, the film audiences viewed this repetition as a way of allowing them a double perspective on a single event. As a trope of montage, the doubled scene was simply an alternative to intercutting, which came into use slightly thereafter and came to dominate film history, effacing the trope of repeated views.

One film historian who does address the issue of flashback use in early film history is Barry Salt, in his book *Film Style and Technology: History and Analysis*. Salt's discussion of the flashback serves as one of his means of clarifying his periodization of early film history between 1906 and the twenties and the manner in which he finds this periodization useful for tracing the development of film techniques. He summarizes the type and frequency of the flashback, analyses punctuation devices for entering and exiting flashbacks, and comments on formal changes. He also cites briefly a number of fascinating flashback examples, some of which we will also consider later on. Though in other aspects of this study Salt is quite specific about the application of his quantitative methodology to trace the use and frequency of techniques as part of a larger stylistic film history, in these flashback sections the body of reference from which the conclusions are drawn remains vague.

The impressionistic aspect of Salt's historical commentary on flashback use before 1930, even in an author devoted to quantification, illustrates an issue related to the problem of origins we addressed earlier. There are simply not enough surviving prints from much of the silent period to perform a very convincing assessment of the flashback technique in a quantitative manner. A statement such as "the fashionable interest in the flashback continued to increase into this period" that Salt makes about the period (1914–1919) cannot be taken at face value.[15] Though we might take the surviving films to be in some manner representative, it is also likely that they are not at all typical, but particularly innovative or even unique. Though one can broaden or systematically select a sample to attempt to assure historical accuracy, eventually the film historian must place his or her analyses of films in a theoretical frame in order to write any kind of history. Similarly, the authors of *The Classical Hollywood Cinema*, David Bordwell, Kristin Thompson, and Janet Staiger—a monumental study that uses a quantitative methodology to discern typical film techniques within a "random sample" of films—have not addressed their research to the early flashback, whereas other film techniques do receive such attention by them during this period.[16] My point is that quantification of a flashback study is perhaps not only difficult, but less theoretically rich than the questions we might ask as to what kinds of flashback are found and what vision of memory, history, and narrative are evoked by them.

As a consequence, the quantitative aspect of my study of flashbacks is admittedly restrained; if I make no claims for an exhaustive historical survey or a random method in choosing films, it is because I enter into the project of history with somewhat different goals. Though such a quantitative survey certainly could be produced, I have made a choice to write this history within a theoretical frame that is not primarily empirical nor quantitative. Films have been taken as examples in a manner that makes qualified claims for what they illustrate, claims appropriate to my goal of film analysis as an historical and theoretical activity.

Employing such a theoretical perspective, we can still speculate on such issues as flashback frequency and about the kinds of functions and uses flashbacks have in certain historical periods. Accepting that we do not have an exhaustive body of texts, we can occasionally arrive at such speculation by other means, that is, by examining the kinds of examples we do have and indications of how the flashbacks in these films were received by critics and theorists at the time.

In the earliest period of cinema, before 1910, any quantitative speculation is extremely difficult. Flashbacks in this period are difficult to distinguish from vision scenes that are meant to be understood as imaginary, or actions that happen simultaneously, but are "seen" by a character in no position to observe them. An example of each of these types of sequences are *And the Villain Still Pursued Her* (or alternatively titled, *The Author's Dream*), a Vitagraph film from 1906 and *Drink and Repentance: A Convict's Story,* a British production from 1905. In the first case, the sequences in question are understood as the imaginary vision of a writer, framed by images of him writing; the film ends with these visions driving him insane. In the second case, the vision sequence is that of a convict in a cell (not unlike the flashback in *Histoire d'un crime*), except that here the vision is that of his wife at home, who lifts her arms forward in a gesture of longing which he matches from his prison cell, as if to meet her. The notion of a "vision" scene seems to have predominated over that of the flashback in films before 1910, sometimes inclusive of what we might term "flashback," but most often presenting another kind of imaginary elaboration in a different register.

A film from 1911, *After One Hundred Years,* shows how the vision sequence virtually accommodates a flashback within it; virtually, because what occurs in this film is nearly a flashback, but remains coded as a dream, a product of the imagination. The narrative first establishes the murder in 1810 of a man at the Royal George Inn. We see him enter the Inn, the beginning of an argument and then an ellipsis takes us to his murderers disposing of his body. Another ellipsis whose magnitude is one hundred years takes us to the story of the murdered man's greatgrandson, Harry, setting off to visit England and the inn murder site. Instead of granting truth value as a story told or read to the near-flashback that will show the grandfather being shot, the film leaves its near-flashback as the dream of its main character. The entire murder sequence is presented in superimposition and Harry remains visible in the background of the shot the whole time, dreaming.

The very notion of vision, of an imaginary seeing, may be closer to the spirit of much early cinema than the more concrete category of temporal inversion. A 1914 text called *Playwriting for the Cinema: Dealing with the Writing and Marketing of Scenarios,* gives us a section on "visions" but none on flashbacks. It suggests abandoning the superimposition for the sequential presentation of dreams punctuated by fades-in and -out, a preference presented as more economical for producers.[17]

This reminds us that the period predating this advice was characterized by a more artisanal mode of production, which rapidly became subject to industrial imperatives.

It perhaps follows from the way in which the many of the earliest film narratives privileged spectacle and ways of seeing events that a different kind of temporal vision is apparent even in certain flashback constructions. Consider two films from this period that take the form of series of clearly historical events framed by a scene in the present. One is Méliès *Le Juif errant* (1903), which apparently cuts from images of the banished Jew in the desert to a series of events that led to his banishment; the theme is Biblical and the structure is that of tableaux illustrations of a series of representative events. Yet the spectacle vision also arranges the past incidents as causal explanations of exclusion implying a symbolic justification of punishment.[18] Another example is J. Stuart Blackton's *Napoleon: the Man of Destiny* (Vitagraph, 1909) in which Napoleon is seen remembering the major stages in his career, as marked by the intertitle: "Napoleon at Malmaison after the Battle of Waterloo. He pays a last visit to the room where the Empress Josephine died. Visions of his past greatness, his triumphs, victories and final defeat." Each of the visions is a tableau image, illustrating the battles of Marengo, Austerlitz, Jena, and Friedland; continuing through the marriage, coronation, and the birth of the King of Rome; and culminating with the abdication at Fontainebleau, the battle of Waterloo, and the exile at St. Helena. If the film departs from flashback logic by having events framed by Malmaison that are posterior to any possible presence of Napoleon at that site, narrative logic (if not historical logic) is possibly restored if we read the exile sequence as a flashforward. These two films recall the popular 19th-century staged tableau and the history painting; that earlier aesthetic of spectacular vision in its theatrical presentation may not have needed a device to smooth the ellipses in the chronology. In film, the framing device of remembering from a vantage point in the present that implies causality or nostalgia serves to connect the tableaux and contextualize the ekphrasis of the posed images.

Imaginary vision is paralleled by the development of the action-adventure narrative and of an aesthetic critical of its power to interrupt and effect shifts in the mode of expression. This tendency found written expression in Epes Winthrop Sargent's *Technique of the Photoplay,* first published in 1911, in which he views "the vision as a device that interrupts the flow of narrative experience" and "cautions against repeated and potentially ambiguous changes in time frames" (as Edward Azlant has remarked in his study of Sargent's influence on screenwriting theory).[19] Sargent's attack on flashbacks ("the spectator spends all his time taking in postdated facts and trying to put them in their proper places," *Azlant,* p. 239) not only indicates a certain prominence of flashbacks prior to 1911 to which he is reacting, but also an attitude that, if not successful in suppressing the flashback, perhaps led to its more dynamic narrative coding and its differentiation from the vision scene.

If before 1910 the flashback is not easily distinguishable from the vision scene or serves as a rhetorical trope of framing a spectacle, in contrast, it does appear that flashbacks clearly marked as temporal analepses were quite common in the teens—

although relatively few of these films have survived. One important indication of the frequency of flashback use is the manner flashbacks are mentioned in review articles by the early twenties. Often flashbacks did not get noted at all by contemporaneous reviewers, but when reviewers did note the presence of a flashback they tended to remark on how common the technique had become with statements like, "the author has resorted to the old device of making it a story within a story" or conversely, "for once a flash-back, as it is made in this photoplay, is interesting." [20] Similarly, discussions of flashbacks in screenwriting manuals, such as Marguerite Bertsch's *How to Write for Moving Pictures* (1917) and Howard Dimick's *Modern Photoplay Writing* (1922), give us an index of the frequency of use of this device (which in each case is referred to as a "dissolve," though a flashback is clearly meant).[21] Bertsch writes, "very often, however, a story is of such a nature that, artistically, its proper point of beginning is near the end of the action. Starting at this point, we tell our story in 'dissolves,' which are equivalent to the recital of happenings in a play" (p. 100). She warns, however, against "dissolves within dissolves" as too confusing and adds, "Neither the double exposure of the 'dissolve' is popular with the audience to-day; for even the smoothest 'dissolve' called the *interpose,* destroys the grip of a photoplay, reducing it from drama to narrative" (pp. 100–01). Similarly Dimick presents the flashback as a "well-known technique" and adds similar cautions against the lengthy "retrospect," as "continuity is given a severe wrench, an inexcusable dislocation" (p. 200).

The action-orientation of such early screenwriting prescriptions against the flashback were countered in the critical writing of Hugo Münsterberg, a well-known psychologist teaching at Harvard. We turn to his work not only as an historical indication that already by 1916 the flashback was considered common and worthy of study, but also because in many ways his study is exemplary. It provides an example of the kind of history of a technique that is perhaps most interesting, one that reaches out to encompass the function and social meanings of specific narrative inscriptions.

Münsterberg's Discussion of Flashbacks and Memory

After a year's intensive viewing of films "projected on American screens," Münsterburg wrote a volume originally titled *The Psychology of the Photoplay.*[22] Since his research is primarily from 1916, Münsterberg's concern with the flashback as device that raised important issues for psychology is of historical importance to us. Apparently the narrative device was common enough for Münsterberg to see it as a major technique of the "photoplay": as well as one that intrigued him for its similarity to his notion of memory processes.

Münsterberg states his project as twofold; first, to explore "what psychological factors are involved when we watch the happenings on the screen," and secondly, "what characterizes the independence of art" (p. 17). He frames his study as an attempt to define cinema's functioning aesthetic specificity, goals shared by most early film theory. Implicitly, however, his work is motivated by the consistent project to see film as a physical, observable manifestation of human processes of perception and intellection. In explaining the ability of cinematic expression to represent the function of the mind, Münsterberg is able to see that films are capable of complex patterns of subjectivity. He argues for serious intellectual study of how films treated temporality and memory at a time when few considered the theoretical implications of cinema from a scientific and philosophical perspective. He makes valuable distinctions and useful linkages between the subjectivity of characters represented in a filmic fiction and the inner thoughts and memory of the film's viewers. Unfortunately, he goes too far in assuming that what he sees in film in some way truly parallels the inner functioning of the human perceptual apparatus.

This is apparent in the short section Münsterberg devotes to "Memory and Imagination." In speaking of flashbacks (though he uses the term "cutbacks"), Münsterberg distinguishes among flashbacks that repeat scenes the audience has previously viewed, those that depict a character's memory of the past, and those that represent a character's telling of the past, with the flashback images substituting for words. The latter he finds a poor instance of the use of the device, because Münsterberg values flashbacks as an analogue of memory, not as an illustration of verbal discourse. He claims that "we must recognize the mental act of remembering" in the filmic flashback. "It is as if reality has lost its own continuous connection and become shaped by the demands of our soul. It is as if the outer world itself became molded in accordance with our fleeting turns of attention or with our passing memory ideas" (p. 41).

As we shall see later, when our investigation of the flashback leads us to consider other theories of human perception, cognition, and memory processes, Münsterberg's formulations are overstated. A rather naive view of human memory is implied by his exaggeration of how completely the flashback embodies a memory. One is led by Münsterberg's hyperbolic tendencies to assume a picture theory of memory, in which recall takes the form of complete images appearing to the mind and in which memories conform to the linearity and clarity of filmic narrative.

Yet one can also assume that he never meant his enthusiasm for the parallels between film and subjective memory to be taken so literally, despite his rhetorical flourishes. Assuming a general audience rather than the scientific community, Münsterberg perhaps generalized the connection between mind and movie. Münsterberg's theoretical contribution in recognizing the manner in which the flashback could be linked to various types of memory should not be underestimated. In many ways his observations serve as the respected antecedent to this present study.

If we examine Münsterberg's writing in another way, an historical source, the vague manner in which he refers to film is somewhat frustrating. In the passage on "Memory," he mentions four examples of flashback film, but in each case it is unclear whether these are examples of actual films Münsterberg viewed or composite models that he invented to illustrate the forms flashbacks can take. Only one flashback film, *When Broadway was a Trail,* is mentioned by name; this is an intriguing example of a frame story flashback where the contemporary hero is shown at the beginning narrating the history of New York's urban development to his companion. The embedded history concludes with the "present" romantic moment, the couple looking out on Broadway. The frame story seems to function to justify progress and urbanization as engendering modern romance, excluding other connotations such as a history of a city might have. Lacking more specific evidence in Münsterberg's description, this reading remains a supposition, as he gives us a limited account of the film itself. In considering Münsterberg as an historical source on how flashbacks function in early film, one is left without any specific sense of his sample or any detailed analysis of his examples.

Another question raised by Münsterberg's writing on flashbacks is whether the different kinds of flashbacks were punctuated by different kinds of filmic transitions from present to past. Münsterberg tells us, "if a person in the scene remembers the past, a past which may be entirely unknown to the spectator but which is living in the memory of the hero or heroine, then the former events are not thrown on the screen as an entirely new set of pictures, but they are connected with the present scene by a slow transition" (p. 42). He then goes on to illustrate this point with a scene from an unidentified film in which a man recalls his romance with a former sweetheart. The scene dissolves from a close-up on the fireplace in the room where he is sitting to one of the couple together years earlier in a garden. Another dissolve brings us back to the man's living room. This subjective flashback is quite similar to the one in the Dickens-Collins stage melodrama of 1837 mentioned earlier; Münsterberg cites this example to show how in the film subjectivity is marked by a dissolve and to celebrate the dissolve as an analogue for the process by which memory operates (moves us from the present to an image of the past). Münsterberg's focus here is on the dissolve, not its specific filmic context. The dissolve suggests the association of images and coincides with Münsterberg's implicit theory that memory operates through association of images. He was probably unaware of another implication he makes that other flashbacks that are not subjective do not use dissolves or fades, but are simple cuts. As a historian of film, one must consider this implication, however, as a possible record of the corpus of films Münsterberg saw that no longer exist. However, even from the limited evidence that remains of the period, it seems as if most early flashbacks, not only those marked as subjective character memories, are set off by filmic punctuation such as fades or dissolves.[23] This historical question of punctuation of the filmic flashback is another for which Münsterberg's writings are of limited use.

These cautionary statements about the ways in which Münsterberg can or cannot be used as an historical source do not in any way reflect on the historical interest the appearance of his writings have. As we shall see when we continue the exploration of philosophical and psychological writings on memory, the connections Münsterberg makes between filmic representation, memory, and imagination are of major historical value, even if his interpretation of these connections is open to question in the ways I've indicated. Münsterberg shows us the importance of a theoretical investigation of film technique, and more specifically begins to show us how the filmic flashback as a form is a particularly rich development in the history of representation.

Functions of Early Flashbacks

Once we continue to assess the uses of flashbacks in early film, we find that they are richer both in form and theoretical consequences than even Münsterberg's writing indicates. For not only do flashbacks represent a unique visual rendering of memory, they contribute to the apparatus of filmic expression and to representation of historical subjectivity in film, both formally and ideologically.

First, consider how flashbacks forge a specific relationship between image and language in silent films. In many instances flashbacks substitute images for dialogue or voice-over commentary, providing a different semiotic means of expression in a medium in which spoken language was absent. These image inserts of the past amplify, complicate, and expand the narrative while avoiding an abundance of written titles. The image is often privileged in the silent flashback as an autonomous and polysemic means of expression. A single flashback tableau image can generate many meanings and functions within a narrative. Montage of the flashback with the images surrounding it in the present often generates rich associations. More elaborate flashback sequences have internal image montage that is often quite extraordinary, so that in addition to an obvious meaning there are also many other implications that are far more subtle and complex.

Titles, freed by an image flashback from the responsibility of narrating the entire story from the past, can be reserved for the equivalent of voice-over commentary, or they can be used selectively to indicate dialogue in conjunction with the image flashback. This opens up a range of possibilities, including humorous or satirical use of the ironic disjunctions between the image narration and the character's verbal account. Flashbacks become an instance in which we can be made more aware than usual of the status of the image and of the voice.

In silent films, flashbacks have a great potential for innovation. In the earliest period any temporal anteriority is itself innovative. Once a certain codification sets in, innovation is pursued in variations in editing and punctuation techniques, changes in flashback form and function. Flashback development should not be seen as progressing from primitive to advanced in any qualitative sense. Apparent complication in flashback form does not necessarily indicate a more sophisticated inscription of the device. A single tableau image might be more polysemic than a more elaborate flashback that organizes its information in a particularly obvious manner, and, therefore, a flashback that appears quite simple may ultimately be more suggestive.

If the substitution of images for language appears to be a practical solution for silent film, it is one with broad aesthetic consequences—ones that will carry over to sound film. For even though sound gives film the possibility of more easily recounting the past verbally, the rich functions of image narration of flashbacks will sometimes be an aesthetic choice.

In fact, the basic functions of flashbacks in early silent film do carry over into sound film, with modifications we will examine later. Often flashbacks completely restructure narrative form, becoming pivotal to both film structure and ideology. This can be seen as serving the need of silent film production historically to diversify. It also allowed individual films to express various modes of narration, for the range of textual differences to be greatly expanded.

In the rest of the chapter, I will analyze several films from this period that display particularly intriguing uses of the flashback, as well as indicate those which I have found to be most common. Here, as elsewhere in the book, discussing the function of flashbacks from the perspective of textual difference means that I must refer quite specifically to the inscription of the flashback within these film's narratives. From the body of silent American films containing flashbacks I have been able to view, or in cases where the films are lost, where detailed enough verbal descriptions remain, seven major functions that flashbacks serve can be delineated. This list is certainly not exhaustive, but it offers a way of seeing the types of commonly used functions in this period; it should be remembered that within textual practice most of these functions occur in combination and that they may be used within various filmic modes (eg. comic, ironic, dramatic, melodramatic):

1. Story within the story—contemporary frame/past history.

2. Trial testimony—presenting the words of witnesses as visual renderings with various ideological consequences.

3. Didactic reminder to the audience of events already seen—almost always coupled with some other function.

4. Haunting of the past—representing a certain character's obsession with the past, sometimes pathological, sometimes an emblem of loyalty or fidelity; a subjective focalization—thoughts rather than a story are told here, thus the voice is internal rather than external.

5. Character's narration—a story of the past to which a character gives voice; a subjective focalization—often used in an extended format for biographies (as is also characteristic of function six).

6. Character's past explained—a means of filling in expository material, the traits of a character through imagery of the past, not necessarily focalized as a subjective view of the character.

7. Revealing an incident withheld from the exposition of the narrative for the purpose of suspense, or to engender comic misunderstandings.

To demonstrate how these functions tend to occur in conjunction with one another, let's consider *Cry of the Children,* a film directed by Lois Weber in 1911. Its flashback is used both as a didactic reminder to the audience of earlier narrative occurrences from which a moral lesson is to be drawn and as a haunting of the past visited upon a character who has behaved selfishly in her own class interests to the detriment of others.

Cry of the Children is a crusading plea for an end to grueling child labor exploitation. It opens with the title, "Do you hear the children weeping, O my brothers, ere the sorrow comes with years?" This archaic, poetic language continues throughout the titles and the initial title sets the stage for the didactic flashback to come both in tone and content. The film opens on a plane of generality before attaining narrative specifics, providing images that depict the factory life of poor workers almost as a reconstructed documentary.

After this didactic opening, the film shifts from the general view of the mill to the beginning of a day at the home of a family of mill workers. With the title, "Little Alice, their one ray of sunshine, is to be kept free from the factory," the film introduces its major enigma—can a working-class family preserve its youngest child from the harshness of factory labor?

Circumstances force Alice into the factory where her death is depicted as an industrial accident. Before the actual flashback there is an apparition scene where Alice reappears to her family in superimposition, arms outstretched as if she were an angel. The real flashback of the film, though, appears in a kind of narrative coda as a vision of the mill owner's wife. From a long shot of the factory a dissolve carries us into a repetition of images of Alice's death, first, the scene at the machine when Alice fainted, then a dissolve to her family at the cemetery gate. The structure of the film establishes the flashback both as reiteration of the scenes of the working-class exploitation and suffering that the audience has already viewed, and as the memory haunting the mill owner's wife. The moral charge of the flashback is double, as indignant reminder of social injustice and as admonition to the wealthy exploiters that their unrighteous behavior will return to haunt them. Early films often display such emphatic moralizing characterized by a rhetoric of reiteration; here the opening title prefigures the flashback and the flashback doubles the climactic scene of the narrative. Flashbacks have a great potential for reiteration, as they can retell what has already been told. This emphatic voice is more common in early cinema than later, although Hollywood tends throughout its history to favor overstatement and repetition.

This same type of emphatic voice and moral advocacy is displayed in *The High Cost of Living*, M. Arnaud (1912), an early example of the flashback as trial testimony and biography. As we shall see later in this chapter, trial testimony and biography are two of the most common instances of flashback structures in American films of the twenties, functions that continue with similar frequency in the sound period as well. *The High Cost of Living* begins in the present as "Old Joel," a former iron worker is brought to trial. As the worker pleads his own case, each line of testimony is accompanied by images from the past that illustrate the action. In a sense, these titles serve as a kind of "voice-over" commentary, presenting the cost of food as too high, the boss denying the worker's demands, the decision to strike taken because the only alternative was "to die." In many instances the image-tableaux that follow these verbal explanations would be difficult to decipher alone and depend on the words for their complete signification. The effect of telling the story of labor struggles in flashback is to emphasize the sacrifices made in fighting for justice by a worker who is now old and broken, appearing before us one last time, pleading for "an end to tears," as the film title puts it. Thus the subjective experience of the past, one person's story told by himself, is deemed the most emotionally effective way to examine labor issues and historical events.

The story-told flashback was undoubtedly used by the mid-teens in rather mundane ways to fill in narrative information. Reviews begin to make negative comments about the device when it appears to be an after-thought of a screenwriter who suddenly decides the audience needs more background information.[34] In such early films as *The Passer-by,* Oscar Apfel (1912), and *Just a Shabby Doll,* directed for Thanhouser (1913), the flashbacks are integral and well-executed. Here, as illustration of the story-told, flashback imagery occupies most of the narrative and is made more complex by the way in which the temporal embeddings that result have the effect of highlighting the uncanny. In *The Passer-by,* a bachelor party invites a stranger in to dinner as part of a traditional ritual of including the first passer-by. He is prevailed to take his turn telling stories at the dinner's end. This initiates a flashback introduced by a striking dissolve from the older man directly facing the camera to a matching shot of him as a young man. The story, narrated by intertitles in the first-person and illustrative images, tells of his being abandoned by his sweetheart for another and as a result of his despair, going through a bankruptcy and finally being reduced to total privation. Upon returning to the present, with dissolves which match in reverse the entry to the flashback, we discover that the bridegroom is the son of his unfaithful sweetheart. The present frame in this case is responsible for creating the sense of the uncanny as the story-told is only made intriguing by the fact that it is told at this moment in this company as a result of random selection.

In *Just a Shabby Doll,* the uncanny is tied to the circulation of an object within the flashback, an object that is also the impetus for the storytelling in the frame. The father tells his daughter (in first-person intertitles accompanied by flashback imagery) the story of the "shabby doll" which she has been given; it is also the story of his romance with his wife. As a child, he gives his future sweetheart the doll as a present; an embedded flashback repeats the doll exchange scene as a superimposed frame within the image of the now-grown sweetheart being denied the right to marry him by her wealthy father. After circumstances reverse the class positions of the former sweethearts and make them strangers to one another, the doll serves as the clue which permits recognition and reuniting. Magically connecting the past and the present, the charmed object is auxiliary to the flashback as a device. This combination of devices will repeat in many flashback narratives that annex the supernatural and strive for surrealism.

Rearranging Narrative Order—Hermeneutics of Early Flashbacks

Many flashbacks in early films had as their primary role rearranging narrative order, filling in gaps structured into the narrative. An early ellipsis leaves open a missing link in the narrative chain that is later supplied as a story told by a character to others who would not have witnessed it. This type of ellipsis and retrospective revelation set the stage for much future innovation in montage and point of view in relationship to filmic narrative structure.

An example is the 1912 western, *Blazing the Trail,* which recounts an Indian attack on the Cooper family who depart from a wagon train accompanied by their daughter's fiancé, Blake. As originally presented the encounter with the Indians begins peacefully; though the Indians are shown looking at the Coopers's wagon from a bluff in a shot which in its deep focus positioning threatens conflict, the Indians approach calmly and are offered food by the Coopers. Blake is off finding water, and it is from his vantage point that the first indication of the attack is given, as his point of view shot reveals the Coopers's campsite burned to the ground.

Only later does one survivor of the attack, the son, Jack Cooper, tell his story of what happened, filling in the ellipsis in the original telling; a single-shot flashback shows the Indians, having partaken of their food and coffee, shooting at their hosts. Although this is a very early filmic western, the Indian attack was already a cliché of the western as literary genre. The flashback here allows for the disruption and postponement of the narration of the attack, giving the cliché an imaginative twist and making the most of shifting spectator identification with the visual image.

Another type of narrative ellipsis filled in by a later flashback is seen in *Little Meena's Romance,* Paul Powell for Triangle-Fine Arts (1916), starring Dorothy Gish as an orphan from the Dutch settlements in Pennsylvania who has come to live with her relatives in New York City. Owen Moore plays a German count who takes Meena to a roadhouse, followed shortly by the scandalized relatives who demand an explanation. There is then a flashback to the wedding ceremony as the count tells of his earlier, secret marriage to Meena. Here the ellipsis and subsequent flashback revelation allow for a surprise, humorous ending, a last minute inversion that has an ideological function. It legitimizes the film's flirtation with unsanctified sexuality by transforming a roadhouse encounter from horror to consecration worthy of a relieved chuckle. We will see that flashbacks are often used to restructure narratives in such a way as to work through the ideological constraints of a given period and to supply ideological legitimation. After the initial voyeurism freely exercised in many of the earliest films gave way to longer narratives that adopted more bourgeois ideologies, the next years of American film production are marked by a greater restraint on sexual display and behaviors. Innovative structures represent one way to circumvent such constraints.

Melodrama, Motivation, and Self-Consciousness

Flashbacks could also offer an explanation of character motivation. In *Regeneration,* a film directed by Raoul Walsh in 1916 for Fox, the inner thoughts and past history of a gangster are exposed in flashback, providing his childhood and early gang experiences as explanations of both his will to reform and his difficulty in escaping his gangster role. The opening scenes of the film depict a young orphan, Owen being brought up by a drunk who is always arguing with his wife. The tenement environment is depicted as one of child abuse and matrimonial dispute that Owen escapes only by taking to the streets.

An ellipsis takes us to Owen at age seventeen defending a hunchback kid, and then another to Owen at twenty-five attaining the leadership of his gang. The first flashback occurs when Owen is shown drinking beer at a club frequented by gangsters. The image dissolves to one of Owen as a child licking an ice cream cone. We have seen Owen's childhood earlier in the film depicted quite differently from this, virtually devoid of such normal childhood pleasures. We might expect a different link to the past from the flashback imagery at this point in the film: a simple moralistic image to remind us of the connection of the adult beer-drinking gangster to the young boy shown in the tenement carrying pails of beer to his father. The ice cream flashback, while still evoking the earlier scenes, gives us another side of the gangster's childhood.

As this contrasting past emerges, we remember the interim image of Owen helping the hunchback boy. We are thereby prepared for a new juncture of the narrative, for it is at this nightclub that Owen first sees and becomes fascinated by Mamie, a settlement worker, who will be his inspiration for the regeneration promised in the title.

The film has already told us through its structure that gangsters are underprivileged kids coming from environments filled with alcohol and violence. The flashback implies in addition that their fast living is to be seen in relationship to the childhood pleasures they rarely enjoyed, while subsequent sequences develop the maternal imagery associated with Mamie and turn their romance into a recovery of the lost mother.

However, Owen's more recent past intervenes to block his reformation, and this too is marked by a flashback. One of Owen's former gang buddies pleads for aid with a dissolve to a flashback of his having covered for Owen during an earlier police chase. Owen pays his debt to the past with another transgression, but the film's denouement, a cataclysm of violence, acts as a purification ritual saving Owen from the evil influences of his past under the sign of Mamie's superimposed image.

In early silent films like *Regeneration,* the flashback was used to emphasize the past as a motivational force within the psychology of character. In *Regeneration*, it is especially intriguing to analyze how different stages of a character's past, recalled selectively in the unfolding of the narrative, serve to explain narrative turns and reversals. The film is preoccupied with the way past personal history forms values and incites actions, a concern which it plays out by stopping its melodramatic action for inserts of past incidents.

A film whose own self-referential mode highlights the flashback as a filmic device for memory and character construction is *Hoodoo Ann,* directed by Lloyd Ingraham for Triangle-Fine Arts in 1916, starring Mae Marsh and Robert Harron. The film's narrative traces the growth of the heroine, "Hoodoo Ann," from orphanage outcast to flapper dressed in modern finery copied from "Vogy" magazine. Here the flashback comes at the end of the film to reverse and clarify the false leads given in the film's hermeneutic coding of a murder; it does so in explicit reference to a film-within-the-film that the characters see, linking the flashback as device to a self-conscious representation.

The reflexive irony begins when Ann enters a movie theater and a close-up on a movie poster announces,"Miss Stella the Broadway favorite, supported by James Kinley, the well-known legitimate star in 'Mustang Charlie's Revenge,' a Western Idyll produced by the Hoboken film company." "Broadway favorite" and "legitimate star" are most certainly digs at Famous Players-Lasky, the studio which tried to boost its appeal by promoting stage and opera greats as film stars. The western's title, "Mustang Charlie's Revenge," parallels the nickname "Hoodoo Ann." The film emphasizes this parallel between the melodrama and embedded western by matching a scene of handholding in the film to a close-up of Ann in the audience holding her boyfriend's hand. In the film within the film, the heroine wields a gun to save her lover, which inspires Ann later to rummage through a trunk for a costume and even don a gun that she is unaware is loaded.

This leads to the incident that will present us with the false lead. As Ann is practicing histrionics, aping the film, her gun goes off. She assumes that her shot kills her neighbor who "crawled away to die like that man in the picture." This generates a first flashback, marked by a fade-out from a long shot of Ann to a fade-in on a scene from the western in which Mustang Charlie crawls away from a saloon table to die alone. The use of this flashback to the fictional embedded narrative comments on this modern woman's character—how her memory and imagination is being formed by film. Ann's memory mimics that of the fictional conventions of the movies she has seen and her logic is so tempered by these constructs that she spends a sleepless night convinced she has committed murder.

The film continues to build on this presumption, as Ann refuses to marry her boyfriend, convinced of her imminent arrest; when her neighbor's wife becomes a suspect, Ann begins a confession, only to faint before completing it. At this point, the neighbor's husband returns to offer the flashback explanation of the misconstrued events and provide the film's denouement. An intertitle gives the "voice-over" narration, "I vowed I wouldn't stand Sarah's jawin' any longer" and we are shown the husband going to sleep under a haystack, accompanied by "I don't know how long I slept." The flashback includes the husband's imaginary view of his wife asleep in their warm bed which serves to explain his return, while the bloodstains turn out to be from a cat who came into Hoodoo's line of fire.

This final flashback turns what appeared to be a melodrama into a comedy of errors. Announced as a "Drama in obscure and peaceful corners," *Hoodoo Ann* turns out to be a sophisticated joke using flashbacks and a film within a film to satirize the melodramatic conventions of early cinema. Interpreted on another level, it operates like *Merton of the Movies* (a 1924 film directed by James Cruze also using flashbacks) to express a cultural awareness that the cinema was transforming contemporary consciousness through its means of expression as well as its conventions and myths. The filmic fantasies depicted within these films are shown as appropriated by a character's consciousness and imagination, with the flashback being one of the ways this appropriation is presented within the visual rhetoric of silent film.

Despite the emergence of this early satirical view of melodramatic conventions, American filmic expression throughout the silent period exhibited the hyperbolic tendencies and knotty narrative coincidences of melodrama. Romantic couples' fates were threatened by intervening events and various evil forces necessitated suspenseful last minute rescues or noble sacrifices in films which provided directly stated moral lessons and pursued elaborately wrought and obviously underscored symbolism. The flashbacks found a home within this genre as a tableau memory image. It became a way of expressing passions indelibly etched in consciousness. Such flashback memories are bound by the conventions of this genre to *cause* other events.

Thomas Ince's 1915 western, *The Deserter,* employs such flashback causality. The narrative concerns a love triangle at Fort Hamilton in 1868; Lieutenant Parker is given a flashback at the moment he realizes his sweetheart, Belle, is attracted to his superior officer. Over a close-up of Parker's face, the image dissolves back to an earlier scene in Belle's parlor when she promised to marry him. A title then tells us that the lieutenant decides to spite Belle by visiting Hell's Half Acre, a gambling house and dance hall, wherein a series of incidents occur that lead to the lieutenant's desertion, exile, and expiation in death in an Indian battle.

The flashback to the unfulfilled marital promise serves not only to inform the audience of the broken vow, but also to illustrate how an image of love and hope, remembered at the moment of betrayal, becomes a source of pain and torment. This pain, in turn, will cause other actions, as the tableau image from the past cuts immediately to the next sequence in a forbidden and shameful milieu. The saloon violates the memory of the domestic foyer, which itself has been negated by the circumstance of rivalry. The flashback thus graphically contrasts sites with opposing meanings, creating for the audience a vivid sense of the character's emotional trauma, as a split between two worlds, one of which is the negation of the other.

The film melodrama depicts emotional states of mind through the flashback representation of not only events in the past, but also sites or images saturated with symbolic meanings within the structure and ideology of the narrative. These become central to systems of character representation and identification. *Knights of the Trail,* a William S. Hart western from 1915 highlights this focus on character memory and emotional state and markedly addresses its inserted flashback to the film's audience as if to underscore the process of enunciation and identification taking place.

The flashback occurs when the heroine, Molly discovers her beau leads a double life as a mysterious bandit. Molly looks directly at the camera, and therefore out at the audience, as the image dissolves to the flashback of an image of a wanted poster for a bandit being hung in the restaurant where she works. The direct address of this flashback, framed as it is by the character's stare into the audience, underscores the next narrative demand, for the hero to destroy this association with the wanted poster through an expiatory good deed.

We can see that while some films like *Hoodoo Ann* could use flashbacks as part of their satire of the mechanisms of melodrama and audience susceptibility to these conventions, other films from the same period were using flashbacks to present the core of the melodramatic problematic. Flashbacks symbolize the conditions that inform a character's emotional trauma and initiate a shift of direction in the narrative. As such they activate conflicts and emphasize the symbolic thematization so central to melodrama.

Flashbacks as Emotional Symbolism in Griffith's Films

Several films by D.W. Griffith, who is today the best known filmmaker from this period of American film, display this highly melodramatic mode of flashback narration. Flashbacks serve Griffith's films both as subjective memory inserts from a character's point of view and as illustrations of stories being told. While the functions of flashbacks in Griffith's films are similar to those in other contemporaneous films, flashbacks are central to Griffith's vision of history, saturated with emotional identification and symbolism. We can see his films as one of the formative stages of the massive effort in American films to subjectivize history (further examined in chapter three). His adaptations of melodramas are constructed with the kind of visual inventiveness and creative montage that allows the filmic melodrama to disengage itself from its theatrical heritage and develop an imagistic realm of expression all its own. So even though earlier cautionary statements in this chapter were meant to avoid taking D.W. Griffith as the "inventor" of the flashback or any of its various uses, we can still look at his works as significant contributions to the inscription of the flashback. Since the Griffith films under consideration here span the period 1915 to 1921, this section will also serve as an historical transition from the teens to the twenties, allowing us to ask in what ways the means of expression developed in the earliest periods of filmmaking continue in later flashback use.

The theme of collective memory as determinant of history and individuals as exemplares of collective memories in their most personalized and subjective form is developed in *Birth of a Nation* (1915) through the use of one of Griffith's melodramatic strategies, the interweaving of personal tragedy and love stories with epic narrations of major historical events. The film portrays the conviction that the South will not forget either its past way of life or the indignities it suffered in defeat.

The story, derived from Thomas Dixon's novel *The Clansman,* centers its narration on the unlikely interaction between the Camerons, a South Carolina plantation family, and the Stonemans, the family of a Northern abolitionist statesman during the Civil War. One of the Stoneman sons falls in love with the older Cameron daughter, while one of the Cameron sons becomes equally enamored of a daguerrotype of his friend's younger sister, Elsie Stoneman. Flashbacks are used selectively in the part of the film devoted to Reconstruction to display the memories and histories which haunt the South.

The first indications of the budding romance of the "little Colonel," Ben Cameron, and Elsie Stoneman (Lillian Gish), are free from intrusive echoes of the past, but an immediate contrast to this idyllic scene of love among the Southern oaks is provided by the next sequence. Introduced by the title, "Bitter memories will not allow the Poor Bruised South to forget," the parallel romance is presented as a less optimistic interaction. Margaret Cameron is shown in medium shot, pausing as she gathers flowers by the picket fence of her family's house to pluck the petals sadly from one of the flowers. A cut to Phil Stoneman shows him looking at her, then another cut shows him entering the shot of Margaret trying to talk to her from the far side of the fence. She makes a gesture of rebuff, then exits on the left side of the image frame. She then enters into a medium close-up shot from frame right and stares off to the left, away from Stoneman. There is a cut back to his further entreaty and a return to her staring away, oblivious to his presence, avoiding his look. A fade-out on this image cuts to a flashback tableau image of one of her brothers dying in the arms of a superior Confederate officer. We cut back to her, still staring and remembering, then cut back to Stoneman, turning away. The segment ends with her still trancelike, turning even farther left and walking away.

This flashback poignantly shows memories of death and the historical opposition signified by the war intruding upon the romantic scene, keeping each of them on opposite sides of the fence, making it impossible for glances claimed by the internal vision of past to meet in the present.

This pessimism then contaminates the first couple's prior happiness, as the title, "Pride battles with love for hearts' conquest," introduces a troubled scene between Elsie and Ben. When they once more meet in an outdoor setting, she turns away from him, entering another shot alone, crying. He comes to her, comforting her with an embrace, but the tensions of North-South romance are now doubly marked, both hinging on the reluctance of the women. Yet only the Southern woman's grief and loyalty to her past are illustrated in flashback.

If Elsie is troubled, her doubts are not graphically clarified—and this is crucial to the ideological project of the film; only later does her refusal of romance focus on Ben's leadership in the Ku Klux Klan, an apprehension that the film will attempt to show is wrong-headed. Elsie, riding in the victorious Klan parade at the end of the film, has been made to "learn that the Klan should be welcomed as heroic saviors of the South's past." She is denied any historical memory of slavery or the abolitionist cause for which her other brother gave his life. Margaret Cameron's flashback, slicing as it does between the double romances, is structurally crucial to the film's ideological slant, for it structures memory as the South's province.

Other representational devices in the film will complete the symbolism opened by this flashback memory image, including another flashback which craftily supports the film's racism and its nostalgia for Aryan privilege and domination. After the blacks are victorious in the post-war election, Cameron is shown telling a group of whites gathered at his house of what, a title tells us, are "a series of outrages that have oc-curred." Here the flashback sequence is meant to illustrate Cameron's statement, "The case was tried before a Negro magistrate and the verdict rendered by a Black jury." Although we never get any indication of the charges against the white family on trial, the images in the flashback attempt to martial one's sympathy for the whites and foster disgust at the notion of a courtroom dominated by blacks. As a black magistrate is shown addressing the jury, the only whites visible in this shot are seated in the back of the courtroom. There is a cut to a closer shot of a black witness animatedly gesticulating during his testimony. A cut to the jury shows one of them asleep, while a cut to the white family shows the little girl terrified, being comforted by a hug from her father. Then the jury is shown bowing to the judge. A final long shot shows the witness being congratulated by his buddies in the front of the courtroom while the whites in the back are being chided by a large black woman.

When the image returns to Cameron telling the story, the film's audience is expected to read this sequence in the most prejudicial manner possible to conform to the notion that what we just saw was a true outrage. We are to assume the whites are innocent (the presence of the child encourages this), the witness is giving false testimony, the jury is inattentive and conditioned by the judge, and the black woman is an abusive creature. Reading the images with those assumptions, the burden is removed from the "spoken" words of Ben Cameron for the spectators; conclusions are drawn from observation of the supposedly objective flashback to the courtroom. What we see in *Birth of a Nation,* then, is the use of flashbacks for ideological argumentation within the fiction; as flashbacks, they allow the narrative to marshall a representation of history that is quite slanted to its own purposes and to pass that history off as a visually "documented" truth.

The power granted flashback images in *The Birth of a Nation* is mirrored in the narrative by Ben Cameron's love for a daguerrotype; the logic of Griffith's emotional symbolism is to permit images laced with sentimental or prejudicial appeal to argue emotionally for the ideological implications made by the narrative and create emotional identification with the Camerons. Once the Stoneman participants in the romances conform to the Southern perspective, the film can end with a double honeymoon without troublesome flashbacks to disturb the closure in love and peace.

We begin to realize from the structural analysis of a film like *Birth of a Nation* how pivotal a device flashbacks can be for the filmic narrative, yet how selective its use often is. Certain characters get certain kinds of flashbacks at given moments, and analysis of a film can benefit from remarking not only on the presence of a given flashback but the absence of others, not only on what information is presented in a flashback, but what is left out.

Griffith's *Intolerance* (1916), a film that weaves together four narratives from different historic periods, is sometimes described as a modern story with flashbacks to religious and political conflicts in the times of Babylon, Christ, and the Huguenots. The footage of the modern story was originally intended as an autonomous film, and its clear, emotional narrative may seem more involving than the epic extravaganzas or the moral illustration of the passion play; still, in the final version of *Intolerance,* the present-day story does not frame the other stories in a flashback logic. Each of these four narrative strands is interspersed within a structure of parallel development, though in somewhat unequal proportions.

However, actual flashbacks do occur within the modern day story of *Intolerance,* including one that violates its announced focalization. This first flashback occurs during the report of the middle-class "reformers" to Miss Jenkins on their moralistic clean-up activities. It is awkwardly introduced with the intertitle, "You were with us when we raided, . . ." before cutting back to an image of young prostitutes being herded into paddy wagons. If Miss Jenkins had been present at the arrest, it would be illogical for her fellow reformers to provide her with a graphic description of the events, as represented by flashback images. Further, the images within the flashback do not correspond to the attitude the reformers would take in recounting the story, since the film techniques and titles often ridicule their activities. A tracking shot across the line of reformers is followed by the title, "When women cease to attract, they often turn to reform as a second choice." This sarcasm from an external, authorial voice is then supplemented by a series of close-ups of the women, as if to prove that all members of the women's reform movement were either old or ugly. A commentary that does not emanate from the original teller of the incident continues as another image of the police herding the women is followed by a contrasting series of close-ups of men looking at the young prostitutes with expressions of lust. The authorial voice further intrudes with the admonition, "But these results they do not report," followed by images of homemade distilleries and young women meeting men on the street rather than in a brothel. The flashback device here is violated, as the filmmaker deliberately abandons midway the constraint of the story-being-told, usurping the female character's voices to allow for his own editorializing on the reform movement.

This gross violation of the posited voice and focalization of a flashback midway in its duration is certainly uncommon in later filmmaking and it is difficult to say how common it was at the time Griffith made *Intolerance.* It was perhaps less obtrusive in the context of the moralistic and didactic voice we have already noted in flashback films of the teens and the shift undoubtedly remained less visible to those who had no sympathy for the reform movement.

The flashback which is central to the modern story in *Intolerance,* in contrast, is far more typical of a flashback intervention at the height of a melodramatic narrative line; analysis of its function will show that it reverberates both backwards and forwards across the narrative, unifying the action and the character motivations according to psychological determinants. The Musketeer crime boss has tricked his way into the "Dear Little One's" apartment while her husband, "the Boy," is not home, only to have "the Boy" return to confront him. Watching this scene through the apartment window from the fire escape, the "Friendless One" has a subjective memory flashback before she shoots the Musketeer who had been her lover. Her flashback is to a tableau image taken from a scene earlier in the film, prior to the departure of these working-class characters for the city after a prolonged strike at the Jenkin's plant forced them to leave their homes. "The Boy," suitcase in hand, is shown kindly wishing his neighbor, "the Friendless One," farewell.

The motivations suggested by this image are multiple. In repeating an earlier scene, the flashback gives the Friendless One a more intense motive for slaying her faithless lover, for the remembrance of the Boy's kindness makes her "fallen woman" status all the more painful. There is a hint that the Friendless One is attracted to the Boy, making her act of violence against the Boss a gesture against the Boy's enemy. Further, the flashback reminds the film's audience of all the opening scenes of the film that set up the conditions of this flashback; the closing of the mill and the corrupting city environment to which they are forced to migrate are recalled at the very moment of these characters' greatest peril.

The flashback also reverberates through subsequent sequences, as it supplies a motive for the Friendless One's incriminating behavior as she follows the Dear Little One's quest for the governor's pardon of the Boy who has been arrested for her crime. The flashback is a pivotal hinge to the structure of the modern story, connecting early segments to the slaying and the slaying to the final last minute rescue of the Boy, supplying sociological and psychological depth to this part of *Intolerance*. It is supplemented by a final flashback that ties up one major loose end in the trial sequence. The Boy testifies that the gun did once belong to him as the police are claiming, but that he didn't commit the murder. This testimony is illustrated by a flashback image of the Boy returning his gun to his boss as a gesture reinforcing his decision to quit his life of crime. On one level, the flashback of the gun's return ties up the loose end of how the Boy's gun was available for the Friendless One to use and gives more evidence of his innocence of the crime. Seen in terms of symbolic coding, it doubles the previous flashback in building a symbolic opposition between innocence as depicted in the flashbacks and guilt associated with the narrative moment in which they occur. These flashbacks take on their own moral thematizing, a return or the longing to a return to innocence. Innocence is found in the past.

This rhetorical figure of nostalgia is strongly reiterated in *True-Heart Susie* (1917), which uses four flashbacks as integral to its rendering of the persistence of Susie and William's true romance, despite William's attraction to and subsequent marriage to a "milliner from Chicago," a flapper. The first flashback is not about a magic recovery of the past, but a trust in past values—one that is depicted, at least temporarily, as misguided.

The first flashback occurs after Susie is shown watching as William walks by with his new flapper fiancée, and she returns home to mimic the modern fashion in hopes of regaining William's attention. The flashback is to an earlier scene at the soda fountain, which a title anchors as Susie's memory of William's remarks at this site, ones disparaging "painted" ladies. The flashback "causes" Susie to return temporarily to her less fashionable attire—only for her to realize that her trust in memory is dooming her to failure, for she has not succeeded in deflecting William's interest in the modern woman. However, Susie's temporary negation of nostalgia is later, finally circumvented by a compromise that reestablishes the values of the past.

Ensuing flashbacks take up this task. Both William and Susie have flashbacks to scenes of their youthful romance; William's comes after he becomes disenchanted with his flapper wife who is less desirable in marriage than she was as a flirt, and Susie's, while she is shown reading William's old love letters. A final flashback occurs at the end of the film after William's wife dies when her partying indirectly leads to pneumonia and Susie's noble attempts to nurse her back to health are of no avail. William is free to renew his romance with Susie, which he does with a final kiss that engenders a flashback image of Susie and William walking together years before. The last three flashbacks counteract the temporary negation of the figure of nostalgia of the first flashback; they partake of a direct representation of a longing for the past which "correctly" guides the direction of the present.

If this return is so neatly circular, we must still recognize that the motor force of the narrative, that which separates ordinary truth from nostalgic return, is the social force of modernity represented here by changing appearances and sexual roles. By killing off the flapper, the film negates the modern woman in her most explicit form. However, Susie adapts her own "true-heart" nature by acquiring some aspects of a modern style, thus reconciling nostalgia with the intrusive inevitability of change as a compromise narrative formation.

As we shall see in chapter five in the analysis of forties' melodrama, flashbacks to past loves and lovers' enunciations will in this later period often be presented as neurotic symptoms. In *True-Heart Susie,* clinging to such memories is instead presented as one of Susie's positive traits, and as William's saving grace when he finally shares in the flashback imagery. Thus the flashbacks counterbalance the modern forces of instability, closing the film with a dominant sense of continuity with past values despite intervening transgressions and slight compromises.

It is intriguing to see many of the same elements of *True-Heart Susie* reworked in another Griffith melodrama, *The White Rose* (1923). Again, a series of several flashbacks is used for the tale of a romantic triangle between a minister and two women; however, in *The White Rose,* the flapper, Bessie "Teazie" Williams (Mae Marsh), is the heroine and the narrative is structured to build sympathy with her that was lacking for the "modern woman" in the earlier film. The difference in the flashback inscription is ever so slight, but significant; instead of being primarily signs of nostalgic longing, here the flashbacks evoke sentimental remembrances of moments of desire tainted by guilt and a sense of loss when they intrude in the present. This textual difference is open to an historical reading as part of a gradual easing of strict moral proscriptions in Griffith's films, but we need to consider that the differences here might not be a matter of evolution or historical determinism. It might also be a matter of variations on the same tale whose elements are 1) a taboo or moral norm, 2) a violation of that taboo, 3) a redemption and reconciliation that modifies slightly the absolutes of the taboo, while maintaining the same value system that structured the taboo in the first place.

These flashbacks to object-engendered memory images of the brief sexual encounter of Bessie and Joseph bind both of them to a Victorian notion of the "souvenir"— the scrapbook, the pressed flower, the heart-shaped love token—as emblems of a romantic involvement. The souvenir here is not a simple evocation of pleasant memories, since the minister (Ivor Novello) is less the romantic hero than a cad and sexual adventurer; though the objects do provoke a flashback focalized by Joseph, the emotional response of this character is suppressed and delayed. The persistence of the emotional symbolism and the accumulation of objects and memory images, however, serve to align the audience with Bessie, to embue the flapper with traditional Victorian sensibility despite her modern appearance and to permit her marriage to Joseph at the film's end.

One can see, then, both a similarity to the flashback structures of *True-Heart Susie* and *The White Rose* and an important difference. The structure, symbolization, and ideology of the first film is far more completely inside the Victorian value system of opposing good women to bad women and holding up the past as a nostalgic repository of values worth recovering. Still, in *The White Rose* the remembrance of past romance is no longer a longing to recover that past, but is tinged with irony, as the promises of the past are recognized as false. This structure recognizes a hypocrisy at the core of the Victorian value system, one that the earlier film effaces under the sign of the Victorian "true-heart."

The emotional symbolism and the systematic interplay of flashbacks found in these films are also apparent in *Orphans of the Storm*, a Griffith melodrama from 1921. In *Orphans of the Storm*, however, the use of flashbacks is more dispersed and reiterative, serving as a systematic leitmotif unifying the narrative.[25] *Orphans*, like *Birth of a Nation* and *Intolerance*, also positions its melodrama of personal interactions against a larger referential canvas, the result being that the ideological function of its flashbacks simultaneously constructs meanings for the political events of history as well as for those of the couple and the family.

In its introductory scenes the film establishes all the material which will repeatedly return as flashbacks. Hoping she will be adopted, the working-class father of baby Henriette decides to leave her on the steps of Notre Dame; instead, he ends up taking both his own daughter and another little girl he finds lying there back home with him. The abandoned baby, Louise, who had been taken from her aristocratic mother, is accompanied with a locket, a letter, and gold coins. We see each object in close-up at the time of the forced abandonment by the mother and at the time of her discovery by Henriette's father.

When the film reintroduces the Countess de Linières as a middle-aged woman whose "past is secret," it reveals this past in flashbacks to the film audience. It is a return to the image of the infant Louise being taken from the Countess's bedroom. The second flashback in this series comes when we are reintroduced to the sisters as young women who are now orphans. A flashback from a two shot of Henriette (Lillian Gish) and Louise (Dorothy Gish) fills in the history of their family being stricken by the plague which kills their parents and causes Louise's blindness. A doctor responds hopelessly after examining Louise's eyes. The scene which follows this flashback in the present provides the image for a later flashback; it is an image of a solemn oath taken by Henriette to "be Louise's eyes, to never marry and to always take care of Louise." The flashback to the image of this oath-taking occurs when the Chevalier falls in love with Henriette after circumstances have separated her from Louise. The remembrance causes Henriette to postpone marrying the nobleman.

Yet here the narrative threads begin to cross in a tangled knot, for the Chevalier introduces Henriette to his aunt, the Countess of Linières. The knot begins to unravel when another flashback intervenes, depicting the story Henriette tells the Countess of her sister, repeating the images of the two babies and Louise's locket. At this moment, Louise passes on the street, below the very balcony on which Louise's real mother and Henriette are speaking. Before this "uncanny" coincidence can combine with Henriette's revelation to unravel the narrative knot, however, Henriette and the Countess are taken prisoners of the revolution.

The Louise/Henriette flashbacks are used to explain or to remind the audience of the circumstances surrounding these two sisters and to develop the connection between them and the Countess and her nephew, the Chevalier. More than this, they develop a kind of psychological determinism to explain the characters' motivations, by emphasizing how past events and personal secrets linger and return. The scene of the infant being taken away determines the behavior of the Countess, just as the oath determines that of Henriette. Particularly due to the French setting of this melodrama, but also due to its flashback structure, one is reminded of the writings of Victor Hugo, particularly, *Les Misérables*.[26] However, the psychological weight granted the past as it returns in memory images is less dynamic and complex here than in Hugo; characters in *Orphans of the Storm* do not shift their emotional associations with past events, but instead the image of the past is a kind of indelible mark systematically constructing their consistent and uniform "nature" as characters.

Witness the semic traits assigned Jean Setain, a tenant farmer on the estate of the Chevalier, ones which are also determined by a memory flashback. Called "Jean Forget-me-not," this character is marked by a nickname that indicates the quality he shares with Louise and the Countess. He is irrevocably marked by an image from the past. When he is first introduced bringing his apples to the manor, his introduction is accompanied by a flashback to the scene of his father's torture with molten lead by the father of the Chevalier. This same flashback is repeated later when Jean Setain sits as judge on the revolutionary tribunal considering the case of Henriette and the young Chevalier. This flashback to the scene of inherited hatred of the aristocracy clinches his own decision to send the relatively liberal son of his father's oppressor to the guillotine.

A third flashback series reiterates the scene of peasants standing in line for bread presented toward the beginning of the film. In this breadline scene, the young Chevalier is shown philanthropically buying bread for the starving peasants. The first repetition comes as a didactic insert within the scene of the aristocratic orgy, providing a contrast between the amusements of the privileged classes and poverty. The second repetition occurs later in the film when a highly fictionalized Danton remembers the breadline scene in a flashback, one that punctuates the condemnation of the Chevalier and Henriette to the guillotine; the flashback memory spurs Danton to stay their sentence in a last minute rescue.

There are thus three series of flashbacks in *Orphans of the Storm*: the Louise/Henriette series, the Setain series, and the breadline reiteration. The Louise/Henriette flashbacks develop the complex links of the two orphan heroines to the "good aristocracy." Personal past tragedies, loss of parents or loss of a child cross class affiliations. The sympathies that are engendered by the flashback revelation of Louise's story allow for a happy ending where double marriages efface class differences. In contrast, Jean Setain's flashbacks depict him as obsessed with a memory that remains an emblem of class oppression and is shown to stimulate his class hatred. Whereas his flashbacks could be seen as illustrating the thesis that revolutionary violence is an outgrowth of the violence done to oppressed classes in the past, this thesis is undercut by the greater empathy developed in the Louise/Henriette flashbacks. It's as if the film needs to contain the force of Jean Setain's flashbacks by structurally opposing them to a more developed melodrama and love story with a contrary ideological message.

In the four Griffith films discussed here, we have seen how flashback imagery is a part of a system of expression that aims at emotional responses by the viewer. Like the close-ups of objects embued with symbolic resonance and emotional investments, integral to Griffith's melodramas, these flashbacks are highly charged. They represent "emotional" remembrances by characters of incidents that have marked their experience and will become traits defining their future actions. The subjectivity of characters is systematically used within the overall narrative structure and ideology of each of these four films, in each case with a specificity of inscription that provides for the development of textual difference. While aspects of this difference *may* constitute an historical development—for example, an increasing challenge of absolute paradigmatic oppositions aligned with an absolute code of morality—we have also noted an overall similarity of style and sentimental evocation in Griffith which remains rooted in a system of Victorian values. For Griffith, the flashback is a tool to express the indelibly marked consciousness; an air of nostalgia, pathos, and even the maudlin accompanies these stamps of the past appearing in the present.

Flashbacks Rendering Verbal Narration Visual

The symbolic pictorial mode represented by Griffith's use of the flashback continues to be used in melodrama throughout the twenties, although like Griffith's stylized character names that border on preciosity ("Dear Little One," "Friendless One," etc.), the exaggerated aspects of this type of symbolic representation will be toned down by later filmmakers to avoid an outdated, maudlin tone. Along with this image symbolism, the flashback image will be used increasingly as a semiotic substitution. As more and more American films of the twenties are adaptations (of plays, short stories, and novels), the flashback becomes a means of filmically presenting theatrical and novelistic modes of narration. Within a form whose signifying elements do not include the spoken word of theater and which must reduce the written text to brief interventions in the form of written titles, the flashback serves as a kind of replacement for voiced explanations.

It is possible to see the use of the flashback in the late silent period as part of the compensation for the lack of sound and as an anticipation of the use of sound. By substituting a flashback for a story told verbally, the silent cinema could express complicated dialogue or monologue scenes without resorting to a plethora of wordy titles. The sound film also lends itself well to the same type of flashback, using a voice-over narration from the present to lead into or even continuously comment on visual returns to the past. As we shall see, the flashback will become a means for the sound cinema to avoid the static aspects of long verbal renderings and to develop complex narrational modes that combine the image and the spoken words, though sometimes as a bifurcated voice. The flashback as illustrator of dialogue is thus a technique that bridges the transition from silent cinema to sound.

The verbal narration need not always be "factually" true. At least two twenties flashback films, *The Goose Woman*, directed by Clarence Brown for Universal in 1925, and *Footloose Widows*, directed by Roy Del Ruth for Warner Brothers in 1926, display flashbacks illustrating characters prevarications.

The Goose Woman actually contains two examples of flashbacks used to replace a character's verbal narration: one true, one false. An economical exposition sets the stage for the flashbacks. Mary Holmes (Louise Dresser), as we find out through close-ups on the newspaper clipping she cherishes, was once the famous opera singer "Marie de Nardi" before an illegitimate child ended her career. In an opening scene that shows her living in poverty on a goose farm, Mary throws her son Gerald (Jack Pickford) out of her house after he objects to her drinking. A stage manager named Eldredge is murdered that same night near the farm. An initial flashback, belonging to Gerald's girlfriend Hazel Woods (Constance Bennett), offers her explanation as to how her pearl necklace was found at the scene of the crime. It narrates a scene which took place in her dressing room the night before, when she rejected Eldredge's advances and forced him to take back the necklace he had given her. This flashback contains clues to the enigma of who killed Eldredge which are all ultimately shown to be narratively true.

In contrast, the second flashback which follows immediately thereafter, when the detectives question the Goose Woman, will ultimately prove false. Seeking attention, Marie tells them a story, illustrated by flashback images, of seeing a car with only one headlight the previous night; she then reports seeing a man in a white coat shoot Eldredge. Periodically during this action, the flashback cuts to images of Marie watching the murder; the editing style seems to authenticate the Goose Woman's story in this regard, by such details as a close shot of Eldredge's face during the struggle. Marie's play for attention has the unfortunate consequence of turning her son into a prime suspect, since she has composed her lie out of elements (one headlight, a white coat) that correspond to his own visit to her house the previous night. When the Goose Woman changes heart and retracts her lie, the police still believe the story she has told in flashback.

By positioning the false flashback so soon after a flashback to which it grants narrative truth value, and presenting the flashback with filmwork that matches that of film scenes we ordinarily take to be truthful accounts of narrative events, the film raises some unsettling questions about the truth value of cinematic narration. However, this questioning of the epistemology of narrative form is not carried to the same intriguing degree of refinement we will later see operative in the flashback used in Hitchcock's *Stagefright* (1950), for example. The Goose Woman's flashback is presented in a context where the audience has already been given the motivation for her lie as well as having been shown Gerald's innocent visit. We know she is not simply narrating a scene lacking from the original narration of the night before, but fabricating a story that never occurred. The audience, unlike the police in the story, are not duped.

The film makes little of the unconscious incrimination by the mother of her resented son. Visually it is all there; the bitter woman unconsciously uses elements of her son's visit to create her false testimony. The denouement of the film, which includes a *deus ex machina* confession from a stagehand that he killed Eldredge to save Hazel, moves away from exploring the psychology of Mary Holmes and simply frees the film to end happily, with the mother reunited with her son and his sweetheart. Despite the potential of its structure, *The Goose Woman* is played only for an odd mixture of comedy and suspense.

Similarly, in *Footloose Widows* the spectators know from the outset that the main characters are only pretending to be wealthy widows to disguise their calculated search for husbands. So when one is questioned on how such a young woman came to be a widow, the other invents a flashback explanation of a fake husband committing suicide after mistaking a brother he had never met for his wife's lover. Here there is no question of fooling the spectators; rather the imaginative story is supplied with concrete illustration to partake fully of the comedic effects of the character's outrageous prevarication.

Most flashbacks that render verbal material visual are straightforward flashbacks, however, ones that are granted truth value within the narrative. Many twenties films tend to motivate such stories with supplemental narrative framing such as the biographical flashback and the trial testimony flashback, each of which were common conventions of twenties filmmaking.

Biographical Flashbacks

In the biographical flashback of the twenties, a life story is either told or remembered by a character, with most of the narrative being encompassed by the flashback and the present, later time serving primarily as a frame. *Secrets,* directed by Frank Borzage in 1924, stars Norma Talmage as an old woman, Lady Carlton, whose husband is critically ill.[27] She falls asleep writing in her diary and the flashbacks which ensue are understood as being the secrets she has recorded. This structure allows for shifts in narrative setting and genre, as well as ellipses that allow for the concentration on three separate episodes: one, a melodramatic elopement; the next a move into the western genre where the young couple fend off an attack by robbers; and finally, a love triangle in which the now wealthy Lady Carlton copes with her husband's infidelity. This flashback of the history of a marriage prepares for a return to the bedside vigil in the present, as her husband overcomes his physical crisis and appears to recover.

Secrets was followed the same year by *The Lady,* also directed by Frank Borzage and also starring Norma Talmadge. It is an obvious reworking of the earlier film, providing a vehicle for Talmadge who was critically praised for being convincing both as the young women and as the nurturing matrons in these two films. In *The Lady,* the flashback is motivated by a scene in which a former dancer tells the story of her life while sitting in a cafe during World War I; it tells of the dancer's marriage, her widowhood, and her separation from her baby. As the flashback ends, on the account of her spending years searching for her lost son, the image returns to the present, where we discover that one of the British soldiers overhearing her story in the cafe is her lost son. Both films have echoes in sound films that will be discussed in chapter four; *The Great Man's Lady* (1942) has a narrative structure quite similar to *Secrets,* while *The Lady* finds its echo in *To Each His Own* (1944). The similarity of these later films to their twenties antecedents indicates how the flashback structure of the biographical silent film provides a solid frame for the development of the "women's film." The diary and the confidential revelation that these biographical melodramas use as their framing convention correspond to the narrative intimacy of the later genre.

Another biographical flashback film from 1925, *Soul Fire* by John S. Robertson, shows how flashbacks can be interspersed with a scene in the present in a structure that modifies the nature of the frame. Since the present scene is a performance by a conductor of his symphonic compositions, this structure also becomes a discourse on programmatic music. The narrator is a music critic whose version of the composer's life is segmented to correspond to the symphony, with episodes in Paris, Port

Saïd and the South Sea Islands. The flashback segments can be understood as the visions called up by the programmatic musical movements of the symphony as heard by the critic and the composer's parents, who had originally thwarted their son's musical ambitions and for whom this musical biography is meant to serve as an object lesson in the ways of the creative soul.

In the original screenings of this silent film, the corresponding music was provided by a live orchestra; the flashback narrative is a way of incorporating in the diegesis (the film narrative) that which ordinarily remain the non-diegetic musical accompaniment. The flashbacks raise the issue of the semiotics of programmatic music. Does music that narrates or evokes images do so in the same sense that this film presents narrative, representational images? The structure of this film sets up an exact equivalence between the flashback narrative imagery and one's imaginary vision while listening to music, implying an affirmative response to that question. The processes of imagination are given the power to fully reconstitute representations of the past, filling in the unknown from the musical cues.

While these biographical flashback films are basically frame-tales, there is a close connection between them and the inserted flashback tableaux that gives us a clarification of a single element of the character's past. Characters are assumed to be mimetic representations of people who have life histories that affect them psychologically. Characters are not always "true-to-life," for not all films operate within a realistic mode, but even within exaggeration and fantasy, characters are given a density through reference to a past and memories.

An interesting variation on these biographical/psychological assumptions is the trope used in some flashback's films of one's life passing through one's memory when one anticipates death. Thus a film from 1928, *The Last Moment,* directed by Paul Fejos, structures its flashbacks as a memory flashback montage insert within the final sequence of the film, the criminal's execution. Here we see a complete inversion of the duration of the biographical flashback relative to the present action from that of the frame story discussed above. Whereas the frame story has a present sequence of short duration framing a long flashback or series of flashbacks, the moment-before-death flashback trope structures films with a long and ongoing present narration and a short flashback near the end. As such they present opposing treatments of flashback amplitude as well; in both cases, the amplitude of the flashbacks covers most of the biography of character in question, but in the moment-before-death flashback this great amplitude is much more condensed, providing a quite different vision of memory. Here memory is not a conscious retelling and not at all like traditional film narration, but rather a collage of elements, elliptically and metonymically represented, gathered together by some unconscious force. This moment-before-death flashback is one instance where the traditional narrative structure that develops in American silent film adopts a narrative mode characteristic of the European avant-garde (a form of memory montage that will be analyzed in detail in the next chapter).

Trial Testimony Flashbacks—the Eyewitness of Film

Trial testimony engenders flashbacks which create an atmosphere where guilt, innocence, condemnation, or clemency are the constant undercurrents of each scene related. The film's spectators become the trial's jury, witnessing both the courtroom drama and an imaginary recreation of the circumstances involved in the crime. As such, these films represent the imaginary fulfillment of the "dream" of trial lawyers and the dread of trial justice, to have verbal accounts transformed into images so vivid that they efface the verbal and subjective aspects of testimony. If film has so readily been appropriated for this type of fictional legal spectacle, it is due to both the mythic charge of the eyewitness, the one who saw the truth that the fictional film can represent, and the taboo on taking photographs or filming inside the courtroom (only recently lifted), a taboo that the fiction film can transgress.

The Woman on Trial, a film directed by Mauritz Stiller for Paramount in 1927, and *The Night Watch,* directed by Alexander Korda in 1928 for First National, are both films that use this courtroom flashback structure. Both films were made at the end of the silent period, and *The Night Watch* even used sound effects and music, but no words, on its Vitaphone sound track. These films display the readiness of such trial films for the transition to sound.

Both films are also characteristic of the kind of narrative that dominated film in the middle and late twenties, the romantic drama of infidelity or jealousy, a thousand versions of the love triangle. In *The Woman on Trial,* Pola Negri stars as Julie Moreland, a murder defendant in a French courtroom who is accused of killing her lover, Gaston Napier. Her subjective flashback account reclaims instead that the murder was the result of a revenge plot arranged by her rich and jealous husband; she fired on Napier in self-defense from his attempted forced seduction, arranged by her husband. This argument depends on recounting her original motivation for her marriage, conceived as a means of helping a consumptive artist, Pierre Bouton, with whom she is in love. Her narration of this complex intrigue wins her acquittal, leaving all legal credibility behind in favor of the emotional identification; we, as audience-jury, are led to identify with her love with one artist and accept her marriage to wealth to support his sanatorium care as self-sacrifice. We are never led to question her assertion that she is the innocent victim of her husband's jealousy and another artist's lust, for their portrayal, within the flashback, shows both of these men to be evil. The subjectivity of this portrayal of the past is not in question.

The Night Watch which stars Billie Dove as the wife and star witness in the court martial of her husband Captain Corlaix, accused of the murder of Lieutenant Brambourg, makes use of the trial frame to rearrange the temporal order of the flashbacks, inscribing them within the hermeneutic revelation in a more complex manner. Testimony provides us with flashback images of the scene of the crime at the time of discovery, including the finding of Corlaix's gun near the body. Only after all the prosecution testimony, depicted in flashbacks, does Corlaix's wife testify in her husband's defense, having withheld her testimony due to its personally compromising nature. The "portée" of her flashback is anterior to all other flashbacks seen thus far, taking us back to a dinner party aboard ship for the officers' wives a few hours before World War I was declared. When Captain Corlaix hurries the women ashore, keeping the declaration and departure secret, Mme. Corlaix's former lover, a Lieutenant d'Artell, urges her to stay behind in his cabin. This allowed her to witness the murder of Brambourg, and finally, to testify that the murderer was not her husband.

Once these trial flashbacks are underway, the imagery is presented contradictorily, as both narrated testimony and objective account. Although different witnesses may narrate different parts of the story, there is little questioning of subjectivity or faulty memories or development of overlapping and contradictory versions as each unfolds—although later trial testimony flashbacks will exploit these alternatives. The emphasis in the twenties is rather on the reconstruction of past events viewed by a witness with a clarity characteristic of the present. Like many flashbacks, once the trial flashback is under way, it is impossible to distinguish sequences within that flashback from other sequences occurring in the present on formal levels of filmic style.

For trial testimony flashbacks, this similarity between illustrated testimony and the representation of the present has ideological ramifications. The effacement of the difference between the spoken account of the past and presentation of the present sets up an unspoken confidence in verbal testimony.

Assimilation of the European and the Avant-Garde

The use of flashbacks in American film occurs in a constant system of exchange with those used in European cinemas. Surely Griffith's flashbacks, for example, find their echo in the work of Abel Gance, a parallel that we have every reason to believe marks an historical influence of one filmmaker on the other.[28] Towards the end of the silent period in American film, the force of influence is perhaps stronger in the opposite direction, with American films borrowing from the flashbacks that appear in European cinema of the twenties. As we shall see in the next chapter, the European avant-garde uses the flashback device as an element in creating an expressive manipulation of the image and filmic montage. The flashback is introduced as a device to explore character psychology and even psychoanalysis in a way that is quite different from the American tradition up until this point: presenting the semes of character as unidimensional and unified, even if determined by the past. Theories of subjectivity and memory and the quest for a cinematic equivalent to the surging of memory images will color the form of flashbacks in these avant-garde movements.

We will examine all of this in much greater detail in the next chapter, but the point here is to recognize that there is a pattern of cross-fertilization of technique and thematic interest as regards the flashback. Perhaps there the role of emigré directors in Hollywood in the late twenties is in part responsible. While the mimetic rendering of memory images never dominates the structure of an entire American film from the late twenties the way that it does in the films of Louis Delluc, for example, montage techniques do appear which show multiple images that encapsulate a memory. It is worthy of note that Stiller, Korda, Fejos, and Feyder, filmmakers discussed in the previous sections of this chapter, are all European emigrés, though in many cases they worked from scenarios by American writers. (Fejos did write *The Last Moment,* a film which demonstrates his ties to the avant-garde in his native Hungary and to Hugo Metzner, known for his innovative film, *Überfall* [1928].)[29] Also worthy of note is the precedent for innovative flashback used in earlier European films by some of these emigré directors. As we will discuss in the next chapter, Stiller's earlier Swedish films characteristically use flashbacks, while Feyder's *The Kiss* (1929) follows his work with flashbacks in such films as *Carmen* (1926) in France and the French-German production of Zola's *Thérèse Raquin* (1928).

Another example of a European emigré is Michael Curitz who directed *A Million Bid* in 1927, and who went on to direct other flashback films in the forties. In *A Million Bid,* Dr. Robert Brent is riding a train to London in an attempt to stop the wedding of his old sweetheart to a millionaire. The preparations for the wedding are intercut with close shots of the train's wheels. From a subjective close-up on the wedding announcement at which Dr. Brent is looking, a dissolve carries us into a flashback montage of scenes from the past, of Dr. Brent courting the bride-to-be.

The Last Command, directed by Josef von Sternberg for Paramount in 1928, is a film that mixes European and American sensibilities. It doesn't use the mimetic memory imagery characteristic of the Europeans, but the psychological dimensions of its flashbacks introduce concerns that evoke those of the European flashback.[30] Its presentation of history as the subjective experience of an individual not only continues the premises we saw operative in Griffith, but serves as an example of how that tradition is passed on to American developments in the sound flashback film of the forties and fifties. As such, *The Last Command* represents not only an assimilation, but also a prototypical precursor of the way various traditions will find a reinscription in films to come.

The film is a gem of Hollywood's reflexive storytelling, for not only does it concern the making of a Hollywood film by a Russian emigré director, it typifies the genre in retaining much of the mystique and mythology of Hollywood narrative. All the while that it supposedly goes behind the scenes into the mind of an extra for a critical perspective on Hollywood practice, it uses a subjective flashback narration to construct a fiction that displays many of the mythologizing aspects of Hollywood film, including the transcendant love story.

With titles by Herman Mankiewicz, the film immediately sets an ironic tone by describing the Hollywood of 1928 as "the Magic Empire of the 20th Century" and "the mecca of the World" while showing us a rather unglamorous version of the Hollywood workday. This opening scene establishes a present which both contrasts with the past and sets up the necessity for revealing the past; as such, it builds the foundations upon which the flashbacks can be constructed under the figure of irony.

Director Leo Andreyev (William Powell) surrounded by sycophantic assistants, selects a photo of an extra to cast as a Russian general after turning over the photo to reveal the man's wage of $7.50 a day. The price tag on the photo is the beginning of a series of scenes which emphasize a degraded form of wage labor at the heart of the "Magic Empire," one whose full irony will only be evident once the film flashes back to the Russian revolution. These scenes include a call by one of the director's assistants to the old man at a dark boarding house; the sunless and dreary enclosure of this hallway itself clashes with the audience expectations for Hollywood, as does the old, forlorn character compulsively shaking his head as he listens to the wall phone. Then a tracking shot along a crowd at the studio gate introduces this assemblage as the breadline of Hollywood; another tracking shot from the interior of the prop and costume department passes by each of the distribution windows to show the old man's difficulty in fighting the mob of extras to acquire his uniform. Hollywood is presented as a factory where some workers are called "extras," while others toss costumes and make-believe rifles at them with disdain.

The flashback is initiated by a scene in the mass make-up room when the old man annoys the others surrounding him by his continual shaking of his head. This motivates his explanation, "I had a great shock once," a remark that is temporally left suspended as the sequence continues to plant cues for the revelation to come— such as having the old man place his own medal on his Russian general's costume. As the others laugh at his assertion that the medal did not come from a pawn shop, but was given to him by the Czar, this preposterous old man is shown gazing sorrowfully in close-up into his makeup mirror, a shot of self-absorption that serves as a bridge to the first segment of flashback narration. The makeup mirror as site engendering a flashback poses as a visual symbol for all the film's ironic speculation on fiction and reality, fantasy and history, a speculation that does not restrain it from indulging in the most fantastic of flashbacks presented as an historical account.

In the flashback to "Imperial Russia of 1917" the old man is a general and a cousin to the Czar, a devoted military commander whose dedication to the "protection" of Russia is contrasted to the extravagant folly of the non-military leadership on one hand and what the film terms "the revolutionists" on the other. He takes as his mistress, an actress Natalie Dembrova (Evelyn Brent) who is actually a revolutionary comrade of the stage director, Andreyev (Powell); she becomes "the General's" mistress only to facilitate his assassination, but is finally unable to kill the man she has come to love. When the revolution is successful, Natalie and the General once more find themselves face to face, she apparently denouncing him to the cheering hoard. As Natalie shouts, "Let's hang him in Petrograd," the film cuts back to the present as we fade in on the General shaking his head in front of the mirror, just as he was before this excursion into his memory.

We might be led to interpret this return of his former mistress to her revolutionary politics and her condemnation of him to death to be the "great shock" that explains the former General's nervous affliction; certainly the return to the present from that moment of the past in which she denounces him seems to indicate a causal connection. However, the film here equivocates, fragmenting its flashback and withholding certain information in order to present a false lead to the audience. Its return to the present is only provisory, only long enough to establish the scene in the present which will inspire another flashback, one which will complete the first and contradict the false interpretation of the past the audience is meant to take as true.

The scene in the present is the scene to be filmed, a battle scene in the snow in which the former general and his former captive meet on the terrain of a Hollywood sound stage, the power relations inverted from the encounter we witnessed in the flashback. Now the theatrical director is in command of the staging of his fantasy, his moment of revenge. As the director hands his former oppressor a whip like the one this man had once used on him, as he is about to send him out to play a part "for which he needs no rehearsal," the General, at this moment of renewed mockery, is resubmerged in his memories of the past.

We return to the scene on the railroad heading to Petrograd, as the General is being humiliated by the revolutionaries. Forced to stoke the engine in the coal car, the General is visited by Natalie who explains her denunciation of him as part of her own plan to save his life, to trick the revolutionaries so that she could aid his escape. She returns to the General a pearl necklace to finance his emigration and uses her sexual wiles to divert the attention of the revolutionary guard, as the General jumps to safety. This turn of events is not only a narrative inversion that reopens the question of what constitutes the great shock buried in the General's past, it inverts the ideological stance of the flashbacks as well; whatever sympathy the audience might have had with Andreyev's and the actress's original struggle against the Czarist class is increasingly negated by identification with the love story, one that is accompanied by increasingly caricatured portrayals of the revolutionaries as drunken and depraved.

The shock, then, is yet to come, and the flashback must continue to resolve an enigma the film has located in the past. As we see the train disappear from the General's point of view, the train bearing the revolutionaries and Natalie falls from a broken trestle, sinking into the water. Cutting back to the General's reaction shot, we see him shaking his head, the compulsive gesture associated with the old man he has become in the film's present. We realize that the death of Natalie (which that but for her help would have been his own death), is the motivating cause of his pathological shaking.

With his enigma solved, as well as an explanation of the General's emigration, the flashback ends with a return to the sound stage where the former revolutionary Andreyev is making a fantasy return to the Czarist war. The filmmaking apparati are set into motion along with fake snow, a wind machine, and even piano music of the Russian National Anthem to set the mood on the set. But as shooting begins, the filmmaking apparati becomes invisible and the film's audience witnesses not only the fragmented action of camera angles being shot, but rather a finished, edited film in projection—the director's realized fantasy transcendant. As the General collapses having given his "last command," the film director Andreyev cradles him in his arms and responds to the General's hallucinatory question "Have I won?," with an admiring affirmative.

The present and past are momentarily interwoven in subjective hallucinations that take place on a sound stage that disguises itself as a projected, finished film; within its fiction of film production, *The Last Command* complexly presents filmic temporality as symbolically multiple, a multiplicity determined by the layering of fantasy and reference within fiction. Then the film returns to a final, unambiguous temporality as Andreyev covers his dead extra, his former adversary, with a Russian flag that is conveniently on the set, and says, "He was more than a great actor, he was a great man." The film thus uses flashbacks to present both the history and explanation of a psychological trauma within its fiction in a particularly clever way, making use of the structuring of the dual flashback fragments for a system of narrative inversions. Within the flashbacks it personalizes its account of history as a love story between a Czarist general and a revolutionary beauty, transforming the ideological positions it initially inscribes; by its end, the revenge fantasy of an emigré revolutionary director has become an homage to the nobility of a reactionary past.

Though we can see the similarities in flashback functioning between *The Last Command* and the Griffith melodramas discussed earlier, primarily in the emphasis on subjectivizing history—that has the ideological consequence of submerging the historical in its broad sense with the personal in its most romantic sense— we can also see the differences. In Griffith, character psychology is shown through emblematic image-tableaux of past events. The coding of character psychology is significant, but in a restricted form that is congruent with the typing of character in the 19th-century melodramatic tradition. The psychological coding of the flashbacks in *The Last Command* is, in contrast, more expansive, allowing for a play of contradiction. The flashbacks take the form of a developmental hermeneutic within the past, a story which unfolds with its own false leads and suspense structure.

This difference between past as emblem and the past as story is significant. The emblematic use of the past in flashback will play far less of a role in American film history than will the structure that presents the flashback as a melodrama within itself. From the late twenties and on, the past-as-emblem coding system falls out of favor and becomes outdated. It is seen as granting less depth to character development, and fullness of character is, at this point, regarded as an emerging style of Hollywood realism. (Sometimes misleadingly called "believability of character," this fullness is not necessarily based on principles of psychological verisimilitude. There is a certain fascination with extremes within Hollywood character coding that disperses with any moderation that might make its characters truly plausible.)

As such, *The Last Command* is closer to the form of flashbacks that will characterize Hollywood flashback films in the sound period and will be the subject of analysis in chapters four and five—even though the roots of this form, the emphasis on the ideological twists of the individual psyche and the subjective experience of history, are also present in the Griffith films. However, a different use of an emblematic past will be a source of innovative modernism for the flashback, both in the European films of the twenties we will examine next and in the modernist films that reemerge in the fifties that will be discussed in chapter six.

3

European and Japanese Experimentation with Flashbacks in Silent Films

The twenties was a time of aesthetic experimentation for European cinema. Impressed by the developments viewed in American melodrama and comedy films, French, German, and Swedish filmmakers produced works whose style and conception redefined the specific character of filmic expression. Often the flashback figured in these adventurous works of film art, for vision back in time coincided with the European avant-garde's various approaches to the exploration of subjectivity and social history, the dynamism and fluidity of junctures of time and space, the creative manipulation of cinematic structures. The focus of this chapter will be on those European films of this period which develop a quite different use of the flashback and of filmic expression than the American films discussed in the last chapter. I will also look at parallel developments in Japanese flashbacks.

Certainly the French films in question, more or less products of avant-garde movements, in no way constituted the norm of European production. Rather, these innovative films were surrounded by an industry producing popular films that followed more traditional narrative lines and had flashbacks similar to the ones already discussed in American films. The German films under examination were more likely to be produced within the mainstream of German film production, yet as Lotte Eisner has argued, these films are linked to developments in the theatrical avant-garde of the period.[1] There are many historical reasons that justify the use of the term "avant-garde" to apply to these films, including their association with avant-garde movements in the other arts, their alternative production and distribution methods (in many cases), their connection to other avant-garde films of geometric abstraction or surrealism. Yet as an alternative to thinking of these films as avant-garde, we might also benefit from seeing them as an exploration of cinematic modernism, introducing a range of textual differences that distinguish them from a more traditional cinematic form. This will help us develop a definition of cinematic modernism that will indicate the connection to be made between these films made in the twenties and the modernist films made after World War II, the subject of chapter six.

For film history the term "modernism" is itself somewhat problematic. In one sense, we can see the development of cinema itself as a modernist impulse, contemporaneous with turn-of-the-century modernist movements in literature, painting, theater, dance, and music. The earliest films can even be seen as influencing modernist tendencies in these other arts. Yet, as we have seen in the course of our examination of the flashback, if the "primitive" period of the cinema displayed a kind of visual innovation and anarchy, in another sense, cinema began somewhat nostalgically, as a recuperation of the 19th century at the turn of the 20th. Within its first fifteen years, film came to replace certain of its performative structures with ones borrowed more and more from the 19th-century structures of the novel and of theater to nourish and legitimize itself as a narrative form.[2] Yet even while films borrowed, they transformed. The melodrama as rendered filmically develops into a more modern and visually complex form, which had as one consequence an innovative approach to flashback temporality which marks silent cinema.

We can see this period of the twenties, then, as a moment of dual impulses. At the same time as an active challenge and expansion of an already-formed cinematic tradition takes place, we can also recognize that this innovation happens within the heart of the tradition of melodramatic and epic narration, as a display of differences struggling through the coded, recognizable, popular forms. Our purpose here is to explore the play of aesthetic and structural differences that include and contextually surround the inscription of flashbacks in these films. This is not a project of aesthetic valorization per se, but rather a part of a consideration of how flashbacks can be instrumental in the changing philosophical implications of narrative.

The Italian silent cinema is particularly illustrative of the two principles of coupling a borrowing from tradition with a filmic inscription of innovation. Italian films used flashbacks early, as part of an epic treatment of history as well as for literary adaptations, two genres that were most important and characteristic of Italian production. *L'Inferno,* an adaptation of Dante directed by Francesco Bertolini and Adolfo Padovan (1911) and *Gli ultimi giorni di Pompei,* Mario Caserini (1913) are films that use flashbacks to visually present literary and epic traditions while at the same time expanding cinematic expression. *Nozze d'oro,* Luigi Maggi (1911) frames through a flashback its telling of the battle of Palestro and *La Guerra e il sogno di momi,* Giovanni Pastrone (1917) presents the reading of a letter to frame a flashback to the war as the inciting incident of a dream sequence; the child transforms the war story he has heard into his dream depicted using frame by frame animation of marionettes. The spirit of cinematic innovation with narrative form and use of flashbacks that these films embody, then becomes integrated in a melodramatic form of expression in *Tigre Reale* (Giovanni Pastrone, 1916), but with a form of melodrama that finds its immediate inspiration in an adaptation of a work of decadent literature.[3] *Tigre Reale* seeks stylistic innovation in the graphic exploration of the design qualities of the image and the narrative construction of the *femme fatale*. The flashback illustrates the heroine's telling of a tragic incident from her past to a present admirer, offered as an explanation of her inability to love faithfully; elements of this past incident will return at the conclusion of the film, effectively curing the heroine of her cynicism and its degeneration into hysteria. By the mid-teens, then, Italian film had established a precedent for the use of the flashback in film to present literary and historical manipulations of temporality for symbolic purposes and as an element of visual innovation. The Italian cinema reached a height in this period and it is possible to see these films as preceding or at least coterminous with some of the forms of flashbacks found in the American films discussed and in French production.[4] Over the next decade of the twenties, there was less of this visual and temporal innovation to be found in Italian cinematic production, especially in contrast to the flourishing of such innovation in French cinema.

French films of the teens similarly drew on literary sources and developed a range of flashback techniques. In *Les Misérables* (1911–12), adapted by Albert Capellani from the Hugo as a feature-length epic, two important flashbacks appear. The first uses a kind of split screen as Fantine is explaining to her employer, M. Madeleine (the former Jean Valjean) how she was abandoned by her wealthy lover after the birth of their child. The scene she is describing appears on the right half of the frame, but the two shots share a common background, so that there is no apparent line of spatio-temporal separation between the two actions; though they merge visually, the idea that the right part of the image illustrates with a past event the telling in the present on the left is clear. Later in the film, a more conventional flashback appears when the old gardener recalls M. Madeleine's kind and extraordinary effort that saved his life when he was pinned under a huge hay cart. The flashback is a repetition of an earlier scene, but from a new angle on this action. *Les Misérables* is a melodramatic narrative that hinges on a reiteration of the past; Jean Valjean is haunted by Inspector Javert's repeated efforts to resurrect his past as a convict, while he is repeatedly saved by people who recall his past kindness. This kindness is in turn motivated by a remembrance, the Abbé's act of faith in him upon his first escape. Further, Fantine's past, her illegitimate child, controls her present situation, and when she dies after having confessed her secret to M. Madeleine, he promises to care for her child as his debt to her past and his own. Given that Hugo's legend still loomed large in French letters, this narrative obsession with the past was to reappear not only in the numerous French adaptations of *Les Misérables* itself, but also migrated into other narratives similarly marked by the melodramatic influence of 19th-century novels and popular theater.

La Sultane d'amour, a French romantic adventure-fantasy from 1919 directed by René Le Somptier and Charles Burguet, for example, uses two flashbacks to narrate the brief encounter of an Arabian sultan (Sylvo de Pedrelli) and sultaness (France Dhelia) who fall in love with one another; each of the flashbacks corresponds to the narration of this situation from one of their points of view. Both are disguised as commoners when they first meet and each takes the other to be a tragically impossible love object. What would be a standard explanatory flashback giving a character's subjective account of a past event is made greatly more interesting by this effect of doubling and difference.

The use of the flashback seems to be a common element of narrative exposition in French films of the teens and twenties, serving both to present new information and to recall events already presented. Surprisingly, perhaps, several of the popular serials of the teens, such as those of Feuillade, do not make systematic use of the flashback to recall earlier events—although the fourth episode of Louis Feuillade's *Les Vampires* (1915–16), "Le Spectre" does offer a flashback explanation to a narrative mystery. In Henri Fescourt's serial *Mandarin* (1924), each episode begins with systematic flashbacks to earlier events, and flashbacks are also interspersed in the narrative to depict characters recalling, telling, or writing chronicles of events. Popular films such as these are the background against which to set the more experimental treatment of the flashback in the French avant-garde of the twenties.

French Philosophical Inquiry Into Memory

The development of a French avant-garde cinema interested in the flashback as a rendering of memory processes can be understood in the context of French inquiry into *l'esprit*—the intellectual and emotional functioning of the mind. A key figure in developing these themes in French thought is Henri Bergson, whose *Matière et mémoire* was first published in 1896.[5] In his examination of memory processes, Bergson draws heavily on William James's *The Principles of Psychology,* as well as on various articles on psychophysiology published over the preceding twenty years in *La Revue Philosophique* by Ribot, Maudley, and others. He also spent seven years studying aphasia. Bergson's metaphysics is an attempt to account for scientific theses on mind-body functioning. The thesis he adopts has great significance for aesthetics and theories of narrative.

Bergson's model of memory functioning is a circuit in which present perception and stored aspects of memory can interact to produce a memory-image:

> Perception is never a mere contact of the mind with the object present: it is impregnated with memory-images which complete it as they interpret it. The memory-image, in its turn, partakes of the "pure memory," which it begins to materialize, and of the perception in which it tends to embody itself: regarded from the latter point of view, it might be defined as a nascent perception. Lastly, pure memory, though independent in theory manifests itself as a rule only in the colored and living image which reveals it. (p. 170)

Bergson distinguishes between spontaneous memories evoked by present perceptions and conscious recall which strives to reconstitute the past. Conscious recall, then, serves as a model to explain how the more spontaneous bursts of memory occur. To clarify our introspective experience of this process, Bergson utilizes a cinematic metaphor, which first evokes the focusing of a lens over a period of time, as if one were racking focus on the object of one's recall:

Whenever we are trying to recover a recollection, to call up some period of our history, we become conscious of an act sui generis by which we detach ourselves from the present in order to replace ourselves first in the past in general, then in a certain region of the past—a work of adjustment something like the focusing of a camera. But our recollection still remains virtual; we simply prepare ourselves to receive it by adopting the appropriate attitude. Little by little it comes into view like a condensing cloud; from the virtual state it passes into the actual; and as its outlines become more distinct and its surface takes on color, it tends to imitate perception. But it remains attached to the past by its deepest roots, and if, when once realized it did not retain something of its original virtuality, if, being a present state, it were not also something which stands out distinct from the present, we should never know it as memory. (p. 171)

The debate over Bergson's description of memory processes and his concomittant dismissal of "associative" memory theories as inadequate received much discussion in French intellectual circles. Numerous books and articles on Bergson were published in France between 1911 and 1930, the years immediately preceding and coinciding with parallel treatment of memory in avant-garde films.[6] During this time, the French ciné-clubs sponsored public discussions of cinema aesthetics which addressed issues such as cinematic temporality and the psychology of the image.[7] The question of the direct influence of Bergson on such filmmakers and theorists as Louis Delluc, Marcel L'Herbier, Jean Epstein, and Abel Gance is not as significant as the more general sense in which Bergson dramatically inserts his theory of memory into French thought of the period.

Another important parallel concern with the processes of memory can be found in the literature of the period, particularly in Marcel Proust's *A la recherche du temps perdu,* published as nine volumes between 1913 and 1927. Proust, in turn, has been seen as influenced by Bergson. At the time of the self-financed publication of the first volume of *A la recherche du temps perdu* after several editors refused to finance its publication, Proust wrote in an article in *Le Temps,* November 13, 1913:

From this point of view, my book will be perhaps a series of *"Romans de l'inconscient"* [novels of the unconscious]; I would have no shame to say "Bergsonian novels," if I so believed, for during all periods, literature is given the task of aligning itself—after the fact, naturally—with the reigning philosophy. But it would not be correct, as my work is dominated by the distinction between involuntary memory and voluntary memory, a distinction that not only does not occur in the philosophy of M. Bergson, but is even contradicted by it.[8]

It is not true that Bergson did not literally address the distinction between involuntary and voluntary memory, but Proust's disclaimer can be taken to criticize the way that, after recognizing the different categories of memory, Bergson models the functioning of one on the other. The somewhat sarcastic tone of this disclaimer and the ambiguity of its view of the relationship between literature and philosophy may lead one to think that Proust, perhaps, was protesting too much. At any rate, it was not to be heeded; as early as 1929 in a chapter called "Proust et le Bergsonisme," in his book *Essences,* Burnet argues for an appreciation of Bergson's influence on Proust.[9] This discussion has continued, with critics taking both sides of the influence/difference comparison between author and psychologist/philosopher.[10] While the *"madeleine* incident" is often a reference in discussions of memory in Proust, narration of memory processes covers many different instances of recall in *A la recherche du temps perdu.* Both spontaneous and studied elaboration of memory traces are described and Proust develops metacritical commentaries on memory's relationship to writing. Proust's "theory" of memory evolves in the play of his narration, revealing memories in poetic language, developing these memories as part of the psychology of his main character and narrator, Marcel. Marcel is modeled from Proust's autobiographical experiences and insights, but the work of fiction is also a work of formal structure which cannot be taken directly as a personal memoire that chronicles introspection as a theoretical example in a phenomenology of memory. The novel recasts the memories of the author into its own imaginary constructs; among the prodigious pleasures of Proust's work is this oscillation between observation and introspection on one hand and fictionalization and writing on the other.

It can be misleading to seek precise equivalences with Bergson, whose aim is toward theoretical universals. Proust's aims as an artist were more diverse; introspection as it coincides with autobiography and philosophic speculation are coupled with a desire to achieve a distance, an abstracted plane of language, order, and structure. The comparison between Proust and Bergson can be useful as long as it never attempts to use Bergson to explain, reductively, the richness of Proust's project. The most fruitful approaches are to be found in textual studies of Proust's novel that derive from this fictional structure an implicit theory of memory.

Still, in a general sense, we can see that both Bergson's and Proust's visions of memory share with the French flashback films a concern with the way memory links the past and present. They also share an interest in the evocative power of objects or sensations perceived in the present to initiate recall of the past. These common threads do provide clues to the shared concerns of the philosophy of the period in both its creative and direct manifestations.

These cross-currents in philosophy, psychology, and aesthetic practice are linked in the comments on filmic temporality made by Elie Faure in a essay written in 1927:

> Cinema incorporates time into space. Even more than this: time for it becomes truly a dimension of space. We will be able to see a thousand years after it has been disturbed from the path beneath the gallop of a horse, the dust rising, billowing, dissipating, the smoke from a cigarette condensing then entering into the atmosphere, all this in the frame of space we have before our eyes, . . . Time has become necessary for us. It is more and more a part of the idea, daily more dynamic, that we have of the object. We can play with it at will. We can speed it up. We can slow it down. We can suppress it.[11]

It is perhaps most useful to see the overlapping concerns of writers, filmmakers, and philosophers as coalescing in this manner, as brought together by conjunctures in technology, the history of philosophy and the formal history of aesthetic change. Rather than trying to prove influence as a direct impact, we can see that the French films were conceived in this climate of thought on memory. Faure's quote also introduces us to another factor in the French development of the flashback: the sensitivity amongst French theorists of cinema to the specificities of cinematic expression and the transformative aspects of cinematic representation.

Formal Experimentation and the Mimetic Rendering of Memory

Theoretical investigations of the properties of the cinematic image and the rhythms of editing lead French artist-intellectuals to proclaim the necessity of aesthetic development of film outside the commercial constraints of the industry. Leon Moussinac, in *Naissance du Cinéma* (1925), summarized the early stages of this creative movement as an extension of the work of Griffith, Ince, and DeMille, but a reaction against the commercial imperative in much of twenties American cinema:

> Since its heroic early period, the cinema has become the second largest industry in the U.S. organized along Ford's principles. They began to make films on an assembly line, as if they were automobiles. Artistic means quickly disappeared, or become functions of the art-director.[12]

As an antidote to this mass production of what they considered non-artistic films, the French theorized about the specific nature of the image.

Louis Delluc used the term "photogénie" to express the poetic aspect of things and people that can only be revealed by cinematography.[13] The French filmmakers of this aesthetic inclination were later to be termed "impressionists" and stylistic criticism collected a series of techniques that characterized their work: soft focus, the use of gels and prisms, various masking and reframing compositional devices, rapid jump-cut editing, and a greater variety and number of camera angles within a scene, especially canted angles.[14] However, the term "impressionist" has often been criticized as confusing and inadequate.[15] A characterization of this filmmaking practice in terms of a repertoire of techniques ignores the shared tone and mood of these films, a tone and mood that inform the specific construction of those techniques. These films are often expressions of mental states of anguish, ennui, or desire. In this charged realm, passion is sometimes blocked, but sputters against the short-circuiting. At other moments, the visual energy crescendos, expressing passionate release or triumph. Images are transmitters of emotional charges, sculpted to convey the fusion of external environment and inner states of mind.

Mise-en-scene and camera angles portray the interaction between the subjective states of characters and the atmosphere of the places they inhabit. The objective world is subsumed in a subjective response to it. In this context, flashbacks play a key role. They infuse the present with the weight of the past, allowing an already subjectively rendered site to give way to another that is even more subjective, in that it is constituted as a memory image. If subjectivity is the site of these fictions, memory is the site that offers explanations for the dark subjectivity one experiences in the present. The flashback becomes a means of expressing the mood of remembrance in instances in which memory is bitter, nostalgic, melancholy, obsessive—anything but simply happy.

If these films share tonal affinities, they also have narrative structures that follow similar patterns. The protagonists are often sensitive and even marginal characters. The flashbacks provide keys to character psychology and fill in the audience on a fictional past which is presumed to determine the present action. The loves that are narrated are often multiple triangulations that can even include, as is the case in Gance's *La Roue* (1922–23), incest. The films are filled with loss and death, sometimes quite violent. The psychoanalytic foundations of these narratives include female masochism and a portrayal of the death drive linked to an aspect of the past that remains unresolved because it is too painful. One can speak of these flashbacks as a mimetic rendering of memory in a dual sense. Many of the flashbacks represent the circumstances and present the initiating causes of memory images. Like Bergson's theory, they link the surging of an image from the past to the presence of objects or the conjunction of circumstances in the present. Further, they attempt to convey the mood of reluctant and disquieting memories. The quest for atmosphere extends to the imaging of the mood surrounding the process of bringing images forth from the crypts of the mind. Finally, a mimetic concern for memory processes will include the obsessive, repetitive, and fragmentary aspects of memory.

Melodrama and the French Flashback

On the level of the scenario, the French films of this period are deeply indebted to the melodramatic heritage of French theater and literature, as well as that of film melodrama. Marcel L'Herbier's *El Dorado* (1921) was subtitled *Mélodrame,* a self-conscious indication of this heritage. Like many other impressionist flashback films, its plot certainly merits this acknowledgment. It concerns a Spanish dancer, Sybilla (Eve Francis) who tries to save the life of her critically ill illegitimate son by appealing to his rich father, Estiria. When he rebuffs her appeals, she launches a vengeance plot that involves locking Estiria's daughter with the daughter's lover in their trysting spot, causing the daughter to miss her marriage to a wealthy man. Later Sybilla reveals her son's parentage to the daughter and her lover and they take the sick boy for a rest cure in the mountains. This sacrifice of her son, even though it makes his recovery possible, leaves Sybilla despondent. After one of her fellow performers tries to rape her, she commits suicide. This plot that interweaves an evil father, a desperate and self-sacrificing mother, a sick child and a secret romance has all the elements of melodrama except a happy resolution.

El Dorado uses five flashbacks within this melodramatic context, most of which are similar in function to those of the American melodrama. They represent a character's thoughts, as when we see the flashback image of the young lovers' meetings to indicate that Sybilla is thinking she can use these meetings for her vengeance. Similarly, Sybilla has a flashback memory image of the departure of the young couple and her son that reiterates this scene that we have already witnessed. Presented as memory, it is marked as motivating Sybilla's suicide, as the return of the moment in which she realized she was losing her son. While there is nothing startlingly innovative about these flashbacks, there is another flashback in the film that is exceptional in its marked subjectivity and in the manner it appears twice, first as Sybilla writes Estiria asking for help, and then later when Sybilla tells Estiria's daughter about the past. A medium shot of a man leaning forward across a table begins the flashback, followed by a subjective angle from the woman's point of view of this man's amorous advances. The image becomes distorted as his gestures approach the camera.

This flashback indicates the ways in which the French films of the twenties avant-garde differ from the melodramatic models from which they inherit so much. Though American and earlier European films established the structural centrality of flashback memory images, these French films will give cinematic moments of recall a new force by creating an image that is more indicative of a mental image, a character's subjective state. Like other images and montage patterns in *El Dorado,* such as the constant intercutting and superimposition of the sick boy during the scenes depicting his mother dancing, this subjectively rendered memory of seduction uses the coding of the image itself to suggest that what we are seeing has been interiorized. No longer a vision of an objective world, the flashback images of impressionist films distort spatio-temporal relations and transform visual codes of representation to indicate the thought patterns, the feelings, and even the functioning of the psyches of the characters.

Obsessive Memory—Flashbacks, Fragmentation, and Repetition

Louis Delluc's *Le Silence* (1921) unfortunately has not survived as a film, and it is only possible to study its innovative treatment of memory through Delluc's detailed screenplay, published in his *Drames du cinéma.*[16] *Le Silence* presents a dramatic transformation of memory images beyond their representation as a unitary event or a coherent linear narration of past circumstance. It is a film that sixty years later still seems like a daring montage of different temporalities with minimal cues to guide the viewer, who is instead expected to experience the jarring temporal displacements of memory.

The film concerns a character plagued by memories of the past, and Delluc's modernism develops from his attempt to describe mimetically the form of memory images. Memory processes are shown as disjunct, repetitive, and yet still associative, having an order that signifies. Some images pass by too quickly to be fully under-stood, others mix events according to a logic which corresponds to a notion of the functioning of the unconscious. Though this view of memory is more modernist than the sentimental symbolism of the American melodrama, the recalled occurrences retain some of the same pathos and a similar functioning within the narrative construction. The very title of *Le Silence* indicates that the images are construed as an interior monologue. They can be seen as the visual equivalent of the literary expression of the mental wandering that Proust, Joyce, and Faulkner explored during the same period. The unspoken is expressed through silent images. Scenes from the past surge through the consciousness of the lead character, Pierre, as he is preparing to leave his apartment for a theater date with friend Suzie. These memory images chronicle a melodramatic narrative that, once rearranged in story temporality, tells of Pierre's marriage to Aimée, the introduction of a rival for Aimée's affection, Pierre's shooting Aimée, and, finally, Aimée dying.

The film avoids a linear narration of these events, and instead shows them as raging through Pierre's mind as they are associated with objects he encounters in the same apartment in the present. In order to grasp this ordering of the flashbacks as associative memories, it is necessary to describe the film in detail, and then chart its rearrangement of story time into a complexly wrought plot order.

The film opens as Pierre walks through his orderly room in the present, dressed in his tuxedo. The image cuts from an angle on his bed to a new shot of Pierre in the bed, looking sick, surrounded by a clutter of medicine and books. Pierre asks why he is in the bed but this question initiates another cut to a similar shot of the bed, this time with a woman, Aimée, occupying it, still surrounded by equal disorder. This associative series involving the bed gives way to another series of shots: first, the young Aimée, then Aimée and Pierre leaving a church, then Aimée dead, in the bed as Pierre kneels beside her. Pierre rages in despair as nurses subdue him.

This quieting brings the image back to the present, as Pierre glances at the clock. Soon, however, a close-up on an open drawer signals how some objects within are drawing his attention. He takes out a photo, then tosses it back. Then his hand reaches to open a second drawer, revealing letters bearing the inscriptions, "Amour," and "Cheri." A cut to a more distant shot shows Pierre handling the letters, then a cut returns the image to the past, showing a series of shots, first of Aimée laughing; then Aimée dead, lying on the bed; then Aimée very sick, extending her arm to Pierre, who turns away as she falls back on the bed. Back in the present, Pierre closes the drawer in anger and opens another, taking out a letter from his friend, Suzie; it extends him an invitation to the theater for that evening. A cut yields an image of Suzie at her house, writing, possibly this letter. Then the image returns to the letters. Pierre is shown taking out a photo of Suzie, but the image dissolves to Aimée, lying on her bed, extending her arm and falling back, a repetition of the scene that was shown earlier. Once more, a return to the present shows Pierre in his apartment. This is followed by a rapid montage of images from the past: Aimée in evening dress falling forward, cut to a puff of smoke, cut to a revolver, cut to Pierre standing over Aimée as he throws the revolver down, then bends down to lift her, then moves away from her. A close-up on Pierre following the murder cuts back to Pierre in the present. The next return to the past is to a time before this murder, as Aimée enters Pierre's office to embrace him. We understand the link, though, when a rival is introduced into this scene. Jean, an attractive young man, enters the office and watches Aimée intently as she exits, a regard that Pierre notices. This jealousy theme is developed in the next shot which shows Jean flirting with Aimée at a dinner party as Pierre watches, disconcerted. Suzie is seated next to Pierre, observing his jealousy of his wife. Suzie's presence here is only revealed in its full significance in the denouement of the film when Pierre realizes, after his memory returns to a letter telling him of his wife's infidelity, that it was in the same handwriting as Suzie's invitation to the theater. Suzie arrives to pick him up at the end of the film to find that her plot has backfired. Pierre, having sorted out the truth of the past, has committed suicide.

Looking at a diagram of these narrative events in their plot order will help us understand the structure of the film. If we assign numbers to the progressive moments of the present time and letters to the events from the past, we can diagram the flashbacks as follows:

A—Marriage of Aimée and Pierre					
B—Aimée happy					
C—Dinner party	1.G	2.B	3.H	4.E	5.D	6.C
D—Pierre shoots Aimée	E	F			
E—Aimée dying	A–B	E			
F—Aimée dead	F				
G—Pierre ill					
H—Suzie writing to Pierre					

This diagram shows us that the image of Aimée dead is repeated once and the image of her sick in bed appears three times. Not only is memory presented as non-chronological (an image of Aimée and Pierre's wedding following one of her dying from the gunshot wound), but it is also presented as obsessively repetitive, with the guilt-provoking images of Aimée's death and her suffering frequently returning to Pierre's thoughts. The bed, which is designated as the site of Aimée's last moments and Pierre's repentance, as well as his subsequent illness, seems to evoke the whole rush of memory images, which are further nourished by the contents of drawers, by photos, and by letters.

This imaginative use of the flashback to represent memory processes was continued by Delluc in *Fièvre* (1921). *Fièvre* has survived in excellent condition (though missing original titles in the print in American distribution), thereby permitting close study of Delluc's innovative use of the flashback. Theorists at the time found this film to embody the creative potential of cinema as an evocative medium of expression; in fact, Léon Moussinac, in trying to explain the power of French films of the post-war period, turned to a flashback sequence in *Fièvre* to illustrate how "photographic material demands a particular kind of treatment."[17] After quoting from Delluc's script, Moussinac asserts that this "*découpage* is conceived essentially in consideration of the proportions, the many angles, and the numerous movements wanted in the images" (p. 30). In stating that the scenario envisions graphic density and variety, Moussinac points out how certain narratives can serve film by generating complex and stimulating image relationships. This is an inversion of a more common notion of how form constructs meaning or suits content, coming closer to a formalist notion of how narrative representation serves to justify the elaboration of form. The two processes here are, however, inseparable; we can speak of graphic, formal elaborations and the growth of complexly articulated narratives as part of an interdependent semiotic process in this film. Flashbacks are key to this process, as we shall see.

Although the flashbacks are not as numerous or as complexly ordered as *Le Silence,* they present a fragmented return to a past series of events in inverted order. Their focalization is divided between two of the main characters, Sarah (Eve Francis) and Militis (Van Daële) and this divided perspective is part of an ambiguous series of oppositions that underlie the structure of the film.

A conversation over the Marseilles bar between the *serveuse,* a woman bartender/ waitress named Sarah and a young woman leads to the first flashback, as Sarah in close-up looks not at her interlocutor, but seemingly back into her memory, she thinks of her former lover. Like all the flashbacks in the film, the shot of the speaker in the present (most often, as in this case, a close-up) cuts to black, followed by a fade-in on the image from the past illustrating the story-being-told. In this case, we see Sarah seated to the left of a small balcony, while a young sailor, Militis, stands next to her. As she rises to embrace him, the image fades to black, and then cuts to Sarah wistfully finishing her tale. This type of symmetry between the opening and closing of the flashbacks is found throughout the film. Now the two women in medium shot look off left, as if they are looking to the outside of the cafe at the port. An iris to the exterior series of shots of the boat arriving follows, but this time the angle is a subjective view from the short of the boat coming into the harbor. The angles of these two shots combine to create the impression that it is the women's look that sees the boat's arrival, a physically impossible suggestion that alludes to another meaning, that in some ironic or metaphysical sense they know about or anticipate Militis's reappearance.

The sailors pour into the cafe. Sarah retreats to the bar, while Militis, in close-up, begins narrating a portion of his story, as the image fades in on a second flashback. The image from the past is a long-shot view of a marriage in an oriental temple with the sailor and his kneeling oriental bride seen from behind in the distance of the shot. A dissolve gives us a frontal view of the couple, then another dissolve returns to the same long shot from behind as the men attending in the foreground kneel in prayer. After this image fades out, the cut to the present is to a shot of Sarah in medium close-up looking distressed, then to a shot of the oriental wife gazing off into space uncomprehendingly. Sarah walks back to Militis, and as he reaches out for her hand, alternating close-ups of Militis and Sarah show their continued attraction for one another.

A third flashback, initiated by an image of Militis, apparently represents his thoughts, yet returns to the same scene as in Sarah's earlier flashback, a similar angle of the two on a balcony. The difference is in the action depicted, for this time he passionately embraces the back of her neck, then spins her around towards him. The return to the present shows Militis still lost in thought as Sarah dances amongst the other sailors in the background.

The final three flashbacks are all punctuated by returns to Militis in the present, ending on a shot of Militis between his oriental wife on his left and Sarah on his right. Flashback four simply shows us Militis alone in bed, suffering from the fever for which the film is named. Flashback five shows him still in bed, reading a letter as the oriental woman comforts him. Then after the image fades to black within this flashback, an iris into the next image discloses a shot of Militis seen from behind, in the foreground on the left side of the image, with the oriental woman on the right and her father in the center background. All the figures are represented by fragments of their bodies only. This extreme metonymic rendering leaves us guessing as to the precise circumstances of the marriage, which could range from love and gratitude to the forced fulfillment of an obligation. Another mystery surrounds the oriental woman, who is always shown kneeling, or sitting, and finally later in the film, crawling toward a white flower that has caught her eye across the room at the bar, leaving us to guess whether she has the bound feet of an upper-class Chinese woman or is lame. One is led to believe that Militis married not out of sexual passion, but rather respect for the woman who cared for him—this interpretation is favored both by the subsequent events in the film and the order of the flashbacks. The four flashbacks surrounding Militis's experiences in the orient become important, if somewhat ambiguous indications of his character. Militis and Sarah are shown dancing together in ironic counterpart to the wife's crawl towards the flower; yet Militis responds quickly when his wife is threatened by the advances of the drunk seen earlier. When Sarah attempts to place herself between Militis and his rescued wife, he shoves Sarah away—a violent rejection that ironically sets into motion the final brawl that ends with Militis's murder perpetrated by the jealous bar owner Topinelli (Gaston Modot). Sarah hovers sorrowfully over his corpse, only to be arrested moments later. The film ends by returning to the oriental woman's fascination with the flower, apparently oblivious to the turmoil.

We see then that the fever, recovery, and marriage to the oriental woman are told in four flashbacks, with the last event, the marriage, told first. This inversion transforms our interpretation of the events, since only the marriage is publicly told, while the fever and the request to marry are private memories recalled later by Militis. Just as he remembers these past scenes of his needs being attended and his marriage, the return to the present shows him positioned between his wife and his former lover. The interpretation of the subjective significance of these memory images is difficult; however, upon learning of Militis's thoughts of the past, we see him walk over to Sarah to ask her to dance, indicating that the memory was not so strong as to interfere with his other desires in the present.

Who, then, is Militis? What does this character, whose return, thoughts, and death structure the film, signify? One way to answer this is to contrast the two flashbacks that recount Sarah and Militis's love affair, since the first one is Sarah's focalization, while the second belongs to Militis. From Sarah's point of view the embrace is initiated by her, seemingly filled with the romantic expression of love. Militis's focalization shows him as initiator of a far more passionate and sexual exchange, as if Militis's sexual attraction for Sarah were another meaning for the title, "fever," a passion as beyond his control as are the other addictions evidenced in the cafe. His love for his oriental bride is under the sign of the flower, contemplative, respectful, peaceful, sanctified, protective, as evidenced both in the flashbacks and in his defense of her from the sexual advances of the drunk in the present. The fragmented and separated representation of their bodies in the scene where Militis requests permission to marry the oriental woman and her distance from him as she kneels in the past and present suggest that Militis's marriage represents the inversion of the Baudelarian notion of the oriental, exotic woman. Decadence and sexuality become the meaning of the Marseillaise cafe, while the orient, far from being the source of this corruption, is removed from any comprehension of its events—as the young oriental widow is left staring at the only object in the environment that seems familiar, the flower.

This interpretation of the film is one that structures the flashbacks into two sets of memories: one set comprised of the flashbacks of desire, the other set indicating remembered obligation and responsibility. Militis is the figure who cannot choose and dies as a consequence of his renewed desire contradicting his sense of duty. Yet the melodramatic structure and morality that anchors this narrative of contradictions between two female characters and two sets of flashbacks is somewhat revised by the film's form of expression. The fragmentation of the imagery and the ambiguity of the representation urges the audience to participate in the movement of desire and the "inevitability" of death. Sarah's flashback gives her an enunciative power that creates sympathy for her when she is shackled and led away by the police at the end of the film, since we remember her standing behind the bar just moments before, remembering an affair that, for her, blended the erotic and the romantic.

In these Delluc films the manipulation of temporality as an element of composition throws into question the status of the narrative event. Events in the past are available only through the filter of a troubled or ambiguous memory; events in the present are subject to the intrusive associations of the past which determine their shape. The kind of subjectivity this implies is not simply a unitary individual's perspective; focalization, while always marked, is itself disordered, impulsive, charged with the forces of desire. Subjectivity here is of a different order then it is in fictions in which a character is assigned a more singular and unified subjective reality and in which conflicts between the characters' perspectives are systematically worked out. Here, instead, filmic narrative becomes the scene in which this tension within the imaginary reality of the fictive individual can be played out.

Female Subjectivity in French Flashback Films

Several other French films from this period use the flashback to convey female subjectivity. This association of memory with the female is certainly worthy of note, for it implies a fascination with how sexual difference affects the very nature of subjectivity. The women characters in these films are often vulnerable subjects, for whom romance, if not life itself has been filled with torments, sacrifice, or loss. For example, the flashbacks in Delluc's *La Femme de nulle part* (1922) portray the memory associations of an older woman evoked by the parallel situation of a younger woman living in the house she once occupied. Here the scheme of associative memory and parallel romances develops an almost uncanny resemblance between the two women's experience at the moment when each debates leaving their home to follow their lover. As a result of this structure of parallelism and association, there is less disturbance of temporal order and less conflictual subjectivity than in the flashbacks in Delluc's earlier films.

The female-focalized flashback in *Menilmontant* (Dmitri Kirsanoff, 1929) occurs in the context of a film that is radically fragmented and rapidly paced in its editing style. The first scene of the film is one of domestic violence rendered as a staccato series of metonymic images, as a man leads a woman and another man from a farmhouse and bludgeons them to death. The representation of these events is metonymic: the lace curtains on a doorway violently fluttering, the anguished expressions of the victims as they are pulled out of the house, the hand of the murderer grabbing an axe and then the axe flung into a muddy puddle after a swing. The film's narration continues in imagery whose spatio-temporal representation is equally as fragmented and indirect as it tells of the two daughters of this family discovering the scene of violence, leaving town, and then leading adult lives in Paris.

The flashback occurs when one of the women leaves her lover's apartment to walk along a quai by the Seine. A close-up of this woman in a cloche hat that echoes her round, innocent eyes shows her looking up at the sky and then down at the water. Her contemplative face is the image that cuts to the flashback that begins with a swish pan across trees, and then a tilt down to show her as a child, dressed in the white dress and bows we saw in the scene immediately following the murder. *That* scene, earlier in the film, showed both sisters dressed in the same manner, playing outdoors and then coaxing their cat down from a tree. When one of them turns down a lane, the sequence of her joyous running is cross-cut with the crowd gathering around the murder scene, until her approach brings her to the point where she can see the crowd. The child's realization of the murder is expressed by a series of jumpcut shots on her. Starting with a medium shot, the camera jumps in five times along the axis of action to show her in extreme close-up as she reacts by placing her hand over her mouth. This earlier scene resonates throughout the flashback as the repressed scene that is not recalled; instead the flashback shifts to another scene that is closely related. This scene shows the girl in solitary play in the forest, then by the side of a lagoon that reflects her joyous scampering, then her swishing a branch as she sits on a riverbank, then turning somersaults and gleefully running off. The flashback shows us moments of happiness, of active pleasure even when all alone, of innocence. It is a scene from before the murder, and as remembered it does not, like the earlier narration, lead up to the murder. Yet in a sense it does. In the return to the present, we turn to the same close-up as before the flashback, but this time the girl touches the edge of her finger to her lips and stares with an unnerving depth. The film then fills in the significance of this deep stare as a close-up shows her feet descending the staircase to the river, then reversing her steps, metonymically presenting her suicide plans and her renunciation of them.

The drama of the sisters' lives in the city continues, as this woman becomes pregnant, only to find out her sister has begun a romance with the same man. The sisters separate, one wandering through the streets with her baby, the other becoming a prostitute, until they are shown circumstantially reunited at the end. Another prostitute murders the man who wronged them both in images whose fragmentation and metonymy echo the opening murder scene.

Both the flashback to childhood and the surrounding narrative of urban drama is like a darker version of *Orphans of the Storm*. The vast difference is one of structuration and tone, derived from *Menilmontant*'s framing and composing of events. Unlike Griffith's sentimental symbolic representation, the flashback here operates through ironic displacement. At the moment of suicidal compulsion, after her sexual encounter with a near stranger, the young woman thinks not of the horror of her discovery of her mother's mutilated body but of a scene of innocent play. Yet this scene of play also represents the surrounding horror by that scene's prior contiguity and its current absence. The sister is also absent from the flashback images, which soon becomes the case in the subsequent sequences, so that the flashback is also a mental image of the remembering sister's ability to survive alone. This gives the flashback another nuance, a motivation for the renunciation of suicide, even as it is meant to explain and be motivated by her suicidal drive. The multiple meanings of this flashback are complimentary to the disruptive and suggestive montage throughout the film.

This brings us to the question of how the difference in the structuration of these flashbacks and of these films in general accomplishes a transformation of melodrama. The elements of melodrama remain, as in the final coincidental occurrence of the sister's reunion and the man's murder that echoes the initial murder. However, in *Menilmontant,* we are left less with a charmed circularity, less with the type of satisfaction that is derived from the completion of a contained pattern, as in Griffith's *Orphans of the Storm*. Impressionist films give us instead another type of filmic expression that evokes a poetic ambiguity and irony, creating a more subjective rendering of mental states and memory processes.

Jean Epstein's *La Glace à trois faces* (1927) uses a three-part structure to depict the lives of three women of different classes who share the same lover; the title, which means "the three way mirror," refers not only to this narrative tripartition in the imaging of French womanhood and the manner in which each woman mirrors this man's desires, but also to a form of representation used in the film. Not only is it composed of three distinct segments, but each segment utilizes a fragmented and multiple mode of representation, a kind of three-way mirror, a cubist refraction of the action.

The film begins with a rich woman, Pearl. After Pearl is abandoned by her lover at an outdoor cafe, she decides to tell an older man there about the history of her love affair. A flashback shows Pearl's lover running through a woods in a tuxedo accompanied by her and another fashionably dressed woman. Later in the segment, there is a scene of great temporal and spatial ambiguity that shows her waiting in a chair cross-cut with the lover, who is preoccupied with business matters, including making numerous telephone calls. Only at the end of a series of shots do we realize that the couple are in the same space in his apartment and that she is in his presence. In the extremely fragmented editing we see close-ups of a ring in a box, another of her taking a ring off her finger, followed by a shot of the ring falling on the floor. This seems to indicate a past remembrance of receiving the ring from him and her present unconscious desire to end the relationship, to take the ring off.

The second segment concerns a bohemian artist, Mademoiselle Athalia Roubin-owitch. While she waits for her lover (the same man as above) to appear at a party, she tells an artist friend about the affair. The flashback sequence from the past first shows them meeting in a woods when she is taking her pet monkey for a walk and he is on horseback. He rescues her monkey which has climbed up a tree. A brief return to the telling of the story in the present is followed by another segment in which she is sculpting him and then he chases her around the studio. She first orders him to leave, then begs him to come back; their romance is characterized by this type of game playing.

The third segment is about a woman from the working class, Lucie. Lucie tells a woman friend about her lonely love affair. The ensuing flashback is bracketed, giving us numerous typical situations in which he is departing or she is alone, waiting for him, sewing or cooking, or standing over a dinner which will be left uneaten. However, his arrival, unannounced, leads to a segment of them enjoying a Sunday boating excursion. This segment of shared pleasure is marked by her awareness of herself as "just a poor girl" whom he does not take seriously, and ends with an image of her alone, picking up the milk bottle delivered to her doorstep that rejoins the earlier imagery of her solitude.

These three parallel segments, each with its flashback retrospection, draw similarities between the subjectivities of the three women, all of whose romances turn out to be with the same man. The brilliant montage of these metonymically portrayed instances of memory creates an illusive rendering of female desire and the meanings invested in the past within romance. Unlike a more conventional narrative exposition, *La Glace à trois faces* gives us fragmented instances, images rich in potential meanings that we are asked to decipher and appreciate within their brief presentation. Here the form of presentation corresponds to the enigmatic situation each woman faces. Unable really to know or possess this man who illicits their desire only to disappear, they are also unable to understand their own fascination with his "tyrannical" force over them. In the parallels and the narrative gaps between these three segments lies a speculation on this force of unfulfilled desire.

La Maternelle (Jean Benoit-Lévy and Marie Epstein, 1933) is a film that continues the impressionist work on the flashback even though it was made after the introduction of sound and other economic factors changed the context of French production away from such avant-garde imaging.[18] The aesthetics of *La Maternelle* remain tied to the earlier, more marginal mode of intense transformations of imaging and montage. The flashback in *La Maternelle* occurs at the end of the film, as a love-starved child considers suicide, feeling abandoned by her prostitute mother who has run off with a man, and by Rose, a worker at her nursery school, a substitute mother figure who is about to marry the school principal. The child's fear of exclusion from adult couples is portrayed by an image that precedes and initiates the flashback, that of a couple embracing. Marie, sitting on a pier, sees the couple and then their reflection in the water. The child is shown throwing stones at this image, as if this violent gesture could destroy not only the image of adult love, but the associative memories that follow—for the rippled water surface becomes the "screen" on which her flashback memories are projected, interspersed with fantasies and punctuated by returns to her looking at the water. The images intersperse shots from the earlier cabaret sequence in which the man seduces her mother in her presence, an earlier scene in which a man makes a brutal advance to Rose, other images of Rose, and images of an anonymous couple embracing.[19] The close-up on Rose appears upside down, not only increasing another element of difference within the fragmentation of the montage, but suggesting Marie's feelings of being inverted, possibly from love to anger and hate. This rush of images from the past is followed by a return to a shot of Marie as she leans forward and out of the frame, falling into the water.

This flashback is devoted to expressing the child's psychic state, as images from the past combine two sets of events, one set involving her mother, the other involving Rose, into a representation of her fear of abandonment. Even the innocent, anonymous lovers are appropriated into this symbolic configuration, which psychoanalysis terms "l'abandonique," the fear of the once abandoned child that such loss of love is bound to be repeated in all new relationships.[20] Ironically, Marie is saved by the man from the anonymous couple. *La Maternelle,* then, is an excellent example of the flashback of subjective memory images composed to reveal the inner workings of a character's psyche. The upside-down inversion of love to hate symbolized in the representation here of the maternal face culminates in the stone-throwing violence and then the turning of that violence against the self as suicide. In both form and substance this flashback is a most complex reiteration of the psychoanalytical constructs of the narrative, while at the same time displaying the mimetic representation of the inner thoughts of a character.

We see how impressionist films develop a fascinating relationship between the reworking of narrative forms and image forms. The films concern inner subjectivity, often focalized as female subjectivity, and therefore a focalization from a position of oppression manifested as lack or as a fissure of the psyche. The flashbacks informed by this project are characterized by a montage of disparate elements that are restructured symbolically within their depiction as memories. These memory fragments have philosophical resonances, for they represent an acknowledgment of a complex human psyche whose constituent elements draw on a fragmented experience of the past, subjectively retained along lines of force. The shadow of a Bergsonian view of memory and the example set by Proust's transformation of the novel are evident in these films which seek image and montage equivalents for a subjective associative memory and intersperse multiple temporalities as co-present to human consciousness. Still, the transformation is relative and some of the factors that control the limits of this exploration are not limitations of creativity. Rather, filmmaking, more than philosophical writing or the novel is constrained financially and subject to distributor and audience comprehension and approval. The more standard melodramatic formulas remained more popular than these adventurous efforts at transformation and apparently held in check the development of these different forms. Despite the differences that appear in this period in French production, many similarities to the American forms discussed earlier are apparent, especially in those films that remain closer to commercial melodramatic forms. The works of Abel Gance that we will examine next are good examples of this mode that keeps the visual experiment within the bounds of popular melodramatic expression.

Memory Symbolization in Gance's Melodramas

Abel Gance's two epic films, *La Roue* (1923–24) and *Napoléon vu par Abel Gance* (1927), tend towards the sentimental and baroque in a manner that differentiates them from the other French films of the twenties discussed so far. Both films use flashbacks as part of their process of symbolization. Gance, like Griffith, emphasizes the symbolic within melodrama. His narratives return to the past not only to provide psychological explanations of his characters' desires and actions, but also to create visual symbolic motifs whose recurrence punctuates the elaborate visual rhythms established in the editing. This visual repetition of imagery also unifies the film, as images become leitmotifs in the musical sense of this term.

Similarly, some flashbacks which consist of montage reprises of images from various parts of the film serve as recapitulations. Flashbacks therefore have an important structural function in the almost musical composition of Gance's melodramas. Some of these characteristics were already present in Gance's earlier films whose dimensions were more like the melodramas and poetic essays of the other French avant-garde filmmakers. *Mater Dolorosa* (1917), for example, uses flashback images to show the memories of characters in a melodrama of doubted paternity. These inserts fragment the action and create, along with the variety of camera angles Gance employs to depict his action scenes, a montage of disparate elements brought together in rhythmic collage.

La Dixième Symphonie (1918) is a melodramatic story laced with secrets that are remembered and revealed in flashbacks. The opening of the film is in fact a sequence set off from the rest of the film in an anterior time; it shows in enigmatic fragments the accidental shooting by Eve Dinant (Emmy Lynn) of her lover's sister. In exchange for his silence, the lover, Frédéric Ryce (Jean Toulout) blackmails her. This is elliptically linked to the other sequences of the film that take place much later, after Eve has married a composer, Enric Damor (Séverin-Mars) and begun a new life. Elements of her secret begin to be revealed through a series of flashbacks. The climactic explanatory flashback comes as Eve is considering telling her husband all about her past in an effort to save her stepdaughter from Ryce's designs; an iris opens on the court hearing concerning the sister's death. However, the necessity for a complete revelation is circumvented by a confrontation by mother and stepdaughter with the blackmailer Frédéric Ryce that leads to his suicide.

This entire melodramatic plot serves as background to motivate the composer's torment as inspiration for his musical creativity, for although he never learns of his wife's past, he witnesses her distress and interprets this as a sign of infidelity. Gance's investment here is not only on the melodramatic situation, but in the effects of misrecognition and the angst it produces on a creative individual.

Gance's epic films which follow also use flashbacks to reveal past secrets and to depict the weight of the past on the formulation of character and desire. The analysis of the use of flashbacks in these films can only be based on the extant prints, which, film historians have established, survive only in mutilated or reconstituted form.[21] The original nine-hour version of *La Roue* shown in Paris in 1923 was cut nearly in half for distribution the following year. The prints that exist today all vary in length and substance. *Napoléon* remained in a similar state of abridged, disassembled, and contradictory versions until the late seventies when Kevin Brownlow reconstituted a long version. One can assume, therefore, a greater fidelity to the original in the case of *Napoléon* than with *La Roue,* but in both cases images have been lost and occasionally reedited.

In *La Roue,* Sisif (Séverin-Mars) is the railway engineer around whose family— a son, Elie (Gabriel de Gravone) and an adopted daughter, Norma (Ivy Close)—the melodrama of incestuous desires revolves. Flashbacks are used to illustrate Sisif's psychological obsessions and Elie's trauma. Both men have long been in love with Norma, but Sisif has come to a point where he can barely control his desires. (Elie believes Norma to be his actual sister, while Sisif knows she is not his actual daughter.)

Twice flashbacks illustrate Sisif's telling other characters about the past, a telling that is confessional and revealing of Sisif's psychological state. The first of these incidents is Sisif's explanation of his obsessive desire for Norma, who has grown into a beautiful young woman. This confession is offered to Hersan, a rich railroad official to whom Sisif eventually will offer Norma in marriage, a solution meant to foreclose his own lust. Sisif tells of the way his desire has led him in the past to climb the stairs to Norma's bedroom once she has gone to bed. The flashback imagery cross-cuts shots of Sisif outside the door with shots of Norma inside the room. This flashback recalls a sequence from the previous night where a tilt up of a camera angle on Sisif to a subjective shot of Norma's door indicates Sisif's desire for his adopted daughter. In this earlier sequence, he approaches the foot of the stairs, but ties a rope across his pathway, restricting his further action. The flashback confirms what was already indicated in an intertitle in the previous sequence; his nocturnal lust for Norma is a habitual behavior, a repetitive struggle with a forbidden desire that necessitates the symbolic barrier.

Another flashback offered to Hersan is linked to the original staircase sequence of the night before; it begins, as that one did, with a shot of Sisif at his workbench. However, the shot which is aligned with his gaze this time shows Norma swinging on a swing outside the window. The subjective shots of Norma fetishize her skirt and legs, recalling an earlier sequence in which Sisif demands that Norma wear longer, more modest skirts. Sisif closes the window, drawing the curtain across the forbidden vision, but then peeks out again, only to collapse with despair. This flashback gives us new evidence of Sisif's obsession, as we see his lustful gaze and witness another of his attempts to control his passion. So although the flashbacks ostensibly serve as a confession to Hersan, they also function to give more details to the audience on the nature of Sisif's sexual obsession and, through reiteration, to indicate the habitual nature of Sisif's actions.

This flashback imagery of obsessive desire is paralleled later in the film by Sisif's flashback account to his engineer colleague, Machfer, of his son's death. Here the flashback consists of a montage of brief images of various angles on Elie hanging from the cliff (he has been fighting with the jealous Hersan) that were seen earlier in a sequence that depicted Elie's death. This time the brief shots of Elie are punctuated by swish pans of landscape that are like the view of landscape one would get from a moving train. These rapid pans are so blurred that they become a metaphorical device to indicate Sisif's agitation as he is remembering. However, this rapid panning of landscape used as punctuation also suggests that Sisif's thoughts of Elie's death have recurred repeatedly following the rhythms of a train's advance; the metaphor can perhaps be taken to encompass the idea that the images of Elie's death recur daily in the same manner that the landscape regularly rushed by him during his career as a railway engineer. This metaphor then becomes part of a larger metaphorical association the film makes between the machinery of the railway and the mechanisms of the human psyche.

Elie's flashbacks are not stories told to other characters, but interior monologues that depict his private agony. Elie begins to suspect that Sisif is hiding the truth about Norma's parentage from him when he finds out her name is not listed in the family Bible. This engenders two short, connected flashbacks to scenes from Elie and Norma's childhood that represent his trying to remember and figure out the nature of the relationship his father had with each of them. One is to a scene in which the father tucks both youngsters into bed in their shared bedroom. The bedroom scene emblemizes the incestuous web of the desire of both father and son for their "daughter/sister." This again echoes Sisif's construction of the rope barrier to this room once the daughter has grown up. The other flashback is to a scene at a well, seen in full earlier in the film.

Elie's death, in its first depiction, is another occasion in which flashbacks occur. Elie's focalization of images of Norma flash quickly through his memory as he awaits death. This montage series depicts Norma at various ages, engaging in activities and wearing outfits that were seen earlier in the film. These subjective shots belonging to Elie's memory are intercut with the image of him hanging from a branch of a cliff; the editing becomes more rapid and the shots of Norma grow closer, until only her eyes dominate the frame. This montage is the most radically fragmented expression of subjectivity in the film; as is the case of the American films *Two Seconds* and *The Last Moment,* montage privileges the instants before death. The intense dramatic instance allows for an "excess" of expression, rapid montage. Even if this sequence can be said to conform to an allowable excess within intense moments of conventional melodramatic expression, it nonetheless also develops a mimetic concern for memory processes; Gance's cinematic montage here strives to approximate the quickness and diversity of inner thought.

If the flashbacks in the film are divided between father and son in their parallel desire for Norma, so is another type of subjective shot, that, while not a true flashback, is closely linked to the flashback sequences. These parallel shots are superimpositions of Norma's face. Sisif's occurs when he is driving his engine, the Norma Compound; the face appears in the steam. Elie's occurs when he is alone in the cabin to which he retreats to avoid his father and forget Norma after she is married to Hersan. Norma's face appears superimposed on his violin. These shots continue the motif of the haunting of memory and the psychological force of the past over the present that is expressed by the flashbacks. One of the strongest elements of *La Roue* is this parallel treatment of an incestuous obsession that is false and true at the same time; not actually incest, since the daughter/sister is adopted, but quite the same experience in terms of the shared childhood experience brought out in the flashbacks, with their concentration on the space of the bedroom, the well, and the swing. That these same flashback devices also play an important role in both the abstract rhythms and patterns of repetition in the film links filmic abstraction to the investments and energies amongst the psyches within the fiction. Gance's melodramas are indeed more baroque and sentimental than the other French films we have looked at; still, this double flashback structure of incestuous desire coupled with the abstraction of accelerating and repetitive montage, is clearly linked to the innovative exploration of filmic expression of mental states that characterizes the other films of the period.

Napoléon flirts with this level of psychoanalytic structure in its flashbacks as well, endowing its historical hero with psychological motivation rooted in childhood experience. However, such psychologism in the context of the historical epic tends to explain the momentous by the trivial. This reductionist tendency couples Freudian notions of the causal determination of childhood with a 19th-century romanticism and a heavy-handed symbolism.

The film inscribes the past, memory, and repetition into a larger mythologizing process. If the eagle is given a psychological symbolization from childhood, by the middle of the film this meaning is transferred to the eagle as symbol of empire. The recurring image-symbol, eagle, links the defense and acquisition of an empire by France to a young Napoléon's similar struggle to assert and maintain his personal integrity when surrounded by hostile school children, who would take from him his only possession, his eagle, emblem of his Corsican heritage and therefore his selfhood. The choice of the eagle in this dual function of actual childhood possession and emblem of the empire works well visually, but this visual triumph results in a loss of subtlety and multidimensionality in both the historical treatment and the psychology proposed by the film. The mélange of an epic structure with the psychological portrait also results in a wide divergence of tone from sequence to sequence; the flashbacks are stretched over these gaps between history and personal fictions in an attempt to forge an explanatory unity, stretched often to the limit. The visual elegance of these flashbacks goes a long way towards easing the discomfort one might otherwise have with them conceptually. In analyzing Napoléon, however, it is precisely this question of visual spectacle versus conceptual development that one must ultimately raise.

There are two important liaison flashbacks in Napoléon; there is also a more mundane one that takes place during the victim's ball to illustrate Josephine's remark "I was summoned to the scaffold on this spot." It takes us back to a close-up shot of Josephine and Hoche as her name is called to be executed, serving to amplify Josephine's historical reference, and also to portray her relationship with Hoche as a longstanding and emotionally involved one. This is significant in a subplot that follows Napoléon and Josephine's romance as a comic interlude, but it is not part of the systematic historical and psychological liaisons the film strives to make.

The first of the film's flashback liaisons is from the climatic moment of the siege of Toulon to a brief extreme close-up of Napoleon's face during the snowball fight as a student at La Brienne. The return to the present is to cross-cut close-ups between Napoléon and Tristan Fleuri cheering the fall of Toulon. The flashback resumes briefly, with a return to the youthful Napoleon in close-up, now superimposed with a longshot overview of the snowball fight, before returning once again to the scene of Napoleon and Trisan Fleuri at Toulon. The flashback resumes briefly, with a return to the youthful Napoleon in close-up, now superimposed with a longshot overview of the snowball fight, before returning once again to the scene of Napoléon and Tristan Fleuri at Toulon. This flashback cements the parallel and the psychological causality that the film strives to establish between the youthful battle, given such extensive treatment near the beginning of the film, and this first battle against the British. Tristan Fleuri is another device used to make this connection, for it locates him as an innkeeper cheering Napoléon in Toulon, just as he was earlier depicted as young Napoléon's supporter when he was the cook at La Brienne. This kind of exaggerated circumstantial reunion of characters is characteristic of melodramatic form and particularly reminiscent of the endless reunions in *Orphans of the Storm*.

The triptych sequence at the end of the film offers a grand recapitulative flashback similar to the rush of images that immediately precede Elie's death in *La Roue*. An extreme close-up of Napoléon's face is framed by images of clouds that fill both side screens. The center screen dissolves into a very rapid series of flash frames from the past, including a map of the siege of Toulon, the eagle at La Brienne, the boat escape to France over the stormy sea, the face of Robespierre from the national convention, etc. A recapitulation of grand images of the past of Napoléon (and the past of the film) is a key element in the pyrotechnic finale. This flashback sequence also weaves together all the psychological determinism of Gance's fanciful history; the outcast of La Brienne has ascended to military and political power in a manner that has sharpened his will to conquer.

If *La Roue* has closer ties to the explorations of subjectivity that characterize impressionism, *Napoléon,* for all its visual splendor remains quite direct in its representation of unified memory visions and uses its memory images as repetitions of symbolic imagery rather than as a complex view of memory processes. In addition, the grafting of historical causality onto the naive vision of psychological determinism and the manner in which both of these elements are put to the service of a patriotic symbolism makes the flashback work of *Napoléon* less of a break with conventional melodrama than other French films of this period. The latter, as we have seen, were more consistent in their "impressionist" pursuit of subjectivity, of the mental processes, conscious and unconscious that constitute our memory.

Psychoanalysis and the German Expressionist Flashback

German expressionist films from the twenties also strongly link the flashback to the psyche of a character. These films are often explicitly or metaphorically concerned with insanity; the narration of the past often mixes memory with fantasy, delusion and dreams. The influence of Freud and psychoanalysis in general on German culture can be felt in these films and a few even make direct references to psychoanalysis. In analyzing these films, it is important to keep theories of psychoanalysis in a double perspective. From the perspective of filmic analysis, I will be pointing out those psychoanalytic concepts that are appropriated by the films and inform their narrative construction, and that are sometimes distorted in the process. From the perspective of psychoanalysis, I will be analyzing the manner in which these films function.

Certainly the most famous and controversial of the German flashback films is Robert Wiene's *The Cabinet of Dr. Caligari* (1919). The aethestic controversy surrounding this film centers on its expressionistically abstracted sets that some film critics and theorists have denounced as an abdication of cinema's ontological definition, or preferred vocation of realism.[22] But another controversy, historical and ideological in nature, concerns the addition of a frame story to the original script of Hans Janowitz and Carl Mayer by director Wiene and producer Erich Pommer. Siegfried Kracauer claims the original version was intended as a political allegory for the German government of World War I, the "prototype of such voracious authority."[23] Kracauer also asserts that for Mayer the film also has an autobiographical motivation as a critique of an oppressive military psychiatrist who had treated him during the war (p. 62). As an allegory without the frame, Kracauer holds, the film would have been a revolutionary critique of one who murders for power, a Hitleresque figure, who is shown to be aided by a somnambulist accomplice representing "the common man, who under the pressure of compulsory military service is drilled to kill" (p. 65).

The frame story adds a prologue that introduces the student, Francis. Francis is telling another man of his discovery of Dr. Caligari's misdeeds. Only at the end of the flashback narrative do we realize that Francis is an inmate of a mental institution where "Caligari" (Werner Krauss) is a well-meaning, normal doctor and where the other characters in the tale are also mental patients. Once the doctor diagnoses Francis's problem as his belief that his psychiatrist is the legendary medieval Caligari, the doctor states that he can cure him.

The addition of the frame story is taken by Kracauer as a key instance in his sociological analysis of the films from the Weimar Republic; he claims that in turning the narrative into a delusionary flashback, the reading as political allegory is abolished, yielding instead the message that those who would suspect or criticize demonic power figures are themselves suffering from paranoid delusions (p. 67). Kracauer also makes the long-term claim that this adulterated version of *Caligari,* like other films from this period, prepared a susceptible public for the advent of Hitler, by "spreading an all-pervasive atmosphere of horror," showing "normality" to be mental aberration and unleashing a strong sadism and an appetite for destruction (p. 74).

Despite its grounding in an historical account of a script changed against the intentions of the authors, Kracauer's thesis necessitates questionable interpretive leaps. Though the flashback in the final version does end with a return to the insane asylum, it never suggests that all the world is like "the crowd of insane moving in their bizarre surroundings" (p. 74). Kracauer laments the loss of a film that might have been an effective political allegory (although it is hard to see why it, too, would not have spread an atmosphere of horror). He is unable to consider that the frame story changes the film not into a completely reactionary film that simply negates the first version, but rather into one that deserves analysis on its own terms as a vision of the construction of a delusion.

Reviews at the time of the film's release in Germany, in France, and its triumphant American screenings tended to view the film as a serious treatment of the subject of madness and saw its expressionist style as a visual analogue for insanity. Allowing for this interpretation, it is possible to see the flashback as accentuating this aspect of the film, doubling its discourse on insanity. The enunciator, Francis, operating under a paranoid delusion, fabricates a story of his doctor being insane, a story that grounds the doctor's pathology in a reference to a legend. The film is contemporaneous with the widespread discussion of Freud's *The Interpretation of Dreams* (which though published in 1900 was in the process of first being assimilated into the culture in the decade that followed).[24] One of Freud's themes both in this book and other essays on the construction of fantasies and delusions is the incorporation of legend and literature into fantasy material.[25] In the film, the delusionary subject does not simply take his doctor to be a legendary evil figure, as his doctor diagnoses at the end of the film, but something subtler, at one step's remove. Though the name Caligari is applied to both the contemporary and legendary doctor, Francis, in fact, imagines that his doctor imagines himself to be the medieval Caligari, and he presents a detailed account of his doctor's illusion.

This account is told within the film in the form of two flashbacks interior to the frame story. These occur when Francis investigates (or more accurately, imagines he investigates) the library and the medical diary of the head of the mental institution. Francis finds a book from 1093 describing the medieval Dr. Caligari. A close-up on a passage from that text explains Caligari's use of a somnambulist to commit murders. Then, after a close-up on an entry in Caligari's diary from March 12 that tells of a somnambulist being admitted to the institution, the image fades out to a flashback of Cesare (Conrad Veidt) being admitted in a wheel chair. The doctor examines him with great joy, points at the medieval Caligari book and looks back at his new patient. An iris back to the present shows Francis once again reading a diary entry, followed by a close-up on the text, "Can he be made to commit murder?" A second flashback shows the doctor pacing first in his office as he says, "I will become Caligari," then wandering through the village as he considers the temptations of practicing the powers of suggestion he has studied. It is at this point that writing appears overlaid on the image, "You must become Caligari!," representing the doctor's compulsive drive to live out the legend.

These segments follow a Freudian notion of the formation of a delusion. If we put aside for the moment the frame story, Francis becomes the analyst discovering the doctor's paranoia. In representing a psychoanalyst as a deluded and evil power figure, the film would seem to be condemning the emerging intellectual discipline of psychoanalysis. (This implicit condemnation is similar to horror films of more recent American vintage such as Alfred Werker's *Shock* [1946] and Brian de Palma's *Dressed to Kill* [1980], where the analyst turns out to be the psychotic transvestite murderer.) The frame story in *The Cabinet of Dr. Caligari* salvages the popular reputation of psychoanalysis in a film whose narrative construction displays, and perhaps even borrows consciously from, psychoanalytic theory.

In this light, the expressionist style—comprised of the angular distortion of space, the woodblock-like delineation of high contrast black-and-white images accomplished through painted shadows and exaggerated make-up and costumes— becomes a metaphor for Francis's delusion and mad vision. Somewhat problematically, the distortion is not completely straightened out at the film's end, when our narrator is revealed to be a mental patient. Although this narrative inconsistency might be merely the result of a striving for stylistic continuity, in retrospect it appears to be the trace of the film's historical conditions of production, the dispute between authors and director over the addition of the frame story. The political allegory is at war with the narration of a delusion, as two different narrative voices remain in combat for our attention and faith as viewers—a conflict that is not resolved until the very end of the film. So the historical debate over which tale to tell and which ideology to express remains communicated to the viewer in transfigured form in the meaning assigned the decor and the believability of the narrator.

The debate between a psychoanalytical and a political interpretation of the film has broad implications given the intellectual climate of Germany at this time. Carl Schorske points out in *Fin-de-Siècle Vienna* that psychoanalytic and socialist organizations during this period were distinct entities offering competing perspectives on the world.[26] If his conclusions concerning the competitive allegiances within German-speaking intellectual circles can be applied to Germany's film culture over the next decades, then *Caligari* can be seen as caught in intellectual oppositions between the focus on subjectivity and the focus on the social mechanisms of power and class.

A similar frame structure raises other questions of interpretation in E. A. Dupont's *Variety* (1925). Also expressionistic in decor, acting style, and narrative concerns, the film's rich camerawork by Karl Freund gives it a density of visual expression similar to the multiplicity of camera angles and rapid editing that Louis Delluc and the other impressionist filmmakers used to signify subjectivity and atmosphere. In this case, the entire film is being told to a prison warden by prisoner No. 28 (Emil Jannings) prior to his release due to a pardon; it is a story he has previously refused to divulge.

However, once the film embarks on its internal narration, the story of the events which led to No. 28's incarceration for murder, the narrator's voice is seemingly lost. Events unfold without his commentary or central figuration and incidents are presented that he never witnesses. Yet the sense of subjectivity remains strong due to the style of camerawork and editing, as if to signify that the viewer is privy to the prisoner's sense of the past, his imaginary vision of what he now understands to have happened. This is important, for the internal story is one of sensuality and lust transformed into humiliation and jealousy, culminating in murder. It is the work of this internal narrative to make No. 28's revenge for humiliation and jealousy pardonable, as the film ends with the warden calmly wishing him God's mercy and allowing the prison door to be opened.

The print now distributed in the United States is a censored version that omits the entire first part of the flashback. This first part depicts the "Boss" (as prisoner No. 28 was known) leaving his wife and the small sideshow he runs, for an adventure with a young trapeze artist, Berta-Marie (Lya de Putti) and a return to active circus performing. The censored version transforms the Boss's mistress into his wife, turning his murder of her into a husband's "crime de passion" and thus reducing the moral dilemmas posed by the original film.

A scene of domestic life after a performance shows their sensuous interaction; the Boss's toweling-off his much younger mistress becomes a game of joyous movement. Later, he is seen darning a hole in her stocking while she is still wearing it, his domestic devotion doubling as a scene of subservience and fetishism. This domestic sensuality is troubled when the famous trapeze artist Antonelli asks them to join his act to replace his brother, disabled by a fall. Antonelli's ulterior motive is the seduction of the attractive mistress, which he soon accomplishes.

The Boss's discovery of this betrayal is made when he finds a cartoon of himself as a cuckold etched into a barroom table. His fantasy revenge is subjectively displayed to the film viewer, as he imagines dropping Antonelli during a trapeze performance of the triple somersault. Yet after the fantasy sequence ends, the Boss and Antonelli are shown in their dressing room, with the only indication of the murder wish a displaced emblem, a skull and crossbones adorning Antonelli's hood. When the curtain is lifted for the performance, the film depicts the Boss's subjective state through various threatening angles on the audience flashing before him. Though he waves an indication not to continue to act, though we see that his vision has become a prismatic configuration of the spinning lights, wires, and audience below, he manages to do the somersault catch successfully, as well as the hooded catch that follows. The subjectively depicted moments of revenge fantasy are thus followed by his overcoming of his fears and psychic distortions so that he does not fulfill that fantasy.

Later that evening, the Boss performs the violent knife murder of Antonelli. After this direct act of retribution, he walks with determination to the police to turn himself in, even as Berta-Marie clings to him, now begging him to remain with her. Given Antonelli and Berta-Marie's deceit and treachery, and his earlier overcoming of his tormented fantasies, his crime is depicted as not a premeditated evil but an act beyond his control (the trapeze fall would have provided him a cover that the knife murder does not). It is crucial to the ideological work of the film that its story be told in flashback, as a remembrance, since it strives to create identification with the convict who is both victim of his own passions and the others' treachery. Upon the mention of his wife, he tells the tale as an act of remorse, and its telling becomes the fulfillment of a contract with the warden. Telling the tale legitimates the pardon. The film is less a tale of crime than one of a confession to a silent analyst. If this film can be seen as an allegory for psychoanalysis, it never discloses its hidden allegory; that there is a psychoanalytical allegory in *Variety,* as in *The Cabinet of Dr. Caligari,* can be seen more clearly when we compare it to another key film of the period, G. W. Pabst's *Secrets of the Soul* (1926).

To tell the past, to be pardoned or cured; these motives also inform the flashback structure of *Secrets of the Soul*. The scenarists Colin Ross and Hans Neumann consulted Hans Sachs and Karl Abraham, famed psychoanalysts and members of Freud's circle, before collaborating on the script. In addition, Dr. Nicholas Kaufman is listed as "advisor." The film was publicized as being based on a case reported by Dr. Sigmund Freud and is introduced by a title that reads:

In every man's life there are wishes and desires in the unconscious mind. In the dark hours of mental conflict these unknown forces struggle to assert themselves. Mysterious disorders result from these struggles, the explanation of which is the actual work of psychoanalysis. The doctrine of Sigmund Freud is regarded as important in the treatment of such disorders.

Despite these attempts to ground the film in actual Freudian theory and practice, its narration of the etiology and cure of a psychosis takes sweeping and fanciful liberties with the reality of psychoanalysis. Freud in fact opposed Pabst's film project in his correspondence with Abraham, while Abraham himself died in the midst of the project, leaving Hans Sachs to play the largest role in supervising it.[27] As Freud feared, Pabst's film presents a condensed and simplified version of psychoanalysis which serves the purpose of filmic narrative economy, offering the audience an abbreviated tale where all that is presented eventually fits neatly together as the enigma deciphered, the puzzle completed. However, Freud's categorical opposition to the filmic rendering of psychoanalytic treatment and mental processes was perhaps inconsistent with his appreciation of literary works such as *Gradiva* that Freud takes to illustrate his theories magnificently.[28] If *Secrets of the Soul* finally oversimplifies, it also does present elements of the psychic process and indicates the great potential for filmic depictions of mental processes.

So we can best regard the film as an historical compromise between certain lessons borrowed from psychoanalysis, the formal imperatives of film construction imposed by a tradition of narrative construction, and the tendency to be overly didactic in introducing the new psychoanalytic discoveries. The dream sequences and flashbacks serve important narrative functions, churning and distorting narrative events already seen. Later, these events are isolated and rearranged as connections and meanings are provided for them. Flashbacks are used to display the verbalizations by the patient during the psychoanalytic sessions, an innovation of historical and theoretical importance.

The film opens by presenting three segments depicting events in the life of Martin Feldman, a chemist (Werner Krauss), before he realizes that he is suffering from a mental disorder. These events will supply the raw material to be reworked later in dream and flashback sequences. The first of these initiating incidents occurs when Feldman is trimming his wife's hair with a razor. A neighbor's scream, shown in a disjunct cut to her apartment startles Feldman whose razor is shown in close-up slipping and cutting the back of his wife's neck. His wife, holding a puppy, remarks wistfully, "if only I had a baby." In a return to the street a bystander in the crowd that has gathered to watch a corpse being carried out on a stretcher explains the scream and the corpse by telling us of the murder: "He did it with a razor."

The next of these initiating sequences occurs in Feldman's chemistry laboratory as a woman friend of his assistant visits with her child. When Feldman presents the child with candy, the little girl blows him a kiss.

This is followed by Feldman and his wife at home that evening. When she shows him a newspaper article reporting the murder, he throws it in the fire. As a detective questions them regarding the murder, a letter and presents arrive from his wife's cousin, Erich. The letter says that Erich will arrive to visit from Sumatra; the gifts are a statuette of the goddess Kwanon and a saber.

After Feldman and his wife go off to sleep in separate bedrooms, his dream is presented in an array of superimposed and distorted images whose montage is intended as mimetic of the flow of dream imagery. Most of these images are transformed recurrences of the previously presented expository material (what Freud would call the day's residues) or other earlier memories that we cannot yet figure out. The oneiric material thus includes references to cousin Erich, the explorer. In the dream Erich becomes a hunter who shoots Feldman into the sky. Feldman plummets back to his own checkerboard-patterned patio. The goddess statuette becomes a large shrine. The dream also contains images of curbing trains, of buildings that grow out of the ground, of a bell tower with mocking women's faces replacing the bells (including those of the wife and the lab assistant) and images of the wife and cousin in a boat holding a baby as they row past a prison cell where Feldman is incarcerated, accused of murder.

More incidents from Feldman's waking life fill the pool of dream imagery, while others repeat, a repetition charged with the force of the unconscious. Feldman drops his razor while shaving and later his barber's sharpening of a razor appears as an ominous close-up. At his laboratory, informed of his cousin's arrival, Feldman drops a vial on the checkered laboratory floor—thus retrospectively showing the dream imagery to have been premonitory or even causative, an aspect of the film's representation that will never be treated within the analytical explanations which ensue. In a sense, "real" occurrences in Feldman's life and the fabrication of his unconscious have merged in the film's visual unfolding; certain psychic processes are explained while others are confounded with the "uncanny" of fiction.[29]

One of the most curious aspects of the film's imagery in this regard is the manner in which it introduces the psychoanalyst who will eventually treat Feldman. Feldman leaves his dinner table because he has become frightened of knives, as a close-up on the knives in the table setting indicates. Then he leaves his house key behind at a restaurant. When he reaches his door, a man hands the key to him with an explanation that he is a psychoanalyst and he knows that if one leaves a key behind there must be a reason. This analyst, Dr. Orth, enters the film in the manner of a dream apparition, coincidentally and absurdly connected to the ongoing mixture of real and imaginary within the film's narrative events. This absurd entrance is reinscribed when Dr. Orth becomes the content of the first flashback image. Over a close-up of his key, held by him as he speaks, Feldman has just confessed to his mother his desire to kill his wife. The flashback image of the psychoanalyst as he appeared at Feldman's door becomes superimposed behind this close-up of the key. This superimposition has a double meaning; the key evokes the memory of the analyst who just returned it and simultaneously symbolizes the possibility of a cure. What this flashback superimposition cannot address is how this image is precisely the same stylistically as the dream superimpositions seen earlier; the filmwork cannot separate itself from dreamwork in order to develop a metacritical level of representation.

This is evident in the manner in which the film shifts to its work of representing the analysis of patient Feldman by Dr. Orth. Flashback sequences relating the events we have already seen are depicted against a white background and are alternated with cuts back to the present, shots of Dr. Orth listening to Feldman speak. These visual representations of verbally recounted memories are then alternated with more dream sequences to give the following pattern:

Flashback—cutting wife's hair
Back to Present
Flashback—crowd talking of the razor
Back to Present
Dream—wife and Martin on a hill plant flowers; then they enter a furnished baby nursery;
      then the baby furnishings disappear, when Martin re-enters alone; then his wife
      is a member of a harem belonging to his cousin
Flashback—wife and cousin together, Martin looking on
Back to Present
Flashback—letter announcing the cousin's arrival
Back to Present
Dream—trains advancing, merging into foreground; cousin in a tree; Martin's levitation;
      trains curving; cousin in superimposition
Flashback—Martin dropping vial in laboratory
Back to Present
Return to Dream—images (structured as a flashback) in front of goddess Kwanon
Back to Present

Feldman then offers some interpretation of the imagery from the dream. The buildings that rose up represented the small Italian town where Feldman and his wife spent their honeymoon and the steeple was a site he visited with his wife at that time. The flashbacks continue:

Flashback—wife holding puppy
Back to Present
Flashback—lab assistant, her friend and the child with the candy
Back to Present
Dream—trial where wife shows scar

Finally, Dr. Orth asks Feldman if he remembers anything from his childhood, provoking a different type of flashback. This returns us not to a previously seen incident against a white background, as has been the pattern, but to an event which occurred long before the time of the rest of the film's narrative. We see three young children surrounded by toys on Christmas day. The little girl and one of the boys begin playing with a toy train, while the other boy looks on, feeling excluded. This flashback becomes the key to the analysis, as the excluded child is Martin Feldman, whose future wife and her cousin would not play with him. As this flashback ends, Feldman's last analytic session shows him acting out his repressed desire, as he thrusts an imaginary sword into the air and finally into his analyst's couch.

An explanatory title connects his "knife phobia" to his impotency in his marriage—desiring sexual intercourse with his wife, he is haunted by jealousy from childhood; guilt and the fear of inadequacy replace this desire for sex with a desire to kill. Once the outline of his condition is explained to him, Martin becomes able to embrace his wife and greet her cousin. Then an ellipsis occurs to a curious segment depicting the "cured" Feldman in the country, fishing. He gathers up his catch to return home, but upon seeing his wife and child, he drops the pail of fish, spilling them down the hill. In closing, the film once again introduces psychoanalytically symbolic imagery to depict the patient's recovery and new sexual potency. Remarkably, the film refuses to limit its "dreamwork" imagery to the dreams and the memory images, or even to the psychically charged events the disturbed patient is experiencing. Events which should be outside the film's project of representating the psyche (the introduction of the psychoanalyst, the evidence of the patient's recovery) still obsessively continue to mimic dream processes and fantasy images. The dreamwork "overflows" the dream sequences because filmwork, the structuration of narrative fictional film obeys many of the same laws of representational logic as does the dream. In *Secrets of the Soul,* dream, flashback, and filmic fiction merge as like processes, making it all the more difficult to siphon out a discourse on psychoanalysis. The film is instead a highly crafted *dream* of the psychoanalytic process.

Kammerspiel Flashbacks: Romance and History

If *Secrets of the Soul* presents the flashback as one of the foci of the psychoanalytic session within the study of an individual's memory, Pabst's *The Love of Jeanne Ney* (1927) returns to a more traditional use of the flashback to signify a character's emotional tie to a memory of the past. The film uses flashbacks to present a personal, romantic attachment that preoccupies two characters' thoughts, a bourgeois woman who is in love with a Bolshevik despite their differences of class and politics in the midst of the Russian Revolution. The use of flashbacks would be quite traditional, if it weren't for the unusual context developed by the film's style.

Set during the civil war in the Crimea shortly after the Bolshevik seizure of state power, the film opens in a bar frequented by the counterrevolutionary forces. The opening shot details the decadent, fetishistic aspects of the right wing, by introducing an informer Khalibiev (Fritz Rasp) in a pan that first shows his shoes propped up against a table where his messages are messily scattered amidst pornographic photos, then progresses to show him smoking with a cigarette holder shaped as a nude woman's torso. The fragmented image of an "undesirable" is echoed in pans of the army bar and is in great contrast to the figure of Andreas, who is a spy on this scene for the Bolsheviks, introduced at the end of this first segment. As he leaves, he changes from his disguise to his Bolshevik uniform, establishing the opposition of decadent bourgeois/romantic revolutionary that will structure the narrative and lend a contextual ambivalence to the film's flashbacks.

The next scene introduces Alfred Ney, a foreign political observer who has been aiding the counterrevolutionaries, then pans to his young daughter, Jeanne Ney standing by a window. A close-up of Jeanne emphasizes her reflection in the window pane as she contemplates her father's announcement that he will return to Paris shortly. We see her trace the word "Paris" with her finger, then cut to the exterior to see Andreas looking up from the street at this window. These shots connect Jeanne and Andreas for the first time, but under quite uncertain terms. If he is there to visit her (something we cannot know at this point in the narrative) then the word "Paris" has literally come between them. When Alfred Ney continues to say "Six years in this country and not one pleasant memory," Jeanne's reaction is to cross out "Paris," negating her father's statement.

At this point, the window becomes a "screen" for a flashback projection of Jeanne's memories, starting with a tracking shot of the city that appears superimposed as if behind the window pane. This dissolves to a shot filled with the banners of a leftist demonstration, then Jeanne's chauffered car enters the image soon to be engulfed by marchers. As Jeanne looks off right, Andreas can be seen giving an impassioned speech. The image dissolves to one of Jeanne, dressed in an elegant suit, with Andreas, again in uniform on the steps of a public building. She runs out of the image to the left, after which he follows. This dissolves to a match-on-action of Andreas still pursuing Jeanne, this time across a field, until Jeanne stops and they embrace. Jeanne's flashback reverie ends with a dissolve to the doorbell that signals that arrival of Khalibiev, the informer, with his list of Bolsheviks to present to Alfred Ney.

The second flashback is a parallel memory insert belonging possibly to Andreas, possibly to Jeanne, or perhaps shared by the two. It occurs a short while later, after the Ney servant informs Andreas of the list Ney received, causing Andreas and another Bolshevik to confront Ney, demanding the return of this list. Alfred Ney tries to trick and overcome his opponents by shooting his gun from behind the paper in question. The shot wings Andreas's forehead, but the other Bolshevik shoots Ney. The camera follows Jeanne's movement as she rushes to her father who is dead. There is a jumpcut in on Jeanne, seen from the back, then a track-in on the reverse shot of Andreas. This close-up of Andreas dissolves to the second flashback, Jeanne and Andreas embracing by a tree. The image of content lovers embracing in nature suggests a continuity with Jeanne's earlier flashback. This second flashback ends by dissolving back to Jeanne, still looking at Andreas. When the flashback begins we assume it is Andreas's memory since a shot of him precedes it, but as it returns to a shot of Jeanne, there is considerable ambiguity surrounding the focalization of this memory image. The interpretation of both flashbacks is made even more difficult by the exchange which follows. Jeanne exclaims "You're a Bolshevik!"

Can it be that this is the first time Jeanne realizes this? The servant tells Andreas and his comrade to escape, fearing the police, a sentiment that Jeanne echoes. Andreas answers, "Jeanne, it's you who must escape—we're taking the town."

This sets up the lovers' separation, but after much narrative complication they reunite in Paris where Andreas is accused of murder and diamond robbery. The rest of the film is burdened with the task of dissolving the political oppositions to reestablish the romance. This *Kammerspiel* film mobilizes a romance in a historical-political situation returning the flashback to a use which is more directly part of the development of a narrative of history than the treatment of the psyche developed in other German films. Its flashbacks sustain considerable ambiguity but the film ends up concerned only with the romance without resolving the political issues it raises. It never takes up the challenge of its opening, the conflict between personal memory and political context.

Swedish Flashback Legends

Swedish films develop a flashback structure that in many ways corresponds to the use of flashbacks in Hollywood melodrama; however, the style of Swedish film narration, particularly in the works of two of Sweden's most powerful filmmakers, Victor Sjöström and Mauritz Stiller, alters significantly the functioning of these flashback sequences. Further, by 1919–1920 a more experimental use of the flashback begins to appear.

Sjöström's early films were primarily melodramatic narratives and comedies of manners, but both genres were tempered by a style that emphasized a specific mixture of folk legend (including a religious and moralizing vision) and character psychology. This emphasis is stylistically accomplished by a slow and studied pace; the camera holding on characters in contemplation, immersed in interior thought, supplemented at times by flashback visions that reveal their concerns with the past.

While Sjöström's *The Gardener* (1912) and *Ingeborg Holm* (1913) do not contain flashbacks, the narratives of both of these early films are involved with the effects of the past on the present and the recurrence of memories. *The Gardener* is a melodrama concerning a gardener's pretty daughter, Rose (Lilli Bech). Her life is a series of seductions and abandonments; at last, following her adoption by a wealthy General, she is disinherited by his real children after his death. Her life ends in hysteria and suicide in the greenhouse in which her father served as gardener, as she is haunted by the misfortunate events which have befallen her. One can easily imagine this memory-haunting being depicted by flashbacks, but instead the film simply shows the character thoughtful, while intertitles explain that she is trying to forget her past while remembering her youth. *Ingeborg Holm* depicts a mother who is forced after her husband's death to place her children in foster homes and enter a workhouse for debtors. The melodrama includes her escape to visit one daughter whom she finds out is sick, only to be recaptured before she reaches the child's bedside. Later, her youngest child no longer remembers her. These deprivations cause her to lose her mind, but the visit of her son as a grown man restores her reason and her memory. Although Ingeborg is often shown thinking about her children and finally recognizing her eldest son, at no point does the film return to the past to display her memories.

However, Sjöström's *Terje Vigen* (1916) uses two flashbacks at similar moments to provide us with the mental images of the sailor's memories. The film is adapted from Ibsen's poem set at the turn of the 19th century in Norway and is strikingly similar to Griffith's adaptations of Tennyson's poem *Enoch Arden*. In both cases, sailors and their families are separated with each sailor loosing his family. In *Terje Vigen* the family itself dies as a result of his absence. The first flashback occurs when Terje is in prison for transporting food during the war of 1809; he remembers two scenes of happy reunion with his wife and his newborn child after a long ocean voyage, then imagines a scene of his wife alone at the window in the present. Later, when as an old man he begins to rescue a crew from a shipwreck, a flashback depicts his realization that the captain of this merchant ship is the former enemy who arrested him and sank his boat, causing his life of misfortune. Similarly another Sjöström melodrama, *The Girl from the Stormy Cove* (1917), recalls Griffith's *True-Heart Susie,* for like the American film it concerns a pure-hearted girl who is willing to sacrifice her own interests unselfishly to patch up the relationship between the man she loves and another woman to whom he is engaged (in the Griffith film the man and the other woman are already married).[30] The flashback reveals a comic explanation for what until this point has been a serious incident in the plot; the hero believes he has killed a man while drunk because he finds his knife broken in the manner described in a newspaper account of the murder. The girl's flashback reveals that she earlier had broken the knife cutting wood, but had kept it a secret out of embarrassment. Sjöström's *The Outlaw* (1917) again uses a typical melodramatic flashback. A former thief Kari (Sjöström) confesses his past of crime, begun as an attempt to feed his starving family. These explanatory and illustrative flashbacks are quite parallel to the Hollywood films of the time, even as Sjöström's visual style differentiates itself with chairoscuro lighting and a greater attention to holding on shots and stretching moments of contemplation.

With *The Phantom Chariot* (1920), Sjöström's temporal structure becomes more complex and his visual style more flamboyant. The film tells the story of the reformation of a drunk, David Holm (Sjöström), on the New Year's Eve on which a Salvation Army worker who cared for him, Sister Edith (Hilda Borström), dies. The narrative in the present takes place in just a few hours, but four intervening flashbacks fill in Holm's prior history, mixing this retelling of the past with elements of legend and dreams. The interweave of past and fantasy is illustrated by the first flashback, a story told by David Holm in a graveyard to his drinking buddies as they celebrate the New Year. His tale is announced as a ghost story, but begins with the image from Holm's past, his friendship with George; it is George who tells the ghost story within the flashback, so that its telling is embedded within the frame of images of George and David Holm at a bar. The ghost story is the legend of the "phantom chariot" driven by the ghost of the last man to die before the New Year. The legend is illustrated by two deaths, after which the ghost driver gathers a "double" (a superimposed image) of the corpse into his chariot: the first is a suicide of a wealthy man, the second a drowning. (The visual rendering of the superimposed and slightly translucent chariot and ghost and the walking of the ghost through doors and beneath the sea is magnificent.) The richly imaged legend is made more concrete by its placement in a "real" past, for Holm's story ends with the comment that George died late on New Year's Eve last year, leading us to assume that the spinner of this tale became the phantom driver.

Ultimately, all the flashbacks are shown to be not supernatural events but fabrications of Holm's own imagination; though the viewer was led to believe he has died, we learn, retrospectively, he was merely knocked unconscious. The flashbacks occur inside a dream vision and their theme of guilt and moral responsibility is offered as the work of his own conscience (and unconscious). Memory of the past links the supernatural, the morality tale, and the dream state in a way that recalls Charles Dickens's *The Christmas Books* (1843–48), said to have been an influence on Selma Lagerlöf, the author of the novel on which the film is based.[31] Sjöström's film is itself, in turn, an influence in its use of a cinematic means of expression for this ambivalence between states of dreaming, premonition, remembering, and the supernatural, a combination of montage and superimposition, techniques that certainly go back to Georges Méliès and the beginning of cinema; here they are given a kind of psychological density that seems particularly characteristic of this period of Swedish cinema.[32]

The use of flashbacks in Mauritz Stiller's films, like Sjöström's, displays some similarities with Hollywood conventions, but again the element of legend prevails, as well as the mixture of dream, memory, and supernatural apparitions. *The Treasure of Arne* (1919) is a melodrama surrounding the theft of a legendary fortune, while *The Legend of Gunnar Hede* (1922) and *Gösta Berlings Saga* (1923–24) are by title, as well as in fact, stories whose proportions are legendary; they all borrow heavily from folktale structure. The flashbacks in *The Treasure of Arne* all involve the memory of the death of the heroine's half-sister at the hands of one of the thieves of the Arne treasure, the same man who, later, having assumed the name Sir Archie and respectability, courts Erselille, the surviving sister. The flashbacks are combined with superimposition ghost-apparitions of the dead sister, a technique that precedes the extended use of this ghostly visualization in *The Phantom Chariot*.

What is particularly interesting in *The Treasure of Arne* is how the narrational present is connected to one of these flashback instances; Sir Archie is fondling the hair of Erselille when the position of his hand evokes for her an association with the hand of the murderer. An intertitle gives us her thoughts, spoken aloud "That is how my foster sister's hair lay round the hand that killed her" and these thoughts are visually manifest by a return to the shot of the murder which graphically matches the shot in the present. In the tradition of the legend/folktale, it is the ghost of the sister appearing to Erselille in a dream that directs her to discover that her lover was in fact a murderer. In the dream, the ghost leads Erselille to the guildhall; when Erselille retraces this path the next morning she overhears Sir Archie confess his remorse and guilt to his accomplices at this site. The sister appears once more in flashback, begging for her life; here the supernatural apparition, the dream thought, and the memory flashback have become merged—the border between the psyche and the fantastic is thoroughly ambiguous and it is possible to interpret all the flashbacks and apparitions in the film either as products of Erselille's unconscious or as visions produced from a power beyond the grave.

In *The Legend of Gunnar Hede,* the hero of the title is told as a young boy the story of his grandfather's rise to fortune, presented as flashback illustration. The grandfather was a violinist, passionate only about music; he made the fortune that enabled him to pursue his art by driving a herd of reindeer down from the Lapp country to earn double their normal market price. The grandfather appears as a small superimposed dream figure, playing a violin, when Gunnar Hede is shown sleeping. Later, when the young man leaves home to become a violinist, a flashback to the story of the grandfather told to him as a boy inspires him to undertake a similar reindeer expedition. However, Gunnar's expedition is a loss, and he is driven out of his mind by the hardships he has endured.

The remainder of the film is a melodrama involving his mother and his girlfriend Ingrid's efforts to restore his memory; here flashbacks appear first to Ingrid and to Gunnar's mother, and later to Gunnar of events in their past that we have seen earlier in the film—their initial meeting, their reunion after Gunnar's loss of memory on the banks of a river. Finally, in a restorative memory flash, Gunnar recalls the events of his accident and is cured, or, as the intertitles remark, "The darkness left Gunnar Hede's mind." Alongside these flashbacks is a premonitory dream sequence—Ingrid imagines an old woman bringing Gunnar back on a sled to his family mansion; she warns the girl that she will not be welcome at the rich household. Ingrid remembers in flashback this dream just as she is about to enter the gates of the mansion when Gunnar returns, causing a delay in her efforts to help cure his memory.

In *Gösta Berlings Saga,* Gösta Berling (Lars Hanson), a former minister, is a horseman-retainer at the chateau Ekeby. An early flashback tells the history of his being defrocked, initially for drinking too much, but finally for berating his congregation for their hypocrisy. This flashback returns in another context later on, when Gösta becomes the object of a plot by a rich widow, Lady Dohna, to disinherit her daughter, Ebba, in favor of her son and his new bride, Elisabeth (Greta Garbo). The widow's plot consists of encouraging a romance between the pious Ebba and Gösta. The melodrama of inheritance at the Dohna chateau is interwoven with a similar intrigue at Ekeby itself, one that involves the past of the Lady Margaretha Cielsing who commands Ekeby; this past is also told in a flashback, one that shows Lady Margaretha as a young woman being denounced by her mother for an adulterous affair. Once again, elements of this flashback are repeated in a later flashback, when Lady Margaretha's past affair is exposed to her husband by one of Gösta's fellow workers at the chateau. The two parallel stories involve many variations on the theme of denunciation and ostracism; a cousin of Lady Dohna's, Marianne, for instance, is denounced by her father for kissing Gösta Berling. This echo of Lady Margaretha's life, serves to prepare another; when Elisabeth falls in love with Gösta, her desire is made clear to us with a flashback to her passionate pleading with Gösta to shake her hand despite her husband's disapproval. When Gösta rebuilds Ekeby after an apocalyptic fire, a series of plot machinations not only restores Lady Margaretha to her position, but leaves him free to marry Elisabeth who, as it turns out, was never officially married to the Dohna son; Lady Margaretha cedes the chateau to the young couple, allowing every "good" character to overcome the hindrances posed by the past.

The flashbacks in these Stiller films are part of the structure of the Scandinavian legends they adapt in which events from the past return in the present either as memories or apparitions or as reenactments in present circumstances of the same configurations. The past must either be listened to and heeded as in *The Treasure of Arne,* or resolved as in *The Legend of Gunnar Hede,* or overcome and transcended as in *Gösta Berlings Saga:* one way or another, it will extract its toll on the present. Interestingly, earlier in his career Stiller made a film, *The Best Film of Thomas Graal* (1917), whose use of flashbacks is part of a more reflexive and deconstructionist gesture. *The Best Film of Thomas Graal* depicts the power of film form to manipulate the past as the imaginary of narrative. Thomas Graal (Victor Sjöström) is a scriptwriter who falls in love with an aspiring actress. She has run away from her upper-class family to pursue a career dream. The scriptwriter first meets his beloved when he hires her as a temporary secretary to type his scripts; in her job interview, she hides her real identity from him, pretending to be from a poor family. There is a marvelous sequence in which her false narration is intercut with flashback illustrations of her bourgeous family life, in sharp contrast with the version she is recounting: images of the butler serving illustrate her claim of dire poverty, images of her playfully knocking her father down when they bowl in the family's private bowling alley illustrate her claims of a drunken father who beats her, and images of her being served breakfast in bed illustrate her claim that she was forced to work hard. Graal then writes a script based on her lies and eventually she is hired as an actress to play the part of the poor daughter in the film he directs from his script. We witness the filming of scenes that, in fact, parallel her narration from the earlier flashback; unknown to him, Graal is satirizing contemporary films' predilection for sentimentally rendered stories of deprivation or disturbance. It is characteristic of the Swedish approach to cinematic expression to use cinematic and narrative techniques creatively, both building legends and breaking them down.

Japanese Flashbacks

One of the most intriguing aspects of this period of experimentation with cinematic expression and its implications for the representation of subjective memory and temporality is that it is not limited to Western Europe, but has parallels in developments in Japan and the Soviet Union. Perhaps the most surprising of these experimental films is Teinosuke Kinugasa's *Page of Madness* (1926), which would seem to belong to the French impressionist group of filmmaking stylistically, and to the German expressionists thematically (with its narrative concerning an insane asylum). In fact, Kinugasa says he had not seen the French and German films at the time he made *Page of Madness;* when he later toured Europe, he brought not this film but *Crossroads* (1928), apparently because he was unaware that Europe would be a receptive audience for the earlier, more flamboyantly avant-garde film.[33]

The flashbacks in *Page of Madness* are highly ambiguous; in a sense, they fill in narrative information about the past of three female characters, two of whom are now in the insane asylum. One woman is a former dancer, the other is the wife of a man who has become a janitor in the asylum in order to stay with her. The third is the daughter of the janitor and his wife. The ambiguity resides in the focalization and reference of these flashbacks—interspersed as they are with fantasy sequences and rapid fragmentary cutting between different spaces, we are often in doubt about the temporality and "reality" of the representation. For example, the dancer is shown in the present wildly dancing in her cell; she is dressed in rags, but her shadow is of a woman dressed in a stage costume. Does this shadow represent her former life as a professional dancer, or her fantasy, or the fantasies of the other inmates who are seen watching her with much enthusiasm that it eventually leads to a riot of repressed sexual desire? Other flashbacks more clearly belong to the asylum janitor/ husband, but only retrospectively do we understand them definitively as flashbacks. In this series, the first flashback is to an incident in which the wife tries to drown her baby in a pond. Another flashback shows us the janitor's family at a fair, marked by a shot which indicates retrospective focalization: a shot of the janitor staring out the window. This flashback represents the janitor's associational memory; it begins with images of a fair taking place in the present, and then cuts to another fair, sometime in the past. The fair, a memory from a more tranquil past, lends its whirring lights and superimposed crowds to the present atmosphere of madness. The carnival becomes a metaphorical image, but more obliquely than in *The Cabinet of Dr. Caligari*. In *Page of Madness* the carnival becomes a recurring visual motif of the distorted, prismatic, and superimposed reality of insanity.

There are two flashbacks of the janitor bringing his wife to the asylum when she was a young woman. The first is quite fragmentary and is introduced by an object association in the present which metaphorizes both the notion of a "break" and of "fragmentation," the breaking of a bowl by the janitor. The second occurs towards the end of the film, after the janitor tries to free his wife from the institution. She resists, and the janitor has his own breakdown after attracting a leering crowd of patients and being stopped by the doctor. This second flashback version of the wife's entry into the asylum gives more details, showing the wife's hysteria and the husband beating her to force her into a submissive entry into the institution. The two moments of resistance and violence, the entry into the hospital and the attempted escape are thus associated and compared. In this very fragmented manner, some aspects of the history of the wife's mental illness are presented. Rather than merely serving as explanation, these flashes increase the atmosphere of shared mental disorder.

Is Kinugasa's innovative use of flashbacks, coupled with the rapid paced montage of disparate points of view and imaginary sequences, an isolated instance in Japanese cinema? This question is extremely difficult to answer, since relatively few Japanese films from the twenties are extant. One source claims that "there is no precedent, at least extant, in the Japanese cinema itself," for the experimental montage in *Page of Madness,* and then goes on to add that "the film remained only an experiment, and the formal means of expression which it explored spawned no larger movement, and never altogether intruded on the other arts."[34] However, Joseph Anderson and Donald Richie contend that the film enjoyed considerable success, and further argue that impressionist film technique was widespread in this period of Japanese filmmaking.[35] At least three of Kenji Mizoguchi's thirties films, *The Water Magician* (1933), *The Downfall of Osen* (1935), and *Poppies* (1935) use flashbacks and impressionist style.

It is *The Downfall of Osen* with its narrative of a man's remembered debt to the woman who sacrificed for him in the past and its opening of impressionistically interwoven flashbacks that most complexly develops a subjective treatment of memory. So-kichi, the man who has become a doctor, and O-Sen, the prostitute who sent him through medical school arrive on the same train platform after many years of living in ignorance of each other's whereabouts. The train is delayed, and each is seen, separately deep in thought. Flashbacks are intercut with shots of the two characters in the present, still oblivious to the proximity of the other. Coming as a fragmented series of interwoven shots, the flashbacks recall their first meeting near a tree, decorated as a shinto shrine, with cord and paper cranes. The past festival atmosphere is echoed in returns to the two in the present on the train platform filled with festival celebrants wearing masks. The mist, the blowing leaves, and the moon that characterize the scene in the past combine with swish pans to create an impressionistic atmosphere. The action that ensues in this setting seems to have a double focalization; first we get So-kichi's memories of being near the tree, then O-Sen's memory of being chased by her retainer's guards to this site. Her first, lyrically rendered meeting with the young So-kichi is the point at which the two memories join each other and the narration of the past continues as a joint remembrance.

We see in these Japanese films a treatment of memory highly similar to some of the French and German films discussed earlier. Memory is the poetic province of subjective consciousness. It is ironic, haunting, almost another world into which characters are drawn and thus serves as a terrain in which filmic expression can take its most impressionist and experimental direction. That the carnival and festival are metonymically linked to memory in some of these films is a striking means of suggesting memory's supernatural quality and its power to overwhelm (like a festival's celebrating crowd) through its condensation of events and their efforts on the psyche. It is in this world that a sort of explanation for the current malaise, pain, or melancholy can be found. Personal history contains the causes of depression and derangement. Yet unlike the German psychoanalytic tendencies, the explanations offered in the French and Japanese films are not cures or even direct decipherings; at most they provide a vision into the mind, its associations pursued as poetic figuration.

4

The Subjectivity of History in Hollywood Sound Films

The Hollywood film finds it almost impossible to tell the story of an historical occurrence or to describe a period of history without focusing on how a small group of individuals is affected by that time in history. Filmmakers seeking an alternative to this Hollywood mode of narration—most notably, Sergei Eisenstein—have sought to avoid this personalization of history, this incessant focus on the plight and the heroics of individuals.[1] In his early films, for example, Eisenstein made attempts to displace the individual hero by substituting a "mass hero" (though, in fact, many scenes in these films—*Strike* (1925), *Potemkin* (1925), *October* (1928), etc.—are constructed to follow the movements of individuals temporarily highlighted by the narrative). American films however, continue to avoid such dispersion in their narration of historical events. The ideological ramifications of this are pronounced. The individual is created as a far more autonomous and sacred self by such narrative focus than any of us are in modern industrial society.[2]

When history is rendered as the subjective experience of fictive individuals, it is often meant to be representative of a universal response, or, at least, a response representative of a gender, nationality, or class. Generalization and stereotyping, when coupled with narrative and cinematic techniques that encourage audience identification, urge us to assume that the subjective reaction of a fictional individual somehow constitutes a collective subjectivity, a shared experience. From D. W. Griffith's *Orphans of the Storm* to Warren Beatty's *Reds* (1981), Hollywood narrates even such collective historical events as revolutions through the eyes of individuals—in sharp contrast to Eisenstein's *Potemkin*.

One can fault the individualist bias of Hollywood narrative for lacking any systematic analysis of class and gender and for reframing history to support its own ideologies; still, we can see in this mode of discourse an attempt to speak to the issues of social history. Subjectivizing history through narratives which concentrate on individuals can also be a means of posing the philosophical issues surrounding the interpretation of history as a subjective experience of the individual or social group.

The flashback narrative that presents a subjective view of history parallels the development by some historians of theoretical methodologies that tend to regard history subjectively. "History as the re-enactment of past experience" is the phrase R. G. Collingwood chooses to describe a subjective methodology for historians.[3] He defines historical knowledge as "that special case of memory where the object of present thought is past thought, the gap between present and past being bridged not only by the power of the present thought to think of the past, but also the power of past thought to reawaken itself in the present" (p. 294).

Collingwood's metaphor, in which past thought reawakens itself in the present, needs to be analyzed closely. There is an element of personification in it, for ultimately only an animate being can reawaken itself. A thought or a system of thought cannot reawaken itself, except figuratively—by which we might mean something parallel to what we mean when we say a thought "comes back to mind." What we actually mean here is that we remember a thought we once had, and, in so doing, rethink it. The kind of past thought Collingwood is addressing, historical circumstance, cannot simply come back to mind; it would seem to have to be the object of present thought, or, as he says in his first instance, "the power of present thought to think about the past." If Collingwood adds to this process a power he can only express metaphorically, he seems to be implying through his rhetoric that past thought is concrete, if not truly an animate being; past thought has an appearance, and that appearance can reappear.

Collingwood's language suggests an analogy to the flashback and to memory. Doesn't a flashback in film often take the form of an image of the past that is reanimated in the present? Further, doesn't this type of flashback both model itself upon and conversely also become the model for a certain concept of the memory image—as we discussed in regard to the theories of Münsterberg in chapter two? This concept of the memory image assumes memory to be an image from the past that reappears. While Collingwood tries to distinguish "subjectivity" from a sensorial response to immediate experience by reserving the term "subjectivity" for a self-conscious thought process, his metaphorical description of this thought process seems to evoke a phenomenological view of memory—one that sees memory as sensory perception. If an analogy between historical thought reawakening itself, the filmic flashback, and the memory image occurs, it may be rooted in Collingwood's use of memory as a conceptual model for history. His historian does not so much seek to understand or analyze the past as to remember and reexperience it.

It follows from this that autobiography is Collingwood's model for the subjective historical process; he suggests that historical writing can use autobiography as an example through what amounts to a process of projection of the writing-self into the imaginary selves of the historical personages. For Collingwood, the historian's access to the past is a creative act that treats accounts and records in a manner similar to the way the autobiographer treats his or her memory of past experience. The historian tries to imagine the past as the lived experience of individuals or groups, and treats documents and artifacts as fragments of a hypothetical memory to be reconstructed. There is an implicit analogy between the project of writing history and a phenomenological view of the functioning of personal memory.

The dangers of this subjective leap of imagination on the part of the historian have been noted by historians critical of Collingwood's theories—though his influence on the teaching and writing of history has been enormous.[4] Detractors of Collingwood oppose his method with various other methods that take history to be governed by general laws,[5] and along with Eisenstein, many more recent filmmakers have sought other models for the construction of historical narratives.[6]

The flashback narratives that create history as a subjective experience exploit the emotional affectivity of identification with characters. They are often highly melodramatic. These films are even more suspect as historical accounts than would be a text written by an historian using Collingwood's method—since the processes of identification evoked by the Hollywood film, the power of film to disguise its representation as "reality," can mask the discursive argument the film is presenting.[7] Attitudes or images from the past do not simply reawaken by themselves in the present, they are framed by mythologies operative in the present; the Hollywood flashback film is never simply a means of reawakening the images of a past life in the present, though it may present itself as one, and may be so received.

Much of the focus of this chapter will be on the process of ideological reframing of history operative in these films, analyzed not in terms of a unitary project, but, rather, as one characterized by shifts internal to each film and multiplicities created by the disjunct elements of filmic form. Many of the films themselves comment on the process of framing or creating history out of the traces one can gather from the past, while others, though apparently less reflexive, still contain elements that point to a more deconstructive reading of the subjective view of history they present.

As we saw in chapter two in the discussion of *Birth of a Nation* and *The Last Command,* for example, the subjective framing of history through the flashback predates the period that will be the focus of this chapter; but this period of American sound film—from the Depression to the Cold War—does present a particularly significant reinscription of a process of historical recounting, one in which the role of sound is decisive. It is from the juncture of voice and image that these films seek to mold their subjective views of history.

It is for this reason that the first question this chapter will examine is how the transition to sound affected the flashback narrative, through an analysis of thirties remakes of flashback films. We will then look at how the subjectivizing of history emerges as a major function of the sound flashback. This will lead us to a discussion of three types of historically focused flashbacks: the biographical flashback, the flashback that binds two different historical periods together, and the Hollywood retrospective flashback. In each case, the flashbacks facilitate the framing of historical occurrences as they affect individuals. Finally, the chapter will address the question of comedy in certain of these flashback films to show how a satirical voice can undermine some of the investment in subjectivity established through the flashback device.

The Introduction of Sound and the Flashback Remake

As we have seen, the flashback was widely used in the silent period. It should also be noted that by the late twenties, the basic structures that would serve the sound film were established; Hollywood films prior to the introduction of sound anticipated the addition of auditory dialogue by developing such editing patterns as shot-reverse shot, in which characters' dialogue could be highlighted. Yet if there was much stylistic continuity between the late silent and early sound period, there were also many changes that came with the introduction of sound—one of the less direct being the relative disappearance of flashback structure in early sound films. The thirties in America produced relatively few flashback films.

The overwhelming majority of films immediately following the introduction of sound tell their stories with complete temporal linearity, advancing from event to event in chronological order. Neither the machinations of the psyche nor another logic of causality are allowed to interfere with or rearrange the present tense of film narration with its cause-and-effect structure of events. This linearity may have been partially conditioned by certain early assumptions about the use of sound, assumptions that are themselves connected to the synchronous sound recording of the first "talkies." Voice-over commentary, one of the major additions sound contributes to the flashback film, was not widely used in fiction films until the forties.[8]

However, the fact that there were some flashback films made in the thirties rules out too strong a reliance on any such technical explanation. Instead, we need to consider an explanation for the rarity of the flashback in the thirties that views this emphasis on the present tense of filmic narration as historically and sociologically significant. Mervyn Le Roy's *Gold Diggers of 1933* (1933) does ask us through song to "Remember my forgotten man," and illustrates the "flashback" indicated in the lyrics by an elaborately staged song and dance number; it includes World War I soldiers marching to the lyric, "You put a rifle in his hand, you shouted hip-hooray, but where are you today?" Such references to the past, either as ironic contrast or as causally determinant, are uncommon in thirties films, and are almost never told in flashback. This can be seen as an avoidance by Hollywood of any analysis of the economic and political causes of the Depression, a virtual taboo in thirties films; instead, the crisis in capitalism is naturalized as a "disaster" without clear historical explanation, or, more often, never even mentioned, avoided in favor of entertainments or concentration on current social problems such as gangsterism.[9] The forties will break with this linear tradition of narration, not only returning the flashback to prominence, but using it to make historical connections, as we shall see.

Still, some early sound films that are remakes of earlier flashback films do retain the flashback form in a decade not otherwise noted for filmic attention to the remembrance of the past. For example, the Elmer Rice play of 1914, *On Trial,* discussed in chapter two as an example of a theatrical staging of flashback narration, was twice adapted to sound film. In both adaptations, the flashbacks used to depict events reported in testimony borrowed heavily from the filmic form of silent period trial testimony flashbacks, but with a noteworthy innovation. As directed by Archie Mayo in 1928, the film took advantage of the introduction of sound to substitute voiced dialogue for intertitles, particularly effective as the voice in the present could bleed-over the dissolves to the past. When this film was remade at Warners in 1939, it was as a low-budget B film directed by Terry Morse; it was typical of low-budget production to ransack scripts of the films the studio had made previously. This remake policy partially explains the perpetuation of the flashback structure in certain thirties films. Another factor is that the sources of the trial scenarios made into films during this period were stage plays. Theatrical scripts were a privileged source for early sound film, as they provided already formulated dialogue.

An example that illustrates some of the innovations possible in sound adaptations of witness flashbacks is *The Silent Witness,* a 1932 film directed by Marcel Varnel and R. L. Hough for Fox (as the title suggests, the witness's testimony is withheld throughout much of the film). The suspense is built on a witness who will not speak, delaying the flashbacks that explain the solution to the murder mystery. The flashback as visual testimony that so characterized the silent film is repositioned in this film as a central demand for verbal testimony. The "silent" witness, who by finally talking can call the flashback images into being, serves as an ironic sign marking the transition of the testimony flashback to sound film.

Smilin' Through's life as a flashback remake illustrates how the transformation of a play to a silent film to two sound versions can result in a series of works all of which exploit the specificities of their form, while retaining a sentimental approach to the supernatural visitation of memories. The play was written by Jane Cowl and Janet Murfin in 1919 (though published under the pseudonym Allen Langdon Martin in 1924). Jane Cowl originally played the dual roles of Moonyeen Clare and her niece, Kathleen, in the three-act play whose entire second act is a flashback to 1864, from the play's opening act, set on the eve of World War I. The second act is the narration by Kathleen's uncle of the reason he forbids her to marry her suitor; it flashes back to the day of his wedding to Kathleen's aunt. Kathleen's suitor's uncle tried to kill Kathleen's uncle out of jealousy, but instead killed his beloved bride as she tried to shield him.

The first film version was directed by Sydney A. Franklin in 1922, with Norma Talmadge in the dual Moonyeen/Kathleen role. The flashback structure is retained, with the second act and its punctuating curtains rendered through the fluidity of dissolves. The film makes use of superimposition to represent the visits of Moonyeen's spirit and was heralded at the time for the pictorial splendors of its ephemeral cinematography.[10]

A sound version appeared in 1932, again directed by Franklin, this time for MGM, with a star-filled cast including Norma Shearer as Moonyeen/Kathleen, Fredric March as the suitor, and Leslie Howard as the uncle. Mordant Hall in the *New York*

Times praised the film as "infinitely more satisfactory than its voiceless predecessor," a quote that indicates to us what the investment in such remakes could be.[11] The film does make clever use of sound in both the flashback narration and the spirit visitations; Moonyeen's voice in her phantom visits remains inaudible to the uncle as long as he is still consumed by hatred, though the audience is allowed to hear her—a fact which, in effect, makes her voice a divine commentary on the action.

A third remake in 1941, directed by Frank Borzaje, has MGM adding color and songs to this mixture of spiritualist fantasy and flashbacks, this time starring Jeanette MacDonald, Gene Raymond, and Brian Aherne. The return of the flashback narrative of *Smilin' Through* may have much to do with the possibilities of its dual roles as star vehicles. However, we can also see its four versions as signifying a fascination for its presentation of the obsessive hold of memory across two generations as presented in flashback. Memory here is limited to the entirely personalized, emotional realms of hatred and true love. The repetition inscribed in two generations that echo each other has a psychoanalytic dimension that one can read beneath the surface of its symbolic mode of spirit visitations.

Flashback and fantasy modes are similarly mixed in another flashback remake of the thirties, *Peter Ibbetson*. Again there was a successful play (by John N. Raphael [1915], produced by the Schuberts and starring John Barrymore and Lionel Barrymore), which was adapted in turn from the George du Maurier novel. Peter Ibbetson is obsessed with a girl from his youth, Mimsey, and in Act II, upon returning to the town in France where they grew up, Peter enters into a dream of the past, introduced by the line, "Old memories—old memories—crowding on us." The entrance into the past dream world is quite literally represented with an adult Peter sharing the stage and walking unseen amidst the figures of himself and Mimsey as children. Later in the play, Peter kills his uncle, revealed to be his natural father, and he and the now-rediscovered Mimsey communicate telepathically, to join each other in death as angelic specters at the play's end.

The 1921 film, retitled *Forever,* directed by George FitzMaurice for Paramount, starred Wallace Reid and Elsie Ferguson and followed the play's structure. The 1935 *Peter Ibbetson,* remade at Paramount by Henry Hathaway, starring Gary Cooper and Ann Harding, rearranges the narrative, displacing the flashback and changing the murder object from an unwitting patricide to a simple act of self-defense against a jealous rival. The material presented by the play and the 1921 film's flashback, the childhood romance, is presented at the beginning as "a first chapter" in what an intertitle calls "a foreshadowed life." The flashback in the 1935 film is to the murder trial and it occurs as Peter Ibbetson's memory once he is already condemned to prison. The eyeline matches within the trial flashback that show the couple trying to communicate silently during the proceedings set up a series of later telepathic cross-cuts between the couple, for whom prison walls and even death are surmountable by imaginary meetings that culminate in ascension to the spirit world.

Like *Smilin' Through*, *Peter Ibbetson* takes as its theme the uncanny realm of the imaginary, as true love determines a narrative reunion of spectral lovers. Flashbacks act as auxiliary narrative devices, supplementing dream sequences and telepathic occurrences. Memory is annexed by the supernatural. In understanding the conjunction of the flashback with the uncanny, it is useful to turn to Freud's essay on "The 'Uncanny'," where he argues that uncanny occurrences are repressed elements that recur in another form; we therefore have inscribed in the notion of the uncanny, the return of the repressed, the past, the material of the psychological flashback.[12] Films often use supernatural means to express psychological phenomenon; but in periods like the late forties, when psychological melodrama is ascendant, the representation is likely to be more directly psychological, whereas here it remains fantastic. As is typical of the uncanny, the distinction between imagination and reality is effaced.

Back Street (John Stahl) is another film whose 1932 version has a flashback, retaining the same structure as the silent film in 1926, where the flashback is a montage sequence recapitulating the heroine's life after her married lover's death and immediately preceding her own.[13] This remake explanation for a number of the flashbacks one finds in thirties films can be read as a sign of the mentality of the early sound period. On the one hand, the flashback is virtually eliminated from most films, perhaps because the immediacy of sound in continuity dominates plot organization. However on the other hand, the desire to remake past successes with the addition of sound leads to the retention of the flashback, although this narrative technique had apparently gone (temporarily) out of favor. Finally, the instances in which the flashback is retained do not make historical connections between two periods as much as personal ones, steeped in romance and even the supernatural.

A circumstance similar to the remake helps explain the appearance of *Two Seconds* (Mervyn Le Roy, 1932); this film has a structure identical to Paul Fejos's *The Last Moment* (1928), discussed earlier, in which the entire body of the film is a flashback representing a dying man's last thoughts. The impending death is not a drowning in the 1932 film, but a condemned man's memories before execution in the electric chair, its story was adapted from a play by Eliot Lester.[14] The last thoughts of the murderer (Edward G. Robinson) in the two seconds after the current enters his body before brain-death are what the film is supposed to represent in its flashback sequences. The protagonist's memories of the emotional and psychic damage done to him as a result of his wife's infidelity also reworks E. A. Dupont's *Variety;* there are moments in the depiction of the husband's rage that recall that earlier film's expressionism. However, *Two Seconds*'s flashbacks portray the circumstances leading up to a man's crime of passion linearly, employing little of the montage compression or rearrangement of temporality that one might expect from such a temporally self-contained memory flash. There is no trace here of impressionist visual rendering of interior thought.

Given these conditions, in which remakes and adaptations of theatrical successes seem to determine the presence of flashbacks in Hollywood films in the early thirties, it is interesting to consider the kind of shift that begins several years later. By the mid-thirties, writers and directors turn to the flashback precisely as a commentary on American politics in its interaction with personal life. A transitional flashback film in this regard is *The Scoundrel,* written and directed in 1935 by Ben Hecht and Charles MacArthur as an independent production distributed by Paramount. The anti-hero, Mallare, played by Noel Coward, is an evil playboy publisher who dies in ther middle of the film, and comes back as a ghost under the orders of a divine off-screen voice to find, in a one-month reprieve from death, one person who will mourn for him. The flashback here is secondary compared to the supernatural device of a return-after-death (the flashback is used to narrate Mallare's plane crash), but the sense of retrospection on a life lived without ethics in a corrupt society is developed by the combination of the two devices. It signals a shift by some of the most sophisticated screenwriters of the period to a use of the flashback as part of an historical and ideological critique.

Voice-Over Narration and the Biographical Sound Flashback

Biography is usually distinguished from fiction in that biography narrates the history of a real personage, while fiction tells the story of imaginary lives. The biographical flashback blurs this distinction, as it concerns the telling of a life of a personage who may be entirely fictional, but unlike other fictional narration, the act of biography, of telling the history of a life, is highlighted within the frame of these films. Often the fictional protagonist is presented as a famous figure whose life story is the subject of an internal inquiry, by a journalist or biographer whose investigation spurs the flashbacks.

In this regard, *The Power and the Glory* (1933) stands out as an original and complex use of the flashback structure, prefiguring in the early thirties a type of narration that will flourish in the forties as the biographical flashback. The screenplay by Preston Sturges introduces a technique publicized at the time as "narratage" (a portemanteau word combining "narration" and "montage") which synchronized the voice-over narration of dialogue with the images of the speakers silently performing the speech acts.[15] Narratage is used selectively during the flashbacks, serving to remind the viewer of the presence of the narrator, as do the frequent returns to the present scene of narration.

The film begins with the funeral of the subject of the biography, Thomas Gardner (Spencer Tracy). The exposition which leads up to the flashback is economical and rich, laying clues for elements which will gain expansion in the flashbacks. As the funeral sermon tells us that Gardner was the President of the Chicago Southwestern Railroad, we see a man who will later narrate the film's flashback, Henry (Ralph Morgan), walking out to cross the railroad yards to Gardner's office. On his way, Henry overhears a guard on the railroad yard say, "I'm glad he croaked," introducing a counterpoint from another class perspective to Henry's sadness and the solemnity of the funeral. In Gardner's office the camera surveys the man's own few monuments to his past, a photo of himself with his son and then a bust of himself in the corner. Having set up these contradictory responses to Gardner's death—the eulogy, irreverent antagonism, and the subject's own self-image—the scene shifts to the conversation between Henry and his wife that will be the source of the flashback narration.

The narrated story is Henry's response to three critical comments made by Henry's wife: the first insists that Gardner should have been happy since he had everything he wanted; the second, that Gardner killed four hundred men during a strike at his plant; and the third, that Gardner mistreated his wife. Henry insists that his wife delay judgment, offering his narration as proof that one can't judge Tom Gardner by ordinary standards—"He was too big."

The flashback narration of Gardner's life alternates segments from two different periods, each of which progresses in sequential order, with ellipses between the episodes. One series narrates his life from boyhood through his twenties, while the second series begins with Tom Gardner well into middle age and continues to his death. We can chart the alternation of the two series:

Younger Series	*Older Series*
1) Henry's and Tom's boyhood fight.	2) meeting of Chicago RR, secret the Santa Clara RR by Gardner.
3) Tom gets a school teacher to tutor him on reading, proposes marriage to her (Sally, his first wife)	4) Tom's son is kicked out of Yale, Tom begins his romance with Eve Bordman.
5) Sally and Tom as young couple, she is ambitious, but supports his advance, taking over his lineman duties so that he can study.	6) Tom ends his love affair with Eve, but confesses his infidelity to Sally.

PRESENT

7) Sally and Tom both tell each other happy news; he got a new job, she is pregnant.	8) Son at Tom's second wedding to Eve; strike at RR, offices burn during strike.

PRESENT

9) Tom forgets Eve's wedding anniversary, learns their child is not his, attends board meeting, kills himself.

The tired melodramatic incidents that comprise *The Power and the Glory* are revivified by being placed in a structure of contrast and ironies. We see Tom as a young man, poor, struggling for an education, then immediately afterwards see the contrast of his son forfeiting his own education, being kicked out of Yale. A segment portraying the happiest point of Sally and Tom's marriage is preceded by the segment showing the dissolution of this marriage and followed by a segment showing his second marriage to Eve, creating a bitter frame for any moment of happiness. Since we've already seen Tom's disappointment with his adult son, his jubilation over the boy's birth seen late in the film's unfolding is taken ironically. Each incident is received differently than it might have been had the story been told in sequential order from Tom's childhood to his death. The audience actively works to comprehend the interwoven narrative series, while the commentary intervenes to foreshadow, underscore, and color the narrated events.

The role of Henry's wife is to keep posing the hermeneutic question. Her three initial comments alert us to a stance critical of Henry's narration by raising issues of labor politics, sexism, and class privilege. She resuscitates this questioning towards the end, when she asks "Then why did he kill himself?" after Henry asserts Tom's happiness in his second marriage. It is her questioning that calls forth each narrative illustration of the weaknesses in Tom's character, culminating in the final segment in which Tom realizes his guilt only when his second wife mistreats him in the same way he mistreated his first wife. The flashback structure, with its repetition of elements within a restructuring of alternating temporalities, develops a portrait of a man, that while framed within the diegesis as his defense, is ironically turned into his condemnation.

The biographical flashback film reaches its height in the forties with a series of masterful films, all of which owe much not only to *The Power and the Glory,* but also to the trial testimony flashback films of the twenties discussed earlier. Unlike much of the biographical non-fiction or fictionalized biography produced in writing and in film, the biographical flashback tends to shun laudatory renditions of famous lives and instead presents extremely critical views, not only of the personal lives of heroes and heroines, but a social critique of the "American dream," of a rise to wealth and power. The retrospective frame of the flashback biography seems to suggest a more critical stance than biographies told in a linear order, typical of the rise-to-fame narrative.[16]

Of all the biographical flashback films of this period, the most famous, controversial, and complexly structured is *Citizen Kane* (1941), directed by Orson Welles from a script by Herman Mankiewicz and Welles. Much has been written about *Citizen Kane,* including some close analysis of the structure and function of its flashbacks. In fact, *Citizen Kane* is credited too often with creating the complexly structured flashback film; as we have seen, the trial testimony films of the late silent period commonly uses the multiple flashback structure and *The Power and the Glory* shuffles narrative temporalities into at least as bold a pattern as the essentially progressive, yet somewhat temporally overlapping flashbacks found in *Citizen Kane.*

However, *Citizen Kane*'s expressive cinematography and acting lend a particularly rich virtuousity to this structure, which may have helped stimulate the proliferation of flashback films throughout the forties. The revelation of the past of a famous, powerful individual is here accomplished through the device of the newsreel reporter, Thompson, whose search for an angle on his story introduces suspense and an ideological frame for the narration. Like the courtroom drama, Thompson's investigation is a quest for testimony, for narration, that provides the film with structural detours and delays—such as narration blocked by the initial refusal of Susan Alexander to speak, or delayed by such circumstances as Leland's cantankerous personality and Raymond's mercenary demand for a bribe.

The reminiscences of these narrators are drawn in contrast to the initial presentation of Kane's life in the newsreel, screened immediately following Kane's death at the film's opening. The newsreel provides a schematic overview of all the narrations to follow, what David Bordwell has termed a "narrative map" of the film.[17] It also provides a version of Kane's life in the style of popular "yellow" journalism, a style that his own newspaper promulgated. The style and structure of the newsreel segment is a clever pastiche that satirizes actual newsreels, while providing an index of reality within the fiction which presents Kane as a "real" historical figure.

The newsreel is a form of flashback. Since Kane is a constructed character within the fiction, presenting us with a pseudo-documentary report on his life is simply a means of depicting events occurring before Kane's death, before the present moment of the narration. But as a film screened within the film, the newsreel has a different heuristic status than the other flashback narrations. It is a document displaying a certain style of ideological argumentation. It mimics the style of the *March of Time* newsreels produced by *Time Magazine,* interspersing political events and sensationalist scandals such as Kane's divorce and his attempts to legitimize his mistress as an opera singer. Everything is presented as human interest and entertainment so that the net result of the alternating structure is to juxtapose critiques from the right and left continually, neutralizing both, to trivialize the political events of Kane's life, and to render the personal much more spectacular than the major events of the day.

Thus the statement, "Kane urged his country's entrance into one war . . . opposed participation in another," accompanied in the first instance by soldiers on horseback leading a charge, and in the second by a military graveyard, obscures rather than illuminates the issue of Kane's position on U.S. involvement in the Spanish-American and First World Wars. Like actual newsreels of the thirties and forties, the voice-over creates an ideologically overdetermined portrait of a member of the American ruling class, in this case deflecting political analysis by means of sensational scandal and personal pathos and mystery. In the screening room discussion that follows, the newsreel is ironically criticized for lacking an angle, a catchy human interest hook, when, in fact, it is a compendium of such devices of popular journalism.

Thompson, who originally composed the newsreel, must please his own editor-boss by even further sacrificing documentary integrity to popular entertainment. Thompson thus bears the same lackey relationship to his boss that Kane demands of his journalists within the flashback narrative. The use of the Thompson device, coupled with the flashbacks, allows for questions about the institution of American journalism to be posed on multiple levels of the fiction, connected to other questions the film raises about the use and abuse of power within the reform movement, business associations, and interpersonal relations.

To a limited extent, the five narrators (Thatcher, Bernstein, Leland, Susan Alexander, and Raymond) define the flashbacks they narrate. The narrators each tell of Kane's life, the time during which they were most involved with Kane, or, in Bernstein's case, the period for which he most wishes to remember Kane. But the narrative within the flashbacks cheats; these segments are not the cinematic actualization of what we might surmise the narrator might have witnessed, nor are scenes depicted in a manner that would correspond to how the narrator most likely would have represented him or herself and Kane. And though the five are portrayed as distinctly different personalities with quite various attitudes towards Kane, there is an overall continuity of style from flashback to flashback. The first-person voice that opens each flashback narration gives way before an authorial voice determining the representation of all characters and events and minimizing the subjectivity of each flashback segment.[18] This is particularly evident in the case of Susan Alexander, as the shrill shrew we see raging over her opera reviews or nagging at Xanadu is hardly an image a woman would present of her former self. The misogynist caricature is the product of a larger authorial purpose.

Even so, elaborate frames are provided for each of the flashbacks, establishing the character of each narrator. The character traits assigned to the narrator condition the interpretation of their flashbacks. Thatcher's austerity and rigid conservatism are represented by the elaborate development of the expressionistic decor and repressive rules of the Thatcher library. This oppressive power, this space without human warmth, contrasts sharply with the exuberant young Kane whose childhood amusements in the snow are transformed into a real power game in the takeover of the *Inquirer* (in the flashback segment Thatcher's writing narrates). So while verisimilitude is ignored by the images that "illustrate" Thatcher's memoirs, a contrast is implicitly developed between the coldness of Thatcher's economically determined perspective on the world and Kane's own youthful sensitivity and longing for familial warmth.

The second narrator, Bernstein, is introduced under the sign of nostalgia. A portrait of Kane hangs over his large desk, dominating his impressively appointed New York office. Before Bernstein embarks on his flashback narration he offers a story that represents his attempt to answer Thompson's question concerning the meaning of "Rosebud," which we might at first take to be a bit of a digression; however, not only does this story set up the actual meaning the film will finally propose for "Rosebud," it serves here to develop Bernstein's character traits, lending them to the flashback which follows. Bernstein tells of remembering having once caught a glimpse of a young girl who was disembarking from the Staten Island Ferry as he was getting on it. This girl has become for him an obscure object of desire that haunts his thoughts even as an elderly man. The story presents us with information regarding Bernstein's own class background, while his ethnicity is expressed through his Yiddish phrasing. These traits present us with a motivation for Bernstein's narration selecting only the ascendant stages of Kane's career and personal life: his build-up of the *Inquirer*'s circulation and influence; his acceptance, through marriage, into a family of established wealth and power.

Jedediah Leland's cynicism and humorous satirical air color his narration of the period of his own disaffection with Kane; the film's style seems to correlate well with Leland's tone. The montage of Emily and Kane's increasingly cold and antagonistic breakfasts over a nine-year span and the depiction of Kane's outlandish efforts to promote Susan as an opera star seem to be analogous to the way Leland might verbally present such material as illustrations of his view of Kane becoming less humane as he became dominated by his drive for power.

The core of Leland's flashback concerns Leland's own confrontation with Kane over the failure of Kane's brand of reformist politics. This elaborates on information presented by Bernstein that Leland had begun to question Kane's jingoism aimed at securing U.S. involvement in a war against Spain over control of Latin America. In an earlier version of the script, this was presented in the scene in Bernstein's flashback of the party celebrating the acquisition of the *Chronicle* reporters, with Leland explicitly refusing Kane's offer to go to Cuba since he does not agree with Kane's premises concerning the war.[19] This dialogue was cut in the final version of the film, and Leland's opposition is only indicated obliquely, as when Bernstein defends Kane's position in the return to the present following his narration by saying, "But do you think if it hadn't been for that war of Mr. Kane's, we'd have the Panama Canal?"

Leland's disenchantment with Kane is most directly stated in his flashback, when, following his election defeat to Gettys, a drunken Leland confronts a demoralized Kane in Kane's empty, littered campaign headquarters. Leland accuses Kane of manipulating the working class rather than supporting trade unionism. He later returns Kane's severence check of $25,000 with the copy of the statement of principles Kane once flamboyantly printed on the front page of the *Inquirer,* as an expression of his disdain for Kane's lack of ethics. Thus Leland is the most critical voice in the film, focusing on the political analysis of Kane as a figure in history in a way that the documentary newsreel cannot.

Susan's flashback fulfills, on an entirely personal plane, the critical stance opened up by Leland. Despite the misogynist treatment of Susan within the flashback, the account of the forced opera career and the isolated kingdom of Xanadu, along with Susan's own parting words with Kane, reinforce Leland's conclusions that Kane's ego makes him tremendously needy of adulation, but unable to act outside of his self-interest.

Leland's and Susan's flashbacks overlap in a manner unique in the film. Whereas Thatcher's flashback overlaps temporally with Bernstein's and Leland's, it covers different incidents. Only Leland and Susan narrate the same incident, the opening night of *Salammbô.* The film marks this repetition by exactly duplicating the opening shots of the sequence, the long shot of the stage and the tilt up to the blinking floodlight, but Susan's version then deviates from the continuous upward pan to the stage rafters shown in Leland's version, to give us a perspective from behind Susan of her vulnerability in the glare of lights directed at her.

The flashbacks thus progress towards an increasingly critical view of Kane, for while Thatcher's view should be perhaps the most antagonistic, he, rather than Kane becomes the villain of his flashback. The final flashback is narrated by Raymond, the butler of Xanadu, who is presented as a shrewd operator willing to narrate only for the pay-off. This adds a final sordid frame for a Kane in total decline, violently wrecking Susan's abandoned bedroom.

So without remaining "true" to the different voices of narration five different narrators could represent, *Citizen Kane* still colors its unfolding of Kane's life by the introduction of these surviving voices speaking of the past. In Jed Leland it creates a narrator who represents the opposite of the ethics and methods of popular journalism that so determine the newsreel, the Thompson quest, and Kane's political life. Leland's critical ironies turn the film from a jigsaw puzzle where everything could fit together as a portrait in vulgar Freudian terms of a psychologically damaged individual to one which asks many questions about American society beyond the meaning of "Rosebud," and which shows how powerful a vehicle for ideological commentary on U.S. history the biographical flashback film can be.

This evaluation of the potential of the biographical flashback film is reinforced by a less well-known film, *The Great Man's Lady* (William Welman, 1942). This film's work on the voice and on conditions of narration transform its exaggerated saga of the West and the life of its hero, Senator Ethan Hoyt, into something other than a typical American legend. Even as the film's heroine attempts to sustain an heroic myth by never publicly telling Ethan's story, an intriguing deflation of the heroic mythology of biography is the undercurrent of the flashback structure of the film generated by her storytelling in private. This internal contradiction hinges on a symbolic opposition of sexual difference indicated in the title. The "Great Man" of the title is told to us by his "Lady" who, while staying in her place (the private sphere), shares with another woman the secret of her historical contribution and the revelation of less-than-heroic secrets about the public hero.

The frame for this tale is built by an opening in which reporters from the East try to find a story in the unveiling of a monument of the memory of Senator Hoyt in a small western town. They press a centenarian, Hannah Semplar (Barbara Stanwyck), who has previously refused to speak with them, for the story of Hoyt's life. The reporters are similar to those in *Citizen Kane,* motivated by a search for scandal to enliven their coverage. Hannah, standing in her curtained doorway, impassive to their questions about her personal involvement with Hoyt, replies that she is "content to remain silent" about her "own private history."

The device that will break this silence and call forth the secret story are the tears of another woman who lingers after the men leave and who introduces herself not as a reporter but as a biographer. Though Semplar chides this display of emotion—"You need more gumption and spirit"—it appears to earn this woman access to Semplar's upstairs and the story of Ethan Hoyt. Symbolically this woman biographer is ushered into a private chamber and given access to the secrets of the past, only after being told that "You'll never learn a man out of books, or a woman, either." Here narrative film is charged with providing a history that journalism and books are denied and portrayed as being incapable of presenting. It will do so as the actualization of a private recounting between two women, evoking flashbacks that are riddled with narrative reversals presented in a continual alternation of serious, even tragic events with lighthearted events and satirical narration. In the end, Hannah is a traditional unacknowledged woman who provides ethical guidance for the male hero, while sacrificing her own needs in exchange for a vicarious and ultimately secret thrill in his accomplishments. Accordingly, the biographer promises her own female sacrifice, to "kiss my biography good-by," while Hannah, herself makes one last sacrifice; she rips up her wedding certificate, the last material key to her secret, insuring perpetuation of the myth surrounding the "Great Man."

Power and glory remain male activities, and while the potential for abuse of power is criticized, Ethan Hoyt's capitalist expansion (unlike Tom Gardner's or Charlie Kane's) is presented as humanized and morally cleansed by the secret influence of the sacrificial woman. The immediate ideological purpose of this film at the time of its release was perhaps urging the female home-front audience to provide behind-the-line support and sacrifices, as did much government propaganda, and less directly, other cultural representations.[20] It is also possible to see this film as exposing its strategy of closure and concealment so as to invite a reading against its grain. The film suggests that there is a male form of history and biography that needs to suppress a female version that must be kept secret. It offers its female-focalized flashbacks as a revelation of history seen from another, inverted perspective, and this paradox may supply the underlying logic of all the narrative inversions that the flashback structure facilitates. The film implicitly acknowledges what needs to be repressed and forgotten in a wartime inscription of a biography of an American hero, and that covert acknowledgment is quite astonishing.

We have seen how the biographical flashback is an important vehicle for historical retrospection, but we have also seen how this looking back at the past implies a framing and mythologizing of the past ignored in Collingwood's theories. The trope of retelling and reevaluating in the biographical flashback provides it with a special ability to perform an ideological critique; or, conversely, to ideologically recuperate a belief or meaning structure from an apparent critique; or even to create a paradoxical textual duplicity where both critique and recuperation coexist. These three biographical flashback films represent this range of ideological differentiation in filmic representation within the Hollywood flashback film; within the space of ten years, shifting historical conditions coupled with the differences generated by different writers, actors and actresses, and directors transform the framing of the heroic life in the retrospective biography. Though all three films employ much the same structure, each enters into the play of difference within this structure, each subtly inscribes a different relationship of the represented characters, and thus the audience, to the heroic individual's power. These differences take the form of shifts of voice and focalization; the choice of events narrated, the filmic form of that narration, and the commentary on these events within the present frame determine an attitude towards that representation.

The symbolic coding of ideological oppositions between genders and classes, and between corruption and legal, moral behavior in these biographical flashback films places the viewing subject in a relationship to power. What *precisely* that relationship is is difficult to say. It does seem that the place assigned this subject is not as normative and confined as certain theories of the ideology of Hollywood films might contend,[21] but we should also remember that the more subversive readings of elements of these films are not necessarily the ones that all audiences experience— for the ironies of disjunctive structures and the play of voices in a text are not necessarily the most obvious readings of such films or the ones most likely to be accepted. On the other hand, each of these films has an element of reflection on its own strategy of narration and raises questions about the foundations of subjectivity.

Elements of biography pervade many other flashback films, films that do not, however, necessarily present the telling of a "great" person's life at its end. For instance, biographical flashbacks blend particularly smoothly into genres such as the woman's film and melodrama, where the life in question is not necessarily that of a great figure of history, but an individual chosen to represent a class or a sex. Whereas we might tend to see such films primarily in terms of their melodramatic and psychological configurations, we should also remember that accompanying the more evident fictional process is the echo of a transposed and fictionalized biography, where the telling of history remains implicit. A look at three such melodramas tinged with biographical undercurrents will examine how these stories repeat and vary a central myth about the rise from the working class in 20th-century America.

The Hard Way, directed by Vincent Sherman for Warners in 1943, is an example of such a blend of genres. It opens with a failed suicide attempt, introducing a protagonist whose reasons for wanting to kill herself are blocked from verbal expression. Instead, a flashback narration of these reasons is offered as this character's interior monologue.

Two policemen have just rescued the well-dressed Helen Chernan from a river and stand over her, musing aloud about what possible motive for self-destruction such a wealthy and beautiful woman could have. The police pose the narrative's hermeneutic question, but no investigation ensues; instead Helen (Ida Lupino) is shown in a high angle close-up, eyes glazed, lips motionless as her voice-over takes up the narration of her past. At the film's close, we return to the present, where Helen is still lying in the police station, with the rags-to-riches-to-misery biography we have just been told through the flashback narration still a mystery to the police rescuers, whose comments ironically hypothesize that "Some little something went wrong, . . . the trouble with the rich ones is they have it too easy all their lives." In between this frame, the unspoken thoughts of Helen retell her life as a woman's version of the Horatio Alger myth, a rise from humble working-class roots in the factory town of Greenhill. The myth is perverted, though, as Helen's rise from the slums is actuated only through her commanding promotion of her sister Katie as a performer.

The cinematic style does not directly correspond to Helen's subjective viewpoint. Indirectly, however, the narrative selects, orders, and emphasizes segments to present us with Helen's motivations for entering into her scheming designs for Katie's life and perpetuating her power over her younger sister. The opening segments establish the factory as omnipresent in Greenhill, dominating the view from the apartment window as well as the mentality of the town's inhabitants. The deprivation of material goods is matched by a lack of emotional attachment in Helen's working-class marriage. If Helen seeks a way out for herself and Katie, it can be seen as the only alternative for women within the working class seeking escape.

Yet Helen is subsequently represented within her own flashback as an evil, scheming, dishonest figure who attempts to so dominate her sister for her own ends that she cannot permit her sister romance or a happy marriage. This self-representation is perhaps unlikely, perhaps equally an example of an author's license with subjectivity of a character as was the portrayal of Susan Alexander in *Citizen Kane*. However, aspects of this negative self-revelation can be interpreted as representing Helen's own guilt, remorse, and recognition of loss of affection. Her portrayal provides us with a reading of the motivation for her suicide attempt, joining a long novelistic tradition of interpreting female suicide.

Biography in the woman's film of the forties is often tied to such explanations of motivations for suicide or insanity as we shall see in *Mildred Pierce* (1945) and *Possessed* (1947), which will be discussed as psychological melodramas in the next chapter. *The Hard Way* does not delve into the psychology in the same insistent fashion as these other women's films; the character motivations it supplies for its anti-heroine instead link the biographical flashback to the personal history of an individual attempting unsuccessfully to rise out of a working-class background. This is the major alternative to the biography of the statesman-capitalist discussed earlier, and was used for male protagonists as well, though with significant differences.

The male version of this use of the biographical flashback to portray a troubled class ascendancy is represented by a pair of films, *Humoresque* (1946) and *Body and Soul* (1947) both featuring John Garfield as a working-class hero whose special talents (in music and boxing, respectively), facilitate his rise from ghetto environments.

Humoresque (directed by Jean Neguelesco for Warners from a screenplay by Clifford Odets and Zachary Scott, based on a story by Fanny Hurst), opens on a sign indicating a canceled performance at a Broadway theater. This is in many ways the male equivalent of the female's attempted suicide. A mysterious dissolve to a shot of the sea intervenes, then the musician who has refused to play, Paul Bouray, is shown in close-up on a balcony in some undisclosed location. He says, "All my life, I've been an outsider . . . I can't get back to the simple happy kid I used to be. . . ." "Kid I used to be" is repeated in a whispered voice-over as the image dissolves to the sea, before dissolving further, into a scene from his childhood as the son of a Jewish immigrant family. This verbal bridge to the past, marked by repetition of a phrase, is coupled with a desire for repetition, for a return; the flashback is marked as a nostalgic desire to repeat. However, this expressed desire will prove to be a displaced desire, and this displacement of desire will become a key figure in the structuration of the text.[22]

Far from the idyllic scene the nostalgic voice led us to expect, conflict between father and mother dominates the scene of childhood, condensed here onto a scene where the mother buys the boy a symbolically significant birthday gift—his desired violin—against the father's wishes. The violin is given under the auspices of maternal understanding, but we also learn that this gift will demand repayment through future submission to maternal control.

Paul's development as a master musician is shown in a montage sequence of the city environment illustrating the programmatic connections of his music. The Depression stymies his career until he becomes involved with Helen Wright (Joan Crawford) a rich socialite whose patronage assures his success. The sea, introduced rather mysteriously in the opening, is now associated with Helen's and Paul's sexual encounters at her beach house. Paul's mother and his former girlfriend, Gina, are both dismayed by Paul's interest in this older, married woman, and the mother finally tells Helen to leave her son alone.

Even though Helen has obtained the promise of a divorce, this prohibition from the mother drives her to suicide. Wearing a black-sequined dress that makes her appear to be an evil mermaid, she walks into the sea as Paul's concert (love/death music from *Tristan und Isolde*) is cross-cut and heard on her radio. If one simply accepts the mother as moral center, what follows is a condemnation of the Paul-Helen relationship; but, in fact, there is underlying the structure of the film an opening towards a more subversive reading, one that takes into a consideration a conflict between verbal enunciation and a reading of the flashback images inscribed in the opening phrase of nostalgic desire.

In a final scene, the past catches up with the present at the moment preceding the flashback, as we realize that Paul was earlier on the balcony of the beach house, and now he walks along the beach with a friend, contemplating his career. This establishes the frame of the present temporally as the day after Helen's suicide. The displaced desire for a return to a happy childhood that serves the narrative by motivating the flashback, might be seen as a desire to return to the mother. The canceled performance and the sea image, however, represent his desire to interpret Helen's gesture of self-annihilation. It is at this juncture, through the play of imagery framing the flashback, that *Humoresque* appears to be a film that establishes a double reading—on the one hand confirming the morality of the family that legitimately guards against illegitimate intrusion, while on the other hand supplying a critique of this normalizing moral power.

The circular structure of the film carries an ambiguous moral tag delivered by Paul's friend, "Nothing comes for free, you pay for what you are." This strange comment floats over the ending like the images of the sea that are both sexual and suicidal in connotation, implying that the cost to women of sexuality and desire is death, while the cost to men of elevation above one's class, particularly by means of devotion to art, must be sacrifice as well. Yet it also returns us to the mother's gift of the violin, a gift that must be paid for through submission to her will. In one sense, the ending is one of a moral rectification, where return to the mother allows a purification that will not come at the cost of a continuation of art (Paul will pursue his career, the cancellation won't signify a permanent retreat from music); in another, much about this ending is a pessimistic compromise, where all is sacrifice and repayment and where pleasure is suppressed. Desire can only go in the direction of a nostalgia, as the hero desires to overcome his loss through a retreat to childhood.

Body and Soul, directed by Robert Rossen from a screenplay by Abraham Polonsky as an independent production, is almost identical in certain aspects of its structure, but it evokes a far more singular reading than does *Humoresque,* containing little of the first film's doubleness. The flashback is introduced by a high angle on prizefighter Charlie Davis (John Garfield) as he is told "the smart money is against winning." The image whirls, then blurs out, dissolving to a celebration of Davis's first fight victory, which was also the occasion of his meeting a young painter, Peg, with whom he becomes romantically involved. Again, as in *Humoresque,* his parents live on the Lower East Side of New York City, where his father dies during a robbery on their candy store, indicating early poverty and violence in this biography.

Temporal condensation characterizes much of the flashback. A montage sequence shows Charlie's rising career in boxing as he fights to keep his mother off the charity rolls. As Charlie moves uptown and fights unscrupulously, he replaces Peg with a series of women, a high life of gambling, and loyalty to a crime syndicate, also shown in a montage sequence.

Finally, Charlie is asked to throw a fight, but a visit to Peg reminds him of his honor. The factor that redeems him from evil influences is directly stated in the film as his Jewish pride—wanting to fight for real, as if he were fighting the Nazis. In a return to the present, Charlie wakes up on the table, his biographical flashback apparently representing his last moment of decision-making before deciding to win.

The difference between *Body and Soul* and *Humoresque* lies not in their general structures, which are virtually identical, but in more subtle differences in narrative configurations and the symbolic exchanges. *Body and Soul* has little of the ambiguity of *Humoresque,* as the allegorical reference to World War II and its aftermath determines the unambiguous treatment of a Jew's struggle for his self-pride.

In both films, however, the hero is portrayed as viewing his life retrospectively, experiencing regret over having betrayed himself to achieve a success that demanded far more than the honest application of talent. A career that entails class ascension is depicted as necessitating perfidious acts or liaisons that betray the working-class hero's principles. Both of these films, as well as *The Hard Way,* are pervasively remorseful narrations, confessions of past sins and transgressions. Unlike the "great man" biographies, narrated by others with flashbacks nominally focalized by others, the working-class biographies are focalized by the anti-hero or anti-heroine as suits a confession.[23] The final moment is not necessarily punishment; unlike the gangster who must die, the working-class anti-hero or anti-heroine fallen from his or her newly won heights may suffer silently alone, but may also gain a knowledge of self that provides the means to continue or even change.

The moral charge of the biographical flashback narrative, however, is always one of judgment, evaluation of a life. Its unspoken project is an ideological statement on class and power in American society. In both types we have looked at, the biography of the great men of industry and the ascendant working-class hero, these flashback biographies display the conviction that wealth and power necessitate a loss of humanity, honesty, and happiness.

It is perhaps curious that a society that apparently worships success and ascendancy should create such a mythos to dominant its fictional biographies. We must remember however, that these flashback biographies are different from those told chronologically, without frames and fragmentation, many of which tend to be more optimistic and euphoric in their outlook, even if at some point conflicts or downturns are introduced. The flashback form seems to be linked with a certain tone of critique and retrospective guilt.

There are exceptions, notably during World War II itself. During the War, a biographical flashback can serve as a celebration of heroism. In the case of *Yankee Doodle Dandy* (Michael Curtiz, Warners, 1942), the biography of George M. Cohan as told in flashbacks by the performer himself (played by James Cagney) to President Franklin Roosevelt shows how rags-to-riches mobility can be accomplished and recounted with the greatest of patriotic flourishes. The hero must overcome dark periods which remain minor compared to his early rise to fame and his return to root for the United States of America, portrayed by elaborately staged dance numbers. In this film, unlike the other biographical flashbacks we have considered, the flashback frame becomes a vehicle for acknowledgment of the true American hero. This shift of the biographical flashback to a more heroic form occurs during World War II and is perhaps a product of a different ideological imperative.[24] As we shall see in the next section on flashbacks that bind together two historical periods, flashback structure in Hollywood films made during the War undergoes a kind of permutation; employing various means, it tends to be used to place the subject in history in a manner that ultimately strives for an heroic identification.

Binding Connections Between Historical Periods

The Second World War marks the appearance of a number of films that not only use flashbacks to subjectivize history (as do the biographical flashbacks), but also to compare directly through their flashback construction two different historical periods. Taking as their present moment the War, either on the home front or active duty overseas, these films compare experience of that War with World War I, or contrast it to pre-war life in American society. Later, the flashback is also used to create a retrospective subjective recounting of war experiences for which the post-war moment or the return from active duty served as the present of the narrative. The flashback continues to perform this same function of historical comparison for other historical periods in post-war films.

These films render historical thought as the subjective experience of individuals by creating both the present and the past which inserts itself in the present as a series of highly personal experiences. The major events of history are represented as they affect the course of daily life, particularly as they affect the course of romance, marriage, or motherhood. Again, the range of strategies and representations within this structure of the binding flashback is rather large and the connotations assigned the past, the present, and the act of remembering can vary. One constant in each case is the comparative nature of the temporal structure. Often, the two historical moments are placed side by side to interact with each other in a series of contrasts that can even incorporate great discrepancies in tone of the film's style, as if two separate films were being laced together. Different principles can determine the act of suture between temporalities. The binding can signify repetition or ironic transformation, explanation or inspiration, or some mixture of these principles. Significantly, much of what is indicated by such structures of temporal binding is indirect and symbolic, and is best indicated by a look at what threads are used to connect the two temporalities, the form of the suture itself.

Consider, for example, *Waterloo Bridge,* directed by Mervyn Le Roy for MGM in 1940, which draws the remembered experience of a World War I love affair into the context of the declaration of war by Britain on September 3, 1940—the moment of the frame story on which the film opens and closes. This frame story is an addition both to the original source, the Robert E. Sherwood play, and to the 1931 film version directed by James Whale for Universal. In the play and the earlier film, the story involves the romance of an American, a private in the British army, with a young American woman he meets on Waterloo Bridge. She turns out to be a prostitute. The emphasis in both cases is class conflict accentuated by conflicting moralities, though the film has a happier ending than the play.

The addition of the frame story flashback structure is used to transform this narrative, to place it, symbolically, into history. The 1940 version opens with the air of documentary, a repetition of scenes filmgoers had seen only months before in newsreels. The loudspeakers announce the declaration of war as cameras pan an assembled crowd of Londoners, then lines of school children are shown being evacuated.

A dissolve takes us to the scene of Colonel Roy Cronin preparing to leave for France by way of Waterloo Station. At the Colonel's request, his chauffeur goes by way of Waterloo Bridge where the Colonel descends to walk across the bridge alone. This walk, this site, is one of reminiscence, first displayed by a track backwards following the Colonel, then a crane shot outside the bridge dramatically moving in to a medium shot of the Colonel as he pauses to take out a charm. A musical theme comes up as the camera moves in to an even closer close-up of the Colonel's hand fingering this object. A voice-over auditory flashback refers to the original exchange of the charm, before another war; a woman's voice begins the dialogue, and Cronin's voice responds:

—Roy, take this.
—Your lucky charm?

—Perhaps it will bring you luck. Do you think you'll remember me now?
—I think so. I think so. For the rest of my life.

This auditory return to the past precipitates a dissolve to the Colonel as a young sergeant occupying the same place on the bridge, while all of the action within the flashback becomes both the explanation and affirmation of this dialogue with its reiterated promise to remember.

Immediately, the flashback serves to mirror and repeat the present, as an air raid siren sounds, sending the passersby running for shelter. The charm that the Colonel held in close-up in the present and that was mentioned in the dialogue, serves as a device to link present to past, as well as a representation of associative memory. It reemerges in the visual flashback, as Myra (Vivian Leigh), the young woman who was the auditory flashback's female voice, drops her purse while running for shelter. The young Sergeant Cronin helps her gather up the contents, and a close-up shows her reaching for this charm. The charm will continue to circulate through the narrative as an emblem of the romance between the Colonel and Myra.

From this flashback beginning in a war setting, the film narrates a melodramatic love story of a romance alternately blocked by circumstances and spurred by overdetermined coincidences carrying a charge of the uncanny. At first blocked by Myra's domineering ballet troupe leader, the romance is further troubled by the war. When Myra is falsely informed of Cronin's death, destitution leads her to prostitution. Prostitution then establishes the coincidence for the young lovers' reunion at Waterloo station, where Myra is soliciting customers, while Cronin simply assumes she is meeting his train. Myra's interiorized shame at her wartime profession will lead to a climactic scene on Waterloo Bridge, where she throws herself in front of a truck. The charm, back in her possession since Roy's return from the front, spills onto the pavement as her body falls, becoming once again the visual link, in a close-up dissolve return to the charm in Colonel Cronin's hand in the present.

The site, Waterloo Bridge, and an object, the charm, are the obsessively repeated elements of this narrative whose purpose it is to bind the symbolic, displaced sacrifice of one war (Myra's death) to the need to sacrifice in the other. As we return to the present, the Colonel, having relived his memories, is inspired by Myra's voice, reprised as another auditory flashback, reminding him of her love.

Waterloo Bridge, retold as a flashback tale, was probably conceived as a vehicle for winning American sympathies for the British war effort. Yet aspects of the embedded Sherwood narrative seem a harsh reminder of the difficulties for women waiting and working on the home front, hardly conducive to that kind of propaganda effort. If the critical edge of Sherwood's social commentary is less emphasized in the 1940 film, it is perhaps due to the fact that the convolutions of the melodramatic circumstances are now given new symbolic weight, in that they link the two wars under the sign of a sacrifice that is in fact a desperate act of love.

Another linking of the two World Wars occurs in *To Each his Own,* directed by Mitchell Leisen for Paramount in 1946. Like *Waterloo Bridge,* it opens during a bombing raid on London. Miss Norris (Olivia de Havilland), a middle-aged American woman, performs a watch duty on New Year's Eve with an elderly English gentleman, Lord Desham, during which time they bicker about women taking on such responsibility. She answers him by informing him that she runs a munitions plant converted from her cosmetics firm, and when he slips off the ledge during their patrol, she rescues him.

This introduction is used to present the context for potential flashback revelations of their pasts, as this brush with death begins to break some ice between these solitary and unfriendly characters. Lord Desham explains his desire to talk about his past by referring to the moment when he slipped on the roof as being "like the legend of the drowning man who sees his life before him." Memories of the past are presented by this dialogue as analogous to the flashback at the moment before death.[25] Yet he only verbally narrates his story of having spent the last war in France and losing his wife and son in a flu epidemic. Miss Norris refuses to divulge her own story, saying it is of "no possible interest." The narrative has posed the issue of recounting the past, then temporarily blocks the narration of Miss Norris's past with her "feminine" devaluation of the story's worth that is also a bid for privacy.

This negation sets up the flashback that occurs shortly thereafter, when Miss Norris breaks a dinner date with Lord Desham upon hearing that "Gregory" is arriving in town. An added cue calling for the flashback is offered when as she waits at the train station for the mysterious "Gregory." A nervous, excited young woman, also waiting for this train's arrival, explains her anxiety by saying, "You can't imagine what it's like to be in love with a flyer!" As Miss Norris is shown saying, "Can't I?," the image dissolves to the past to reveal the story of the romance of Jody Norris with a young pilot who visits her small town on a bond tour during World War I; the romance leads to the birth of an illegitimate son born after the pilot's death.

The flashback has prepared us for the arrival of Lieutenant Gregory Pierson, a young American flyer who is Miss Norris's son (though he knows her only as his aunt), and also the young woman's fiancé. Her long-awaited reunion with her son takes second stage to his marriage to his sweetheart; but due to Lord Desham's efforts to expedite the wedding, the secret of his parentage is finally revealed. Gregory at last acknowledges his mother at the film's end.

To Each his Own, like *Waterloo Bridge,* depends on the torturous twists of melodrama to provide the connection between the World Wars. The issues of the Wars as repetitive cycles of world politics and the "déjà-vu" aspects of similar adversaries and battlegrounds, of one generation ceding the horrifying duty of war to another, are displaced onto personal traumas of loss and recovery. Still, on a symbolic level, the films are the working-through of these historical repetitions. Both attempt to compensate for the potential pessimism of even a disguised recognition of this parallel by somehow turning the memory of World War I into a reason to fight again.

Jody Norris loses her potential husband to World War I, but regains her son in the same flyer's uniform because of World War II. The War is, in one sense, merely a backdrop for the maternal melodrama, but in another, it symbolizes the gain, rather than the loss, of a son. The circumstances of war indicates a project of recuperation operative across the film. A critical view of war-bond patriotism is represented in the first flashback, when the naive enthusiasm of the small-town flyer is contrasted with his own fatigue and desire both to escape and profit from his role of hero through sexual encounters. Patriotism is futher dampened by the young hero's death, overheard as a news item on the radio. World War I thus receives a somewhat negative portrayal, as the flashback memories are visions tainted with senseless cruelty and loss rather than nationalistic purpose. In contrast, the present-day frame story "corrects" this lack of dedication to ideals, as son replaces his father in all symbolic functions to mother, wife, and country.

These films represent social history and perform ideological identification primarily through displacement of the meaning of the two wars onto interpersonal relations within melodrama. Concern about the repetition of the alienation and trauma associated with remembered war experience are allayed through these films. World War II is presented with the promise of a meaning that remains absent from the memory of World War I.

In contrast, other films which flashback from the war period to the pre-war period or to an earlier stage in the War make a far more direct statement about the function of memory in establishing the patriotic determination to support the war effort. In these films, *Joe Smith, American* (1942), *Casablanca* (1942), *So Proudly We Hail* (1943), *Tender Comrade* (1943), and *The Immortal Sergeant* (1943), the memory is often personal, but it is offered through the flashback as a collective memory, one which transcends its reference within the film to become a memory image for the film's audience.

The conversion from American isolationism to involvement in World War II is symbolically represented by Humphrey's Bogart's portrayal of Rick, the detached cynic converted to Resistance supporter in *Casablanca,* directed by Michael Curtiz for Warners. Rick is motivated in this conversion by a reexamination of his past through a flashback. This leads eventually to the transformation of his contempt for his former lover Ilsa Lund (Ingrid Bergman) into renewed love and respect. However, the immediate motivation for the flashback in the narrative is born of Rick's personal sense of betrayal when Ilsa reappears in Casablanca; he tells the story of their past to her as a form of revenge for the abrupt end of their affair.

Presented in the film as a subjective flashback marked by Rick's voice-over commentary, the Paris segment depicts not only Rick's disappointed expectations, but also the fall of France to the invading Nazi army. The historical context is minimized in the discussion of the incidents during and immediately following the flashback, as Rick is obsessed with his personal experience of being rejected at his moment of need. Yet the images contain vivid accounts of the political conflict and military repression occurring on the Paris streets outside Rick's apartment.

It is not until later in the film, when Ilsa explains her own predicament at that same moment in the past, when she tells of learning that her husband, Lazlo, was still alive and not killed in a concentration camp as she believed, that the full political significance of the Parisian flashback is indicated. Not only is Ilsa worthy of understanding rather than reproach, not only is Rick convinced he was truly loved by the one person he most desired, but Ilsa and Rick can now consecrate their love by engaging in the Resistance effort as a delayed response to the invasion of France that they once witnessed together. The flashback and its retrospective assimilation clears their love of recrimination and self-doubt.

For the American audience this flashback became both a reminder of scenes they had witnessed in newsreels and through newspapers, the collective memory of history inscribed through visual and textual sources, and a supplement to that memory. Now fictionalized as the memory of Rick, this scene evokes a new kind of identification, augmented as well by the emotional involvement provoked by the bombing of Pearl Harbor.

Flashbacks offer a different motivation for patriotism and courage in *Joe Smith, American,* directed by Richard Thorpe for MGM, also in 1942. Images of American life before the War presented as subjective flashback memories serve to strengthen the character within the film, while propagandistically suggesting "why we fight" for the wartime audience.

Robert Young plays Joe Smith, a worker in a defense plant who is commissioned by the government to design a bomb installation site. When he is kidnapped by enemy agents, he weathers the brutal interrogation by consciously making himself remember "the nice things," as his voice-over tells us. These reminiscences are intercut with scenes of violent interrogation and torture. They recall Smith's personal history, his romance, marriage, and child.

The remembrance of even the most banal aspects of daily life are depicted as being the source of America's will to fight, with a sexual division of labor being a source of male pride and gratitude (Mary Smith is shown in a montage sequence rising early, ironing, and darning Joe's socks while he's bowling). The film exploits the transitions to the present scenes of torture for their dramatic contrast, cleverly linking occurrences in the flashbacks with the torture (Mary faints when her son's tooth is pulled as Joe faints from the pain inflicted by his interrogators). This gives the surging images a psychoanalytic dimension, in reference to Freud's theories that dreams and fantasies incorporate immediate sensory experience as elements of their imagery.[26]

The last "flashback" in Joe's series of subjective reveries is actually an imaginary projection rather than a memory, for it shows how Joe imagines his family's response when he didn't return home because he was kidnapped. The torture interrupts with its most gruesome manifestation yet, as pliers are used to break Joe's fingers. His extreme pain brings up an image of his son Johnny's writing pad, seen earlier in the film. It is decorated with a flag and the motto "E Pluribus Unum," which becomes the cue for a montage sequence that links Joe's face, resisting the torture, with spinning images of school children saying the Pledge of Allegiance, and learning about Nathan Hale.

The movement of the flashbacks has brought us through personal memories to patriotic symbolization: the memories of everyday life and the political emblems interfuse each other with meaning, becoming that which one can hold onto during a test of strength. One individual's memories are ideologically represented as normative experience, and the "average" American in the audience is asked to identify with them in order to reach his or her own patriotic convictions.

This use of remembered images of the pre-war period is inverted in *The Immortal Sergeant*, directed by John Stahl for Fox in 1943. Rather than serving as a motivation for patriotism, the past of the hero, Canadian Corporal Colin Spence (Henry Fonda) is presented in ironic contrast with his current call to bravery. Intercut with harsh desert battle scenes that decimate his patrol, Spence's flashback memories are to his rather trivial inadequacies in everyday male social performance before the War. Each of these flashbacks is introduced by tracks into close-ups, as Spence contemplates his own cowardice, and each serves to illustrate the inner thoughts of a man stationed in a forbidding and frightening desert war. As such, these flashbacks would seem to suggest that subjective memory is not always a resource for the hero; a haunting memory of insufficiencies in the past may foreclose heroic action in the present.

However, this implication is introduced only to be overcome. After the heroic and sacrtificial death of Spence's commanding officer leaves Spence in command, the remainder of the film traces Spence's decision-making processes in voice-over interior monologues as he tries to decide what Sergeant Kelly would have done in each new situation. The resolution will not be found in the past but only after the battle, when the trajectory of the flashbacks joins the trajectory of the present. In a narrative condensation—a process similar to Freud's notion of condensation in dreamwork[27]—Benedict, his former romantic rival, reappears in the present as a reporter in Cairo seeking the story of the hero, Spence, who has been evacuated to a hospital after winning the decisive battle in Libya. Spence tells his rival that he had "to meet sergeant Kelly to be fit for Valentine," the woman they have both courted.

The two parallel narratives, the war story and the romance told in flashbacks symbolically merge as the War serves as a proving ground and the woman as the prize, awaiting the man who has learned from the father figure, the immortal sergeant, how to command. If *Joe Smith, American* structures subjective memories of the past as that which gives the hero strength to perform his role, *The Immortal Sergeant*, in contrast, structures the present as that which helps the hero overcome his past insufficiencies. The two films display diametrically opposed functions of the past in relationship to the present in the development of the hero, but this opposition might not represent as much difference or ambiguity surrounding the hero as might first appear, in that these films take different men as their potential heroes. Joe Smith has already succeeded as a father figure commanding the microcosm of the family, while Spence is unformed in his civilian past, and must first be initiated into a paternal role. The past should be a resource, but if it isn't, one must take inspiration from a father figure. Underlying both films, then, is a notion that performing a certain role within the patriarchal family as linked to success as a heroic soldier.

What happens to the function of the past in flashback when the hero is a woman in the wartime film? The flashbacks of *Tender Comrade* (Edward Dymytryk, 1943, from a script by Dalton Trumbo) provide a retrospective view of a character prior to her wartime emergence as a heroine on the homefront. The fact that she is a woman and that the film traces her development within a collective living situation gives the film certain unique qualities, but in many ways *Tender Comrade* parallels in structure to the coming-of-age thematics of *The Immmortal Sergeant,* where the past represents immaturity and the War teaches lessons. The flashback structure provides a complexly ironic alternation of tone, contrasting the serious moments of war with the frivolities of peacetime romance, and the ideological strands woven through these contrasted moments are quite ambiguous.

The film opens on the morning of Chris Jones's (Robert Ryan) departure for overseas as his wife, Jo (Ginger Rogers) hurries him off to Union Station. A teasing banter reminiscent of sibling squabbles sets a light comedic tone for this initial scene, which is dispelled in the actual departure scene whose camera angles emphasize the characters' subjective views of being torn apart from each other.

After this opening of contrasting moods, the film chronicles Jo's homefront occupation, exploring the possibility of wage-earning women cooperating in an experimental form of socialism. Again, the flashbacks contrast sharply in tone with the frame story. The first two occur at night, after the household members retire to their separate bedrooms, leaving Jo alone with her photograph of Chris on her nightstand and her thoughts of the past, while the last flashback occurs when she is alone in the hospital after giving birth to her and Chris's child. Sentimentality is suggested by the introduction and conclusion of each flashback with an image of a couple meeting in a soft-focus landscape dominated by sky and clouds, yet the tone of each flashback recalls the comic treatment of the film's opening, and each narrates a fight between the young couple, each presenting an ironic view of the remembered past. Considering that Jo performs a leadership role in the women's collectively run household, the disputes between Jo and Chris point out the sharp contrast between the headstrong bride and the mature autonomous person she becomes by the film's end.

The flashbacks are not just comic, they are ironic, as each theme is quickly counterpointed in a manner that refers to the present action of the narrative. Even though frivolous and personal, the flashbacks involve serious references to the War; Chris ignores Jo because he is preoccupied with increasingly frightening international news, and during the difficulties of handling their neighbor's baby their own fears of parenthood are overshadowed by the newspaper headline that announces the drafting of married men. The irony of this flashback is doubled by its maternity hospital frame. The flashbacks also convey Jo's dissatisfaction with her role as a housewife, though her complaints are undercut by the comic treatment and the contrast to Chris's concern with the impending war. Whatever resonance there is to the complaint of this future defense plant worker that she is merely a "cheap housekeeper," as she piles unironed shirts at her inattentive husband's feet, is subsumed in the aura of guilt that the flashbacks acquire as her complaints are remembered in Chris's absence, while he is fighting overseas. It is as if the reminiscences are wrought with regret, "If only Chris were here now I wouldn't complain about a thing." This edge of guilt surfaces as Jo tells her friend after she returns home with the baby, "Most of the fights I had with Chris were over nothing at all." The War is marked as a maturation process, one which turns children into parents and selfish individuals into collectively minded persons whose fulfillment comes as a direct outgrowth of their participation in a social process. The ironic tone of the flashbacks and their insertion in the present as moments of reminiscence spurred by loneliness and longing for the absent male generate ambiguous and sometimes contradictory messages. Much of the feminist potential in the focus on Jo and the woman's collective is actually mitigated by the flashbacks and their framing.

The final sequence suggests a way that the audience might have absorbed any lingering contradictions. Upon receiving a telegram announcing Chris's death in action, Jo wakes up her baby. As she holds the child, there is an auditory flashback to Chris's serious words of farewell at Union Station where he stated his plans for after the War. Then Jo addresses her infant son, telling him of the meaning of his father's sacrifice. This final presentation of dead father to infant son represents the incorporation of the past into the future, and of the flashbacks into the present drama. Jo's monologue suggests the importance of memory images in the formation of human values, so that this closing scene serves as a meta-commentary on the flashback strategy of these wartime films; even when the past is presented as comic, ironic, or insufficient, it bears within it another promise for the future than the present of war seems to allow.

Memories, even those of individual foibles and marital differences, are endowed with the power to establish identity and serve identification with a heritage and a cause. In the case of other films that do not use flashbacks, it is the narrative as a whole that can become this sort of fictional "memory," that can be taken as a representation of our social memory. Flashback films, on the other hand, embed the process by which memory forms the individual and the social group within the narrative. They narrate what it means to remember. They indicate what the power of memory can be for a fictional character while becoming a similar extension of that memory formation for their audience. Through their structuring of memory sequences as subjective recall of historical and personal experience, these films structurally underscore the process by which memories are granted the power to define the individual and the social group that identifies with the remembered experience of another's story.

No wartime film makes this meta-commentary on film as constituting social memory more evident than *So Proudly We Hail,* written by Alan Scott and directed by Mark Sandrich for Paramount in 1943. This film's narrative incorporates the battles at Bataan and Corregidor. Its flashbacks are offered by a group of surviving nurses who reject the label "heroine" and who have been reluctant to tell their story. On board a U.S. Navy ship, they are persuaded to help a doctor treating their commanding officer, Lieutenant "Davie" Davidson (Claudette Colbert) by narrating "everything they remember of their ordeal." Davidson lies on a stretcher beside them on the deck, catatonic, perhaps amnesiac, the heroine who cannot speak or remember, whose story must be retrieved for her by the others.

This flashback is similar to many in later post-war films, as it is offered as a stage in a cure for battle shock. Since the trauma victim herself does not narrate, the flashback tale can be a coherent history of the nurses' entire service experience without straining credulity beyond the limits of convention. Voice-over commentary intervenes often throughout the flashback, with the initial narrator, Lieutenant Schwartz, being replaced by Lieutenant Joan O'Doul midway. Despite this change in narrators, the sequences within the flashbacks remain stylistically consistent.

The selection of incidents marks a female experience of the war effort, though along very coded and often sexist concepts of feminine interests. These details of personal behavior, of individual reactions to the wartime experience, are interwoven with major battles and military decisions, to give the story-told a strong subjective dimension.

Three strands emerge in the narrative offered by the nurses, each of which is directly connected to the traumatic cure. One involves Olivia D'Arcy (Veronica Lake) who is added to the nurses' ranks when she is picked up as a survivor of a bombed ship. Morose and disagreeable, Olivia's behavior is contrasted to the bouncy comraderie exemplified by the flirt, Joan, and the sweet generosity of Rosemary Larson (Barbara Britten). Later it is revealed that Olivia's hatred of the Japanese is in fact a violent, pathological symptom of her response to her loss of her husband at Pearl Harbor. Olivia recovers, renounces her plans to kill Japanese wounded prisoners and finds new acceptance among the others; later, however, when the women are trapped inside a hut surrounded by enemy soldiers, it is she who volunteers to become a human bomb by walking out in a gesture of surrender with grenades strapped to her body.

Olivia's sacrificial death is joined by others of a similar nature in the flashback segments. During the worst of the strafing and bombing of their hospital on Bataan, Davie frantically tries to stage an evacuation, while Rosemary and a young Philippino doctor, with whom Rosemary is in love, continue to perform an operation. On learning that Rosemary is still in the operating tent, Davie rushes back through the flames, but is unable to rescue Rosemary. Davie's command is not only characterized by the great stress of repeated attacks on her nursing facilities, but also by personal loss of these two nurses. Yet, while many possible reasons for her trauma are presented by this flashback narration—including increasing battle shock at the horrors witnessed, and guilt at her own inability to prevent the deaths—the film points away from these causes towards another, more conventional one: Davie's endangered romance with John, a young physicist-turned-soldier, whom she meets as a patient.

Davie, the career soldier, is said to be inspired by the memory of her deceased father, a World War I general, to put service in the Army above her personal life, but this adoption of a male role is modified by her romance with John. Their romance is punctuated by battle separations, but John returns to comfort her after each one of the attacks on her hospital, after each time one of the nurses is lost. Towards the end of the flashback narration the nurses are evacuated from the Army fortress at Corregidor as it comes under siege; Davie is forced to leave without knowing whether John is still alive. The apparent loss of the man she loves and military defeat are collapsed upon each other temporally, but the film singles out the love story as providing the explanation of the etiology of Davie's illness. The revelation by the nurses' flashbacks that Davie fears John is lost forever is the clue for which the doctor has been listening. He produces a letter from John that he begins to read. Shortly thereafter, John's face is superimposed over the image of Davie and his voice actually speaks the words of the letter, supplanting the doctor's. Davie opens her eyes and appears cured.

The film proposes to give us the subjective history of women in war, and, of course, in many respects it doesn't do this, obsessively concentrating on romances that rework Hollywood narrative formulas and presenting a mere love letter as the psychoanalytic cure for shell shock. Yet even given the exaggeration of love as the determinant structuring device and the perpetuation of certain stereotypically female behavioral myths, the film does raise the question of what constitutes the day-to-day perspective of people in an historical crisis such as a war, and how women became "heroic" participants in this struggle.

The narrative enigma posed at the film's opening, "Why are these women heroines and why are they reluctant to be acknowledged as such?," is answered through the reenactment of their memories of daily battle pressures. Even moments of selfless sacrifice are not shown as grandiosely heroic, but rather as appropriate responses to the demands imposed by the situation (even, in a more subversive reading, shown as slightly neurotic responses).

Part of Hollywood's input into the social history of the War was to create, through such flashback narratives, modern heroines or heroes whose fictive subjectivity could be shared through processes of identification by those who never shipped out for the War. Fictional memory becomes our memory as viewers, so that even the weaknesses inscribed in our heroes and heroines have the potential to reinforce identification with these myths. For the American audience of 1943, the flashbacks of So Proudly We Hail were flashbacks to their own immediate experience, except instead of being mediated by newspapers, newsreels, and radio reports, this time the fall of Bataan and Corregidor were told and remembered as the experience one might have had if one had been there. Subjectivizing history through flashbacks has ideological functions in these war films that perhaps explain why the discrepancies in tone and psychoanalytical inaccuracies occur. It appears that a more consistent narrative tone, or a more accurate picture of the multiple causes and difficulty of recovery from a mental breakdown might jeopardize the propagandistic program of the film. Not to have a miraculous cure for Davie in the form of a love letter would imply that war destroys even its surviving heroines, a far bleaker notion than the acceptance of death as a celebration of unself-conscious heroism. Similarly, to be consistent in tone in such films as *Tender Comrade* or *The Immortal Sergeant* would enforce a more penetrating and critical consideration of pre-war experience than the comedy allows. This would darken considerably the overall mood of these films, whose need to provide heroic and inspirational individuals outweighs the filmic writing of a social history of the War.

These films nonetheless do establish a rich symbolic structure of comparative historical moments, in which one can see the potential for a more revealing analysis of social history and the way the mentality of one period creates a context for the actions of a later period. As we shall see in the last chapter of this book, one of the recent and international developments of the flashback is a further taking into account of the underlying concepts of this symbolic structure.

Flashback Psycho-Histories of Hollywood

As it looked back on its own history in a number of films in the fifties, Hollywood made use of flashbacks to introduce subjectivity into its retrospection. *Sunset Boulevard* (1950), *The Bad and the Beautiful* (1954), and *The Barefoot Contessa* (1954) all make use of the flashback device to present a "remembering" by individuals of participation in the boom years of Hollywood production. As was the case with earlier Hollywood "backstage" reflexivity, some of this memory searching and social analysis was displaced from the cinema to the theater—as is the case with the flashback film, *All About Eve* (1950), written and directed by Joseph Mankiewicz, adapted from a short story by Mary Orr. All four of these films from the early fifties argue that show business can cause strong psychological deformations for those involved; that breed of monstrous or tragically compromised or failed superbeing is depicted as created by the exigencies of Broadway and Hollywood.

I will call this sub-genre the "Hollywood retrospective flashback," noting that it combines the structure of the biographical flashback with the flashback used to display a subjective view of history. Critical analyses of the industry are presented emblematically through the psychoanalytically flavored accounts of the lives of the industry's most noted (fictionalized) luminaries. Tales of ambition and neuroses serve as the means through which Hollywood can be self-critical; psycho-history of the individual provides the narrative basis for an implicit and distorted psycho-history of an environment, the studio system, the industry. By rendering the tales as individualized accounts, the films avoid critical analysis of the economic structure and ideological functions of Hollywood, converting the moment of self-criticism into another melodramatic entertainment to be exploited commercially like any other.

In this light, it is intriguing that the first voice we hear in *All About Eve* is that of Addison Dewitt (George Sanders), whose official function within the fiction is critic and acerbic commentator on the theater, but who turns out to be the most unscrupulous and self-serving character in the film, except, possibly, for Eve herself. Dewitt introduces a theatrical awards ceremony that will serve as the present-tense frame story for the film's flashback narration. Each of the major characters is introduced by Dewitt's voice-over commentary and the images that accompany his commentary are constructed to connote the unspoken story underneath the surface, to establish the desire for the flashbacks. For example, the reaction of Margo Channing (Bette Davis), the former star whom Eve is replacing, is depicted through her displaced attention to the lighting of a cigarette and the pouring of a drink, displaying a troubled insecurity despite her efforts to appear at ease. Then Dewitt says, "We have arrived at the reason for being here," as we see a close-up of Eve Harriman's (Anne Baxter) expectant hands, as the young actress waits, perhaps too anxiously, for her award. A cut back to Margo shows the older woman lowering her eyes, negating the spectacle to follow. Then, as the award is announced, Eve stands to applause and the image freezes on her advance to accept her prize.

From this frozen image of the present, a voice-over that shifts its source from character to character will evoke images of the past. This flashback narration will be charged with explaining the cryptic elements introduced in the opening frame sequence, the gloating acrimony in Dewitt's voice, the troubled yet eager glory of Eve, Margo's detached yet wounded behavior.

The narration of this fragment of theater history will disclose a bitter conflict hidden beneath the public celebration, and provides us with the moral tale that show business corrupts; those who would seek to preserve their humanity, especially women who wish to preserve their "femininity," are better off retiring to private life. Yet the development of the narration of the past celebrates theatricality, reaching its heights when its characters behave flamboyantly and petulantly, introducing a contradiction between the film's own pleasures and its didactic tone.

The flashback series begins with Eve's introduction into the world of Broadway star Margo Channing. Karen Richards (Celeste Holm), Margo's best friend and the wife of Margo's director, Lloyd Richards, narrates. While the voice-over intervenes only periodically, Karen's role as narrator is crucial here, as in the other scenes she is given to narrate. For to mark from Karen's perspective the scene which shows Karen ushering a loyal fan, Eve Harriman, into Margo's dressing room, only to have the star sarcastically rebuff her admirer, sets up Karen's critical view of her talented and famous friend. Eve wins everyone except Margo's sympathy by telling her life story, a tale of being a war widow totally enraptured by the theater and its star, Margo Channing.[28] This embedded biography signals the power of the narration of the past to captivate (though in this case, presented verbally), adding a level of self-reference to the flashback structure itself.

Margo, herself, is eventually taken into the sway of this story of Eve's past; she becomes the narrator of the next segment of the flashback, which chronicles Eve's growing prominence in Margo's life as her "girl Friday," until Margo's gratitude gives way to suspicions of Eve's intentions. Here Margo's voice leads us to begin to empathize with her fears about Eve, while the scenes of confrontations that she stages, her wit spiced with alcohol, build audience admiration for her grand flourishes (that include the famous warning to her guests, spoken at her fiancé Bill's welcome-home-from-Hollywood party, "Fasten your seat belts, it's going to be a bumpy night"). Theatricality invades the filmic narration of Margo's real life, as her gestures and dialogue are filled with references to the theater and her stage persona. This confrontational theatricality culminates in a scene that takes place on the theatrical stage, when Margo feigns ignorance of Eve's having been hired as her understudy in order to play out a scene of innocently inspired, fresh anger. Despite the fact that the others respond negatively to Margo's actions, her narration inscribes much sympathy for her and begins to taint Eve with an aura of sly contrivance.

However, the narration is shifted away from Margo, to alternate between Karen and Addison for the remainder of the film. This temporarily forecloses sympathy with Margo's perspective, shifting instead to a greater identification with Karen's plot to retaliate against what she perceives as Margo's arrogance, until Addison's own investment in Eve's career takes center stage. In the conflict of personalities that ensues, Addison and Eve come to represent the type of ruthless self-concern that the film posits as necessary for a rise in the theater, but Karen's revenge tactics taint the non-theatrical world with evil passions as well. Eve is caught by Addison at her manipulative schemes and enslaved to him by means of his knowledge; his investigation of Eve's story of her past proves it to be entirely a fabrication. If we noted earlier that her telling of her past was an instance in which film embeds a reference to its own flashback structure, this reference now becomes tinged with irony, and the value assigned the past within the narrative shifts. The performing female goes astray when she covers her real past with a fabricated story; if Broadway and Hollywood are dangerous it is because they encourage deception through the construction of a false public self. This does not make the theater any less effective— Dewitt tells us Eve nonetheless "gives the performance of her life" as the innocent Cora. The recognition of corruption at the heart of the theater is located symbolically by the film's structure in the discrepancy between a fabricated biography and the actual history of the past. This brings the film back to the present, at which point we return to the freeze-frame image, which is reanimated.

In the structure of *All About Eve,* the past literally interrupts the flow of images in the present and undercuts the present's superficial recognition of theatrical success with a revelation of the events not just "behind the scene," but anterior in time. Past history is granted not only a truth value but the power of a judgment on the present, as Eve's acknowledgment speech is met with reverse shot looks of disgust from all the people she thanks and whom we saw her double-cross in the flashback past.

The implicit critique of Broadway is extended to Hollywood by means of two references. First, the aspiring actress who originally reads for understudy to Margo (Marilyn Monroe), is sent to Hollywood by Dewitt when met with failure on Broadway, and Eve herself announces in her acceptance speech that she intends to move her career to Hollywood. The film industry is thus represented as an even tawdrier version of the "legitimate" theater. Secondly, the film indicates that its story of degraded aspirations will be repeated, by introducing Phoebe, a second-generation Eve, who repeats Eve's usurpation of Margo's glory when in the final images of the film she tries on Eve's cloak and holds Eve's award while rehearsing a bow in a three-way mirror.

This triple vision recalls the repetition construction of the triplet, Margo/Eve/Phoebe, and reminds us that the film locates its social critique of a milieu and an industry primarily within the female psyche. Needing to be the center of attention and admiration, vain, self-centered, afraid of aging, unable to perform the nurturing roles of mother and wife, the stars and aspiring starlets are given traits from which only Margo is allowed to retire, by marrying Bill and forfeiting her career. Mirrors abound in the crucial scenes of replacement, and though Margo once fights back with the powerful line that her "cynicism was acquired the day I discovered I was different from little boys," this knowledge of the sexual discrimination a career woman faces is mitigated later in the film by Margo's attempt to recover her sacrificed "femininity," or as she puts it, "the things you drop [during a career] that you need again once you decide to start being a woman."

If "Eve" as a name makes a Biblical reverence to an originary female as a source of evil, the film's symbolic coding locates its critique not simply on fame in the theater as source of corruption, but rather on how the theater is specifically liable to deform the female. The structure through which the film alternates its three narrative voices in its flashbacks to introduce, investigate, and overturn its paradigm of innocence and corruption allows finally for much of its critique of the theater industry to be displaced onto a critique of denatured females.

In *Sunset Boulevard,* the critique of the industry is even further displaced onto a woman's psychic disorder. Written by Charles Brackett and Billy Wilder, and directed by Wilder for Paramount in 1950, the film infuses its flashback structure with the pessimism of *film noir* style that we will consider in the next chapter. In *Sunset Boulevard,* the flashback is just a simple frame structure, but it presents the symbolically rich and theoretically fascinating trope of the narrating corpse, a voice-over from beyond death.

This conceit is presented with considerable restraint and metonomy in the film. A tilt up to show the street sign on Sunset Boulevard introduces a voice that confirms the location verbally; it continues to comment wryly on the scene as the camera turns its high-angle gaze on the police gathered around an eerily glowing swimming pool where the corpse of a young man is floating. A cut to a shot from underneath reverses the natural order of things, becoming the visual accompaniment to this "impossible" narration in which the corpse of Joe Gillis (William Holden) can tell how he reached his demise in this watery grave.[29]

The device of the deceased narrator conforms to the garish exaggeration of the film's stylized treatment of Norma Desmond (Gloria Swanson) and her mansion. The mansion itself is a tomb, sealed off from the world; a monument to Hollywood's past. The frame of the corpse in the present floats over the unfolding of the film as the inevitable conclusion, a predetermined outcome. It allows the film to loop its circular structure back to Gillis's shooting by Norma at the end of the film, when he attempts to walk out on his gigolo relationship with her. The murder scene becomes charged with the uncanny, as everything falls into place with the already-seen corpse in the pool. This circular return, however, is not the film's ending; the film cheats on its trope of corpse-narrator by adding one more scene—the elaborate ruse of luring Norma downstairs by pretending that the newsreel cameras covering her arrest are filming her.

Norma replays her former glory in the present, and everyone supports her delusion with an appropriate mise-en-scene for her fantasy return to the past. Norma lives out a "flashback" here, just as when she projects her old films in her private screening room. The old films also serve as an informational flashback for the audience. So while the flashback structure of *Sunset Boulevard* is technically only a narrated frame story, the re-emergence of the past in the present, the force of an obsessive memory, permeates the film, as does the vision of the darker side of the glamorous dream of Hollywood.

All of this is embodied in Norma Desmond, a figure of delusional senility and the perverse quest for youth. As in *All about Eve, Sunset Boulevard* creates a symbolic positioning of a woman as the locus of a displaced critique. If her portrait as a diseased decadent symbolically represents a critique of a film industry longing for a comeback as it obsessively repeats its past acts, this symbolism nonetheless exists alongside a contrasting vision in the film of a Paramount Studios that has successfully evolved into the fifties.[30] The retrospective flashback film toys with this dual reflection, alternating between the presentation of the case in question as specific (and often female) biography, while at the same time reaching out towards a reflexive symbolic structure that contains a critique of its own psycho-history.

Dark dreams and death imagery also haunt *The Barefoot Contessa*, written and directed by Joseph Mankiewicz for United Artists in 1954. The film begins with a star's funeral in the present. A film director, Harry Dawes (Humphrey Bogart), describes the scene of mourning as if it were any other Hollywood set, "the staging, setting, lighting are what Maria would have wanted." Harry's narration is not only clever and ironic, but continually reflects on the film's representation of life as a mirror of filmic tropes, as when he says, "sometimes life behaves as if it has seen too many bad movies." A crane shot connects our narrator/mourner with the statue of the "barefoot contessa" that marks Maria Vargas's (Ava Gardner) grave. Then the image dissolves to images of the past as Harry says, "Where I *faded in* Maria was not yet a contessa, not yet a star, . . ." inscribing the fact that while others will narrate, his voice is the self-conscious verbal center of the film.

The film obsessively returns to the grave, varying slightly each time the manner in which the crane shots pass the narration from Harry to Oscar Muldoon (Edmond O'Brian, a supercilious press agent) back to Harry and back to Oscar. Their flashbacks narrate the deracination caused by Maria's rise to stardom, which leads to personal unhappiness in romance. After Oscar's narration introduces Count Vincenzo Tolato Favrini, it is to the Count mourning his wife's death that the film returns in the gravesite present. The Count engenders a flashback that jumps out of the simple, linear, progressive chronology the film has established for the other flashback segments. For while Oscar has already narrated Maria and the Count's first meeting in a casino, where the Count rescued her from her lover's mistreatment, the Count's flashback goes back to an event that occurred before that casino meeting, his drive past a gypsy camp where he stopped to watch Maria dancing barefoot with the poor migrants. The Count then retells the casino encounter from a different perspective, replete with different camera angles (reversed 180 degrees from the earlier shot). This temporal disturbance, an analepse and reprise, marks the Count's introduction under a sign of disruption of the pattern of linear reprise in continuity. This marking will soon be incorporated as significant to the symbolic coding of the narrative.

To see how, first let's look at the statue imagery. At the end of the Count's narration, Maria, wrapped in a towel, runs up from the sea to his villa; she graphically matches a draped statue next to her. This establishes the barefoot contessa statue imagery within its past context, symbolically marking Maria's social ascent from dancing gypsy to the heights of European nobility. Then, the actual grave monument statue is created within the next flashback, narrated once again by Harry; Maria is posing for the sculptor when Harry arrives in Italy for her wedding. This flashback reinscribes the gypsy motif, when Harry notes that Maria would have been happier if instead of attending the formal party at her husband's villa, she had been able to dance outside to the peasant music with the servants. It also contains the key flashback-within-the-flashback, which illustrates Maria's confiding to Harry the secret of her unhappiness in her married life, only thirteen weeks after her wedding.

Maria narrates this embedded flashback of the bridal chamber scene during which her husband hands her the 1942 document that gives the reason for his military release; as the film puts it, his "body was blown apart" by a landmine. After revealing the letter that indicates his castration, the Count walks out of Maria's bedroom, leaving her alone with the sounds of peasant dancing still drifting up from the window. These sounds gain their full significance after the film comes out of its embedded flashback; not only do they represent Maria's sexuality (to be repressed in her marriage due to the secret her husband revealed only after their vows), but the music foreshadows Maria's solution, one which will prove fatal. As the film comes out of the embedded flashback, she confesses to Harry her desire to bear a child for her husband; Harry's flashback ends with his narration of the discovery of the murder of both Maria and her lover by the Count.

The barefoot contessa statue looks out of the last image of this flashback, binding the flashback series to the funeral in the present. The narrative hinges on the disjuncture between genuine sexual expression and the representation of sexuality in images; Maria's innocence and talent are corrupted by Hollywood commercialization, but indirectly. The film annexes the fairy-tale mythology of European nobility leading a charmed life of grace and elegance, and then emerses itself in the flip-side of this myth, that of upper-class sterility. This is, of course, a reference to a number of Hollywood stars whose "royalty" in the film world provided them with liaisons to titled foreigners or to the kings of American industry. But we can also note a parallel here to the symbolic coding Roland Barthes finds in Balzac's tale *Sarrasine,* especially as concerns class ascendancy, denaturalization, and castration.[31] Intriguingly, the narrative locates this castration as caused by World War II. By locating the castration of European nobility at this historical juncture, the film implies history's role in both creating and destroying its myths. Within the film's terms, this castration by extention contaminates the Hollywood myth; the belabored returns to the statue, the redundant symbolization, are crucial to the film's functioning, and even attain a sublime presence in the wake of Harry's brilliant, sarcastic lines. The statue graphically represents the star perverted by her sexual glorification, monumentalized as a stone statue of her former self.

A similar view of Hollywood as dehumanizing is presented in Vincente Minelli's *The Bad and the Beautiful,* made for MGM in 1954, from a script by Charles Schnee, but alongside this vision is a continual effort to recuperate the Hollywood myth from this critique. The actress, Georgia (Lana Turner), is less central than in the other films, for in this case the producer, Jonathan Shields (Kirk Douglas), is the focus of the flashback commentary, and two other narrators, the director, Fred Emile (Barry Sullivan), and a writer James Lee Bartlow (Dick Powell), get equal attention as victims of Shields.

If the producer is consistently presented as a demonic figure, the present frame of the story serves to justify such industry tactics. The frame that opens and closes the film chronicles Shields's attempt to regroup the successful talent with whom he has worked over the years on Oscar-winning films. While waiting for a transatlantic call to Shields, the director, actress, and writer each narrate his or her devastating past experience with Shields to explain their impending refusal of his project. Once the three stories are told to Shields's middleman agent, the three begin to leave his office, but find themselves glued in fascination to an extension phone—a three-shot that closes the film on the conciliatory note that a little unscrupulous behavior in the service of megalomania can be tolerated if an exciting project is involved.

The three flashbacks which form a single chronology each contain elements of critique of Hollywood filmmaking that are later mitigated by locating in these same procedures certain practical virtues. For example, the first flashback, the director's, which covers Shields's rise through B movies to his own production company, tenderly mocks Hollywood's artificial means of building illusions, then comments sharply on the calculated, profit-motivated repetition of genre production. However, it is out of the same commercial imperatives of low-budget horror genre production that Shields and Emile come to film "Return of the Cat Men," using only shadows instead of the tacky and deteriorating costumes they have been issued. The film argues that commercial interests create limitations that breed creative solutions and innovation, and this fictional flashback contains historical references to Hollywood genre production such as the Val Lewton and Maurice Tourneur collaboration at RKO. However, innovation is not born spontaneously of low budgets, and in Tourneur's case his link to European production is a more convincing explanation for his particularly intriguing cinematic techniques. In its flashback fictionalization of Hollywood history, the film creates a myth that ignores all of the other factors in this historical instance.

Georgia's and James Lee's flashbacks contain a similar mixture of critical commentary and celebration of the industry. In the end, the compromise of this critical analysis is suggested directly by the agent, when he points out that in each case of misfortune caused by Shields a greater good was achieved. *The Bad and the Beautiful* mixes strange melodramatic plot machinations with scenes that present Hollywood production critically, while the tone of the film infuses comedy into its most dramatic and tragic developments. This melange of tones is perhaps more pronounced than in the other Hollywood retrospective flashback films we have discussed—but the light tone is characteristic of other examples, such as the flashback sequences in *Singin' in the Rain* (Stanley Donen/Gene Kelly, MGM, 1952) and the number "Born in a trunk," in the 1954 George Cukor/Warner's version of *A Star Is Born*. For Hollywood, retrospection is marked by contradiction, and these films certainly lend themselves to a range of readings, depending on whether one extrapolates from the symbolic coding and emphasizes the allegorical or whether one concentrates on the film's efforts to contain and soften the symbolic critique it unleashes.

It is significant that the early fifties produced these films that use flashbacks to recall the history of show business and Hollywood, to examine their means of producing entertainment and the cost of those characteristic methods of operation in creative and human terms. Death and corpses dominate the flashback structures of two of these films, while the two others reveal personal treacheries behind the scenes; sardonic voices echo through all of them. The films are like nightmares, troubled distorted memories of a painful experience; the entertainment principle of Hollywood film production may lighten or modify this bleak recall, but the films remain symptoms of an awareness that the past of Hollywood contains a history that is dark and disturbing.

Comedic Inversions and Parodies of Life Stories

In this chapter on the subjectivity of history in the flashback, a number of mechanisms by which Hollywood presents a specific view of history in relationship to the subject have been explored. I have mentioned ironic moments in many of the films, as well as gaps and contradictions that color what might be seen as dominant ideological positionings at specific historical junctures. In closing, let us turn to some flashback comedies that extend mechanisms of irony and highlight contradiction for the purpose of satire, unstitching the logic of ideological containment of the subject in history that other flashback films attempt to bind. This is not to say that simply by comedic inversion all of these films finally depart from the tendencies mapped out in the rest of this chapter, but only that comedy opens the fissures to a scrutiny whose danger is deflected by the mark of the non-serious, the humorous. Also, the

The flashback superimposition in *Histoire d'un crime,* Zecca, 1901.

Zecca's flashback repeated in *Drink and Repentence: A Convict's Story.*

The ambiguous dream-bubble flashback in *The Old Chorister*, James Williamson, 1904.

The graphic match on present and past in *The Passer-by*, Oscar Apfel, 1912.

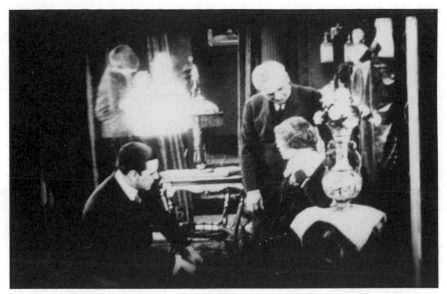

The flashback within the flashback in *Just a Shabby Doll*, directed for Thanhouser, 1913.

The dissolve connecting past and present, *After 100 Years*, 1911.

A flashback embedded in the love letter whose rereading evokes the memory image in *The On-the Square Girl*, Ireland, 1917.

Margaret Cameron represents the South in *Birth of a Nation,* unable to forget the past, as her flashback image to her brother's death for the confederate cause forcloses her romance with the northerner, Phil Stoneman.

In D. W. Griffith's *True-Heart Susie*, a rereading of old love letters and a visit to the site in which names were carved in a heart recalls flashback images of the earlier romance.

From the present day vantage point of *Casablanca* the former lovers look back on a romance encapsulized in their smiles, but which flow into images of the Nazi occupation.

The contemplation of suicide embodied in a look calls forth images of childhood in Dimitri Kirsanov's *Ménimontant*. The images are displaced from the scenes of horrific murder that we see as marking the sisters' youth at the beginning of the film.

Objects and gestures circulate between present and past as poetic, ironic linkages in *Le Jour se lève*.

The highlighting of François' eyes makes the dissolves to his interior vision of the past a particularly effective treatment in *Le Jour se lève*.

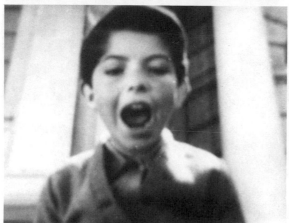

Graphic matching on a close-up of a face "descending" into the
past marks the resurgence of the repressed memory in Hitchcock's *Spellbound*.

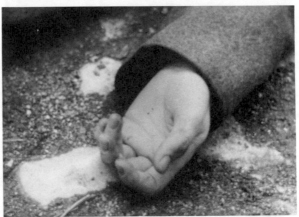

The gaze at one hand recall a flash image of another and the repressed but unreconciled memory of death, in *Hiroshima, mon amour*.

The love affair in the present in *Hiroshima, mon amour* is spurred by a desire for narration and transference.

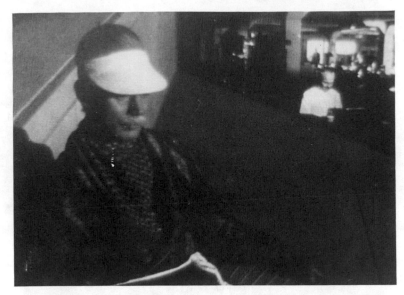

As Jed Leland narrates, a process shot introduces a flashback in *Citizen Kane*. Though narrator and the scene of past are copresent in the same shot, the angular composition still echoes the motif of a gaze into the past.

In *Rashomon*, a stark and straightforward visual centering of a narrator in the present contrasts with the flowing images of his flashback version of the past.

"fun" is not at the expense of an ideologically determined subjectivity alone, but multivalent.

The Marrying Kind (Columbia, 1952) written by Ruth Gordon and Garson Kanin and directed by George Cukor, is perhaps the most pronounced riff on the subjective flashback's integrity and its ability to testify in a fictional court of law, or, to put it differently, to obey the laws of narrative fairness. Here the flashback testimony of a couple in a divorce trial is given informally in the judge's chambers. The most innovative moment is the first flashback sequence, portraying their initial meeting; not only does each have their own version that contradicts the other's, illustrated by the film with a certain equanimity, but the images in each case contradict the verbal narration of the party supposedly "controlling" the flashback through his or her discourse. Although many other films have flashback illustrations which deviate from the enunciation that supposedly evokes them, this discrepancy is nearly always unmarked and clearly meant to slip by unremarked by the viewer. Not only does this comedy unhinge this cinematic convention, it invites the spectator to laugh at the notion of a character's subjectivity. By extension, historical witnessing even of one's own life is not the privileged experience it is in the dramatic films of similar structure.

Another satire of the trial testimony flashback, *Les Girls* (1957), written and directed by Herman Mankiewicz, unveils the personal histories of three showgirls and their manager Barry (Gene Kelly), in three flashbacks, whose precipitating cause is a slander trial. The first two flashbacks told by Sybil and Angele, respectively, are contradictory in their characterization of each other and of Barry, whom each woman claims is the object of the other's affections. They differ in focus on selected details and overlap temporally in the narration of two major events, the performance of a dance number, "Ladies in Waiting," and a gas leak in the women's apartment that each reports as the other's suicide attempt. Barry's version mediates the conflict by proposing a third story, chronicling different but simultaneous events which end on the same gas leak, this time a pure accident. The film self-consciously questions truth values within fictions as emblemized by the punctuating appearance of a sandwich-board picketer bearing the slogan "What is truth?" and a fragment of dialogue pointedly about flashback structuration as illustrative of testimony, "How can you remember scenes you didn't see?" Still, the comedy is mainly derived at the expense of the two females; the fiction portrays jealousy as the motive of a misshapen subjectivity. The philosophical and cinematic challenge of the comedic inversion is constrained by a satire directed against characters and by the service-function the narrative plays as a vehicle for spectacular dance numbers.

That such comedic endeavors have their ideological threat is evident from critical reaction to *Roxie Hart,* an adaptation by Nunnally Johnson of Maurine Watkins's play *Chicago* (1927), directed by William Wellman in 1942. The satire struck Bosley Crowther, for example, as untimely: "This is a most unsuitable time to be calling to mind the follies, the court-room circuses and vulgarities of this brashly eccentric nation during a period which might better be forgotten."[32] As we have seen, World

War II is a time when flashbacks are solicited for their ability to locate the viewing subject in a defined view of history through identification with fictive subjectivity and memory. Here the story of the past is told as a barroom legend rather than as the subjective account of the principal, Roxie Hart (Ginger Rogers); in contrast to the legend-telling of *The Great Man's Lady* (which also mobilized hyperbole and some humor, though mixed with pathos, and ultimately conformed to heroic reinforcement), here the humor depends on outrageous exaggeration that mocks the seriousness of historical retrospection and the purposeful inspiration to be drawn from it.

Perhaps the most sophisticated of the American flashback comedies is *Lady in the Dark* (1944), directed by Mitchell Leisen from Frances Goodrich's adaptation of a Moss Hart play. It is not in the form of the flashbacks, however, that the film distinguishes itself; they do not in fact have a comedic inflection. The flashbacks illustrate a fashion magazine editor's confessions to her psychoanalyst, in which her memories of her childhood competition with her mother for her father's affection are seen as determinate of her drive to be a successful career woman. Again, the humor is directed against a female who attempts to deviate from a proscribed role (the glamor industries of fashion and film are also mocked, though mildly). A popularized version of psychoanalysis, heavily male in its perspective, is reinforced by the film, giving it much in common with the psychoanalytic flashback films discussed in the next chapter. The distinguishing trait of the film is the staging of the dream and fantasy sequences to music by Brecht's collaborator, Kurt Weill, with lyrics by Ira Gershwin that call for comparison to Brechtian theater. If spectator distanciation and ultimate ideological purpose are less vigilant here than in Brechtian drama, the tone of the representation is an intriguing departure from Hollywood norms. All the more striking then, that the flashbacks should take themselves so seriously and remain so unself-critical.

That flashbacks should remain one of the elements of this satire to escape satirical handling suggests how rare subversive structuration of this trope is. We have seen throughout this chapter how flashbacks are mobilized to evoke subjectivity, identification, and the framing of the past in the service of ideological representations of history. Comedy and shifts in tone, when present, rarely interfere with and often are incorporated into this shaping of perspective and attitude. The films frame a way of viewing and remembering the past; they frame the subject in history. While we might view these films critically, deconstructively, transgressing those frames to seek the play of metacritical allegories, the framing process should never remain as invisible to our analysis as it perhaps can be under certain modes of reception that stay neatly within the frames.

5

Flashbacks and the Psyche in Melodrama and Film Noir

Besides subjectivizing history, another major tendency in flashbacks in American films of the forties and fifties is to bind flashback structure to the psyche, either overtly, as is the case in the psychological melodrama, or covertly, as is the case in film noir, the stylized detective/crime film that emerged in this period. In both cases, the films' hermeneutic structures entail investigation or confession. The secrets of the past need to be told or found out.

The two structures overlap on many levels. Voice-over often plays a fundamental role in both genres, at least as a lead-in to the flashbacks. Though crime is usually thought to be the province of film noir, psychological melodramas also often concern crimes that are being investigated. The bleakness of tone, and sometimes even the high contrast lighting, the decor, and the camera angles associated with film noir are used in the psychological melodrama, so much so in the case of *Mildred Pierce*, for example, that this film is often considered as part of the film noir genre. As we shall see, a thematics of evil, particularly associated with women, informs both genres, giving many of the narratives a more or less misogynist aspect.

Yet there are important differences; the psychological melodrama is primarily a narrative centered on a female character whose psyche becomes the structural basis of the narrative, while film noir is centered on a male protagonist, often caught between parallel desires for a good woman and a *femme fatale*. The genres also differ in focus in ways that are directly linked to differences in the functions of their flashbacks. In film noir, there is an overall pessimism or fatalism to which the flashback structure greatly contributes, but in the psychological melodrama, the flashback is part of, or at least provides the promise of a cure or a resolution of problems. Film noir is a genre devoted to abjection; the psychological melodrama explores a stage of abjection through which it moves to a somewhat happy ending. Still, the deconstruction of the psychological melodrama that I shall undertake will show that this difference is less fundamental than it might first appear. The proposed cure is no more or less a confirmation of positive values than are the criminal arrests that end many noir narratives. In both cases, the films are fascinated with the psyche as an agent of evil, causing the destruction of self and of others.

The emergence of both the psychological melodrama and film noir in the United States in the forties might also be traced to another influence besides that of German expressionism as mentioned above. Many of the French films of the thirties, especially those known as "poetic realism," develop similar structures and stylistic traits. It does seem appropriate to examine these predecessors in French films of the thirties both for their possible influence, but, more importantly, for their differences from the American genres which use psychological flashbacks in the forties.

Two films in particular seem of interest here, Jean Renoir's *Le Crime de M. Lange* (1935) and Marcel Carné's *Le Jour se lève* (1939), both of which have scenarios on which Jacques Prévert collaborated (he is generally credited with the dialogue). The flashback in *Le Crime de M. Lange* functions as a variation on the trial and biography flashback patterns, while *Le Jour se lève* creates a similar structure and even uses similar characters, but with significant differences in tone.

Poetic Realism and Flashbacks in French Thirties Films

Le Crime de M. Lange is a fascinating variation on the trial flashback frame story, for rather than an official courtroom, Renoir's film represents a recounting of the crime in question to an ad hoc jury of peers in the dining room of an inn. Their judgment and verdict will determine whether they will turn M. Lange (René Lefevre) in to the authorities or aid him in his clandestine escape across the border. The story is narrated on Lange's behalf by the laundress, Valentine (Florelle), who is in love with him, while he sleeps in an adjoining room, unaware of this moment of perilous narration.

Once the film dissolves from this frame to the actual flashback narration, focalization is not rigorously maintained. The story of M. Lange's writing of *Arizona Jim* and the formation of the publishing collective to substitute for the corrupt practices of the publisher Batala (Jules Berry) are chronicled by a camera that is at once masterfully omniscient, yet almost participatory, whose framings and movements have their own marvelous and quite specific function. There is a consequence to the frame story, however; we are aware that somewhere within the tale Lange will commit a murder, for Valentine has already indicated that in a sense Lange is guilty as charged. We also know, however, that the story is intended as an argument in his defense and that Valentine has an emotional investment in Lange's exoneration. The frame story thus positions the audience in regard to the flashback narration, doubling the spectator's role by representing auditors within the fiction. It displaces the enigma of the story's outcome as it is unfolding to that of the group's judgment of Lange in the frame story—although romantic subplots do maintain a hermeneutic suspense within the embedded tale. The displaced enigma lends interest to the community's will to pursue its own creative capacities collectively and to defend them against oppressive and exploitative forces. As such, the film is structurally imbued with a Popular Front perspective of enthusiasm for collectives and worker control, urging its audience into a position of sympathy by the manner in which the tale is framed.[1] It is similar in some aspects of its structure to the biographical flashbacks of American films of the thirties and forties examined in the last chapter, although the thrust of the mythologies of these narratives is quite different, centered as they are on the American hero and legend of the great man. A large part of *Le Crime de M. Lange*'s unique historical interest is the specificity of its political geography, in the way it locates a collective venture in a French working-class district of residences built above small enterprises, a difference built formally through the means of filmic expression itself.[2]

If the flashback in *Le Crime de M. Lange* functions as a variation on the trial and biography flashback patterns, *Le Jour se lève* creates a similar structure and even uses similar characters, but with significant differences in tone. Again, knowledge of the murder is given the audience within the frame story, in this case as an intertitle: "Un Homme a tué, enfermé, assiégé dans une chambre. Il evoque les circonstances qui on fait de lui un meurtier" (A man has killed. Shut up and besieged in his room, he evokes the circumstances which made of him a murderer).[3] The flashbacks are offered as the subjective thoughts of this man, described as "assiégé par des mémoires" (besieged by memories). In a sense, the past is again offered to the audience as explanation and justification—though due to this trope of interior thought, the narrative does not present itself as trial as directly as does *Le Crime de M. Lange*. In fact, as the film progresses, the hero rejects the crowd's sympathy for him, misleading it as a perverse fascination and will not acknowledge his friends who urge him to surrender to be given a real trial. Rather than directly appeal to the audience's judgment, *Le Jour se lève* shows us a man who rejects anyone who tries to help or understand him; it problematizes judgment before the inner workings of a psyche, but, paradoxically, proposes to show us how psychic tension can reach such an explosive level, encouraging our sympathy.

The flashbacks in *Le Jour se lève* create a specific atmosphere of fatalism that is not present in *Le Crime de M. Lange*. This atmosphere, which has structural determinants in the film, is a strong prefiguration of the structure and tone of the American film noir flashback. The analysis of *Le Jour se lève,* then, will set up many of the principles and philosophical questions that are important to the psychological melodrama and the film noir. *Le Jour se lève* did open in New York, under the title *Daybreak,* but to less than completely enthusiastic reviews.[4] A remake, *The Long Night* (Anatole Litvak, 1947), starring Henry Fonda, Barbara Bel Geddes, Ann Dvorak, and Vincent Price, attests to the interest in *Le Jour se lève* by an emigré director known for film noir at the beginning of the peak period of production of this genre of film. Taken together, these facts suggest that the film was perhaps historically influential in the development of American film noir. Even if this were not the case, however, a comparison of structure between *Le Jour se lève* and the noir genre will prove intriguing.

The structure of Carné's film reverses cause and effect order, giving us the effect, murder, first, and the cause, an overwhelming psychic tension, following that. This reversal of cause and effect can function in different ways in different films; in *Le Crime de M. Lange* it encourages a sympathetic judgment, while in *Le Jour se lève* it is coupled with the increasingly pessimistic progression of events within the "causal" segments, the three flashbacks whose internal temporal structure is a linear progression. This is paralleled by the degeneration of the hero's mood as the sequences set in the present progress through the night towards dawn. This double temporal organization of the film and the object associations which link the present to the past are fascinating. These object associations are both an application of a notion of associative memory and a particular inscription of the object symbolism typical of poetic realism.

The first flashback presents the working-class and marginal *café-concert* milieu of the film's characters, which it will depict as an array of symbols. For example, François (Jean Gabin) is interrupted at work by the visit of a young florist's assistant, Françoise (Jacqueline Laurent), whose chance appearance at his factory bearing azaleas on their mutual saint's day begins his infatuation. In the protective suit of a sandblaster, he takes on the almost surreal appearance of the modern industrialized man, while Françoise appears as an ideal vision, innocence bedecked with flowers. There is a temporal jump to an evening three weeks after their initial meeting, when François visits Françoise in her room, a scene of sexual rebuff that introduces several of the objects that will circulate through other segments: the mirror, the teddy bear, and the broach. That same night François follows Françoise to a *café-concert* where he discovers that he has a rival, Valentin (Jules Berry), who performs with a dog act. The triangle is doubled when François begins talking with Clara (Arletty), Valentin's co-performer and mistress who has just walked out on Valentin. The flashback ends with a confrontation between Valentin and François, not over Françoise, but Clara.

The return to the present shows François at the window whose pane has been shattered by bullets. He imagines an escape by boat, and repeats a gesture, a look in the mirror while holding a teddy bear that he made in Françoise's room in the flashback just seen. He lights one cigarette from the butt of another, a figure of waiting that is joined in its temporal marking by exterior shots of the accumulated crowd. Clara appears in this crowd, pleading with the police not to shoot. The next flashback is introduced by a failed gesture to secure the interior against the encroaching exterior space. François moves his armoire to cover the door, then a bullet which hits the armoire swings open its door to reveal a picture of Françoise. François shuts the door, concealing the picture, but continues to stare at the armoire, as a shot of it dissolves to the armoire in the past, as he dresses to meet Clara.

This next flashback continues the narration of the uneasy substitution of Clara for Françoise, returning to the broach as visual symbol that will bridge the next transition between past and present. Valentin devises a complicated psychological torture for François in which he uses Clara's jealousy of Françoise to extract his revenge. Clara explains that the broach signifies Valentin's sexual conquest of a new woman, that is, Françoise, and she now gives a similar one to François as a souvenir of their affair which he has just ended.

In a transitional shot that brings us back to the present, François throws the broach at the armoire. Françoise shows up below in a state of hysterical delirium, and ironically, it is Clara who takes her away to comfort her. With the women bound in their anguish, the scene inside François's room reaches a state of degeneration. The last flashback covers the time from Valentin's entrance to François's room to the gunshot we have already heard, but not seen in the opening sequence. A final return to the present ends the film with François's suicide at the moment the police would have forced him out with tear gas.

Objects are charged with meanings by the film and their recurrence is key to the structure of the narrative. This circulation of symbolic objects can also be seen as forming the psychoanalytic narrative economy of the film. The objects provide a metaphorical rendering of imagination and the psyche in relationship to death. The room itself embodies the restriction of freedom through a limitation and closure of space. The response to this restriction is a withdrawal, an interiorization which has as its slogan François's shouts of "Fous-moi le paix" and "Fichez-moi le paix" ("leave me alone," but also "give me some peace"). The window, mirror, door, and armoire become symbolically rich elements of this architectonic shell. François's barricade against the world is destroyed element by element, first the shattering of the window, then the breaking of the mirror which fragments his self-image, then the penetration of bullets through the door and the armoire placed in front of it. The final penetration of his space, the ominous explosion of the tear gas occurs fruitlessly, next to his corpse. If these objects become elements of withdrawal, restriction, and annihilation of the self in the present siege of the room, in the flashback past they are imbued with other meanings. For example, the armoire shifts from being a treasure chest whose interior is decorated with photos of Françoise to being François's armor, shielding him from the police. There is a constant exchange and contrast between the meanings objects had in the past and the ones they acquire in this new context of the present. For example, when the bullet causes the door of the armoire to swing open, revealing the photos in the present, François slams it shut again, a metaphor for his attempt to not remember, which nonetheless triggers the next flashback. Each of the objects represents in microcosm this difference in two states of being, one in which there are restrictions, but also dreams and hope for change, and one in which hope is lost and death is inevitable. Objects also permit dialogues to be spun around them poetically, and here Prévert displays his similarity to his contemporary, Francis Ponge, in using the object as the basis for an ironic series of philosophical speculations.[5] The broach inspires an ongoing discourse on the relationship between objects and memory that thematizes the associative memory links the film makes in its flashback structure. This is especially developed in the double entendre in the French world "souvenir" (which means both a memory and a memento), which is developed in the dialogue between François and Clara. This word play reminds us of how objects become invested with memories, for in the Prévert's poetic condensation of "souvenir," objects and memories are inseparable.

The recurrences of these objects also operate abstractly to engage structures of repetition and return. These structures contribute to the fatalism of the film, a film in which the past and the present join on the "seam" of the murder, and once the murder is regained across this temporal fold, the suicide follows.

There are many possible readings of the gloomy poetics of a film like *Le Jour se lève*: as an expression of the mood of despair after the collapse of the Popular Front on the eve of World War II, as the migration into French culture of Nietzschean philosophy, or as Carné and Prévert's personal fascination with and reworking of the U.S. gangster film of the thirties.[6] All of these have some validity, and the historical thesis is particularly intriguing, given the marked difference in the films from the end of the thirties and those from earlier in the decade. What we will see, however, is that in addition to these readings *Le Jour se lève* prefigures the psychoanalytic narrative economy of the forties melodrama and the film noir in its configuration of a compulsive desire forcing repetitions that can only be stopped with death. In developing this trajectory of desire, Nietzschean thought and the Freudian theory of *Beyond the Pleasure Principle* are both represented, in ways we shall explore later in this chapter.

Psychological Melodrama in the Forties

In the forties, the melodrama adds to its increasing concern with the psychology of character an explicit psychoanalytic narrative dimension.[7] Perhaps the German films of the twenties that established such Freudian character studies achieved a delayed impact in the U.S. through an expatriate corps of screenwriters and directors—certainly the precedent had been set by the German films discussed in chapter two. Another explanation, though, is that Freud reached Hollywood in the forties in the same manner he did the rest of the country, through assimilation into popular literature and magazines, as well as by way of his followers' couches.

The latter argument, that there was a general cultural fascination with Freud's theories in America at that time, points not to the emigrés as an explanation for the prevalence of certain genres, but looks to melodrama's own history to explain why it became a suitable host corpus. We saw in chapter two, in the examination of Griffith's melodramas, how the emotional symbolization of character was presented through flashback memories. We can now see how these early melodramas prefigured the filmic components of the psychological melodrama. In *Enoch Arden* (1911), for instance, objects are used to symbolize a character's thoughts and memories. Enoch repeatedly handles a locket which is shown in close-up to contain a swatch of his infant son's hair. This object represents Enoch's longing for his family during his shipwrecked isolation on a desert island and, in a sense, it substitutes for an actual flashback by representing his thoughts of the past symbolically. A similar form of object symbolization of thought often appears as a transition to a flashback in the psychological melodrama. The extended flashback is an amplification of the psychological subjectivity of a character. Again, silent melodramas offer similar tableau representations of a character's psychology. Recall the earlier discussion of Griffith's *Birth of a Nation,* in the scene in which Margaret Cameron turns away from a romantic encounter with the Northerner, Phil Stoneman, to stare into the space of the past, a tableau image of one of her brothers dying in the arms of his superior Confederate Officer. We saw how this flashback poignantly indicated how memories of death and the historical opposition signified by the war intrude on the romantic scene, making it impossible for a glance claimed by the internal vision of the past to meet the other in the present. This use of flashbacks to fill the character psychology and of close-ups on objects symbolically saturated with psychological meanings can be seen as establishing both the iconography and the narrative structure from which the psychological melodrama will develop.

Further, the heritage of melodrama provides conventions for the psychological melodrama that exert a pressure to revamp Freudian concepts to fit their frame. Chance meetings, convoluted plots which intersect to reach, somehow, a clear denouement are melodramatic conventions that ensure that Freud is misread and abused in his incorporation in the Hollywood narrative. Not only are analysts presented as committing acts and performing interpretations one would hope no analyst would ever dream of, but dream interpretation, etiologies of complexes, neuroses, and psychoses are distorted for the purposes of dramatic revelatory scenes and film conventions of hermeneutic truth.

The psychological melodramas of the forties, such as *Mildred Pierce* (1945), *The Locket* (1946), *Leave Her to Heaven* (1946), *Possessed* (1946), and *Letter from an Unknown Woman* (1948) use concepts of memory and psychosis loosely borrowed from Freud. There is a particular fascination with the mechanism of psychic dysfunction, especially with disorders suffered by women, for which an historical explanation has been offered as a response to the largely female home-front audience of World War II and its reintegration into post-war domesticity.[8] All of the films mentioned use flashback narration to illustrate prevailing popular Freudianism. And while the evocation of Freudian notions was far more widespread than just the flashback melodrama, these films offer a particularly lucid example of how the hermeneutics of narrative hold out a single key to psychic disorder. This single key to truth renders the narrative revelation orderly *and* psychoanalytically false. But another reading of the embedded flashback form, a more deconstructive look at these films, indicates another psychoanalytical analysis of these films on a less obvious level. There is more given than is being directly said, there are concepts structured into these films that direct us away from their obviously stated narrative resolutions towards some surprisingly contemporary rereadings of Freud. The embedding of secrets, and specifically of secret objects or images, renders narratives that fold through absurd convolutions. These convolutions can themselves be seen as figuring the psychoanalytic concept of the "crypt" (as developed in Nicolas Abraham's and Maria Torok's *Cryptonymie,* with its introduction, "Fors," by Jacques Derrida).[9]

To see how this process works, and what it can tell us about the flashback, let's look at some length at John Brahm's *The Locket,* released by RKO at Christmas in 1946. The narrative begins and ends at the scene of a wedding. The flashback excursions into the past of the bride interrupt the ceremony, which finally never takes place. Three embedded flashbacks, each with its own narrator source, perform the disruptive narration, creating a pattern that, as was stated in a contemporaneous review, resembles a series of Chinese boxes.[10] The first flashback, the outermost shell, is formed by the narration of Nancy's former husband, a psychoanalyst, Dr. Blair (Brian Aherne). He gains access to the study of the husband-to-be, where he insists on telling the story of Nancy (Lorraine Day), the story of a "twisted personality that ruined three men's lives." Within this flashback, a second flashback is introduced when Clyde (Robert Mitchum), an artist, enters Dr. Blair's office shortly after Blair starts dating Nancy. He warns Blair about Nancy and informs him that, due to her schemes, a man's life is in danger. Within Clyde's narration is Nancy's own flashback narration of her childhood memories. The heroine's childhood is at the core of the puzzle, the central zone that the narrative hits dead center. Inside the male narrations of each of the traumatic romances with Nancy is the revelation of Nancy as an evil harbinger of doom. Inside Nancy's own narration is the revelation of the locket. Discussion of the flashbacks in *The Locket* entail the way this symbol functions in the film.

Locket—the title and object can be seen as the "word-thing" in Abraham and Torok's meaning of that term, since the locket lies at the center of encryptment and circulates as symbol affecting all other symbolization. As a word, as the title of the film, "locket" is perhaps an admonition, perhaps a command—"Lock it." What is it that needs to be locked? Libido as in the "IT girl," or by way of the French, *Ça?* The film will reinforce such interpretations by presenting in its final scenes an image of a Pandora's box. In the closing segments, as Nancy prepares for the wedding ceremony, she accidentally overturns a music box, setting off an ominous tune. Once released, the tune will not go away, even after Nancy once again closes the box. It returns to overwhelm the wedding march on a sound track that has come to symbolize Nancy's subjective state. This haunting of the music from the box precipitates Nancy's collapse into madness. If the tune persists here, it is because it is returning from the past, from the encrypted center of the film, as it was the same tune that came from another music box during the traumatic childhood scene Nancy relates in her flashback. Nancy is presented as always unable to lock it; her desires (for jewels, for class ascendancy, and as we shall see, for the brother) are her undoing.

As object, as thing, the locket is never unlocked. A gold heart on a chain with a diamond embedded on it, the locket remains closed throughout the entire film, yet what it contains of signification remains only partially a mystery, as its symbolization process invades other sequences, words, objects. Its diamond ornament is a mark of value that exceeds both the exchange value and the sentimental value with which the narrative designates the locket. The locket has a gem stone at its heart to mark its precious quality of impenetrability. This quality slides over to Nancy's character as well, creating a metaphorical link between the locket and Nancy, as she deceives all around her, covering her interior turmoil with a seductively decorative exterior. The publicity ads and posters for the film depicted the heroine surrealistically wearing an oversize locket bound to her forehead with large chains. The locket is a lock on Nancy's psyche, an emblem for her state of emotional bondage.

The locket is also a lock for the filmic chain. For as the locket circulates in the narrative, it functions as a device in formalist terms to bind sequences and provide closure. The locket is a lock. But as we have already seen, the locket is a hermeneutic key. Lock and key are joined in a single figure; the locket is both concerned with disclosing and remaining sealed. The locket is both lock and key, for the film cannot really answer its hermeneutic question, "What is wrong with Nancy?," even though it offers the story of the locket as the answer. The locket symbolizes both a structural and an ideological dimension, as it resonates with the questions, "What is the nature of women?"/What do women want?" Freudian terms might suggest an interpretation of the locket as a typical symbol of dreams; though all dream symbols have multiple interpretations, Freud notes that the female genitals are symbolically represented by objects enclosing a hollow space which can take something into it.[11] In *The Locket,* the object is given to the child Nancy by her best (girl) friend, then taken away by the stern mother of that friend. It is later given to that same girl when she has reached adulthood by the same mother, but now on the occasion of the young woman's marriage to the mother's son. This suggests a female coming-of-age parable of heterosexuality as the sanctioned act, an element as we shall see, but not the whole range of meanings the locket suggests. Like all of Freud's suggestions about typical symbols, this association with female genitalia needs contextualization through consideration of the specific exchanges the locket undergoes.

To explore this further, let's trace the appearances of the locket in the film. It first appears in Nancy's flashback. The flashback with Nancy seated with her lover, Clyde, in an alcove of his loft. He has discovered Nancy's theft of a diamond bracelet at a private exhibition of his work, and demands an explanation. As Clyde and Nancy are shown in a shadowy, dark two shot, Clyde's voice-over says sardonically, "I was sure Nancy would think of something to say," introducing the flashback to follow as possibly a prevarication meant to elicit sympathy. This note of cynicism is underscored ironically with a movement of the camera forward into a tight close-up on Nancy's handkerchief moving up to daub her cheek. The image then dissolves into the flashback of Nancy as a young girl, narrating a series of bizarrely depicted events involving the gift of the locket, the parental retraction of the gift, the loss of the locket, its accidental rediscovery, and Nancy's forced, false confession that she stole the locket. Within this series of events are representations that startle through excess. When the wealthy Willis daughter, Karen, gives Nancy the locket, the two girls, almost identical in looks, are shown embracing in a closet, binding their exchange with a promise of eternal fidelity. When the sinisterly thin and darkly dressed Mrs. Willis literally shakes a confession out of Nancy, the music box falls open, underscoring the horrific violence of this scene of torture. Thus the evil mother (named Willis), the definitive barrier of class difference, and the interruption of childhood homosexuality are the elements surrounding the gift and the loss of the locket. The locket operates within the symbolic code of narrative to inscribe the paradigms of exchange, barriers, sexuality, and class opposition.

The locket reappears later as the gift of Mrs. Willis to Nancy on her wedding day at the close of the film, when Dr. Blair's narration has failed to halt the marriage ceremony of Nancy and John Willis. The evil mother has become benevolent, the sister has become a phantom, having died somewhere in between the flashbacks, her death nowhere represented in the film. We only have Mrs. Willis kissing Nancy and presenting her with her deceased daughter's locket, an act which precipitates Nancy's breakdown depicted by subjective high angles of the floor, faces superimposed on the carpet, voices from the past echoing on the sound track, coupled with the recurrence on the music box turn. This climactic scene of psychic dissolution is the reversal of the elements of Nancy's childhood flashback, with Nancy replacing the sister, marrying the brother, with the locket being given instead of taken away.

Kleptomania, the obsessive impulse to steal when there is no desire for the object or economic gain, is represented by the film as one of Nancy's mental disorders, as she steals other jewelry apparently to substitute for the missing locket. Yet this narrative foray into psychoanalytical character development is particularly unconvincing. To call Nancy's thefts of a diamond bracelet at the art opening and of a royal jewel called the St. Anne's locket from an evacuated British museum during World War II "kleptomania" is to engage in grand larceny of the symbolic order. Her thefts of objects may be meant to indicate the desire to steal love, but as the film unfolds, her purloined jewelry is also an implicit displacement of a desire for class ascendancy, as the values of the jewels and the class context augment progressively. The housekeeper's daughter eventually will take a crown jewel, and later crown that victory with a marriage into the family for which her mother was a servant. The film clouds its psychoanalytical pretext by introducing symbols it wishes to maneuver within a calculated economic representation. Each of these two jewel thefts also introduces us to other important aspects of *The Locket*'s cryptonomy. One of the points Derrida makes about the crypt in his essay, "Fors," is that it is not a metaphor but a topography, a connection forged between topoi, death, and the cipher. In this context the two theft scenes are the mise-en-scene of this topography, where place, deaths, and anasemic signs meet. Banner's penthouse apartment presents an elaborate modern architectural space to develop an architectonics of looking, display, desire, theft, discovery.

Two scenes occur there: the first is the art exposition in which Clyde's portrait of Nancy receives first prize at the moment an announcement is made that a diamond bracelet was stolen. The portrait looms over these scenes as an ominous figure of vision, for it is entitled "Cassandra" (a reference to the *Iliad,* where the prophetess Cassandra, daughter of Priam, is fated by Apollo never to be believed). The painting is in the style of Tamara de Lempicka, a mixture of realism, surrealism, and art deco; its most noticeable feature is the lack of seeing eyes, an absence represented by opaque orbs. The painting is a cipher, and, as such, a supplement for the locket; its absent eyes and name take it out of the realm of portrait. It becomes both a non-entity and a secret code establishing the problems of witnessing, foreseeing, telling the truth or telling lies, applicable not only to Nancy, but to the male narrators, Clyde and Dr. Blair as well.

Having established the cipher and the theft in this place, the film veers off into Nancy's flashback to explain her stealing of the bracelet before returning to the apartment site for a scene in which Clyde witnesses, from the corridor, Nancy's exit after she has murdered Mr. Banner and left evidence that will incriminate the butler. (One is reminded here not so much of the game of melodrama but rather that of the detective serial that slips into surrealism, as in Louis Feuillade's *Fantomas* (1913–1914) and of Fritz Lang's *Dr. Mabuse* trilogy (1922, 1932, 1961), as the conjunction of place, cipher, and death opens a narrative space whose borders are the crypt.) Clyde is a witness who has in this portrait of Nancy as Cassandra unwittingly provided the film with his self-portrait, for as this cipher shifts to become the portrait of the artist, its references suddenly make more sense. It is Clyde whose vision will not be believed, as Nancy can dismiss it through verbal deflection, as she first says to Clyde "it's neurotic to be jealous of a dead man," and later to Dr. Blair as she responds when confronted with Clyde's story of the theft and murder, "You are not a psychiatrist if you don't know the truth from lies—you're just a lovesick quack." Strange enunciations, narratively true, in the Barthesian sense of equivocation, these words are beside the point, but somehow they manage to perform for Nancy, covering her own guilt by refracting her mental disorder onto the others.[12] Clyde has no recourse but an architectural suicide, throwing himself out of the window of the psychiatrist's high-rise office, leaving behind the Cassandra portrait as his suicide note. The film represents Nancy's cryptonomy through actions in the present rather than the past; it creates a horror story emanating from the crypt, one which like a patient's dreams reworks the elements of the crypt and its symbolizations in a fantasy context.

This fantasy quality to the narrative is even more pronounced in the second jewel theft, narrated in the second half of Dr. Blair's flashback. As the image depicts London flickering with the bombs of World War II, Dr. Blair tells of Nancy helping him with his work. But the expected images of wartime hospitals, shell-shock victims, war neurosis are never shown; instead, he narrates a trip of supposed respite from psychiatric work, a trip to the country where a chateau with its basement jewel museum evacuated from London serves as the site of Nancy's most daring theft. An incident at a party at the chateau reinforces Dr. Blair's faith in Nancy before the theft occurs—when their hostess's necklace accidentally slips off, Nancy picks it up to return it. This dissimulative act covers Nancy's subsequent theft of the St. Anne's locket whose absence is discovered just before Blair's return to their work in London. It is in the aftermath of a bombing raid that reduces their house to rubble that Dr. Blair learns of Nancy's theft of this royal locket, when he finds among the debris, a jewel box, which opens to display Nancy's considerable hoard, including this most precious jewel. To open a box amidst debris and to find yet another locket—the film has represented the psychiatrist, the lovesick quack, finding out about a woman's psyche. The figuration here is delirious—it dissolves from a close-up of Nancy into a graphic match on a close-up of the Cassandra portrait. The locket returns to give way to itself as cryptic cipher. It is at this point that we must ask what, in its attempt to give figuration to psychology in melodrama, is *The Locket* disfiguring, in terms of the psyche, women, and society?

In the case of the Wolf Man, the formation of the crypt in the psyche was initiated by an incestuous love of the sister, a traumatic misrecognition of the primal scene, an expansive fear of castration, and, finally, the inability to mourn the loss of the sister after her suicide and the father after his death.[13] The inability to introject the lost sister resulted in the incorporation in the crypt of the sister as a phantom of the self, haunting the self.

The Locket gives Nancy some personal history parallel to the Wolf Man's. We are told her father died three months before the time of the childhood locket incident recounted in the flashback, about the same time that Karen's brother left to go to boarding school. These two male absences, along with the Willis father who is never mentioned, place the Nancy-Karen closet vows and the conflict with the evil mother in a new context—but this is a context somehow outside the film's own architecture. For it does not want to, nor could it ever perform or represent the performance of a psychoanalysis of Nancy who is herself a cipher in the text. The film's desire is elsewhere, to maintain the crypt, to seal the architectonics of narrative with its own closure, one that will not let theories penetrate or pry open its cryptic stratagems. We have seen some of the armature through which the film protects its own cryptic structure, but there is another dimension to the seal. The caulking on the crypt is provided by mythologies that the film annexes so that it can escape the intrusion of science and remain in the realm of fiction. One such mythological base is the realm of the supernatural, introduced in the opening sequence of the wedding, prior to the flashbacks. Here we get first the telling of Nancy's fortune by her horoscope, where she is presented as "loyal, generous, self-sacrificing, a devoted friend and an ideal marriage partner, tolerant, kind, clear-speaking and dependable." These positive traits are interrupted by the appearance of Dr. Blair; after he leaves for John Willis's study, a series of bad qualities follows. Nancy is astrologically marked as also "exceedingly cruel, selfish and destructive." This astrological fatalism is reinforced when Dr. Blair uses his knowledge of Nancy's birth date, November 3, to gain credibility in John Willis's mind, so that the husband-to-be will hear his stories of Nancy's ruinous personality. The illogic of this knowledge of a date of birth as proof of authentic knowledge of Nancy is obvious—any stranger could have found out when Nancy was born from a birth announcement, a driver's license, or even by overhearing an astrologer. But in the mythologies generated by the film, knowing Nancy's birth date, knowing that she is a Scorpio, is knowing all. For the film is only using its references to the psyche to project a stronger fatalism and fear of women and the underclass.

It whispers strangely encoded messages from its postwar vantage point of 1946, a point of view from history that is marked by the rubble to which the London home is reduced after war's bombings. It whispers a fear of women, ignoring that men were the primary custodians of psychic crypts, while women were the professional nurturers and mourners in a world perverted by fascism. The film inverts these roles, and scapegoats women as the evil in the world, a cryptic message it stamps on their foreheads like a scarlet A. As a result of this manipulation of the supernatural for ideological ends, the film distorts its psychoanalytic premises.

Leave Her to Heaven, directed by John Stahl for Fox in 1946, uses a flashback structure that is far less intricate than that of *The Locket,* but equally dark in its vision of a mentally disturbed, seductive murderess filtered through a frame structure of male narrators.[14] The flashback is introduced by a conversation between two men, concerning the return of Dick (Cornell Wilde) after two years of prison to his lake home in Maine. As Dick is seen paddling away in his canoe, one of the men, who was Dick's defense lawyer, offers us the story that "couldn't be told in court—I was the only one who knew the whole story."

What ensues is a narrative with a female protagonist, Ellen (Gene Tierney), whose love for Dick, whom she eventually marries, is coupled with a jealousy that develops into a neurotic obsession. The film supplies a psychoanalytic commentary on Ellen, through pronouncements on Ellen's character by her mother and sister, as well as Ellen's own admissions. Ellen is said to be overly fond (incestuously in love) with her father.

The two violent incidents, Ellen's drowning of Dick's handicapped younger brother and her abortion, accomplished by throwing herself down a flight of stairs, are depicted in ways that emphasize Ellen's careful and emotionless planning of these acts. The lawyer suggests that even Ellen's own death from an overdose of sleeping pills was a calculated scheme to destroy Ruth and Dick's happiness from beyond the grave. The flashback, presented as the evidence withheld at the trial, has as its strategy to "argue" that Ellen is evil. The ideological similarity to *The Locket* is striking; the crucial events that condemn Ellen in this account are obviously beyond the knowledge of the narrator or any of his possible sources, Dick or Ruth. It is possible to imagine a counter-narrative, especially since Ellen's worst fears of being replaced by Ruth are actuated by the ending following the flashback. Yet the flashback structure bears detailed witness to the deviant behavior of Ellen, foreclosing any sympathy with her. The audience is conditioned by the filmwork not to question the lawyer's account and other elements of the mise-en-scene (Ellen's cold stare and the frenetic funeral ride ritual in memory of her father, for instance, serve to enforce the psychoanalytic interpretation suggested within the film itself). However, if we address the film's cryptic mythology, those elements act as indices of the text's truth being stretched to cover its ideological structures a bit too tautly.

As excesses, these flamboyant images, offered as a male exchange, extra-legally, without the authority of first-person witnessing, point to the ideological frame that constructs the film itself.

The Locket and *Leave Her to Heaven* use their flashback exploration of the female psyche as a contemporary reinscription of an evil female protagonist, validating the male frame of narration through the force of the filmic image. The genre of the psychological melodrama can lend itself to the inverse operation, however, during roughly the same historic period: the incursion into the past as a means of sympathetic exploration of the female psyche and position in society. It is important to bear in mind, though, that this operation is always filled with contradictions and strategies of containment during this period in narrative film history.

Take, for example, the flashback narration of *Letter from an Unknown Woman* (Max Ophuls, 1948). Here the flashback is offered as the filmic rendering of a woman's letter sent to a former lover after her death; the letter itself provides the voice-over narration. Though it begins, "By the time you read this I'll be dead," the voice that is heard is that of Lisa (Joan Fontaine) the character who has written these words, not the man, Stefan (Louis Jourdain), to whom they are addressed and who is reading them. Lisa's speaking voice ironically asserts desire and self-expression even as it chronicles the years of repression of that voice. Death is the price that ironically allows the secret of a female's desire to be told. The film offers its flashback as a lesson to the male character who first does not notice, then later cannot remember Lisa. It re-establishes the memory of the man, who, until he reads her letter, is ignorant of the depth of her obsession with him and of the birth of their son after their encounter, one that remained for him the affair of a single evening. Re-establishes, because after the flashback that illustrates her letter unfolds, Stefan has his own flashback, a brief series of images from the past we have just seen, now presented as a montage in reverse order.

Although this film has been seen by others as the epitome of a male-oriented Hollywood cinema, for the way it represents the woman as object of spectacle and the gaze, and as a lost object, confined to the past, unknown, I believe there is simultaneously another aspect to the film, in direct contradiction to this pattern.[15] There is a sense in which the letter, the fictional written text, gives us a female narrator who is in fact making herself known, undoing a voyeuristic passivity of the past by voicing her history, even though that history was one of conforming perfectly to the role of woman as absent and blocked from expressing her desire. These contradictions can be traced back to the text of Stefan Zweig, published in 1924, from which the film is adapted. Zweig focuses a psychoanalytical eye on his heroine, whom he sets in 1890. The voice he creates for her attempts to reveal socio-psychological oppression. His imagery is particularly impressive in terms of Jacques Lacan's later theorization of the feminine relationship to desire, that of entrapment as the object of the desire of the Other.[16] Even though the film's ending is transformed to a much more decisive conclusion, Stefan's inevitable death in a dual (rather than the pensive regard on the part of Stefan that ends the novel), Ophuls's lyrical descriptive camera throughout creates images of watching, chance meetings, and the circularity of an inexpressible desire. These images invite theoretical speculation, offering the voice of the woman as a commentary on the great symbolic tension of desire, admissable only as it is lost, this loss caught in the two impending deaths, hers and Stefan's, and already symbolized in the death of their son. As we shall see in the next section, once the Hollywood film really attempts to represent the female psyche with a subjective voice and an internal focalization the system of representation changes—if only so far as to represent structurally, the internal contradictions between the woman's voice and her image, articulated across the gap of two different temporalities, past and present.

Female Insanity and the Gender Focalization of Memory

Some psychological melodramas such as *Possessed,* directed by Curtis Bernhardt for Warner's in 1947, aim to represent the memory processes of the disturbed psyche of their heroines. However, *Possessed* has its own crypt to protect. The flashback structuration is a concealed compromise between two different mimetic aims on one hand and Hollywood conventions of storytelling and filmmaking on the other. On one level, the film is meant to be understood as a psychotic patient's memory. Its flashback memory structure is crucial since it allows for the segmentation of the narration into three "sessions," and the positioning of the audience as "listening" with a psychoanalytic regard, like the patient's doctors represented in the fiction. However, once the dissolve takes us inside the flashbacks, the concern with memory is abandoned as a mimetic goal in favor of a re-experiencing of the descent into madness. This reliving of the past is in turn compromised by the conventional imperatives of Hollywood film narration. Even so, the subjective experience of the woman reacting to her distorted vision of the surrounding world is given a mimetic rendering through the inclusion of both auditory and visual hallucinations. Contained in this complex narrational compromise is a view of female madness nearly as warped as that of *The Locket,* bent out of shape both by ideological premises and the effects of the compromise strategy itself.

The film opens with images of a woman lost, "possessed" by desire, absent from the present in which she circulates, as we see Louise Howell (Joan Crawford) roaming the streets in a distracted state. She looks about her for a man whose name, "David," she addresses to strangers on the street. A high angle on her laid out on a hospital cart introduces us to her introduction into medical care. For a moment, we are asked to identify visually with her situation, as we see the path of this cart from her point of view, in a subjective low angle of the hospital ceiling. With the return to the high angle on her, the doctors who are examining her announce that she has drifted into a coma and should be taken to "psycho."

"Psycho" turns out to be not merely an element of hospital jargon; it is reiterated by a wall plaque indicating this ward. It serves as a sign for the bizarre vision of psychoanalysis that the film conveys. While the psychoanalytic treatment itself is the motivational source of the flashbacks, it is implausibly represented as a drug-induced magic that can extract an explanatory story. Three sessions produce three episodes within a linear narration of the past, a coherent retelling by the patient of the past years of her life. "Narcosynthesis" is the term given to the injection that will make the patient, diagnosed as in a catatonic stupor and suffering from complete "mutism," talk.

As Louise Howell first begins her verbal narration, her enunciation is markedly incoherent. She mumbles the phrases, "in Los Angeles to get away from them, mustn't ever know, I want to disappear." The phrases are fragmented, concealing as much as they reveal. Like the language of psychotics, words are generated that conceal other words that must remain unsaid. And the film form soon invites the spectator into further participation in Louise's mental state by presenting her auditory fantasy as the reality of the sound track. We hear the sound of a Schumann sonata that she is supposedly imagining, while her plea to "make them play it softer," results in the volume being lowered. This rendering of an auditory phantasm in conjunction with the disjunct and relatively opaque verbal narration serves as the film's transition into the first flashback. Yet within the flashback, the filmic rendering of Louise's verbalization of her memories is virtually indistinguishable from other Hollywood films. Continuity supplants the awkward phrases of a jarred psyche; the film images fill in, creating a misleading non-disjunction. If the audience is placed in a position parallel to Louise's doctors, allowed to analyze her story, we do so without access to her language, receiving only a series of events that are to be taken as the causal factors and signs of her deteriorating mental condition. Each scene is offered as part of an explanation, with occasional subjective hallucinations that provide a more direct access to Louise's thought processes.

It is significant that the first such symbolic narrative event is the loss of David Sutton (Van Heflin) as lover. In a scene in David's lakeside house, Louise is shown dressing after their afternoon swim, a discreet double entendre that the film uses to suggest their sexual activities. David announces the end of their relationship, as his response to her bold declaration of love and possessive desire, "I want a monopoly on you." A boatride across the lake is the means by which David returns Louise to her employer's house, depositing her on the dock. It is to this same dock that David returns in a later sequence after having gone to Canada on a business venture financed by Louise's boss, Dean Graham (Raymond Massey). The intervening sequences establish Louise's position as private nurse to Graham's invalid wife who suffers from jealous fantasies of her husband's infidelity with Louise. David's return evokes Louise's humiliating supplication for his attention, alternating with vicious threats and accusations. Her manner of speaking becomes increasingly agitated, manic, until the sequence ends with an image of turbulence on the water as David once again "leaves." This dissolves to Louise in the present, once again calling "David."

The loss of David is thus repeated with the first flashback, presented both times in conjunction with the dock and water imagery. This repetition is characteristic of dream structure; the film, like a dream, is doubling its representation, compulsively marking the loss of the man as a symbolic cause of Louise's psychosis. The return to the present shows Louise once again rambling, voicing paranoid delusions. The doctors begin their diagnosis on the basis of the narrative we have just "heard." They call it the "beginnings of a persecution complex" and a "schizoid detachment" that will grow nourished by her "obsessions." While Louise's verbal narration in the present is a disjointed discourse that might suggest possible paranoia or schizophrenia, the film's audience must ignore the contradictions imposed by the convention of the coherent flashback storytelling in order to accept this diagnosis. On the other hand, analysis of the sequences as suggested above give us a different perspective on Louise, as a woman, not yet psychotic, but with neurotic tendencies who is deeply marked by loss.

The water imagery continues to provide the liaisons between past and present, as well as linking the various narrative threads within the flashbacks. As a nurse pours a glass of water for Louise in the present, the camera tracks into a close-up on the glass, and a superimposition of waves accompanies Louise's return to her narration of the past. "It was black then, cold and black" is the phrase that initiates the dissolve to an image of the water at night by the Grahams' dock, leading up to another traumatic event in the past, the investigation of Mrs. Graham's death by drowning, questionably a suicide.

Mrs. Graham's death and David's rejection of Louise are linked by the film through water imagery and location. This visual link suggests the link of the two events in the etiology of Louise's illness. This link is further reinforced by the entrance into the narrative of the Grahams' daughter, Carol, who has been away at school, as the voice of accusation. Carol suggests that Louise, who will replace her mother by marrying her father, was responsible for her mother's murder. The ironic incestuous liaisons will continue to cross and knot throughout the remaining flashback narration, as Carol then replaces Louise as David's love object, their first encounter taking place at Louise's wedding to Dean Graham. Louise eventually assumes this connection as the basis of her hallucinatory reality, which the film expresses by renewed representation of her subjective auditory fantasies, adding visual fantasy enactment to express an even worsening condition.

These subjectively rendered hallucinations prepare a context for the final scene of the flashback narration, that in which Louise murders David; having witnessed such completely convincing fantasies generated by Louise's psyche, the audience is led to experience her act of murder as undifferentiated from hallucination, and equally motivated by an unconscious that she does not control.

After Louise shoots David at point blank range, a dissolve blends a low angle on her firing the gun to a close-up of her in the hospital bed screaming, "David, I killed him." This dissolve marks the conjunction of the climax of the flashback narrative, the murder, with the climactic revelation of the direct cause of Louise's amnesia and catatonia, a double climax, which maximizes dramatic impact. However, Louise will no longer be aware of her enunciation once she is no longer under a magical narcosynthetic narrational spell. The denouement then has the task of guarding the crypt of this narrational compromise intact. The doctor's explanation to Dean Graham gives us both the clinical diagnosis "psychosis," and a "literary" explanation of Louise as a "person possessed of the devil," a tag which emphasizes the religious reference inherent in the title "Possessed." Like astrology and fate in *The Locket,* this devil-possession metaphor secures the fictional mode against too serious an analysis of its premises. Narcosynthesis is the magic Hollywood potion that can give us a story from a subject who could not possibly remember it the way it is told. Our narrator is stripped of her own narration. Each return to the present shows her doctors categorizing and labeling her mental condition. It is up to the viewer to derive a reading of Louise's loss, fear, and guilt, as well as her similarity to both Mrs. Graham and Carol, which the filmwork does suggest and which has deeper cultural resonances.

Possessed is a film that divides in two along the axis of its narrational strategy, a division marked by opposing ways of seeing the film. The view that contains a woman's insanity within the confines of pseudo-psychoanalytic, and finally conventionally male, point of view dominates—if one accepts the film's doctors and the impossible compromise narration uncritically. But the moment one crosses out any truth value assigned itself by this overlaid discourse, another film emerges from within the contradictions and from the subtle graphic signs of the dissolves and the patterns of repetition within the flashback narrative structure. In this "other" film, one hears more of Louise's subjective experience, more of the functioning of the unconscious, more of the social circumstances that limit a woman's options to deviant behaviors. Implicitly, *Possessed* exposes some of what might possess a female psyche to strike out with violence, even though it simultaneously covers that knowledge with structural and discursive encasements whose function it is to regulate and thus obfuscate this view of the female unconscious. This contradiction is ideologically determined, a cultural trace of a society that cannot ignore a problem, nor face it honestly and analytically.

What does a film adaptation do with a story of female mental breakdown that is narrated exclusively from the point of view of the female protagonist? The stream-of-consciousness voice of the heroine that dominates Mary Jane Ward's novel, *The Snake Pit,* is utilized in the film of the same name (starring Olivia de Havilland and directed by Anatole Litvak for Fox in 1948) as an intermittent voice-over commentary. This voice-over occurs not only over the two flashback sequences Virginia narrates, but also in the sequences in the present, as a sounded interior monologue, accompanying shots of her looking quixotically at her surroundings and experiences in the mental hospital in which the action takes place. This narrative technique, one which breaks into the flow of events with a superimposed commentary, lends the film a greater degree of fragmentation than most Hollywood films, accentuated by the scattered and contradictory patterns of the thoughts thus articulated. Though fragmented, the female voice in its state of "madness" often attains a troubled lucidity, for Virginia's observations often display an ironic and perceptive intelligence.

Despite this innovative narration, the structure of the narrative remains quite similar to the other films in this sub-genre of the flashback psychological melodrama, especially to that of *Possessed*. As in the case of that film, the patient's forgotten past is recovered in a series of flashbacks that represent her talks with a psychiatrist, again with the help of a truth serum, and, in this film, shock treatments as well. However, in *Possessed* we noted that although the patient's voice initially was marked as struggling to remember and to tell its story coherently, this troubled voice gave way to an orderly filmic narrative within the flashbacks. In *The Snake Pit,* the mode of narration bears much greater witness to the patient's state of mental confusion; not only does the voice remain active throughout as a voice-over, but also the order of events narrated reflects the patient's mental disorder. The narration is not simply chronological, but selects instances from the past in a way that is much more consonant with memory processes, especially those of individuals whose memories are disturbed by a nervous and psychological repression. This selection and reordering process does more than increase the verisimilitude of the film. It becomes, as we shall see, highly significant in the symbolic schema of the film.

Another difference in the narrative form of *The Snake Pit* is that it gives much more amplitude to the sequences in the present. Virginia's daily life in the hospital is elaborately chronicled. Also, one of the didactic points the film makes is that state hospital doctors are limited in the time they can spend with each patient. As all the flashbacks are products of Dr. Kik's (Leo Glenn) treatment (even those of her husband, Robert [Mark Stevens] and Kik himself) the film presents these revelations of the past as isolated moments in a tenacious mental illness whose cure is hampered by limited personal attention and contravened by a harsh and insensitive institutional environment.

One of the changes the film makes in the narrative it adapts from Lowe's book is to give two of the flashbacks to male characters. Whereas the novel is narrated entirely in the first person, the first and last flashbacks are the focalization of, respectively, Robert and her doctor. The film uses this male frame of husband and male analyst to transform the ideological critique implicit in the novel.

Robert's flashback is the most linear and in a sense, uncomplicated. It narrates the period from his first meeting Virginia, through their marriage and the point where she began acting strangely and then suddenly disappeared. What is striking is how much his voice-over rendition of their romance and marriage sounds film noir in style. For example, he tells of seeing her standing in front of the concert hall at which they first met after a six-month hiatus in their courtship (she had simply vanished). The shot of her shows her lighting a cigarette on the street, and his first recognition is "of that same lighting of a cigarette." Then he says that even if her secret was murder, he doesn't care. This stylistic flourish in Robert's narration is part of a series of elements that the otherwise didactic film never remarks upon. It never addresses the image of Virginia screaming at her husband, "You can't make me belong to you—I can't love anybody," followed by a subjective close-up from her point of view of a knife. Such images are part of a doubling that occurs between the directed interpretation of the flashbacks controlled by the voice of Dr. Kik and other meanings embedded in the imagery; the neglect that they receive once introduced in the narrative is part of the avoidance of any direct discussion of the sexual politics of both marriage and psychiatry in the post-war period, an avoidance that is consistent throughout the film, even though the imagery is loaded with the material for such an analysis.

The second flashback, Virginia's remembrances under the truth serum, are more complex. First she remembers needing to catch the train by five o'clock on the day she leaves Robert; her memory appears to begin just where Robert's ends, and for a moment we expect the two first flashbacks to be contiguous chronologies. However, this necessity to rush is then associated with another, earlier memory of hurrying to be ready for a date with Gordon, her steady boyfriend when she was an adolescent living with her parents. Her flashback takes us back to a point earlier in time than did the previous flashback, to a point that we soon surmise is causally linked to her flight from her marriage which preceded and precipitated the nervous breakdown. Initially the flashback is concerned with the anxiety about keeping Gordon waiting— which gets localized on tying a bow in her hair, an act which Gordon finally does for her. In presenting this bow incident, Virginia associates Gordon's fixing her bow to her father's similar gesture, a connection that anticipates the structure of the next flashback. There is an ellipsis to later in this same evening when Gordon proposes and she responds first distractedly, then symptomatically, asking to be taken home on account of illness. This leads to a remembrance that is in fact a reexperiencing; on the way home Gordon is killed in a car crash. Throughout the flashback, Dr. Kik's commentary intervenes making interpretative suggestions. Unlike the doctors in *Possessed* who refrain from commentary until the end, at which point their role is minimal, Kik explicates the narrative structure and symbolism of the flashbacks. The film offers a key to its own crypt, telling us that its structure bears another level of meaning. However, the film pursues only one interpretation of this reordering, therefore maintaining itself within a traditional mode of narration.

Virginia's next flashback actually inserts an earlier moment in the midst of the narration of a single incident told in two parts. This insert is disruptive enough to make the flashback appear to be a bracket sequence in which three distinct moments are grouped together. The first is a childhood incident in which she meets her mother's disapproval for trading her new doll for her playmate's. This segment ends with her certainty that her father will let her keep the doll she prefers. The next segment jumps to another incident involving her father and a doll, one that occurred when she was much younger. Her father wins a prize for her at a shooting gallery and she selects a soldier doll that reminds her of a photo of her father in uniform. The third segment of this bracket flashback is to the scene which took place following the first segment, that is when her father responded to the incident with the doll, but not in the manner she had hoped. He asked her to obey her mother, then sends her away from the dinner table to her room when her refusal becomes annoying. Her response as a child in the flashback was to smash the soldier doll. The flashback jumps ahead to a doctor arriving to attend her father's illness and ends with a scene of her standing in the rain with her mother at her father's funeral; over this image her voice-over leaps forward to tell us that her mother remarried and then disliked her for reminding her of her dead husband. This bracket flashback sets up both dolls as symbols of the Virginia's childhood relations to her parents. Dr. Kik responds to the connection between smashing the doll and the father's death by saying, "wishes sometimes seem to come through." Kik, however, does not offer an analysis of the doll imagery that connects these separate achronological incidents. The achronological recounting makes this connection appear to be hidden to Virginia (and perhaps to the spectator) so that the symbolic connections can be made by Kik in the next flashback.

The fourth flashback is another bracket configuration, this time more of a series of illustrations of Dr. Kik's explanation in which he sites scenes told him in the other flashbacks. The ordering of these scenes is his contribution, for now they appear in a comparative order that helps Kik make his analysis clear. The first segment is actually a hypothetical flashback illustrating the doctor's theory that "It may have started when you were a few weeks old, you were hungry and weren't fed." It is illustrated by a close-up of a baby crying, followed by a shot of Virginia's mother putting her to bed as a young girl, but refusing to give her a second goodnight kiss. After the doctor says that her mother's distance made her turn to her father, we see the scene at the dinner table when Virginia refuses to give back the doll, her father won't take her side, and Virginia is sent up to her room. This is coupled with the return to the flashback of Virginia as a child smashing her doll. Similarly, the point that Gordon was like Virginia's father and therefore a father replacement is illustrated with flashbacks of them both commanding situations in which they address Virginia: the father is calling Virginia from the stairs, whereas Gordon at the door reminds her that she is late for their date. This establishes the background for the doctor's contention that Virginia's feeling of guilt at the death of Gordon is linked to her feeling that she killed her father by smashing the doll and wishing him dead.

The flashback continues its comparative mode, this time juxtaposing shots of Robert to ones of the father, showing each of them at dinner tables. It then connects visually Virginia's leaving Robert to her smashing the soldier doll. Virginia's recognition that she "felt like a child" in her marriage is illustrated by a dissolve from her as a married woman to her as a child at the fair where she first got the soldier doll. Finally, there are two shots comparing Gordon to Robert; the first is of Gordon tying her hair ribbon (an act she has said her father customarily performed in an earlier flashback) and the second to Robert and Virginia marrying. Virginia responds to this attempt to have her compare Gordon, Robert, and her father with the phrase, "Husbands and fathers can't be the same thing."

Dr. Kik's retelling of Virginia's history then has a comparative and developmental *parti pris* to which Virginia responds on cue. The role of the doctor is to deliver the wife back to the husband, cured of her guilt and her tendency to confuse all the men in her life with her father. The last shot of the film is Robert putting her wedding ring back on her finger. There is another analysis possible in this fictional case history, however, one of an intelligent woman, an aspiring writer struggling against an infantalized paternalism in a way that manifests itself as a violent hatred of men. This version corresponds to the post-war atmosphere of the psychological melodrama and film noir, both of which concentrate on psychological disturbances in resuming traditional male-female roles and the "good-citizen" productivity, consumerism, and morality of the suburban nuclear family. In this context, the doll imagery that links the childhood flashbacks is significant, for Virginia at once refuses to accept the expensive doll, the consumer product chosen for her by her mother and she trades this model for one of her own choosing that does not have the same commercial value. Secondly, she smashes a soldier doll, an image that jumps out of Virginia's personal childhood history to assume a 1948 context. To reject the image of the soldier and veteran is a negation of the dominant ideological position assigned women, that of welcoming home and nurturing the veterans.

As is the case with the other psychological melodramas, this film is as or even more interesting for the concepts it presents obliquely and tries so hard to disguise, than the narrative meanings and representations it engages directly. These oblique meanings are often located in the flashback imagery and the reordering of events and images conditioned by these flashbacks.

Psycho Thrillers and Suspense of Memory Images

The psychological suspense thriller that we will examine next is linked closely to the psychological melodrama. Of the five thrillers by Alfred Hitchcock that use flashbacks, four have many elements of the psychological melodrama: *Spellbound* (1945), *Stage Fright* (1950), *Vertigo* (1958), and *Marnie* (1964). *I Confess* (1953) also has a flashback, but it is one which frames the whole narrative, and is therefore a somewhat different case. Especially in *Spellbound*, psychoanalysis figures prominently in a manner that has much in common with *The Locket, Possessed,* and *The Snake Pit*—but even in the other films in which no psychiatrists figure directly, the narratives are built on psychological character disorders. The emphasis on suspense and surprise in the temporal structure and hermeneutic coding in these thrillers creates unique aspects of their flashbacks, similar to the crime/detective narrative structure typical of film noir and its use of flashbacks. It is in recognition of their similarity to both sub-genres that I have chosen to discuss them as a group in between the discussion of the psychological melodrama and the film noir.

The flashback in *Spellbound* comes at a moment of climactic revelation as the protagonist, John Ballantine (Gregory Peck) attempts to recover his identity after having renounced his delusionary masquerade as Dr. Edwardes, by piecing together clues to his lost memory with the help of his lover, Dr. Constance Petersen (Ingrid Bergman), a psychoanalyst. The couple are on the run together from the police who believe the false Dr. Edwardes has murdered his namesake. The search for identity therefore takes on the aspect of a race against time. The race is presented imagistically as the pair ski together down a slope at Gabriel Valley, a site they are led to by the false Dr. Edwardes's phobia of parallel lines (ski tracks) and his recall of the name of this resort. The site will later be revealed as the place where Ballantine witnessed Dr. Edwardes's murder, an event that precipitated his delusional identity. The flashback, however, is not to this murder, but to the event in his childhood that made him susceptible to assuming the guilt for Dr. Edwardes's murder and assuming the identity of his "victim" to hide that guilt. In a graphic match from Ballantine skiing towards the camera, the image cuts to a boy sliding down a railing. A shot from behind this child reveals him sliding into another youngster, impaling him on the ironwork. It is one of the most disturbing flashbacks imaginable, partially for the horrifying childhood violence it depicts, but moreover due to its utter implausibility. The representation here is itself a bit delirious, presenting the notions of displacement and association through a filmic condensation that is quite remarkable. Yet it is the graphic match on skiing and sliding that works as a charm to supplement a narrative logic stretched mighty thin. At a meta-critical level it is precisely this outrageous attempt to bind through image puns that makes this moment far more surreal than the self-conscious dream sequence.

The opening flashback of *Stage Fright* (1950) sets up an intricate web of suspense. The flashback has been called a "lying flashback" in that it presents a version of events that is later shown to be not the way these events happened.[17] However, this "lie" is not one told by the film directly, as we shall see, for the lying images are not claimed by an omniscient narration, but rather by a single character. The audience is led to ignore this difference, however, and in that sense the film plays a "trick" on its spectators. This sleight of hand on the part of the film makes it an example of how focalization can be used as a crucial element of narrative and how the questions of focalization, subjectivity, and the retelling of the past become a central concern of narratives in the post-war cinema. A close examination of the flashback sequence will show how this mechanism operates.

After the theatrical "Safety Curtain" image of the credit sequence lifts to reveal a long shot of London, the "stage" of the films "performance," the next image in the film is of a car driving toward us. Eve (Jane Wyman) is driving, as a young man, Johnny Cooper (Richard Todd), tells her why he needs her help in escaping the police. His narration begins by citing Charlotte Inwood (Marlene Dietrich) as the person who got him into this "jam," then leads into a dissolve to a flashback accompanied by the line "I was in my kitchen at 5 o'clock when there was a knock on the door." This dissolves into the first image of the flashback sequence, a high-angle subjective shot on the bloodstained hem of Charlotte's white dress as she appears at Johnny's door. It is significant that Johnny gives such a detailed statement of his location and the time, as this mention of specifics is intended to offer credibility to his account of the event. The subjective shot on the blood stain then lends visual reinforcement to his verbal account; it aligns the audience with him as observer of this clue, encouraging identification.

The sequence that follows is presented from Johnny's focalization, marked by

Johnny's presence in every situation he is said to witness, by a number of subjective shots like the one on the dress and by a moment of voice-over narration. This voice-over is parsimonious, intervening only once to mention a somewhat banal detail, "I told her I had some brandy," which is then reiterated by Johnny's handing her some brandy with the comment, "Here drink this." This redundancy links the voice-over account to the imagistic rendering and is another "effect of reality," a signifier which persuades the spectator that what is being presented is "real."[18] Inherent in this parallel is just the opposite effect, of course; by matching the voice-over to the images, the effect could be to confirm that the flashback only corresponds to Johnny's verbal retelling and not to a reality outside of his subjectivity, or even his devious purposes, as the case may be. Here the text equivocates, by presenting information that can signify two opposite interpretations designed to protect its hermeneutic enigma while not actually lying to the spectator. If this flashback is a lie, its lie is Johnny's. The flashback is truthful to Johnny's narration. However, there are auxiliary reasons why the audience does not suspect that Johnny is lying and is misled into believing the flashback account of the murder, which is in fact a lie, from the first image. Let's examine the reasons why the audience is led to believe this account.

First there is the overriding sense, somewhat naive, that anything presented by concrete imagery in a film actually happened, at least in terms of the filmic fiction's narrative truth. A character can lie verbally, but images, especially flashback images were usually employed to correspond to a fictionally true version of events and often have the additional function of contradicting verbal lies. Obviously the films to be discussed in chapter six systematically contradict this heritage, and an audience accustomed to the questioning or absence of a central fictional truth in films such as those of Resnais, Oshima, or Saura, is not as susceptible to this naive equation of film image and narrative truth as was an audience groomed on Hollywood films prior to the forties. As concerns flashbacks in particular, there are a very few examples of earlier "misleading" flashbacks, although *Hoodoo Ann,* which we discussed in chapter two, does use its flashback as a false narrative lead as early as 1916.

Secondly, there is the attention to detail already mentioned in Johnny's voice-over, but which is increased many times over by the flashback images which support and replace this verbal narration. Details, such as the dancing figures that decorate the door of Charlotte Inwood's closet, are given in the image though they would never be mentioned in a verbal account. These are joined by more significant inclusions of details, such as the photo of Charlotte performing a stage number surrounded by men in formal dress that Johnny picks up off her desk. He is shown gazing at it obsessively (first an insert close-up on it from his point of view, then a cut in to extreme close-up on Charlotte and the man immediately to her right) just at the moment that the maid, Nellie, enters, an event we first are shown by a scream on the sound track, then by a cut to a deep focus long shot from Johnny's position at the desk as he looks up from the photo. Given this much self-revealing detail, one assumes the accuracy of the images in their totality. One is led to grant more credence retrospectively to the opening of Johnny's narration (Charlotte appearing at his door after the crime) given the details which follow.

If Johnny had been present at the scene of the murder, if he, in fact, perpetuated the crime, scenes such as the gaze at the photo could still be accurate. We can imagine the character, Johnny, to have composed his story with a different beginning onto which he simply grafted the events as he experienced them, although we have no way of ever knowing this even at the film's end. We do get immensely plausible details that have the texture of an accurate narration.

There are two more means by which the film amplifies and extends this proliferation of detail and plausibility. One is the insertion of Johnny's flashback within the flashback which extends into a fantasy sequence. Johnny pauses in his room, after Charlotte has left in the blue dress he has brought her to exchange for the bloodstained white one. A close-up of Johnny shows him deep in thought, then the image dissolves into a recapitulation of his running down the steps of Charlotte's apartment as Nellie rushes to the landing. This then segues into a fantasy sequence where he imagines Nellie speaking to the police, including a close-up image of their search in a telephone book for his address. A dissolve from this fantasy sequence to the present shows Johnny phoning Eve's mother; during this call, Johnny sees the police arriving at his apartment, indicated by his point of view shot out the window. Johnny's imagination is therefore granted a logical validity, as the arrival of the police allows us to deduce that the police were informed as he imagined. This assigns Johnny's imaginary focalization a narrative truth value. If his imagination narrates a plausible truth, one becomes even less suspicious of what he offers as his conscious perception. This is seconded by the fact that his flashback narration continues through the scene in the theater where he finds Eve and disrupts her rehearsal to enlist her aid in fleeing from the police. As he is retelling this scene to a character who was present, his version is authenticated by her acceptance of the retelling. Johnny weaves his lie into a fabric that contains true elements, plausible suppositions and a number of convincing details. The film, while never itself lying, deceives its audience by conforming in its filmic means of expression to the interwoven fabric of Johnny's subjective account, and, in addition, lending it the assumed truth value of the filmic image.

Another factor in constructing the false lead of the initial flashback is the withholding of evidence of Johnny's psychosis; signs of his quick temper and selfish comportment increase in their severity and frequency as the narrative progresses, but this process is gradual and parallels Eve's disaffection for Johnny as she falls in love with the detective, Wilfred (Ordinary) Smith (Michael Wilding). Perhaps the pervasive metaphor of theatricality, most evident in the multiple roles and self-consciously marked in the deft dialogue, covers this parceling out of signs of Johnny's long-term illness. As is so often the case in Hitchcock's psychological thrillers, character psychology can be distorted to the service of suspense and the narrative hermeneutic.

Stage Fright also has two key auditory flashbacks that confirm the traditional function of a flashback to reveal, verify, or reiterate a narrative truth. They make the misleading flashback of the beginning all the more of an anomaly, even within this film.

If the flashback in *Stage Fright* serves to set up a false lead within the hermeneutic coding of the film from the very opening sequence, the flashbacks in Hitchcock's other thrillers come at later stages of the hermeneutic puzzle. These flashbacks reveal a secret that as long as it was hidden kept a hermeneutic question alive; they are climactic flashbacks. However, they are all shorter in amplitude than the flashbacks of the psychological melodrama. If they reveal psychological causality in fictional terms, they are not a lengthy investigation as in most of the flashback psychological melodramas. They do so quite briefly, as an insert of a particular moment of tension.

The flashback in *Vertigo* is similar to that of *Stage Fright,* in that both are tied to a misleading representation of a key incident to the narrative hermeneutic. Whereas in *Stage Fright* the flashback itself narrates this false version, in *Vertigo* a misleading representation is established in the first depiction of the incident as it is shown in the present unfolding of the narrative. The flashback later gives us a second version of that incident, clarifying for the audience the systematic duping of Scottie Ferguson (Jimmy Stewart) so that he can give false testimony to a suicide that serves as a cover for a murder.

Up until that point, the spectators need to be as duped as Scottie so that they can be drawn into the mystery evoked in his attempt to figure out the elaborate morbid fantasy of Madeleine Elster (Kim Novak) and in the suspense built by his attempts to keep her from suicide. She believes that she is driven by the reincarnated spirit of her grandmother, Carlotta Valdes; Scottie is hired to follow her as she reenacts aspects of this woman's 19th-century existence in a contemporary San Francisco. What is fascinating here is the mise-en-scene of an obsession with the past, the haunting of memories that have the supernatural aspect of being inherited across two generations. In a sense, Madeleine reincarnates elements of a flashback to Carlotta's life (afternoons spent in a Victorian house Carlotta once inhabited, the exact mimicking of Carlotta's clothes and hairstyle), as well as visits to artifacts that mark Carlotta's former existence (a painting in the San Francisco Museum of Art, her grave). The audience is led, like Scottie, to believe in the intrigue of a woman haunted by the past, the explanation for which can either be supernatural or psychoanalytical. The film lays out a terrain somewhere between the fantastic and the psychological melodrama, between a ghost story and the story of a woman who has lost her mind. It is a game of double meanings that keeps both possibilities simultaneously alive for the audience.

The culmination of this doubling reveals it to be an act of duplicity. Madeleine takes Scottie to the mission where she breaks away from his embrace to commit suicide by jumping off the bell tower. Scottie's acrophobia stops him in pursuit of her as she runs to her death, a fall that is imaged in the film only indirectly, once the leap is completed. The film thus leads its viewers to believe that Madeleine died in this fall; it reinforces this conclusion with the findings of an official hearing and

Scottie's hospitalization for traumatic catatonic shock. It is only then that the narrative begins to introduce a third possibility, in the form of a return of the ghost. Scottie meets a Madeleine look-alike on the street, Judy Barton, who is revealed to the audience as in fact being "Madeleine" long before Scottie realizes the masquerade. Her discomfort with her own role in the duplicity motivates a subjective flashback illustrating how the suicide of Madeleine was, in fact, staged by Madeleine's husband who hired her to play the part of the wife he intended to murder and hired Scottie as an unwitting witness. The flashback fills in the camera angles that were suppressed in the first depiction of this event, angles that reveal her role and the substitution of the wife's corpse.

Judy does not tell Scottie what the audience has seen, but instead reluctantly allows him to work out his obsession with Madeleine, culminating in yet another death scene at the mission tower. This time Judy Barton will be frightened of a nun she takes to be a ghost and will fall backwards to her death.

The theme of the "double" so central to supernatural tales becomes a tool for creating misleading hermeneutic branchings of the narrative.[19] The film uses Scottie's obsessions to provide a motivation for the film's own obsession with repetition and variation, the charm of replaying the scene. Again, the flashback is deftly employed in this project of narrative sleight of hand, for framed by the two other versions in real time, the flashback is the central revelation that makes this triad of repetitions so effective.

The flashback in *Marnie* is quite different than *Stage Fright*'s and *Vertigo*'s. It occurs as a moment of psychoanalytical revelation in which the precipitating cause of Marnie's (Tippi Hedren) personality disorder—kleptomania and sexual frigidity, above all—is shown to be an incident from her childhood. One of her prostitute mother's clients turns his attention towards her. The mother misinterprets the gesture and begins arguing with the sailor. This quickly escalates into violence which results in Marnie killing the man.

The film calls forth this supposedly entirely repressed childhood memory without recourse to the figuration of a psychoanalyst. Instead, Marnie's wealthy new husband, Mark Rutland (Sean Connery) literally shakes it out of her in the presence of her mother. Of course, we can read this representation symbolically as an intriguing figuration of the analyst as detective/husband whose methods are violent and whose counter-transference is a kind of love.

We also see how the childhood scene of male attention to child, mother's anger, child's trauma, comes close to a representation of a child molestation—though the film avoids this issue by representing the events on another register, as a repression of murder. The sexual abuse of Marnie as a child might explain the psychological disorders she is shown to have as an adult more plausibly and complexly than the murder trauma we are instead offered. Once we understand how the film must itself repress such sexual trauma as causal in the etiology of Marnie's disorder, we can read quite differently the farfetched psychological motivations given within the narrative as themselves a result of a substitution and a covering-over in secondary elaboration of the repressed sexual material. In this schema, the murder of the man by the mother is substituted for sexual abuse by the mother's lover, indicative of the narrative economy of the psychological thriller which feeds on such substitutions to serve its exploitation of psychological motivation.

There is also something remarkable about the form of this brief flashback sequence. It is tinted red and shot with a lens that distorts the space of the apartment in which the traumatic scene takes place. Through these two formal markings, the image of the past is given as cause of Marnie's particular combination of frigidity, thievery, deception, and horse fetishism, for it is presented as the climax of a series of associations with the color red and metaphorically imaged as a distorted occurrence.

We have, then, particularly clever uses of flashbacks in Hitchcock's films, where they function as integral elements in a weave of tightly conceived hermeneutic threads, twisted one more time by the work of the flashback itself. Twists through misleading information or withholding of information are to some extent characteristic of narrative structures, essential in the ordering of most stories. The suspense thriller and the detective story exaggerate these structures, while the best of them cover and embellish these false leads or omissions with an elaborate filigree of visual and verbal embellishment. In the discussion that follows of film noir we will see how elements of a distinctive narrative style support and cover these hermeneutic structures. Like the Hitchcock thrillers, these films present a world of double meanings where repetition is pervasive. However, the film noir is a darker world than that of the Hitchcockian thriller where jokes often color the symbolic exchanges tied to death and murder, even if the humor is black. As a consequence, the flashbacks in film noir have a somewhat different function, as meditations on the meaning of the past.

The Fatalistic Flashback of Film Noir

Fatalism pervades film noir. Not only is destiny unfavorable, not only do characters fall into impossible situations or meet with death, but these declines and demises are presented not simply as mere outrageous circumstances, but as fated. The aura of inevitability bathes the action.

Flashback and voice-over narration are two of the formal devices that help film noir create this fatalism. These devices become part of the psychoanalytical symbolism mobilized by these films, presented indirectly. The version of psychoanalysis from which these films draw is a determinist and pessimistic version of popular Freudianism. This dark fantasy can be seen as a fiction of an historically located imagination.

The flashback introduces a reversed temporal order that creates the past as the site of the fiction, as a terrain, a privileged subjective realm of the imaginary. The stylistic traits of the film noir, such as highly directional lighting, attention to shadows, extreme angles, and nocturnal settings are not always limited to the past sequences alone, but even so, they help create the figuration of a filmic otherness associated with the noir realm of anteriority. For even though there may be a stylistic consistency between past and present, transitional dissolves and the bleeding voice-over commentary marks off the past as distinct and different. In a sense, the past is the cause of such disquieting stylistic tropes in the present sequences.

Great weight is placed on the voice-over to direct us caustically through these images of recalled anteriority. It is left to this voice to bridge the gap between present and past, a bleeding which bandages a temporal wound. It also frames the significance of the flashback, returning periodically to punctuate the images. It marks the return to the past as subjective recall, always reinscribing an interpretive tonality located in the grain of the voice, in syntax, diction, and metaphorical usages.

It is possible to hear this voice-over as a transcription of a literary device—as the voice derived from the hard-boiled detective fiction of Dashiell Hammett, James M. Cain, Raymond Chandler, and Cornell Woolrich and the French *série noir*. This is corroborated by the fact that nearly all the film noir flashback films are adaptations of stories or novels whose use of narrating voice is more or less directly transferred to the films.

The voice of this popular literary form is in fact divided between authorial description, first person narration, and dialogue. Its language has been characterized as immediate, tough, swift, terse, concrete, simple, vernacular, colloquial, racy, vivid, stylized, manneristic; as engaging in wildly exaggerated similes; as evidencing a suppression of emotion; and as exhibiting a self-reliant masculinity.[20] Certainly all these qualities belong to the film noir flashback's voice-over as well. Many of these qualities are meant to recreate the spoken language of the contemporary urban dweller, particularly those who frequent backstreet bars and mafia night clubs. Such language already sounded in films throughout the thirties, particularly in the gangster genre, but also in the fallen woman cycle, the backstage musical, and the screwball comedy. The voice-over of film noir is distinguished, then, not by its colorful mimesis of the colloquial, but rather by the manner in which it narrates, marking this act of narration with mannered flourishes. Unlike earlier fictional sound film, which was dominated by dialogue, language emanating from the space of the image, the voice-over is a disjunct verbal enunciation. Its use in the thirties was common in newsreels and documentaries. While thirties flashback films did introduce the bleeding voice-over transition, it is only in certain forties psychological melodramas, and certainly in film noir, that this disjunct voice attains a strong narrative motivation and continues beyond transitional moments. It celebrates and exploits film's ability to conjoin literary antecedents with sound film's own affinity with colloquial language. The voice's autonomy from the image track is slight; though coming from a different space and time, it calls the images into existence and provides a running commentary on them. The disembodied quality of voice-over is thus covered by a dramatization of the present speaking about the past and by the high degree of verbally manifest characterization. The voice sutures itself to the image by its attitude and references, associating itself with the images of its prior bodily self portrayed in the flashback images.

Investigative and Confessional Noir Flashbacks

Film noir flashbacks are of two basic types. One, which I will call the investigative structure, examines the past to solve a crime. It then leads us through a maze of clues and false leads constructed within the flashbacks. This investigative structure shares much with the trial testimony flashback, though here the preliminary stages of law enforcement are guided, not by the civilities of the judicial bench, but by the hunches of private detectives and less than scrupulous district attorneys. Many of the characters and the language they use are familiar for the gangster film. The emphasis of the narrative, though, is no longer on criminal exploits, nor on the legal sifting and retelling for legal justice. In the investigative flashback of noir films, the process of gathering and deciphering motivates the journey through the past with the investigator's own desire to know becoming a major narrative spur. We are constantly made aware that violence threatens to arrest the investigation and few witnesses are reliable. Ambiguity, contradiction, and the threat of death characterize the reconstruction of the past. The biography-research structure we examined in *The Power and the Glory* and *Citizen Kane* here lends the investigative flashback its multiple returns to the past, often from different perspectives presented as the enunciation of various characters.

The second major type of noir flashback construction is the confessional flashback, characterized by the protagonist's retrospective examination of the ways he was introduced to his current criminality. The confessional noir flashback is the male counterpart to the primarily female-centered psychological melodrama. In psychological melodrama, as we have seen, the introspection or clinical examination of the psyche is usually restricted to the female psyche—though in *Spellbound,* the male amnesiac does receive a flashback explanation of his past trauma. However, such male introspection is rare when a Hollywood film of the forties and fifties focuses on the male psyche, it typically does so through the symbolic action of noir flashbacks rather than through the more directly introspective flashbacks of the psychological melodrama.

The early flashback film noirs provide examples of each of these two basic structures. *I Wake Up Screaming* (H. Bruce Humberstone, 1941, 20th Century-Fox), is an oddly fascinating version of the investigative flashback. Its title is a nonsequitur that has virtually nothing to do with the film's narrative; when the film was remade in 1953 by Harry Horner, again for Fox, its title was changed to *Vicki,* the name of the enigmatic murder victim whom we meet only in the flashback segments. The phrase "I wake up screaming" indicates a far more personal psychological reaction than is ever taken up by the 1941 narrative. This displaced indication of a non-attributed psychological torment floats over the whole of the film, as if waiting for a suitable assignment to claim its first-person proclamation. Several of the characters could be the psychopathic sufferer or the surprised victim that the title so mysteriously suggests.

This ambiguity also conditions the flashback structure. When Vicki Lynn (Carole Landis), the pygmalion protegée of a trio of show business impresarios is murdered, each of them becomes a suspect. Frankie Christopher (Victor Mature) emerges as the prime suspect among them and the victim's sister, Jill Lynn (Betty Grable), is also questioned. Jill's love/hate relationship with Frankie is interpreted by the detective questioning her as a jealousy motive for revenge on her sibling. The flashbacks are introduced by interrogation scenes, with the transition between questioning sessions and flashbacks accomplished with great visual flourish. Also of interest is the shift from Jill's interrogation to Frankie's, accomplished by a pan of the architectural separations in the police station. This serves as liaison between their two flashbacks, which though different in focalization, are contiguous in terms of the periods they recall.

One of Jill's flashbacks prefigures a narrative twist that occurs later in the film's present-tense narration. It introduces Cornell (Laird Cregar) as a secret admirer of Vicki, voyeuristically watching her from the street through the plate glass window of the restaurant. The film's audience is given the visual information to connect the shadowy voyeur to the current investigator, even though at this point none of the characters in the film remark upon the connection. This inscription prepares us for the suspects to become the detectives and the detective, Cornell, to become their prime suspect, along with the night clerk at Vicki and Jill's apartment house whose behavior arouses suspicion.

As Frankie and Jill become allies in an effort to combat Cornell and clear Frankie, their alliance leads to the romance that the flashback sequences intimated could occur. The noir aspects are considerably diminished in the rest of the film whose action is all in the present. Cornell is revealed to have fetishized Vicki; he decorates his apartment with her photos and returns to her bedroom after her death to ruminate on her memory. Despite this, the film settles on another perversity to solve its enigma, as the clerk is revealed to be the quietly psychotic murderer. Cornell knew all along that the clerk was guilty, but he set Frankie up out of jealousy and ends this narrative by poisoning himself. The flashbacks function to set up a series of clues while concealing others. The inverse temporal structure not only allows the audience a participatory entrance into the investigation, it establishes a realm of hesitation between guilt and innocence that the film noir can mine to its advantage.

Similarly, *Stranger on the Third Floor* (Boris Ingster, 1940, RKO) is an early example of the noir flashback, this time of the confessional mode, though not a confession of an actual crime committed. The self-revelation of the past is evoked by a strange series of circumstances that connects two murders; the exploration of the past reveals how circumstantial evidence that might implicate innocent men by supplying a plausible motive in their past actions toward the murder victim. *Stranger on the Third Floor* marks its huge debt to the German expressionist tradition not only in its flashbacks, but in an hallucinatory montage sequence that follows them.

Mike Ward (John McGuire) is a reporter whose Riverside Drive apartment is the scene of a murder. He uses his personal connection to the scene of the crime to professional advantage by writing a by-line story featuring his own testimony against his neighbor, Briggs. This earns him a pay raise that encourages him to propose to his girlfriend, Jane (Margaret Tallichet). However, Jane becomes upset when she hears Briggs reiterate his innocence at the trial; her disapproval sends Mike into a soul-searching questioning of the basis of his testimony. Auditory flashbacks first replay Brigg's denials, then the doubts Jane voiced.

The image flashbacks come as a series interwoven with new events. Annoyance in the present with his neighbor, Mr. Main, leads to a flashback to the unpleasant behavior of this man in the past. When Mr. Main is murdered, uncanny events begin to implicate Mike. The second and third flashbacks further develop Mike's attempt to work through the comparison between his situation as falsely accused and that of the man he helped convict, Briggs. The three flashbacks are linked within the narrative logic with Mr. Main's unpleasant behavior, his complaining to the landlady and leering at women's legs; they are the means through which the hero comes to recognize murderous, violent impulses in himself. As confessional flashbacks, they explore a past containing previously unremarked-upon hostilities that circumstantially could supply the psychological portrait of a murderer. The form of the flashbacks here tries to mimic interior thoughts, a surging from the unconscious of incidents that contradict the character's conscious construction of himself.

These lead to a guilty dream in which surreal sets, deep shadows, canted angles, and flashing lights present Jane and the landlady's testimony against him at a trial for Main's murder; the noir stylistics are most prevalent in the handling of interior and dream thought. The rest of the film dramatizes Jane's efforts to clear Mike's name, which eventually expose a figure seen earlier in the shadows (played by Peter Lorre) to be the murderer of both Nick and Main; his motive for the crimes is simply an advanced state of paranoia.

It is ironic that though these two early film noirs establish the two narrative paradigms of the investigative and confessional structures, they share many qualities with each other that set them apart from the later film noirs. In each case the hero-suspect turns out to be innocent, the woman he is in love with is a good woman who saves his life and redeems his reputation, rather than the noir *femme fatale*. Though *I Wake Up Screaming* casts aspersions on the detective, in both films the conclusive perversity and insanity belongs to strikingly similar, relatively marginal and anonymous characters. These structural similarities include happy romantic endings with evil apprehended and innocence cleared and freed. The ideology is clearly less cynical and pessimistic than the later noir films, and the films are concomitantly less consistent in tone. In the next few years, however, noir flashbacks emerge which use the structures of investigation and confession with an intensity of narrative symbolization beyond these early noirs. While this early pair of films demurred from the full exploration of the fatalistic parable possible in the noir use of flashback and voice-over, the next pair I will discuss fully partake of a fascination with determinism and death.

Death, Repetition, and Fate Neurosis

Out of the Past, The Killers—even the titles of these two films, made just a year apart at competing Hollywood studios, evoke the entire problematic of this fascination with a dark, deterministic view of the subject. In referring to both a return from the past and to death, these titles suggest the intriguing reverberations of Freud's theses in *Beyond the Pleasure Principle*.[21] The return of the repressed, the repetition compulsion, fate neurosis, and the death drive moved Freud beyond a faith in the centrality of a quest by the subject for pleasure. Pleasure remains as only a partial motivating force in Freudian theory. It comes to share an uneasy dialectical relationship with a force seeking the reduction of excitement, change, a homeostatic equilibrium ultimately achievable only in death.

The films of the noir tradition go farther than Freud, or to put it another way, they choose a neurotic position within the theory as their central truth. They create a dark world beyond the fate/free will struggle of even the bleakest Shakespearean tragedy, for unlike *Hamlet* or *Macbeth* they do not locate the tragic flaw in the psychology of character. They protect their male hero from psychological condemnation for acts of his own responsibility. Their model is the fatalistic Greek tragedy, where destiny creates a trap, prepares a fall for a hero who could not know and who could not act otherwise. In an age of popular freudianism, where heroines are being diagnosed in nearly every psychological melodrama in which they appear, the noir film avoids dramatizations of Freudian concepts and diagnoses; it inscribes them instead on an unconscious level for a symbolic reading. The filmic symbolization should not necessarily be taken as representing the truth of psychoanalysis (a precarious concept in any case). Noir films do not simply illustrate psychoanalytic speculation at this symbolic level of unconscious inscription, rather, they create a romance of the death drive, unmitigated by any will to survive.

One way to approach the dark transformations the noir parable performs on the principles of psychoanalysis is to analyze how compulsive or neurotic behaviors are sympathetically represented in male protagonists. The protagonists seem to request empathy, counteracting their anti-heroic behaviors in the past. The heroes of film noir are depicted as suffering from a fate neurosis whose symptoms are manifest not only in the series of actions they undertake, but often in their own commentary in the voice-overs. Such metaphorical expressions as "Fate dealt me one from the bottom of the deck," serve as introduction to the subsequent action. The heroes believe themselves to be unable to escape a pessimistic trajectory and a compulsive attachment to the other who will destroy them.

In *Beyond the Pleasure Principle,* the concept of fate neurosis is introduced by Freud as an explanation of behavioral repetition. Freud links this fate neurosis to a repetition compulsion spurred by the death drive.[22] He speaks of individuals who seem to be "pursued by a malignant fate or by some 'daemonic' power" as actually driven to this repetition of unpleasant recurrences by a force operating within the unconscious (p. 15). The examples Freud gives of patients whose life histories follow this pattern are concrete: "The benefactor who is abandoned in anger after a time by each of his protegés, however much they may otherwise differ from one another, and who thus seems doomed to taste all the bitterness of ingratitude; or the man whose friendships all end in betrayal by his friend; or the man who time after time in the course of his life raises someone else into a position of great private or public authority and then, after a certain interval, himself upsets that authority and replaces him by a new one; or, again, the lover each of whose love affairs with a woman passes through the same phases and reaches the same conclusion" (p. 16).

A useful outline of the components of the fate neurosis is offered by Jean Laplanche and J. B. Pontalis that distinguish it from the more general supposition that "the course of every life history might be treated as having been arranged by the subject in advance."[23] They list three specific aspects: 1) events are repeated despite their unpleasant character, 2) they unfold according to an unchanging scenario whose sequence implies a lengthy temporal evolution, and 3) the events appear to be governed by an external fate, whose victim the subject feels himself to be.

However, Freud does not elaborate on how what he terms a *"Schicksalzwang"* (fate compulsion) can be seen as a neurosis beyond the passage I have cited, though other psychoanalysts have developed a theory of the fate neurosis. Karen Horney is one who develops the theory of fate neurosis extensively.[24] Her work on this subject critiques Freud's insistence that the fate neurosis provides evidence of the repetition compulsion and the death drive. This critique, combined with her work on masochism, constitutes the key to Horney's alternative theory of the cause and treatment of neurosis. In *New Ways in Psychoanalysis* (1939) she writes:

> Concerning repetitive painful experiences in a person's life, we understand them easily, without having to assume a mysterious repetition compulsion if we consider that certain drives and reactions in a person are bound to bring with them repetitive experiences. For instance, the propensity for hero worship may be determined by such conflicting drives as an exorbitant ambition so destructive in character as to render the individual afraid to pursue it, or a tendency to adore successful persons, to love them and to participate in their success without the individual having to accomplish anything himself, and at the same time an excessively destructive and hidden envy toward them. . . . , such a person will easily have repetitive experiences in which he finds idols and is disappointed in them, or he deliberately makes idols of people in order to crush them afterwards (pp. 137–138).

This alternative view of the fate neurosis stems from a link Horney suggests in *The Neurotic Personality in our Time* (1937) between the fate neurosis and masochism.[25] She says that one manifestation, the masochist's "feeling of intrinsic inferiority," is "a feeling that good and evil come from the outside, that one is entirely helpless toward fate" (p. 228). The argument leads Horney to a discussion of masochism that is not gender specific (Freud's view of masochism is associated with the feminine) nor primarily sexual as in Wilhelm Reich. Horney says:

Whether the neurotic subjects himself to a person or to a fate, and whatever the kind of suffering that he allows to overpower him, the satisfaction he seeks seems to be the weakening or extinction of his individual self. He ceases to be the active carrier of actions and becomes an object, without a will of his own, . . . the tenaciousness of masochistic strivings in neurotics is then accounted for by the fact that at the same time they serve as a protection against anxiety and provide a potential or real satisfaction (p. 234).

It seems that Horney at the furthest extension of her argument circles back to Freud, at least as concerns the death drive, when she speaks of the subject's desire to seek extinction of an individual self (symbolic annihilation) and to become an object with no will of his own.

Horney's debate with Freud, coming some twenty years after his speculations and at the brink of World War II, points to the fascination the inversion of pain as pleasure holds on even a theoretical level. Possible to interpret either as a dialectic between opposing forces (death and pleasure) or as a circuitous domination of the pleasure drive by any means necessary, the fate neurosis becomes all the more important for the way in which it poses this crucial theoretical dilemma. Fate neurosis seems a perfect source of parable for an increasingly industrialized and alienating society. It is in this context that the male protagonist of film noir provide American culture with their life stories exemplifying neurosis as truth.

One can also compare the repetitious structures of noir narrative to Nietzsche's concepts of the eternal return and to the state of forgetting that he describes as necessary to the cycle. However, this comparison omits the joy in knowledge inherent in the Nietzschean moment of recognition, made repeatedly possible by the act of forgetting; recent theoretical discussion of Nietzsche has stressed this optimism as opposed to earlier readings of Nietzsche that emphasized his fatalism and determinism.[26]

Existentialism has been proposed as another philosophical comparison to film noir, and one can certainly take some noir narratives as fables of the existential view of the human condition in the same way that French poetic realism and Godard's films are seen to share certain existential motifs.[27] However, the comparison here too, seems only partially appropriate, for the development of the motifs in noir is again not favored with a *prise de conscience* that is an element of existentialism in its diverse forms. Both Nietzsche and existentialism face philosophically the psychoanalytic state of abjection and its state of powerlessness and go on to redefine a theory of empowerment; it is in the description of this first instance that the philosophies rejoin the psychoanalytic theory and the film noir narratives.

In the opening sequences of *The Killers* (Robert Siodmak, 1946), two strangers appear at a filling station in Brentwood, New Jersey. They cross to enter a diner where their clipped, caustic, and finally violent interrogation of the cook and customers reveals that they are looking for a man they call "The Swede." When warned by his friend Nick that these men are after him, The Swede (Burt Lancaster), who has been known in Brentwood as Pete Hunt, seems to accept his pending death with the lines, "I'm through running. I did something wrong once." When, moments later, the assassins perform their murder, his resignation is metonymically reiterated. A close-up shows his hand slipping down the bed post. This opening sequence leads to an insurance investigation into The Swede's life that is the source of the film's flashbacks.

Out of the Past (Jacques Tourneur, 1947) also has its intruders enter a gas station in a small town. They are looking for Jeff Bailey, formerly Jeff Markham (Robert Mitchum). Jeff is off-duty and only his deaf-and-dumb assistant is there. The visitor crosses to a lunch counter where he questions the waitress, who reveals out of jealousy that Jeff is at the lake with his girlfriend, Ann. The assistant runs to warn Jeff in sign, but the visitor is able to find Jeff and deliver his message: Jeff is to see his former gangster boss, Witt (Kirk Douglas), in Lake Tahoe. Jeff complies, offering Ann the explanation for his mysterious command appearance at a gangster's retreat as the two of them drive to Tahoe that night. Jeff tells his story as a voice-over flashback confession. The dawn arrival at their destination shifts the recurrence of past events from the register of memory and retelling to repetitive actions in the present.

Both films thus begin with a claim on the life of the protagonists by former criminal associates. In both cases the lead characters have reformed and covered their illegal pasts with small town livelihoods and normal routines, when they are confronted by emissaries from their previous lives. Both open in settings defined by a gas station (working-class, honest employment; a fixed locality servicing the mobility of others) and a diner (meals and leisure space for a working-class hero who lacks a real home). The opening sequences both present the violation of this symbolic space. Their similarity may be due to a common inspiration by Ernest Hemingway's short story, "The Killers," which the film of the same name credits (though Hemingway's story concerns only the time and events of the film's opening sequence). In the case of *Out of the Past,* this similarity was never acknowledged.[28]

One film, *The Killers,* has a hero corpse who mysteriously accepts his death because of some guilty debt to the past. The other, *Out of the Past,* has a hero called back into his past by an obligation, fear, and, eventually, by his own desire. The flashback structures of both films embody different symbolic inscriptions of a pessimistic determinism. Neither hero can escape his past, transform his life to attain the safety one might associate with refuge in a small town, let alone build a future with a wholesome bride. The beginning of *The Killers* establishes that the character we follow throughout the flashbacks is already a ghost, a memory image. The inevitability of death is the initial statement with everything following in its wake. *Out of the Past* presents us with a different determinism, for it leads us to believe through its hero's flashback narration of the past that he is telling his story with hindsight and insight, that he has come out of the past able to end his account with a statement of rededication to his new love and the future. Yet this promise is essentially a promise to "return" to the future. No sooner is the promise stated than contradicted and lost, as the hero walks back into his past never to return. Jeff's reentry into Witt's domain involves him in a repetition of a schema that varies only slightly from the story he has told, and whose goal, ultimately achieved, is his death.

The investigative and confessional frames present different focalizations of the retelling of the past. *Out of the Past* incorporates its confessional as a single linear narration of events occurring in the hero's life three years prior to his account of them. Ellipses are covered by his verbal explanations, and other remarks present actions as habitual. But the voice controls more than temporal understanding, more even than his present attitude towards these past events. Like first person voice-over narration in other film noirs, it reinhabits the past images, giving us precise and detailed thoughts that belong to the Jeff who is in Mexico, who is obsessed, still, by Cathy Moffitt (Jane Greer), the former girlfriend of Witt whom he had been hired to retrieve. The voice intermittently becomes the interior monologue of the character we see in the flashback.

Only in the punctuating returns to the present is the interlocutor, Ann, directly acknowledged and the judgment due the present fleetingly passed: "It was the bottom of the barrel but I scraped it." Then the voice of obsession returns, "I didn't care, I had her." The life of this flashback is in the voice/image relationship in this mixture of confession, inner thought, and symbolically loaded mise-en-scene. The voice points out the effect of Cathy's white dress in sunlight then in moonlight, accentuating the lighting effects inscribed for our vision. It even cites self-consciously the stagesetting of the decor, discussing the American bar and the Ciné-Pico theater across the street as an architectonic place of waiting, watching, and being observed. It presents the Los Angeles dwelling as a "movie house apartment in North Beach." The voice continually reinforces the film's oneric symbolism and cinema's relationship to the phantasm with such passages as:

> What was left of the day went away like a pack of cigarettes you smoked. I didn't know where she lived, I never followed her, all I ever had to go on was a place and time to see her again—I don't know what we were waiting for—maybe we thought the world would end. Maybe we thought we were in a dream and would wake up in Niagara Falls.

This habitual nightly ritual, "every night I met her," this cinematic dream fantasy amidst fishing nets has a hypothetical happy ending—if the substitution of good woman for bad woman could be made. The male frames his own obsession with the evil woman, reveals himself as continually deferring reality. His commentary is given to the ear of the analyst, speaking that to which the patient himself cannot really listen even as he speaks. Here the film splits the regime it establishes for the spectator, allowing us to listen analytically, but at the same time inviting us into the fantasy along with the hero, inviting us to accept the fatalism of the final fatality, the repetition and the symbolic death drive car crash through the blockade of the law.

It is in this way that eros and the death drive become bound by the narrative chains of film noir. Whatever elements of eroticism that might be attached to the life forces of a pleasure principle are severed by a deterministic coupling of hero and lost object: the evil woman. The lost woman object, always incapable of love, always betraying love for money, looms as the lure within the noir flashback, enticing the hero to his own destruction.

Many analysts have seen the evil woman of film noir in relationship to an oedipal triangle or, alternatively, to a pre-oedipal obsession.[29] Both schemas are rich in implications, but neither is complete without the other, and both imply another symbolism as well. The evil woman of noir, the naughty lady of so many shady lanes, is also the queen of the night, the dark chamber where the death drive ends. This is, of course, a perverse sexual metaphor, but this perversity is exactly what is projected upon her to embody. She is the sexual woman of demonic death; the snow queen, Yuki, of Japanese legend portrayed in Noh and Kabuki. It is this personification of death as a sexual woman that links *Out of the Past* and *The Killers* as parables of the fate neurosis.

The voice in *The Killers* inverts *Out of the Past*'s confessional voice, as it is multiplied and parceled out, belonging to everyone from the Swede's past except the Swede himself. The first two narrators are incidental friends, acquaintances whose distanced observations of the Swede towards the end of his life give the audience the most recent past events before the investigation delves back further for explanations. Queenie's flashback poses one of the hermeneutic questions and leads us further back: Who is the "she" figured in the cry, "She's gone," the woman whose absence leaves the Swede raging across the image?

The investigation is framed as an insurance probe to recover money that the head of the insurance company doesn't want returned—the money is a figure of the ridiculous within the film's economy. Ridiculous, unless one turns to the economy of the unconscious where the ridiculous makes sense. The investigation continues, as if to insure the audience against the Swede's death drive, his acquiescence toward death (that was the place where Hemingway left his short story). At the center of the film is the account of the Swede's obsession with Kitty, the film's evil, unfaithful seductress, narrated from the tenement rooftop apartment of police Lieutenant Loubinsky and his wife. Loubinsky narrates the Swede's last fight; then Loubinsky's wife Lily (who was the Swede's former girlfriend) tells of the Swede's first meeting with Kitty; then Loubinsky depicts the Swede's arrest, in which he takes the rap for Kitty who is wearing a stolen broach. These flashback framings are highly symbolic, since Loubinsky and his wife were formerly the Swede's best friend and the Swede's girlfriend and the alternation serves to match the segment of narration with the narrator most immediately involved with the specific incident narrated. The exposition plays dramatic games with the spectator by withholding a full understanding of the triangular configurations until mid-way through the flashback rooftop triptych. Crime and the obsession with the evil woman are framed by the law and the forsaken, good woman, who have now married each other.

While the flashback focalization can be highly symbolic, the film can also abandon any rigor of focalization when it deems another rhetorical strategy to be more forceful. For example, Lily's flashback to the Swede meeting Kitty joins with Charleston's account of the Swede's reunion with Kitty after his release from jail in emphasizing the parallel presentations of the Swede's obsessional desire for Kitty. The Swede's gaze dominates the editing and the mise-en-scene. Even when he tries to look down or away, it is only to the fetish object, her green silk scarf decorated with shamrocks, her gift of luck which instead becomes an emblem of her as bad luck, evil fate. Then he must return his eyes to her. Focalization within the image is not mimetic, as it departs from the narrating voice in *The Killers,* sometimes providing a special irony.

The newspaper account of the Hat Co. Payroll robbery yields to a long-take flashback rendering of the robbery that greatly supplements the verbal account with additional information and an added charge of documentary that the verbal journalism lacks. Similarly there is a tension between Blinky's disjointed, fragmented delirium on his deathbed and the coherent flashback imagery of the hide-out and the Swede's double crossing escape with the payroll fortune. As a finale to this series of flashbacks, Kitty herself is made to testify, but not before another series of symbolic references are brought into play.

One of the gang is named Blinky, another Dumb-Dumb. These names which mark a lack of sight and sound are joined by the cinematic self-conscious references that occur at two critical junctures. Lily introduces the flashback which narrates her loss of the Swede to Kitty with the line, "I thought we had a date for the movies, but we went to a party in a kind of hotel instead," this being Kitty's suite. The insurance agent tells Kitty to meet him in front of the Adelphi theater, which turns out to be a cinema showing a technicolor feature, called "Claude's Wife," a pastiche of the melodrama *Craig's Wife,* which features a wife who uses her marriage to satisfy her obsession with material acquisitions (the melodrama was famous both for its stage run and the Dorothy Arzner film of 1936). This reference to the women's film inside the film noir makes an oblique connection between the women depicted in both, a point we will come back to shortly. Just as in *Out of the Past,* the film mobilizes cinematic references to point obliquely to its symbolic project, its projection of symbolization, knowing that while the audience is both Blinky and Dumb-Dumb—intermittently blind and repeatedly deaf to the covert enunciation—in another sense it sees and hears even the most secret codes. This is represented through another circumlocution, the ruse the investigator plays on Kitty before he gets her to speak. He refuses to meet her at a bar called the "Green Cat," demanding the Adelphi rendezvous instead. Once she is in his car he drives her to the Green Cat, saying he only goes there when he knows no one else knows he's expected. The ruse for which Kitty—the Cat emblemized by green silk—falls is more complex than this, for the investigator wants her to think he doesn't know he's being taken to his assassination; he wants Kitty to say too much, knowing that her cohorts will kill him. Kitty speaks of no longer being Kitty, of being a new woman, who will finally tell the truth because she is now a "married woman." The old Kitty needed to be instrumental and deceitful, but the new Kitty can confess as to how she set up the Swede. This is also a ruse; Kitty believes she still has death as a weapon. The investigator is neither seduced nor killed, while the evil woman dies, repeating, "Tell them Kitty is innocent." She is told that this time she has no fall guy.

The fall guy, the male masochist whose fate is embodied by women—noir and the woman's film are two sides of the same coin in Hollywood's forties symbolic circulation. In *The Locket,* we saw the woman-fate-harbinger of death configuration as a study of women's neurosis. In *The Killers* and *Out of the Past,* the noir blacks out the direct psychoanalytical configuration, but the high-key lighting spots the same perverse figure.

Proliferation and Reiteration of Noir Flashbacks

One of the most significant aspects of the film noir flashback in the forties is its proliferation. While most fall into the patterns I have analyzed already, this constant reworking of the same narrative structures is striking historically. There are also variations within the structure in certain films that are worthy of note, including a blending with the women's film that produces a sort of hybrid between the melodrama and the investigation or confessional noir narratives. The final section of this chapter will look briefly at a number of examples that amplify and extend our findings on the flashbacks in these films; detailed analysis of each film has been foregone in favor of a commentary on the most salient features of difference from the narratives discussed in detail earlier.

One example of a noir investigation narrative that matches the pattern of *The Killers* fairly closely is *The Enforcer* (Bretaigne Windust, 1951).[30] An assistant district attorney, Martin Ferguson (Humphrey Bogart) loses his evidence in his case against a murder-for-hire gang boss Albert Mendoza when his chief witness dies the night before the case is to come to trial. The film covers the twelve hours in which Ferguson and a police captain try to piece together their case from the collected prosecution files, which leads to a series of flashbacks telling the history of the investigation. The interesting difference from *The Killers* is that there is both a frame story (the final hours before the trial) and a frame flashback (the first flashback in the investigation, motivated by a search for a clue that is running through the D.A.'s head). The individual witnesses then offer their testimony as a series of flashbacks embedded inside this frame flashback, and the returns to the "present" between each flashback in the series are in actuality returns to the unfolding of the past of the investigation in the flashback.

Like the investigation in *The Killers,* which begins as an insurance investigation and grows to involve a large criminal gang, Ferguson originally was called in to investigate some strange aspects of the murder by Tony Molloy of his girlfriend, aspects which hint at a larger crime. The flashbacks represent his interrogation of various witnesses until he finally obtains enough of the story to lead him to a crime ring and the brains behind the scene. Though the district attorney in *The Enforcer* takes on more heroic proportions than the insurance investigator, a consequence, perhaps, of the growing tendency in America in the fifties to lionize law enforcement, this film, once inside the frame flashback, is characterized by a series of flashback witnesses that gives it an almost identical narrative structure to the earlier film noir.

Some of the witnesses are able to offer a fragment simply because they never knew the whole story. *The Enforcer* develops a particularly intriguing dimension of this fitting together of story fragments, since several promising sources of information are cut off before they can be heard; others who know more are not able to tell it. One gang member is killed, another goes crazy, mumbling from his hospital bed only incoherent elements of incriminating evidence. The film cheats on this seemingly hopeless source, however, offering a flashback that tells his fragment with enough coherency to have this flashback function like the others as a piece of the puzzle of the past falling into place, allowing for a successful incrimination of the gang boss by the film's end.

The Mask of Dimitrios (Jean Negulesco, 1944) is another investigative flashback film. It is an international spy tale that can arguably be considered a film noir. The structure is again similar, but the variation in this film lies in the fact that like the journalist's tracking of the Kane legend in *Citizen Kane,* the investigation here is carried out by a writer, Mr. Lyden (Peter Lorre), after the death of his subject of interest (a notorious criminal, Dimitrios Markopolous). Since Lyden writes detective stories and his subject of investigation is supposedly dead, his quest is not presented as legal, but rather literary, a search for a good story that can be turned into fiction. This quest for fiction gives the film a self-reflexive element and eventually provides a twist ending in which the dead Dimitrios (Zachery Scott), meant to be the subject of a future fiction, is revealed to be still alive when he bursts violently into the writer's present reality.

The story of Dimitrios is told in three flashbacks, each introduced and closed by elaborate ripple dissolves. The first is offered by Colonel Hachey, an official in Instanbul who draws Lyden into the case, knowing that as a writer of mysteries he will become fascinated by Dimitrios's character and carry on an investigation that will perhaps save the police the trouble. Eric Peters (Sidney Greenstreet), another former accomplice betrayed by Dimitrios, begins to shadow Lyden's investigation, first discreetly, then as an intrusive and violent threat to Lyden's own safety. A belly dancer who was a former conquest of Dimitrios provides the flashback narration of his involvement in the assassination of a Bulgarian official in 1923. The third flashback, to the theft of Yugoslavia's Italian mine charts, is narrated by another criminal associate, Gradeck, whom Peters directs Lyden to find in Geneva. Lyden's travel is necessary to the quest structure of the narrative even though the information might have been presented more directly. Once Lyden has learned this much of the story Peters can manipulate him as the bait to blackmail Dimitrios in Paris. The film's baroque narrative twists reveal the past as a particularly threatening object of investigation, as the past can return in the present as a live threat. This symbolic danger implicit in seeking to investigate the past reiterates that of *The Killers* and

Out of the Past in the entirely different context of a reflection on the genesis of literary fiction.

The film goes to considerable length to make this spy intrigue set in a volatile part of the world in the years preceding World War II free of any direct political implications for a wartime audience. As the plot steamrolls over political assassinations and military espionage, it carefully covers its tracks by turning the countries in question into fictional realms whose history is as vague and incomprehensible as possible. The film, whose structure could have served as a model of how flashbacks can be used to explain pre-war political events and negotiations, is instead an example of the way history is allowed only a symbolic entrance into Hollywood films of this genre in this period. Dimitrios is an evil charmer who betrays all with whom he negotiates only to be shot by the writer, Lyden, a bystander whose courage is spurred by his indignation. The Mediterranean spy setting serves as an oblique war reference rather than a direct, historical one. The Dutch writer becomes a figure for the working out of a U.S. victory on a symbolic level, mobilizing through allegory some of the same narrative elements popular culture used to depict U.S. involvement on the European fronts, i.e. a bystander-nation brought into the scuffle by circumstances not of its making whose moral indignation will provide its strength to win.

The confessional flashback also has interesting variations in several other films, prime examples of which are *D.O.A.*, and in another sense, both *Double Indemnity* and *The Postman Always Rings Twice*. The later two films never really enter their flashbacks, but have voice-over narrations that are present from the opening shots of the film, though these voices are located in the present in relationship to the images that the voice-over marks as the past. The voices confess and explain the murders that the heroes planned and attempted while under the influence of the wives of the murdered men. In *Double Indemnity* (Billy Wilder, 1944, script by Raymond Chandler and James Cain), the past catches up to the present when the dying narrator-murderer (Fred MacMurray), who has been dictating his story into a dictaphone as a note of explanation to his boss, completes his story and life in the presence of his boss. In *The Postman Always Rings Twice* (Tay Gannett, 1946), the confessional voice of the narrator (John Garfield) comes from his jail cell, where he tells his story to gain a final absolution. Both films therefore display the full symbolic function of the confessional voice in retelling the past, to mark the past behavior with the sad knowledge of what the outcome was destined to be. As the hero says at one point in *The Postman Always Rings Twice,* "I should have walked away just then"; the confessional narrative is laced with hindsight, but the direction of this new consciousness is unilateral. He confesses in order to place the guilt elsewhere, with the woman who tricks men weakened by desire. In a sense, then, the confession serves to protect the hero, as it never exposes his psyche to examination nor allows for his own responsibility in desiring to kill off his rivals. In the name of self-revelation, it is a consistent disavowal, a psychoanalytical term for an indirect process of denial.[31]

D.O.A. (Rudolph Maté, 1949) is a frame story flashback whose major anomaly is that its narrator/confessor is almost a corpse. *Sunset Boulevard,* as we discussed in the last chapter, is narrated by a corpse, through a poetically licensed foray into the surreal. In *D.O.A.*, the fascinating aspect of the narration is that it occurs in the length of time that it takes for the protagonist (Edmond O'Brien) to succumb to the effects of a poison that he has been given to drink. He begins his flashback with the response to the question "who was murdered," with the impossible enunciation "I was."

These words inscribe the paradox of this narration; not only is the "dead man" not yet dead, but this statement seems to put temporality itself into question. The flashback extends from a moment of innocence, in the past, when the narrator started off on a vacation trip (albeit refusing to take along his secretary whom he was dating steadily) through his unwitting involvement in a complicated business swindle and private scandal which results in his being first framed and then poisoned. The film is characterized by an absurdly exaggerated and highly subjective sound track, a filmic *écriture* which along with the noir scenography create the atmosphere in which its murder plot of the innocent bystander can be thrust into the realm of the symbolic. Bigelow dies as a little man caught by forces outside him, just at the moment he first dared to leave home alone.

In a sense all of the confessional flashbacks I've discussed have elements of an investigation embedded in the confession. A more complex hybrid between the confessional and the investigative flashback, however, is offered in *Dead Reckoning* (John Cromwell, 1947). The voice-over belongs to a former paratrooper, Mike (Humphrey Bogart), who is telling his story to his former chaplain now returned to his church. Choosing a priest in a church as the interlocutor for the tale emphasizes its symbolic confessional aspect—although the narrative offers another explanation by describing the former chaplain as the only man the narrator can trust.

The confession is the story of the investigation into his army buddy and personal hero, Sergeant Johnny Drake. Mike discovers that Johnny led a double life, one part of which includes involvement in a romantic triangle and gangster conflict. In seeking Johnny's past, Mike takes on the same role that Johnny had occupied. The symbolic operation here is similar to *Out of the Past,* in which the hero repeats his past once having confessed it; in this case, Mike, in the process of discovering Johnny's past virtually becomes Johnny, an operation of identification and repetition.

Other sorts of anomalies are possible in the flashback voice-over during this period. The flashback in *Laura* (Otto Preminger, 1944) is a fascinating extension of a voice-over narration present from the beginning of the film. It belongs to the film's most verbally adept character, Waldo Lydecker (Clifton Webb). Lydecker's voice begins with the lines,

> I shall never forget the weekend Laura died. A silver sun burned through the sky like a huge magnifying glass. I, Waldo Lydecker, was the only one who really knew her. I had just begun to write Laura's story, when another of those detectives came, . . .

Having announced his privileged status for telling Laura's story in his opening line, Lydecker will later be given his chance to make good on his self-promotion as narrating voice. After having been preoccupied with shadowing the detective in his investigation of other suspects, he gets his chance to speak of Laura's history, while sitting with the detective in a bar. His voice-over is illustrated by a lengthy flashback, the first time we actually see Laura (Gene Tierney) in the film, as she is assumed dead at the beginning of the narrative.

Waldo's version of Laura's life is a self-serving chronicle of his "discovery" of her when as an advertising copy assistant she approached him for an endorsement, through his grooming of her as his sophisticated protegée. It is a flashback that begs for a double "hearing," from both detective and audience—one ear lent to finding out who the mysterious, deceased Laura was, and the second to the character of the narrator. It is Lydecker's cunning expertise as storyteller and his *sang-froid* as well as his privileged opening voice-over narration of the film that keeps us from suspecting that Lydecker himself is the murderer, and of another woman whom he mistook for Laura. This double secret maintained by the hermeneutic code of the film is protected by the authority film has traditionally assigned the narrating voice.[32] It is an authority which is called into question somewhat when we come to realize that there is no possible time and location for this voice to locate itself diegetically: its "I shall never forget" is a future perfect that attaches itself to the past "Laura died," and is presumably said in some time posterior to the present of the film's opening in which Lydecker luxuriates in his bath. Midway through the film, the bluff of this memory game is called when this voice that we never meet at its point of spatio-temporal articulation would have to have known that Laura remained alive and that the events of the weekend could never be simply categorized as those surrounding Laura's death. Furthermore, unlike the voice-over of Mike Donovan in *Lady from Shanghai* (Orson Welles, 1949), one that also never receives spatio-temporal location but can walk away with the character at the end of the film, Lydecker's voice is simply lost, for he dies before the film ends.

In retrospect we can hear this voice as marked with paranoia and possessiveness, from its first image of the sun as magnifying glass, examining and burning, to its claim of knowledge which is figuratively bound to the tropes of sexual possession and jealousy that structure the narrative. The power of *Laura* as a film, besides its exquisite portrait-dream fantasy sequence that serves as the center of the narrative, is its ability to mobilize this narrating voice whose status is so ambiguous and which reveals and hides each time with every utterance.

Another anomaly occurs in *Experiment Perilous* (Jacques Tourneur, 1944). As was the case in *Letter from an Unknown Woman,* a diary serves as the flashback narrator. Again the woman character's voice issues forth from the diary, though it is a man reading her pages after she has died. However, the function of this diary flashback is quite different than the one discussed in *Letter from an Unknown Woman* due to its placement and duration. It is placed in the center of the unfolding of the fiction in the present and it creates a pause in the narrative in order to shift the semic and hermeneutic coding of the narrative. Its revelatory material from the past of the characters re-launches the narrative on different terms.

Another sort of hybrid between sub-genres is *Mildred Pierce* (Michael Curtiz, 1945); it has elements of both the women's psychological melodrama and the film noir. The film is framed as an investigation of the murder of Mildred Pierce's (Joan Crawford) current husband, Monty (Zachary Scott), to which she immediately confesses. It would seem to be, then, a mixture of the investigative and confessional flashback with, from all appearances, very little left to drive its investigative mechanism. However, Mildred's flashback confession has a greater amplitude than strictly necessary for police purposes. It begins with the narration of her first marriage and her divorce, her struggle to survive as a single woman, her rise to financial power, and her romance and marriage to the deceased, all of which turns the film away from the detective/noir tradition and towards the women's melodrama. Laced in this narrative is Mildred's motive for the crime, her stormy, jealous, guilty, but protective relationship to her eldest daughter, Vita, whose secret love affair with her husband Mildred presents as motivating her confession. The twist to this flashback confession is that it is diegetically true in all particulars except one; Mildred was not the murderer. It is an elaborate false confession that despite itself reveals the circumstances that motivated the fictional crime perpetrated by another.

A reintroduction of didacticism in the flashback is another path of variation films take in their use of the flashback structure in the late forties. Two noteworthy examples are *Crossfire* (Edward Dmytryk, 1947) and *Knock on Any Door* (Nicholas Ray, 1949). *Crossfire* uses an investigative flashback structure to develop a psychological portrait of an anti-Semite and a social critique of the community that accepts and shields such attitudes. *Knock on Any Door* is a trial flashback film that does not motivate its retelling of the past as a hermeneutic revelation of innocence, but rather as a plea by the district attorney (Humphrey Bogart) for social responsibility and understanding about the circumstances that led to his juvenile delinquent defendant's crimes. These films of social commentary graft their discourses onto structures previously used for tightly drawn suspense narratives and less didactically developed symbolic representations, seeking to situate their lessons in the genre expectations of their audience and to introduce them as a more interesting twist in the narrative development.

It is precisely these sorts of twists, hybridizations, and variations that make the flashback viable during this period, one of its richest. As we have seen, a few basic structures rest at the base of all the films discussed in this chapter. The proliferation of examples repeat the symbolic paradigms, which in any case demand repetition, being themselves the inscription of the force of repetition and the circularity of desire. Looking at all this repetition in forties Hollywood flashback films, several questions arise: Where could filmmakers go on from here with the flashback? What was left for Hollywood sound film to do with this narrative trope of the return to the past—to further varying its duration, twisting its narrative coding, inverting its symbolic paradigm along the axis of sexual difference? What would be the result but a series of minor variations that in some sense had all been seen before? These questions are not idle ones. In fact, the flashback becomes less common in late fifties and sixties American film; an apparent impasse is reached within the only form this system of representation apparently could allow. The change and renewal of the flashback comes from elsewhere in this period, from a modernism developed in Europe and Japan, the "new waves," which will be the subject of the next chapter.

6

Disjunction in the Modernist Flashback

Modernism—for film history this term is itself somewhat problematic, and for the flashback in film, the problems are compounded. In a general sense, we might want to consider the flashback as a modern technique whose use within film—itself a modern art form—always implies a departure from the continuity assumed by linear narration. Yet we have also seen the modernist potential of the flashback tempered by highly coded transitions and explanations that rendered the flashback as a conventional device within early commercial cinema. The flowering of an early cinematic modernism in the form of avant-garde movements in the twenties presented a more modernist inscription of the flashback, restoring some of the energy of dislocation and mimesis of thought and memory inherent in the flashback. This early modernism was followed by a return to more traditional cinematic structures and styles in the early sound period. Still, certain films from the "classical period" of sound cinema (from the late twenties through World War II) bear witness to the preceding innovations as well as developing some new stylistic and structural features of their own, particularly, experimentation with the temporality of the sound track. After World War II, a series of changes in cinematic expression begins to occur, not just in avant-garde cinematic production, but on the margins of or even well within commercial production. These films react to the Hollywood genres and reintroduce forms that are beyond the limits of the conventions of genre and spatio-temporal continuity. It is this post-war shift in expression that we shall try to analyze as a determined renovation of the flashback as an element of modernism in film.

The emergence of a European "art cinema," the new wave, auteurism—all of these terms try to describe changes which occur in filmic expression in the post-war years. In addition, Japanese cinema becomes known to Western countries, and the differences of aesthetic impulses in this non-Western cinema tend to be assimilated as modernist expression (although seen in a Japanese context, the traditional and modernist dichotomy undergoes some inversions).[1] A new literary influence is exerted by the modern novel on screenwriters and filmmakers. These changes take place not all at once, but gradually and differentially; there are changes at the level of production and distribution, as well as changes at the level of filmic articulation, the patterning of cinematic expression. One of the elements of change is the treatment of cinematic temporality. This final chapter will discuss these modernist post-war uses of the flashback. The integration and recuperation of these techniques into mainstream Hollywood cinema will also be considered as a prelude to a speculation on what form further temporal innovation might take.

The filmic experimentation of the twenties is a point of reference for some key post-war filmmakers (particularly, as we shall see, for Ingmar Bergman and Alain Resnais) who reinscribe the temporal experiments of the past in new contexts. Time is once again treated as an element to be shaped and designed. Temporality is subjective and relative. It is linked to a conception of the functioning of the psyche, and once again, like the psyches in Hollywood films from the forties, these are often wounded and damaged either by the War or by personal trauma. The modernist difference is that the mode of filmic narration seeks mimetically to represent mental processes, to show the memory flashes and brief disjointed or distorted images which come to a character's mind.

If the "art film" becomes a distinct category of filmic production and consumption, it has a different significance in the United States than in Europe and elsewhere. In the United States, this term was almost exclusively reserved for foreign films shown at certain theaters in cities large enough to support such activity.[2] In Europe, the art cinema does not acquire the connotation of "foreign." Many European countries developed their own "art cinema" with a distinct production and distribution network feeding into an international circuit of exchange. France, Italy, Poland, and Sweden are particularly important centers of art cinema production during the late fifties, while other European countries at first provide an audience for these films, then in many cases begin themselves to produce films for this circuit. This smaller market of distribution encourages the production of films that would appeal to more sophisticated and intellectual audiences, but it also revitalizes and differentiates the national cinemas from Hollywood domination. Japanese cinema, however, is an example of how tenuous the boundaries between mainstream and art cinema are, as a few of the major Japanese directors producing for major Japanese studios become known as the equivalent of the Western art cinema auteurs.

Several films that become famous during this period play an absolutely key role in a changing flashback epistemology and practice. These films in turn were often part of developments in their respective national cinemas or individual filmmakers' careers, the earlier manifestations of which were unknown at the time outside the filmmakers' own countries. Such modernism also directly evolves from a reaction to the classical paradigms of Hollywood cinema, the films looked at in chapters four and five. Modernist films often seek a reordering that is drawn in relationship to the codes and structures used in these films that immediately preceded them in history.[3] Kurosawa's *Rashomon* and *Ikiru* and Ingmar Bergman's *Wild Strawberries* are such breakthrough films, yet they are not the first films by these directors to experiment with the flashback. In the next two sections of this chapter the innovative flashbacks in Kurosawa and Bergman will be examined in this historical context and in relationship to some earlier or less well-known works that are important to consider alongside them.

Relative Truths and Subjectivity in Japanese Flashbacks

In chapter two we saw that flashbacks were important to certain Japanese films of the twenties, including those of Kenji Mizoguchi; Mizoguchi continues to make films during and after the War, and his three historically set flashback films from the post-war period will serve as a means of reintroducing and expanding upon some of the issues the flashback raises in the Japanese context. This will serve as prelude to a discussion of Kurosawa's flashback investigation of subjectivity in three post-war films.

Some flashbacks in Japanese films display the influence of Western narrative traditions on Japanese storytelling; the *gendai-geki,* or modern tale, is an obvious place to expect such emphasis on individuality, as was true of the Shimpa-influenced films of Kinugasa and Mizoguchi that we looked at earlier. Certainly the flashback emphasis on an individual's past, or to put it differently, the relationship of the past to character psychology, constitutes more of an innovation in the context of the Japanese narrative arts than within the Western tradition where it confirms a major tendency of the epic and novel. However, the Japanese have their own tradition of reflection on the past in legend and theater, more epic and apparently less individuated. *Jidai-geki,* Japanese films set historically, have the possibility of borrowing from the Japanese theatrical and novelistic traditions that can be traced back to the aristocratic late Heian dynasty. Since the *jidai-geki* is often a mixed form, historical in subject matter, but modern in filmic form, the flashbacks found in *jidai-geki* often take a more modern and more Western vision of the role of the individual's remembrance of the past.

Three of Mizoguchi's *jidai-geki* from the fifties use flashbacks. Each creates a portraiture similar to the *gendai-geki,* including notions of how the past marks and distinguishes specific focal personalities. However, these historically set films can give the revelation of an individual's past a legendary dimension.

Mizoguchi's *The Life of Oharu* (1952) is adapted from a tale written by Ihara Saikaku, the writer credited with establishing a literary genre based on the lives of samurai and the merchant classes in the early Tokagawa period. Saikaku's work transformed the Heian memoir tradition by shifting its class perspectives and languages.[4] *The Life of Oharu* is a film in which an aging prostitute tells her life, in flashback, to a group of Buddhists whose leader has held her up as a model of depravity. Her narration is a vindication of her character and an indictment of the society. This flashback narration is followed by a scene in which Oharu takes refuge in a temple gallery filled with boddhasattvas; the faces on the statues dissolve to take on the appearance of various men who treated her badly throughout her life, an apparition that acts like a reprise of the flashback itself while it serves as coda for the film. The flashback functions here as it did in Mizoguchi's earlier *jidai-geki* as a powerful vehicle for social argument linked to character identification. The individuated past is valorized against collective standards in a manner that turns the victimized woman into a heroine of pathos.

The conjuncture of symbolic narrative structures of the *jidai-geki* and the *gendai-geki* in Mizoguchi's other two *gendai-geki* flashback films is tied to an exploration of power and ability to revolt against the abuse of power. The flashbacks in these films evoke the historical tradition of the patriarchal inheritance of power, but in both cases the flashbacks use the interruption or disturbance of patriarchal inheritance as a motivating factor for a heroic rebellion against injustice.

Sanshō The Bailiff (1954) is the story of two children and the wife of a disenfranchised noble who are sold into slavery and prostitution following the father's banishment. Mizoguchi's immediate source was the 1915 novel of Morai Ogai, which itself was based on a traditional oral legend, or *sekko-bushi*. This oral legend is itself the story of the evocative power of an oral legend; Mizoguchi's film version seeks a parallel lyricism in its creative manipulation of images which transcend time and space.

The attempt of the mother and children to leave their estate and travel to safety is presented metonymically in the opening scenes. The flashback occurs very close to the beginning of the film and recalls the time when the father was still in power. In giving us this aspect of the exposition in flashback, the film sets up the father as a highly symbolic element; he is the source of the name and unity of a family within the Japanese historical value system, but significantly, he is only remembered in the past, already lost.

An ellipsis that follows the children's enslavement takes us to a point where they have forgotten their past. Their mother, whose story has been told parallel to that of the children, remembers her family by creating a song, which the daughter hears sung by a new slave sent from the district that the mother inhabits. The song is the impetus for the brother's recalling his past, which in turn causes him to escape and struggle for the causes of freedom his father believed in. The initial flashback then floats over the entirety of the film as the characters strive to recall once more what was already a memory at the outset and which subsequently had become lost even to memory.

The flashbacks in both *Oharu* and *Sanshō The Bailiff* provide visual analogues to the remembered family ballad or to the samisen ballads of the geisha/prostitute tradition. The melodramatic narratives are given the elegance of a traditional Japanese legend rendered as song; the phrasing of each filmic sequence is of a rhythm and a tonality that establishes this lyricism.

In Mizoguchi's *Taira Clan Saga* (1955) the flashbacks revolve around the question of paternity of the lead male character, Kiyomuri, who, though raised as the son of a samurai, has heard rumors that his mentor-father may not be his true sire. Both of the flashbacks recount an incident which occurred just prior to Toyamuri's marriage to Kiyomuri's mother, a woman whom the flashbacks contend was a courtesan to the emperor (a revelation for the son). However, the flashbacks relate contradictory versions of the incident and name different fathers. The flashbacks are used to introduce multiple possibilities into the narrative hermeneutic, similar to the play of different versions of the incident in Kurosawa's *Rashomon,* made six years earlier, whose structure and impact we will take up shortly.

Like *Rashomon,* the setting of the two flashbacks and the basic lines of action in each case remain constant; in both cases, the ex-emperor, Toyamuri, and his guard arrive at the pavilion of the ex-emperor's favorite courtesan. In the first instance they surprise the figure lurking in the garden who turns out to be just the man who lights the oil lanterns. Toyamuri impresses the ex-emperor with his calm handling of the situation and the ex-emperor gives him his courtesan in marriage as an act of gratitude and acknowledgement, knowing she is pregnant with his own child.

In the second version, the ex-emperor's entourage surprises a monk who is the courtesan's lover. Again, the samurai Toyamuri proves his good judgment by allowing the monk to escape, saving the ex-emperor embarrassment. The ex-emperor demands an additional act of duty from Toyamuri, asking him to marry the courtesan to cover the scandal further.

The play of these variants in the ensuing narrative establishes an identity crisis for Kiyomuri of great symbolic import given the politics of the historical moment being portrayed. Kiyomuri is either the son of the ex-emperor, a "lewd" monk, or a samurai—at the time when the mobility and the monasteries are jockeying for land and political power, while samurais remain an unrecognized force entirely subservient to the nobility. The uncertain paternity of Kiyomuri marks him as the figure who will successfully challenge the lines of power and bring his Taira clan of samurais to dominance. *Taira Clan Saga* is a film marked by the self-conscious representation of the theatricality of history as it attains the status of a legend. The confrontations in the film are all treated as formal encounters whose declamation and visual gestures bear the traces of the theatrical presentation Kiyomuri performs for his samurai clan early in the film at a banquet celebrating their recent military victory. For Mizoguchi, melodrama, high tragedy, and legend merge into a form where the echoes of a past explain, justify, or determine a philosophical or political position in the present. In the post-war period, such play with historical causality is not without important ideological overtones in Japan; like the forties American films that use flashbacks to connect the war period to the pre-war period and the post-war period to the War, Mizoguchi's fifties films make a symbolic argument about history, interweaving personal history with the history of power.

The flashbacks in Mizoguchi's *jidai-geki* introduce a character who has links to the nobility in the past but finds him or herself disenfranchised by the power structure in the present. Due to this past of elevated rank, the main characters are in the position to question the power structures that oppress them. Ultimately these films thematize remembrance or revelation of the past as a key element in the formation of a legend.

In contrast, Kurosawa's post-war flashback films make the flashback into key elements of modernist film form. Kurosawa's *Waga seishun ni kuinashi (No Regrets for our Youth,* 1946, though the title actually translates as "no regrets in my life") also makes a fascinating comparison with the American films we examined in chapter four, but the manner in which it uses the flashback to symbolize the weight of history is quite different from Mizoguchi's and, in fact, is quite singular in Japanese film up to this point. This film, based on the real events surrounding the political censorship of a professor and his student in the thirties, adds a love story to the tale of political opposition to provide a personalized chronicle of Japanese leftists during the rise to power of the military and the right wing. It uses the flashbacks as part of a discourse on the ideology of memory, tradition, and nostalgia, a discourse it works out in terms of fictional symbolic representations.

The film begins in 1933 at Kyoto University when the professor's daughter, Yuki (Setsuku Hara), is picnicking at Mt. Yoshida with a group of her father's students, including two rivals for her affection, Noge, the leader of a radical faction, and Itakawa, a more sedate personality who eventually drops out of the struggle to become an official within the military government. The romantic rivalry gets played out with a series of matched traveling shots on a chase by the two men of Yuki through the woods (the chase is characteristic of Kurosawa's graphically rich style of filming action sequences). The hike and picnic surrounded by wildflowers, an idyll at springtime so dear to Japanese notions of pleasure, provide one image of youth to which the film will return later on. This pleasant scene is interrupted by gunshots and the discovery of a soldier wounded during war-game exercises.

From this introduction of contrasts the film turns to the Zengakuren (student group) struggle for academic freedom. Yuki's father is fired by the Ministry of Education and the student rebellion is crushed by police repression. Yuki's father tells his former students, "Your struggle was not wasted. When Spring comes flowers will bloom again," establishing with these words a reference to the first springtime picnic scene. The radical Noge continues the struggle and is imprisoned. Yuki's bourgeois tastes and loyalty to her father separate her from Noge in spirit. In a ration line in 1938, Yuki meets Itakawa who has become a government employee in Tokyo where she has become a secretary. Itakawa tells her of Noge's whereabouts and also that he thinks that Noge has changed as a result of his five-year imprisonment. However, Itakawa's perception is superficial; Noge seems different only because his activities are more clandestine. Yuki watches Noge from a distance through several seasons depicted in a montage sequence. Finally they meet, rekindle the romance and marry; however, Noge's political activities are not directly discussed. Yuki is still a somewhat passive and traditional Japanese wife, whose sphere is their apartment.

It is at this point that the flashbacks and the complex commentary on nostalgia for the past and the relationship of the past to the present and future of Japan begins. A first flashback to the picnic occurs when Yuki evokes their youth. For Yuki, like her father, the springtime idyll represented a lost and idealized past for which she longs when confronted with the threat to their security posed by her husband's antiwar activities. Noge's memories are verbal rather than visual. He simply recalls the struggle to "defend freedom in school."

This contrasting retrospection introduces two sequences which depict a difference in attitude and political maturity between Yuki and Noge. The first is a scene of them in the audience of a movie theater. Noge laughs heartily along with the film, while she cries at his side, apparently lost in her thoughts of fear about the future. Following this scene, they return home where they discuss the role of the past, present, and future in providing the meaning of their lives. Noge explains to Yuki his philosophy of personal and political history. His philosophy not only establishes his character, but sets the precedent for Yuki's later conversion to Noge's credo. First he says he knows the truth will be known ten years from now and people will thank the resistance. Then he tells of a moment of "weakness" when he left home ten years ago to his father's scolding and his mother's tears. This moment of doubt has since been resolved and his comment on it now is the assertion that there are "no regrets in my life." This rejection of filial subservience in favor of other ideals, in this case a commitment to political struggle characteristic of the communists, is an especially strong departure within a Japanese context that prizes self-sacrifice to the family unit and to authorities. Underlying the difference between Noge and Yuki's visions of the past is the ideological conflict between the tenets of political activism and Japanese tradition. However, as the film resolves this conflict it is not simply Noge's view which triumphs, but rather a complex synthesis in which Noge's parents will return later in the film as part of Yuki's means of formulating her own version of her husband's credo.

When Noge is arrested as a spy, Yuki is also held for questioning; in jail, as she looks out the cell window, there is a second flashback to the picnic, this time to the scene of the chase through the woods. Yuki is again shown contrasting her present situation with a moment of happiness in the past. Her memory is still primarily nostalgic, unlike Noge's view of life that sees the past as the foundation of the present struggle and the future as its vindication. However, after Noge is tortured to death in prison, Yuki undergoes a transformation. She comes to subscribe to Noge's perspective of life and political struggle, but adds to his lesson a reconciliation with his past that he never made. This is made clear when Yuki decides to move to Noge's natal village to live with his present father and mother, to earn their respect for herself and her dead husband despite the villagers' persecution of them for being a family of spies. Working in the rice paddy, she has an auditory flashback to Noge's words in the earlier scene of philosophical explanation. His voice-over echoes from the past with such lines as "I have no regrets for my life" and "ten years from now people will know."

The final flashback in the film indicates how Yuki's values have changed; during her visit to her parents' house in Kyoto following the War, the image dissolves from her hands at the piano keyboard to an image of her hands in the water of the rice paddy as she worked. This memory image from her recent past is interpreted by

Yuki as also an indication of what her future now should be, as she once again decides to leave her middle-class home to return to her husband's family. This resolution is an odd mixture of traditional Japanese behavior (a widow traditionally was expected to remain with her deceased husband's family) and a Maoist position on solidarity with peasants as an expression of commitment to leftist politics. In a sense, Yuki's final position is much more a return to nostalgia than it is the assimilation of her husband's credo. The difference is only in the object of her nostalgic longing. Rather than a sequence of youthful play and seduction, her nostalgia is now aimed at her husband's past. When Noge stated that he had "no regrets for my youth," it was a statement of a decisive break with tradition that was not at all nostalgic, whereas Yuki's means of incorporating this credo is to substitute her husband's past for her own bourgeois heritage and to construct a life that combines elements of this past and of tradition as her means of approaching the present and the future. Though the film might appear to be one of the few flashback films to date to represent the nostalgia inherent in flashbacks critically, finally it backs away from the radicality of this position to one which reconciles, symbolically, nostalgia with a new set of principles and objects of that nostalgic longing.

Further, the displacement of the nostalgic object has as its ultimate consequence the dismissal of a bourgeois and urban life in favor of solidarity with peasant farmers. This can be interpreted as a political allegory, especially given the influence of the Japanese Communist Party on the scenario through the pressure exerted by the labor union of film technicians at Shochiko studios, cited in several sources.[5] In fact, the historical figure after whom Noge is modeled was a Communist Party member, though this is not mentioned in the film, probably due to the censorship authority of the U.S. Occupation forces. The anti-bourgeois and anti-liberal message is easily explained in this context, a position quite different than the kind of humanism one finds in other Kurosawa films. Beyond this, it is fascinating that at the level of political allegory the film suggests a Maoist solution rather than one more characteristic of Soviet Communism, though to some extent this constitutes a prefiguration within a Japanese context of the Maoist philosophy that will gain such currency after the Chinese revolution of 1949. Explaining the narrative in these terms, we find that the wife of a former student radical who died as a war resister, specifically one writing against Japanese imperial penetration of East Asia, finds her means of continuing his goals by working in the fields alongside the peasants, working to modify their right-wing nationalist sentiments. As a Maoist parable, this film suggests the significance of the peasants as a force of resistance, though the film modifies this by reference to the traditional aspect of Yuki's act of returning to her husband's family. The final flashback that substitutes the image of hands working the fields for hands playing the piano is the quintessence of Maoism. One finds then in *No Regrets for our Youth* a complicated use of flashbacks for historical/political commentary, a precedent set not only for Kurosawa's later work, but whose direct impact can be seen on Nagisa Oshima's construction of flashback allegories, and which are more indirect parallels in other modernist films.[6]

Rashomon (1950) is a quite different film project whose acclaim in the West was a major breakthrough for the international distribution of Japanese films. Adapted from two short stories by the modern writer, Ryunosuke Akutagawa, *Rashomon* is a *jidai-geki* set in the late Heian period. Along with *Citizen Kane*, *Rashomon* is one of the films whose flashback structure has generated the most written commentary.[7] The film opens with a scene at the Rashomon, a major gate to the city of Kyoto, which has been partially destroyed during the fighting of the civil wars. A downpour emphasizes the bleakness of the scene at this moment, as three men, a priest, a woodcutter, and a vagabond thief, gather there for shelter. Their conversation introduces a series of flashbacks to an incident involving the attack of a robber on a samurai and his wife, though the incident is told with so many significant variations that all that appears constant is the samurai's death.

Kurosawa begins the flashback series with two first-person narrations that set the stage of the police inquiry, giving information that surrounds the incident though they claim not to have witnessed the incident itself. The first flashback, told by the woodcutter, shows his discovery of the murdered man in the nearby countryside. It ends with a cut to his testimony at the police inquiry. The flashback thus doubles as a telling at the Rashomon gate and a telling at the inquiry itself. Like the flashbacks to follow, it is primarily a visual sequence, with very little dialogue and no voice-over during the flashback itself (some of the others use minimal voice-over commentary); the testimony at the police inquiry which follows supplies the verbal rendition of the story, which acts as a summary recapitulation. A wipe makes the transition to the priest's testimony at the inquiry which is followed by a flashback to his viewing the couple before the man is murdered. Here the same verbal/visual separation is used, but the verbal summary precedes the more elaborate visual rendering of the flashback. In both instances, as well as in the flashbacks to follow, the virtual absence of voice-over is emphasized by long sub-segments in which the characters move through the woods without any voiced accompaniment, be it voice-in or voice-over.

Since both the priest and the woodcutter heard the entire proceedings as well as giving their testimony, they can supplement their accounts of this past event with their versions of the other trial testimony. However, the transition to these other narrators is initially made in such a manner as to minimize the audience's awareness of this narrative embedding that makes most versions of the actual incident second-person narrations told by the priest.

The thief's version is preceded by contradictory accounts of his arrest by an officer and by the thief himself. In the arresting officer's account of the arrest, he comes upon the thief on the beach after he has been thrown from his horse. A return to this shot in the present shows the derisory laughter of the thief signaling his disagreement with this version. He then provides another version of his arrest, which shows in flashback his drinking from a stream that he contends was polluted, explaining his groveling on the beach as illness, rather than the wounds and humiliation of being thrown by the horse, as in the arresting officer's version. At issue is the thief's pride and personality as well as a subsidiary marking of contradictory stories.

Tajomaru's narration of the earlier events of that day is also characterized by defiant and cynical laughter. He claims, boastfully, that he indeed killed the man whose death is in question. This cuts to a flashback of his version of the incident itself. In Tajomaru's version, what begins as a depiction of rape, with the wife defending herself with her dagger, becomes the portrayal of a pleasurable seduction, indicated by the dagger falling from the woman's hand, whereupon the hand erotically embraces the back of her assailant. One more return to Tajomaru's testimony introduces his ribald commentary, "I could have had her without killing him," but the motivation for his murder is supplied in the last segment of Tajomaru's flashback, as the wife begs him to kill her husband. A lengthy sword fight follows, after which the victor, Tajomaru, discovers that the woman has betrayed him by leaving, a fact remarked upon in his final commentary in a return to the trial.

The marked embedding of Tajomaru's flashback occurs only retrospectively, when the narration not only returns to the Rashomon gate, but there engages in a philosophical dialogue on the truth value of stories and the human's capacity to lie before continuing on to the other versions.

The priest offers a sympathetic introduction to the wife's version of the incident when he describes her comportment at the trial ("her face was peaceful, not violent"). This cuts to an image of her testifying, bowed in grief and shame before the tribunal. Her behavior here is consistent with her portrayal of herself during the incident as a properly demure and self-sacrificing Heian woman, whose own suffering is of secondary concern to her husband's pain at watching her being raped. She begins narrating the incident at the point where the rape is finished, and the bandit announces his identity. In her version the gaze which unsettles her is not that of the bandit before the rape, but that of her husband, afterwards. A close-up of him staring at her cuts to her at the trial remarking on the chilling effect of his leaden gaze. In a return to the flashback she runs toward her husband, cuts the ropes that bind him with her dagger, and begs him to kill her. The exchange of gazes continues between her and her husband in a rhythmic alternation of shots of each of them as she circles around him. In another return to the trial, she says she then fainted, and discovered in horror when she awoke that her knife was in her husband's body. Whether the husband killed himself or she attacked him before fainting is left ambiguous even within her storytelling; in either case, the spectator is not allowed to see either of these possibilities as a flashback image like the others that illustrate the trial narrations. Our vision of this version is subject to her fainting; what occurred is blacked-out in the elliptical montage between disparate temporal moments. Further, her claim that she tried to commit suicide in a pool by a mountain but failed, is illustrated only by a quick cut to an image of this pool from which she is entirely absent. Her flashback ends with her lament that she is only a "weak woman," a perfectly ambiguous self-declaration, since it could be an apology for being too weak to resist the bandit and too weak to commit suicide, but on the other hand, it could carry the implication that she was too weak to kill her husband and therefore would be a clever statement of defense.

Another return to the Rashomon Gate provides another introduction by the priest to the next witness, as he introduces the testimony of the priestess who will voice the version of the dead husband. Her introduction by the priest is colored by his religious conviction that such communication with the dead is indeed possible, but a visual cut from the fallen statuary that adorned the Rashomon Gate to her scepter as she begins her testimony adds a touch of irony. If the Gate's religious icons can lie crumbling in the mud and rain, then the entire power of religious iconography and ritual is perhaps called into question. The purpose of such statuary on a gate is to embody the guarding of a holy site; its defilement could indicate a certain crisis of faith, although perhaps it is more of a self-conscious remark on the difference between representations and truths. The iconographic representations of religious beliefs, then, would not themselves be imbued with special powers, but serve as representations of faith. According to this interpretation, the film introduces the fallen icon to once again underscore its paradigmatic investigation of the gap between truth and representations.

The testimony of the priestess is presented with similar ambiguities. She is depicted in accordance with some of the codes of Noh theater, including the slow chanting accompanying her story, characteristic of the Noh musicians who accompany the declamations of the actors in the drama. However, as these conventions of Noh drama were themselves representations derived from earlier religious rituals, as well as being taken up by the Japanese ghost story in its oral and literary traditions, the meaning of such a convergence in Kurosawa's mise-en-scene is possible to interpret in more than one way. Further, in the structure of Noh, the priestess's evocation of a dead spirit would be split between two characters, the *waki,* or introductory secondary character taking the role of the priestess, and the *shite,* or main character taking the role of the ghost she summoned. In the film, this summoning is indicated by a substitution on the sound track; from the lips of the priestess, the male voice of the dead husband is heard. This establishes a mimetic indication that the medium is indeed in touch with the spirit of the dead and not fabricating a story. So Kurosawa's representation is ambiguously structured as either the theatrical representation of a ritual or as the manifestation of the ritual itself, including the successful supernatural visitation, depending on which codes one takes as determinant.

The Noh reference implied by the introduction of the seer permits us to see a fascinating manner in which the Noh tradition could be seen as nourishing the Japanese flashback film in general. As Faubion Bowers remarks in *Japanese Theatre,* in the Noh play "action is generally recollected and . . . the plot hinges on an event that has already taken place in the past. This means that the dramatic situation is not necessarily acted realistically before one's eyes. Rather it is poetically recalled and discussed by the characters and chorus and their movements become dreamlike glosses to the idea carried by the words."[8] This commentary on Noh is not only suggestive for *Rashomon,* but for all Japanese flashback films. It evokes the same theoretical principles as the flashback, for it adds to the notion of retrospection the concept of a special poetic dimension inherent in a marked retelling. This may be most apparent in an archaic narrative form, entirely devoted to such structured retellings and less apparent in the filmic flashback, but *Rashomon* serves to point out the correspondence between the poetic theatrical tradition and that of filmic retrospection. The immediacy of filmic action so vital to the filmic style of *Rashomon* is subservient to its reframing devices that create even filmic action as in no manner immediate, but either already inscribed action or merely potential past action.

The dead man's version also begins after the rape. The ghost recalls how radiant his wife's face appeared when the bandit asked her to accompany him, but in repeated intercut returns to the trial, the ghost emphasizes that this bothered him less than her subsequent request that the bandit kill her husband. The flashback ends with the husband stabbing himself with the dagger after the bandit has refused the wife's cold-blooded request and untied the husband in an act of sympathy.

As we have seen, the principals in the incident each narrate the husband's death differently, but the versions vary, not as one might presume (especially if one is conditioned by a Western perspective), with each claiming innocence and assigning guilt to the other. Rather the bandit claims to have killed the husband in a sword fight, the wife claims he was killed with a dagger under circumstances left mysterious, and the husband claims to have killed himself with the dagger. The inversion of the motivations one might have anticipated lies in the codes of honor and behavior each character must follow to uphold his or her reputation within a Japanese historical context. Both men's versions focus on the wife as the truly unworthy figure, exonerating each other in the first instance as a worthy adversary, and in the second as equally appalled by the woman's treacherous shift of allegiance. The woman's defense of herself as an innocent pawn to their desires to possess her is coupled with her disdain for the both of them. The differences distill to oppositions aligned with sexual difference; male pride and mutual respect create an alliance that blames the woman, displacing their guilt for both the rape and the inability to protect her from the rape onto a depiction of her as treacherous.

The woodcutter offers his interlocuters at the gate a final version, no more definitive than the others, but one which reinforces the contradictions between versions. The woodcutter claims to have withheld this version previously at the trial, but offers it now to explain his dismissal of the husband's version as false. Once more the flashback begins after the rape, this time with the bandit pleading for the wife to marry him, while threatening to kill her if she doesn't. In this version it is the wife who unties the husband, suggesting that she will belong to the victor of this sword fight, but the husband at first refuses to risk his life for her. He tells her she is dishonored and demands that she kill herself. The wife then becomes the center of the action, as she goads both men to fight, while reaction shots show each of them responding to her verbal jabs at their warrior status. The sword fight that ensues is unlike the bandit's version of the sword fight, as it takes place quite close to the ground, with the camera positioned to capture the groveling action with straight-on or only slightly high angles. The fight involves several instances of loosing the swords entirely and is more of a game of dodge than a parry. The fight ends pathetically with the husband deprived of his sword, begging in vain for his life, after which the wife runs away, and the bandit is left to go off alone with the two swords. No character is heroic or even empathetic; all are engaged in a battle of pride and power that reaches a derisory conclusion.

The woodcutter's version counterbalances the other flashback renditions of the event, in that it shifts our attention away from deciding which of the three principals are worthy of our identification. The modernist impulse behind this narrative seeks to ensure that the series of variations remain equally hypothetical. Each must be seen as merely a variation on possible actions and positions. Plausibility and identification, if not entirely arbitrary, should remain highly subjective investments on the part of the audience, for part of the modernism of the text is to play out this complex design of narrators and versions under the sign of undecidability and the pervasiveness of lies, and ultimately to evoke a reflexive gesture towards fiction as practice, and filmmaking at the service of fiction.

The fascination of Kurosawa's rendering comes from the construction of shifts of voice within a mode of representation that remains relatively constant. Each version contains images that transpire without much voice-over to mask them as subjective narration, confining the subjective voices to the trial scenes that surround or interrupt the image flashbacks. Each one holds the full imaginary lure inherent in filmic fiction of depicting a reality, but as the events depicted are in some contradiction to one another, if one is "true" the others cannot be. Reaction to such a systematic exploration of narrative illusionism ranges from taking the film as a philosophical statement on relative truth values and subjectivity, to interpreting it as a discourse on lying, to understanding it as a deconstructive play with the mechanisms of fiction.[9] Though spectators might also choose a version as the one to be believed (usually the woodcutter's final flashback[10]), there is no definitive textual evidence for this.

These flashbacks to the incident itself are therefore the priest's and the woodcutter's renditions of what the three trial witnesses, the bandit, the lady, and the seer gave as testimony. For the interpretation that takes *Rashomon* to be a rationalist philosophical inquiry into truth, the seer poses a strange problem, for within the frame of the tale the seer is a witness like any other. However, outside this frame, the seer is a poetic convention. She is marked as a device and therefore particularly susceptible in a modernist context to act as a deconstructive clue. Despite their placement as testimony at a trial, each of the narratives is a fabrication, appearing through the imaginary vehicle of fictional characters. It is the character of the medium, herself, who serves as a clear allegory for this process.

This film's modernism is tempered by other impulses; first, Kurosawa's film ends with a humanist coda to the novel's pessimistic view of the world bereft of truths or morality. This optimistic reversal of tone doesn't finally undo the framework of the earlier flashback tales, but it allows for the forgetting of the decentering propositions that their structural balance implies.

Returning to the earlier analysis of the tales aligned along an axis of sexual difference, we find a second problem. There are particular constraints framing the woman that interfere with the hypothetical equality of the tales. The flashback variations all shift the portrayal of desire and power represented in the act of rape and the subsequent possession/meaning of a woman. The female character, even in her version of the narration, is limited; the semes that can be assigned her are a conventional suicidal shame or an evil betrayal, a limitation drawn directly by the Heian setting, but in another sense also by twentieth-century Japan. This basic structure of sexual differentiation and antagonism complicates the balancing of the tales one against another. A more deconstructive play with the film can look at its balancing structures with an eye to what remains opaque and fixed in the process of construction of this fiction and why.

Ikiru, in contrast to *Rashomon,* is a *gendai-geki* and uses its flashbacks at two different moments to depict the past events in a civil servant's life. Shinobu Hashimoto and Hideo Oguni collaborated with Kurosawa on the original script to produce a film that fulfilled Kurosawa's desire to have a contemporary Japanese story reach an international audience as successfully as had *Rashomon.*[11] The first set of flashbacks occur after the civil servant, Watanabe (Takashi Shimura) finds out he has cancer; they represent the moments of his life that echo in his mind upon the realization of his imminent death. The second group of flashbacks occurs at his funeral as the group assembled in mourning debates the significance of his actions months between the discovery of his illness and his death, months devoted to overcoming the bureaucratic refusal to answer the complaint of a group of mothers concerning the dangers of an open drainage ditch in their neighborhood. Most striking is the number and amplitude of these flashbacks and the doubleness of the construction. One might expect either a film constructed around the first set of flashbacks and then a linear conclusion or a different film constructed around the funeral and its flashback debate. Instead, the narration begins in the present, goes back to a distant past, continues briefly in the present, but stops short at the moment that Watanabe returns to his office. An ellipsis of five months occurs, bringing us to Watanabe's funeral for the flashbacks which fill in the elided action in great detail. The effect of this structure is to emphasize retrospection; except for the visit to the doctor where Watanabe learns he has cancer, the most significant events in the narrative are presented in flashback. These retrospective segments that have an almost staccato rhythm, though this is used to different effect in the two series of flashbacks.

In the first series, the flashbacks are linked by returns to Watanabe in the present as he thinks about the past, the eve of his realization he has cancer. Four disparate past events are linked in this flashback series: (1) his wife's funeral, (2) a discussion with his brother Kichi in which he says he will not remarry because of his son, Mitsuo, (3) a baseball game during which Mitsuo suffers an appendicitis attack and the subsequent hospitalization, (4) Mitsuo's departure on a train for the War. Watanabe's movements in the returns to the present match the movements in the flashbacks, an associative editing pattern that creates a lyric flow between past and present that unifies the imagery. The most striking example of this occurs with an insert of the present in the middle of the baseball/appendicitis flashback; Watanabe's sitting down in the stands in shocked reaction to his son's injury is matched with his sitting down in the return to the present. Besides the visual lyricism gained through these graphic matches, they portray Watanabe's complete psychic involvement with this past. His own death links associatively to his wife's death, which was also the moment at which he renounced his life in favor of his son's. This is the link to the two sequences of threats on his son's life (appendicitis, mobilization) which become the major events in Watanabe's own sacrificed life. The discussion with his brother includes a prefiguration of the sense of futility which the audience already has witnessed. The brother asserts that Watanabe's son won't appreciate his sacrifice, a statement that has already been proven to have come true in the present sequences that have preceded this flashback series. The flashback series might be summarized thematically as the remembering of a useless sacrifice, but its interest lies far more in its form than in its signified.

Similarly, the flashbacks that take place at the funeral are brief in their extension (*durée*), though as a series they form a roughly contiguous temporality. The retelling of the past is interrupted incessantly in order to serve the debate in the present. The emphasis is on the interruptions, on the commentary that ironically raises questions in order to provide answers in a manner that makes the film a self-interrogating morality tale. These brief flashbacks respond to three controlling questions; the first group follows a speech by the mayor in which he tries to deflect criticism by suggesting that Watanabe, and not himself, was responsible for the park project— so that the first question could be phrased as "What role did Watanabe play in bringing the park to fruition?" To contradict a ranking official directly is impossible within Japanese bureaucracy, so this indirect method has a series of low-level clerks innocently remember Watanabe's efforts. The flashbacks manage to suggest politely another truth, one that the mayor is trying to suppress through Japanese indirect discourse. When the series culminates in the revealing scene in the Mayor's office where he flatly refuses the project until Watanabe insists, the polite means has ironically brought us to the most direct of contestations. The next series of flashbacks is introduced by Kimura, the one colleague of Watanabe who honestly appreciates the dead man and responds to the question of motive: Why did Watanabe struggle so hard? This series shows that Watanabe indirectly revealed his motivation at several junctures: he was excessively tired, indicating illness, yet he relentlessly continued; he defied some gangsters who wanted to build a nightclub on the site by continuing the project, unafraid of their threats on his life; and, finally, in the completed park, he remarks how he never appreciated the sunset until now when there was no more time.

The sum of these positions leads those assembled to conclude that Watanabe knew he had cancer and that it was this knowledge that gave him the will to complete the project, something the film's audience knew all along. Is this series of flashbacks merely redundant from the audience's point of view? The answer lies in the realization that the controlling questions are not hermeneutic puzzles for the spectators' benefit. The questions and the flashbacks they engender are a playing out of an argument in a particular form. The final question is more indirectly presented, but follows from the others: If Watanabe saw his efforts claimed by others, how did he feel in his dying moments about the cause to which he had dedicated himself? The response is provided in a single flashback offered by a policeman who was so struck by the way Watanabe appeared on the night of his death that he came to the funeral to pay his respects. The flashback shows Watanabe sitting alone in the part on a child's swing singing a favorite song of his, apparently completely content.

By framing the flashbacks as an argument used within a debate in the narrative, the didactic elements of *Ikiru* as a humanist morality tale are underscored. This emphatic voice, however, is used to create a particularly Japanese structure of argument, the indirect revelation of numerous examples that leads to a biting ironic overturning of the opponent's position.

In its own way, each of Kurosawa's flashback films, *No Regrets for our Youth, Rashomon,* and *Ikiru,* makes a significant contribution to the modernist flashback and modernist narrative temporality in general. This heritage of the flashback will be renewed by the younger filmmakers that emerge as the Japanese "new wave" in the sixties; the work of one of them, Nagisa Oshima, will be discussed in a later section of this chapter.

The Swedish Dream Flashback

Having traced the parallels between some Japanese directors' use of flashbacks in the post-war period and that which occurred in the twenties in that country, it is interesting to note that a similar parallelism of flashback experimentation exists amongst the major figures in Swedish cinema. The flashback imagery of Ingmar Bergman, that is so much a part of the innovations his post-war films represent for Swedish cinema and the art cinema in general, rests on the historical precedent set by the films of Stiller and Sjöström we examined in chapter three. Further, there is another intriguing parallel in that Bergman's early films, in which he first began working with flashback and dream devices, did not get international distribution. Bergman's *The Prison* (1947), which was his sixth film but the first for which he wrote the scenario, uses several devices to embed its flashback sequence in a manner that presages his later innovative mixings of narrative techniques. It was discovered by international art cinema distribution only in the late fifties, after the success of the later releases evoked interest in Bergman as a director.

The Prison takes as its embedding device a journalist who has been investigating prostitution in Stockholm and decides to write a scenario for his filmmaker friend. The imagined scenario, whose recounting is presented by filmic illustration that comprises the body of the film, is based on the life of a seventeen-year-old prostitute the journalist has discovered while doing research. She is forced into prostitution by her fiancé. At the film's end, the filmmaker rejects the scenario as too pessimistic to work as a film, but in the interim the audience has followed the bleak narrative of a girl whose husband and sister-in-law steal and murder her newborn infant. This crime is repressed by the young woman so completely that it is only in the form of a dream towards the end of the scenario-film that she remembers her repressed past. The images surrounding the baby's birth and disappearance are represented in a film style simulating the dream imagery in which they are understood as having reemerged.

In *The Prison,* the blending of alternative realities is not at all the product of differing versions or accounts of reality as in the Japanese films we discussed, but rather the presentation of different versions of a reality that are conditioned by the imaginary and the unconscious. This, of course, makes the fictional presentation of the past through flashback somewhat problematic; are these images drawn from the past but filtered through the filmic simulation of dreamwork really flashbacks? Any "real" version of the prostitute's life is held at a distance from the viewer by the film's embedding devices. Even from this remove the "real" plays the significant symbolic role. The film, while marking more strongly than most traditional films the difficulty in postulating a "real" past, ironically presents its work on levels of the imaginary through the introduction of a journalist, a character who represents the form of writing most centered on reporting reality. As the "real" past is embedded within an encrustation of imaginary fictions and the imaginary unconscious of characters, it manages to escape the censorship of a fictional mode that rejects "unanswerable" philosophic questions. These questions concerning the nature of reality are voiced in the hypothetical mode of address, a journalist interrogating the possibilities of producing fiction.

In *Wild Strawberries* (1957), the relationship between the past and the imagination of the main character is even more blurred, as the series of flashbacks and dreams that interrupt the narration of an aging professor's trip to accept an honorary degree alternate between registers of representation. The return of Victor Sjöström to the screen to play the part of the professor accents this film's relationship to its antecedents in silent Swedish cinema, and it in turn became very influential on the kinds of modernist structures that would emerge in the art cinema to follow. A very similar structure will later inform Alain Resnais's film *Providence* (1977), where a famous author remembers his life on the eve of his death, his memories conditioned by the baroque fantasies of his psyche—but *Wild Strawberries* had a more general impact for the presentation of psyche and memory as the inspiration of a modernist practice. Mai Zetterling's *Night Games* (1966) uses similarly baroque fantasy-flashbacks to depict the memories of a man as he returns to the house in which he apparently passed an extremely unhappy and perverse childhood, the elements of which are exaggerated by the film into a surreal dream vision of grotesques.

This narrative practice of Bergman and Zetterling parallels contemporaneous explorations of memory in not only psychoanalysis and psychology, but in neurophysiology. There is an effort by science to describe and theorize about memory, even locate it physically. Ironically, in order to describe memory imaging, science often has recourse to the most modern means of imaging and information storing available to the culture; in this period, immediately preceding the dominance of cybernetic metaphors, there is a tendency to assume that mental processes are the equivalent of cinematic representations. In a sense, scientists take the flashback or the Proustian novel's verbal description of memory to be evidence. The process of memory still needs to be compared to known mechanisms or inventive fictional descriptions. In the films themselves, as well as in the larger culture (even in scientific/medical paradigms), cinema becomes an operative metaphor for the brain's imaging capacity. A next section of this chapter will consider the scientific conception of memory that is the background for film's treatment of memory.

Cognitive Shifts Inherent in Modernism

We can see in the reemergence of filmic modernism a shift in the presentation of memory processes and cognition, both as pertains to the delineation of character psychology and to the film spectator. In earlier chapters we saw how early filmic expression affected the writings of psychologist Hugo Münsterberg, providing illustrative evidence of his theories of memory functioning, and how avant-garde film of the twenties could be seen to parallel the writings of the philosopher Henri Bergson. These comparisons pose the question of confluences of theoretical thought and creative work. Filmic treatment of temporality and memory might inspire scientific inquiry or it might simply run parallel to it; in few cases historically can film artists be said to be *directly* schooled in their filmic research by scholarly writings—though, as we saw, the twenties avant-garde is one moment where some evidence of intellectual cross-fertilization is evident. The writings of Freud can be seen as having a more general impact, but primarily through the pathway of the popularization of certain Freudian notions and the general assimilation of a version of psychoanalysis by the public.

Similarly, indirect effect and/or parallel development are appropriate ways of characterizing the impact of research in cognitive psychology and neurobiology concerning memory processes on the modernist filmic forms that emerge beginning in the late fifties. Again, a generalized popularization of the scientific theses may be responsible for whatever parallels we find between changing filmic representations and research into the way humans recall events. The filmic use of fragmentation representing memory as fleeting, highly selective images governed by an individual's subjective experience (as distinct from the highly secondarized retelling of events that dominated the previous coding of the flashback) might not depend on theoretical sources at all, but rather on a lineage of experimentation in literary and filmic narration. As scientific research has pushed itself away from the expressive essays of philosophy and towards more self-contained discourse and more empirical methodology, it has nonetheless explored areas that are of immediate consequence for the representation of memory. An exploration of the parallels between theoretical research in this area and filmic expression is worth illuminating, as we seek to explore how this fascination with the mind's functioning dominates a shift in epistemologies evidenced in certain of these modernist films and in the flowering of cognitive science.

We can note, for example, that the concept of "image memory" has undergone a distinct evolution. At present, cognitive psychologists are concerned with exploring the relationship between verbal and visual memory, as well as considering how such memory is linked to memory traces inaugurated by the other senses.[12] If a kind of "mind's eye" camera image metaphor of memory dominated Hugo Münsterberg's theories and allowed him to celebrate the way cinema incarnated human memory,[13] more recent research circumscribes this metaphor. Image memory, or as it is alternatively called, visual memory, is still discussed as such, but it is now being shown to be an ability held differentially by various individuals. It is also now believed to be mostly a process of encoding and decoding information. This information was originally perceived visually, but the model of visual perception itself currently incorporates into perceptual processes a continual consultation with memory. As Ulric Neisser states, "perception is generally the result of an integration of many snapshots, which creates something different from any of them; seeing itself is a matter of visual memory."[14] The term "snapshot," of course, retains the earlier camera model, but here it is used not to refer to what the subject sees but to the patterns that are registered on the retina. These patterns are never individually directly understood, but combine with each other and schemata the subject possesses to produce the percepts. Visual cognition is for Neisser an "active and constructive process."

This model of cognition has consequences for the model of memory. Percepts are encoded as memory in another form and must be reconstituted to become a visual display. In other words, an information-processing model has supplanted the camera-image model of memory in most instances. Cognitive psychology has not traded in the camera for the computer, it has moved from a machine metaphor to a computer-programming metaphor, one that considers the vicissitudes of the flow of symbols, or seen more abstractly, information.[15]

In the special cases of "photographic memory" or "eidetic memory" as it also is called, something closer to the camera-image model of memory is sustained in current theory; these terms refer to the ability found in only certain individuals to retain analogues of visual displays in short-term memory.[16] Subjects tend to describe their eidetic memories as "projected on some external surface" and in the present tense.[17] The first description of photographic memory, by Johannes Evangelista Purkinje, dates from the period immediately surrounding the development of photography itself, 1819, while additional work by Johannes Müller was published in 1826.[18] This points, perhaps, to a convergence within the scientific imagination of interest in the image as reproducible both mechanically and mentally.

Twentieth-century research on eidetic memory is primarily in terms of geometric figures and pictures that can be so reconstituted by some subjects as to be measured or described in detail purely from the subjects' memory images of them. Some research suggests that eidetic memory is stronger in young children and disappears with maturation and the development of language skills.[19] It is also possible that "eidetikers," subjects with strong eidetic memory capabilities, may be able to retrieve material from long-term memory more vividly as images. Some eidetikers project their recalled images as three-dimensional images that have more cues of spatial reality than the original stimulus, while others have the ability to make their recalled images move and change in time, like the cinematic image.[20]

If true, these scientific findings have intriguing implications for understanding the powerful imaginative impact of the representation of memory as strongly eidetic in flashback films. The cinematic representation serves to recall and reinforce the eidetic recall of childhood that is for most adults lost to some degree. Our nostalgia for our childhood perception is perhaps tapped at some unconscious level. Further, as an ability that only certain adults possess, vivid visual memory has a magical, mystical quality to it, a quality reinforced by the finding that certain drug experiences such as mescaline produce eidetic memory capabilities.[21] R. R. Holt suggests these qualities in his explanation of why eidetic memory is discouraged in American culture:

In a factually oriented, skeptical, anti-intraceptive, brass-tacks culture like ours, where the paranormal is scoffed at and myth and religion are in decline, the capacity for vivid imagery has little survival value and less social acceptability. We live in an age of literalism, an era that distrusts the imagination, while at the same time it develops its beat fringe of avid seekers after drugs that may artificially restore the capacity for poetic vision. It is little wonder that our children rapidly lose their eidetic capacity and that adults are made uneasy by the admission that they can experience things that are not factually present.[22]

While we might wonder if Holt has overstated his case, particularly in light of certain developments in American society since the sixties that make it appear on the whole as less literalist, his perceptive usefully indicates how films that manifest such imagery might function to provide a kind of poetic and mythic vision. Modernist films from this period which code such imagery as completely mimetic borrow on this charmed magical quality.

Modernist films also work with the flash memory image, the involuntary intrusive brief flashback that gradually leads to a more expansive recall. We can see how brevity can be taken as a sign of mental processes meant to enhance the mimetic aspect of the representation. A short image correlates with the rapidity of human perceptual and cognitive processes. The isolation of a brief instance of recall serves to augment the coding of an unconscious recall breaking through repressive forces. Still, does the notion of a single, isolated visual flash of memory, vivid and complete as an image, or a series of such images linked together, correspond to scientific views of memory? Can such flash memory images be distinguished from phantasy and secondary elaboration?

A series of scientific experiments by William Penfield throughout the fifties on electrode stimulation of the brain may have spurred acceptance and utilization of this notion of brief vivid visual recall.[23] Penfield found that electric stimulation during brain surgery provoked extremely detailed visions on the part of his patients of incidents from their past. He argued that this recall constituted evidence of a "permanent record of the stream of consciousness," though this conclusion has been widely discounted by other scientists who hold that his experiments provide no new evidence that nothing that registers perceptually ever escapes being permanently recorded.[24] For our purposes here it is fascinating that Penfield's terminology is already borrowed from literary usage. This points to the circularity of artistic and scientific influences, a circle that is perhaps made full by the fact that Penfield's studies were widely enough publicized to have been a factor in encouraging a literary and filmic treatment of such direct visual recall. That Penfield's theory of a permanent stream of consciousness has been largely refuted does not dispel the effects of the widespread dissemination of such a theory in the mid-fifties and early sixties.

Electrode research on memory process continues at present to search for the exact electro-chemical processes that result in memory storage. There has been some speculation on mechanisms which differentiate short-term and long-term memory, as well as unconscious and conscious recall.[25] Several hypotheses on the specifics of an electro-chemical tracing and transfer of memory information are still being debated. However, the research into the biological infrastructure that results in information being registered grows out of investigation of the biology of neurons in rats. For the purpose of this research the source of the information is irrelevant; so far, such research concerns what happens after unique or mixed sensory impressions or simple concepts are translated into rhythmic patterns of electrical impulses.

There may be no way to isolate experimentally human perception from its elaboration as cognition in order to differentiate the specifics of different sources' registration. We do know that cognitive psychologists argue that it is likely that all forms of sensory input are part of a perceptual-cognitive cycle in which no such thing as a whole image simply exists in an unreconstructed form. The flash image of memory by which films represent the actual process of memory are best seen as figures, metaphors for memory fragments.

The process of reassembling fragments as more complete memories, one that informs the narratives of so many modernist films, is in actuality less of an additive montage (revealing the truth as the sum of evidentiary elements) and more of a secondary elaboration, like the telling of a dream. Few films acknowledge the fictional aspect inherent in memory, residing at the core of its process of storage and retrieval. They substitute the image-as-truth for the reconstructed memory and have us believe that while memory is subjective, it is not fractured and recombined intra-subjectively. Occasionally, though, certain modernist films will merge dream and memory imagery, explore the surreal aspects of memory and investigate intra-subjectivity, mapping out through poetic vision a terrain that science can discuss theoretically, but not yet measure experimentally.

Memory Flashes and the Modernist Literary Conjunctions

If films since World War II give us the sense that a resurgent modernism is developing different filmic forms in which the expression of cinematic temporality will undergo major transformations, it is with one cut between two graphically matched, but temporally disjunct images of two different men's hands that *Hiroshima, Mon Amour* clinches this sense that a new tendency in flashbacks emerges in the late fifties. The key role of *Hiroshima, Mon Amour* can be discussed in many different ways; here it shall first be presented in the context of a grouping together of a series of films made by Resnais as one example of the modernist literary influence on script temporality that characterizes a form of filmic modernism. This modernist literary influence on films parallels the emergence of the *Nouvelle Vague* in France; in fact some historians and critics never made much of a distinction between the two parallel and simultaneous movements, but there are good reasons historically and theoretically for doing so, especially as concerns the mode of film production.[26] For our purposes, here, the distinction permits us to note that the *Nouvelle Vague* films, while often elliptical, introduced their temporal absences and jumps within a linear temporality which for the most part avoided the flashback.[27] On the other hand, many of the films whose authors or coauthors were first literary authors or those by director/screenwriters outside the New Wave group not only frequently use flashbacks, they produce a new richness in flashback structuration.

It is paradoxical that the filmmaking of Resnais should represent one of the most consistent explorations of the flashback and cinematic temporality in this reemergence of modernism, since he is among the few "auteurist" directors not to write his own scripts. Grouping "his" films together like this becomes one means of tracing the variations on flashback function and memory representation during this period, as well as the literary/scriptwriter role in the explorations of variations on the flashback in this reemergence of modernism. Certainly Resnais's shorts already introduce the concepts of memory as a major filmic preoccupation of his: *Nuit et Brouillard* (*Night and Fog,* 1955) situates its footage of the concentration camp as a virtual flashback within the space of shots of the present site of the former camp; *Toute la Mémoire du Monde* (1956) presents France's Bibliothèque Nationale within a metaphor that makes it a collective mnemonic system, and *La Chant du Styrène* (1958) constitutes through the voice-over commentary the investigation of the production of plastic as a flashback into the birth of this material.

Hiroshima, Mon Amour, (1959), Resnais's first feature film, has a script by Marguerite Duras that develops this concern with memory and the flashback in the context of filmic fiction. It narrates the romantic encounter of a French woman (Emmanuèle Riva) who has come to Hiroshima to act in a film about peace, with a Japanese architect (Eiji Okada) whose family had been in Hiroshima at the time of the bombing, but who, himself, was away in the army. The narration is quite selective in its mimesis of this situation, at times presenting these two characters within a stylized realism, at times using them as points of departure for a decidedly abstract play of language, images, and concepts. Over the course of the film, the woman reveals her past, events which took place in France during the occupation and liberation in a series of three flashback segments, the first of which is a single image, the other two more extended image sequences.

The first flashback is quite extraordinary. Its direct cut to the past is devoid of the usual filmic punctuation, a technique which is further accented by its brief duration and the fact that it remains thoroughly unexplained until much later in the narrative.

While its complete narrative signification remains temporarily opaque, two aspects of this flashback which even first time viewers can grasp are its focalization and, to some extent, the context that inspires it. The focalization is clearly that of the female lead character, a French actress who is never given a name in the film. The morning after she spends the night with a Japanese man, the woman apparently wakes first, for we open on shots of the street retrospectively focalized as her subjective shot from the hotel balcony. This is followed by a shot of her in the balcony doorway of her hotel room as she looks back at the man with whom she has slept. This establishes the inserted flashback as her memory association upon looking at his upturned hand lying against the sheet (shown in subjective close-up). The woman focalizes another scene, the meaningful elements of which pass by perhaps too quickly for complete recognition, though they constitute a swish pan from a hand of a soldier in a German uniform to his face as he lies, dead, on the ground.

Despite the clarity of this focalization, the narrative context of this flashback is only partially apparent due to the plane of poetic abstraction on which the film opens. A dialogue between two voices about Hiroshima is accompanied by a montage of images in counterpoint. These images include close-ups of bodies in an embrace that may or may not be the bodies of the couple who will be introduced shortly, mixed with images of hospitals in Hiroshima, the museum that commemorates the bombing and footage from documentaries of that bombing (films which are in fact shown regularly at the museum). The dialogue mixes an abstract exotic exchange with a discussion of the subject matter of the images, the museum, the bombing, the evidence of the damage, the attempts to document this damage. It prefigures the narrative scene to follow, shots of the French woman and the Japanese man in the bed of her hotel room at four o'clock in the morning. The dialogue between them becomes more concretely that of fictional characters, the representation of lovers, though echoes and reprises of the earlier abstracted dialogue can be heard in their exchange and the voices are the same. We can retrospectively hear the opening dialogue as the poetic abstraction of a possible dialogue between the two lovers that is at the same time "impossible" in the manner of much of Duras's fiction—too abstract to be "real."

The balcony flashback, then, is grounded in a nascent fiction whose allegorical elements have been anticipated by the abstract introduction. The spectator knows the female character associates the hand of her Japanese lover lying against the bedsheet with the image of another hand. Some spectators may recognize the German uniform of the dead soldier, yet despite the marked focalization, this flashed image is not even necessarily understood as one specifically from the woman's memory, her past.

The ensuing narrative and the flashbacks posterior to this one will fill in the signification of this image, too rapid and enigmatic to be anything but a superb visual clue to a story that for the time being is unknown. The form of this visual enigma is a truly radical departure in narrative form; certainly Hitchcock could give us the visual clues of parallel lines marking the patient's repressed memories in *Spellbound,* but this enigmatic flashback in *Hiroshima, Mon Amour* seems to be of another order altogether, far more minimalist and left to dangle longer over a narrative. It hangs, alone, unremarked upon by another character's recognition that constitutes it as sign. It is therefore a far more disruptive trace of a new and different mode of *écriture*.

Since these Nevers flashbacks are so integral to our current sense of the film, it is curious to learn, as Duras tells us in an introduction to her published script, that the flashback passages were elaborated not in the original version of the script, but in a later version: "The passages on Nevers, which were not included in the original scenario (July 1958) were annotated before the shooting in France (December 1958), . . . They therefore represent a work apart from the script (see the Appendix: Nocturnal Notations)."[28] The published scenario, then, includes the Nevers flashbacks as they were incorporated into the earlier script before shooting, but also the preliminary descriptions of this aspect of the narrative, a treatment in the form of a fragmented short story, elements of which are quite different from the shooting script. This double rendering allows us to examine how the flashbacks add to the ambiguity of character motivation and the irony of voice.

Duras's script is divided into parts, like scenes in a play or chapters in a book, though these divisions are not evident in Resnais's film. These divisions do signal a certain literary conception of the work that remains apparent in the work, which is not to say that its visual rendering is any less dynamic. Instead what emerges is a new fusion of literary and filmic treatments of the past, as presented by voice and image, a fusion that needs to be examined in some detail.

Except for the brief flashback described above that occurs in Part II of the script, the other flashbacks to Nevers begin at the end of Part III and then dominate Part IV. In terms of the film, the two distinct scenes that generate the flashbacks become more clearly places when presented in the mise-en-scene of Resnais. The flashbacks occur in alternation first with a scene of the couple lying on a bed in the afternoon in the Japanese man's apartment, and then later that evening, with a scene in the present that takes place in a bar in Hiroshima as she continues, with much more detail, the story of her first love. The bed scene generates flashbacks that accompany her narration of the past, similar in form to a standard flashback to the story-told and the voice-over uses the third person to describe the German lover and the past tense which indicates a distance from these historical events. The flashbacks generated by the bar scene are quite different in form; the telling is an acting out. She addresses not the Japanese man, but the German soldier whom he has tacitly agreed to embody for her by acting the part. He questions her in a manner that urges her to continue her story as he adopts the German's persona. She seems to be in a trance, while her voice-over is in the present tense and addresses the German in the second person. There is none of the emotional distance that we sense in the bed scene flashbacks. Instead these flashbacks rejoin the first brief flashback as representing involuntary memory, a surging of a memory image outside the control of the voice. The voice shifts to the plane of abstract figuration of a psychoanalytic acting out, rejoining the voice-over dialogue of the opening sequence. As such voice-over commentary and the image editing develop a special rhythm that makes this flashback so lyrically unique.

In fact, these three sets of flashbacks are highly structured in correspondence to one another. The first flashback introduces the lover with his German identity visually marked by his uniform, but so quickly that even an audience who lived through the War and for whom that uniform is an indelible memory might, in other contexts, not fully realize what they've seen. When the Japanese man asks the question that initiates the second bedroom flashback, he asks, "Your lover during the War, was he French?," a question conditioned by the poetics of a modernist narrative leap since we have no textual evidence of how the Japanese lover knew she had a lover during the War. It is possible that this indicates an ellipsis, other conversations that we are to have understood as having already taken place, but he seems, rather, to be embodying an extra-narrative knowledge, the knowledge of the text and author, if you will, and in some ways giving voice to a question marginally available to the viewer. Having seen the earlier flash-image the reader could perhaps have wondered, "Is the man she kisses after his death her lover from the War period and what uniform is he wearing?" The Japanese man then, never having "witnessed" the memory the spectator saw as a flashback, asks this question for the spectator, after what constitutes a considerable delay. Her response to her Japanese lover is simply a negation in the terms the question was posed, "No, he was not French," without going on to specify that he was German, with all the additional referential information this might convey. However, the image that accompanies this, the soldier crossing the square of Nevers, allows the audience a better view of his uniform and leads anyone who possesses any knowledge of the Occupation to deduce that if he was not French, he must have been German. Still, within the second set of flashback images, the full weight of the ideological taboo crossed by this love affair is unspoken, and the lyricism of the images, the racing across fields for clandestine encounters, counteracts the charged context of the War. This segment ends abruptly on the German's death, repeating the moment presented in the first flashback.

At first, then, the past is flashed in condensation, the love affair with the enemy is represented by a single element, his death. Then the second flashback series presents the passion of the affair as a lyrical expression of desire, outside the political context, except for the intrusion of death as a result of that political context. In the third flashback series the images repeat, but quite differently, given new connotations by the shift in context and subjective commentary, and by the force of repetition. This time the flashback is introduced by an almost documentary presentation of Nevers, focusing on its geography: river, walled inner city, fields. This gives us the landscape devoid temporarily of the narrative elements of the love affair. Then we are introduced to the political transgression such a love affair signified. The weight of the flashback is on her punishment after the end of the War and what she calls her "madness." The temporality of this flashback mixes a linear progression of certain events with a sort of flashback within the flashback to earlier events, while presenting two stages of her punishment, being locked in her bedroom and being locked in the cellar of her parent's home, in an atemporal alternation.

A look at Duras's preliminary treatment of the Nevers flashback is particularly intriguing, for in her original text concerning Nevers the girl speaks in the midst of the love affair that she knows is forbidden. In the film, this voice of the girl in love is present only in the third segment of flashbacks to Nevers where she presents herself as initially far more innocent of the situation than in the written version. In the writing, the girl, presented as having a Jewish mother who is in hiding, is aware of her attraction to the enemy, whom she labels as such. The film, in contrast, withholds the verbal identification of her lover as the enemy. He is simply described as "not French" and shown wearing a German uniform. None of the other characters or the town receive as much semic development in the film as the treatment. What emerges in the film is more ambiguity concerning the social condemnation of a romance with the enemy than exists in written form. The treatment more directly explores the force of desire, desire that is spurred by the fact that it is forbidden, desire that is tinged with hatred and self-effacement, desire that ignores the history that might condemn it, not out of innocence, but because it is driven by a stronger force than conscious will. In the film traces remain of this overwhelming desire, but it is more a condition of the innocence of young love, a youthfulness that motivates and permits such a forgetting of circumstances. One question that the Nevers flashbacks raise as they are presented in the film is the differential readings they might evoke in various audiences. A French audience would bring to these sequences more referential associations that might fill in some of the material presented in the written work but omitted from the film precisely because stating it, for such an audience, would be redundant.

This leads me to make a more general comment about the way in which some modernist flashbacks present brief images whose signifiers lack verbal redundancy that fixes their meaning. This tendency towards a style that works on repetition and reference without redundancy of coding, especially as concerns verbal cementing of signifieds to signifiers, constitutes the spectator as participant in the formation of the text. The more references a spectator brings to the decipherment of visual images, the more information these images will relay and deflect into new configurations. *Hiroshima, Mon Amour* provides considerable information concerning the history of the Hiroshima bombing in its documentary references in the opening montage, earning it acclaim for its innovative mixing of fiction with documentary codes. Within the film, Nevers is being explained to a foreigner, a device that introduces some elements of defamiliarization in the description and images which open the third flashback sequence, a brief quasi-documentary on the town, yet the film directs its discourse more at an audience in possession of the French frame of reference.

Instead, we are invited to partake of the French woman's subjective recall, in a manner entirely parallel to the subjective recall and shuffled temporal order in Delluc's *Le Silence*. The temporal structure of this third Nevers flashback can be interpreted as a particular instance of associational memory whose jumps and elisions are themselves elements that signify the position of these events in the subject's mind. The subjective recall does give a linear account of her punishment. We are invited to read this as an inability to differentiate developments and reproduce a chronology. The cellar and the bedroom confinements are interwoven, apparently because they cannot be remembered as a distinct progression of hours and days. The death of the German is interwoven with this punishment perhaps to indicate that it remained a memory throughout this time. Each temporal inversion or embedding is at least possible to interpret as itself imbued with meaning, with being a signifier of the unconscious of this fictional character. To say that a form of cinematic expression is meant to allow one to appreciate the characterization of an individual's unconscious is to say that the images and sounds invite psychoanalytic interpretation in order to be understood even at the most basic level of intellection of the text.

A series of paradigmatic oppositions and inversions surround the flashbacks. "Having seen" versus "not having seen" various aspects of Hiroshima opens the dialogue debate in the abstract beginning of the film, giving way to another abstracted opposition which in the French is "Tu me tue, Tu me fait du bien," roughly translated as "You destroy me, you are so good for me." Presented abstractly, this last opposition seems to suggest the paradoxes of erotic encounters, a pleasurable, yet painful desire, the self-effacing aspects of loving. One another level the opposition indicates the potential for perverse motivations inherent in any interaction with the Other, be it at the level of interpersonal male-female relationships or in international affairs. This antithesis characterizes the bombing of Hiroshima, at the time celebrated as a victory even as it caused annihilation and suffering. Duras's poetic dialogue suggests perhaps that if humanity could raise but a single voice during any war, it would be a voice infused with such paradoxes.

Remembering is paradigmatically opposed not only to forgetting but to not remembering, as remembering and forgetting are played against each other not simply as parallel and opposing terms, but ones that garner a whole series of differing connotations. In the repetition of the word "forgetting," the Nietzschean sense of forgetting within the theory of resentment is brought into play. Nietzsche considers forgetting as a letting go of the pain attached to events in the past, pain that would have been directed either at the self as guilt or the Other as revenge. At one point in the opening dialogue these concepts are presented in particularly evocative language, suggesting at once the multiple meanings associated with memory and forgetting, and the temporality of each process:

She: Listen to me. Like you I know what it is to forget.
He: No, you don't know what it is to forget.
She: Like you, I have a memory. I know what it is to forget.
He: No, you don't have a memory.
She: Like you I tried with all my might not to forget. Like you, I forgot. Like you I wanted to have an inconsolable memory, a memory of shadows and stone. Like you, I struggled with all my might, every day, against the horror of no longer understanding all the reasons for remembering. Like you, I forgot. Why deny the obvious necessity for memory?

The terms of this dialogue are taken up repeatedly in the Hiroshima imagery with its "shadows and stones" that mark the atomic bomb damage, and also by later dialogue and the flashback imagery that concerns the woman's past in Nevers. The two tragedies are structured by the text to be mirror reflections of one another—not the same, but containing the same elements in a somewhat inverted configuration, different alignments of personal pain and the political signification, different alignments also of desire, celebration, and suffering, the pleasure/pain opposition discussed earlier. The film persists in displacing the terms of the oppositions, in realigning them against our common sense and in evoking new meanings for the words and images. Its force is this reconstruction of the meaning of memory.

Most of Duras's writing and films, and most of Resnais's films (all the rest by other authors) continue this work on memory, though not always through the use of flashbacks. Duras wrote another quite different film script about memory and its reconstitution, *Un aussi longue absence,* which was made into a film directed by Henri Colpi (1960). This film pivots on the appearance of a tramp who may or may not be the amnesiac husband of the owner of a cafe in a small town. The woman struggles to resuscitate her husband's memory, but the tramp remains outside her efforts to identify him or elicit his recall of their shared past. Rather than use flashbacks, the images remain fixed in the present; only dialogue is used to evoke this past, but in elaborate ways. Talking about the past while others do not hear, or do not want to talk about the past, structures the unrelenting present of this film. This incessant verbalization of the past is present in many of Duras's other works, but flashbacks appear again only in *Natalie Granger* (1972), in the form of one repeating image from the characters' past, the image of Natalie's school teacher reporting to her mother on Natalie's state of mind. One phrase from this report, "Une telle violence dans une si petite fille" (so much violence in such a young girl), echoes as a metonymic refrain across the film.

In contrast, several of Resnais's films rework the flashback structure, with different scenarists reworking the memory flashes of *Hiroshima, Mon Amour* to distinct ends. The flashes are not always identifiable as memories of the past, however, so to be more exact, it is necessary to modify and generalize this statement to say that the subsequent Resnais films rework the structure of the temporally disjunct insert. This twenty year investigation of the disjunctive temporality can be traced over the following films: *L'Année Derniere à Marienbad* (scenario, Robbe-Grillet, 1961), *Muriel, ou le temps d'un retour* (scenario, Jean Cayrol, 1963), *La Guerre est finie* (scenario, Jorge Semprun, 1966), *Je t'aime, Je t'aime* (scenario, Jacques Sternberg, 1968), *Stavisky* (scenario, Jorge Semprun, 1974), *Providence* (scenario, David Mercer, 1976), *Mon Oncle d'Amerique* (scenario, Jean Gruault, 1980). Some of these films have true flashbacks, some other sorts of temporal jumps (such as the imaginary leaps into a hypothetical future in *La Guerre est finie*), and some have other devices that operate somewhat similarly to flashbacks. In many ways this series of variations on the flashback that one finds in Resnais's films has to do as much with his powerful and sensitive talent for montage rhythms as it does for a thematic concern with time. Let's briefly explore what the temporal strategy of each of these films signifies for a modernist reworking of the flashback, then ask what these series of films represent in terms of the reemergence of a cinematic modernism.[29]

L'Année Derniere à Marienbad poses all its narrative events as somewhat hypothetical occurrences in a formal universe in which design and pattern tend to dominate reference, but somehow, despite the rigorous beauty of the game board, elements of reference and narrative take hold. Thus the repeated vague references to the past that punctuate the film, to events from last year, could be entirely without story behind them, no last year, no event, just an imaginary, fictive reference with no referent. Or last year could mean the time in which the film itself unfolds, frozen in time, repeating and interrogating itself. Or there could be a last year imbued with fictive density, that haunts the memory of the fiction in the present and it is this tease of a possible temporal map to the fiction, a posited reality that establishes one year and the next and a movement of diegetic memory between them. The pseudo-flashbacks augment this tease within the film's unfolding.

Even the title *Muriel, ou le temps d'un retour* suggests flashbacks; the French for "flashback" is "retour en arrière" though the English term is more commonly used than its translated equivalent by most French speakers. The title takes the temporality of "en arrière" in the French idiom and places it in front of the "retour"—a literal translation of this would be the time of a return or a going back. The spatial transition of temporality in the title is itself an analogue for the filmic flashback, which transposes space and time, placing two non-contiguous moments next to each other. Each of the double strands of the narrative entails events in the past that remain to be clarified over the course of the film. Bernard's (Jean-Baptiste Thierée) experience as a soldier in Algeria and the significance of Muriel constitutes one strand while the other concerns the love affair between his step-mother, Hélène (Delphine Seyrig), and the visitor, Alphonse, some twenty-four years earlier. Whereas the past of Hélène and Alphonse is revealed through a series of fragmented verbal enunciations, the revelation of Bernard's past comes as a voice-over monologue when he shows a home movie to a friend accompanied by a voice-over explanation. This screening of the film from Algeria operates like a flashback within the structure of the film. Still, the difference here is also significant, first, because in constituting its "flashback" as a film screening within the diegesis, the film discharges this sense of anteriority without itself assuming the narrative omniscience to evoke the past through devices. Second, the film clip presents different images than Bernard narrates verbally. The verbal images tell the explicit story of the torture and death of a member of the Algerian resistance, while the images in the film are mundane images of the soldiers' daily life. These routine home movies mark a displacement of the visual from the censored event to an acceptable banality, whose contingent relationship to horrors nonetheless serves as backdrop for the confession. In contrast to *Hiroshima, Mon Amour, Muriel*'s diegetic unfolding remains fixed in a present which is disturbed by the past, which evokes the past at every turn, but which precisely can't embody this past as flashback memories. It has access only to the exterior of what is manifest in words, or through the material evidence from the past, a film clip that can be reinscribed (though of course this film artifact is ultimately part of its own fiction). This "limitation" is by no means an aesthetic "lack" of the film, but rather a constructed boundary inside of which its energy and difference as a fiction is manifest.

On the other hand, the mental images that interrupt the present narrative moments in *La Guerre est finie* are structured much like the first flashback in *Hiroshima, Mon Amour*. Brief inserts referring to another time, introducing events that are decipherable to the audience only *après-coup*, the difference is that only some of these are flashbacks, while others are imaginary images of possible simultaneous or future events. Diego (Yves Montand), the anti-Franco militant, engages in secret political organizing in Spain while in exile in France, crossing the forbidden border to his homeland regularly under false identities as part of a movement to coordinate a leftist resistance. These flashes to potential events are all focalized by Diego, the embodiment of his fears, anxieties, but also sometimes, his desires. Though they have often been called flashforwards this is not truly accurate, not only because only a few are projected as occurring in the future, but also because these segments do not necessarily represent events that will happen within the narrative; rather, they exist as an imaginary potentiality, a speculation. Rather than the omniscience of an authorial voice that can reveal a narrative future in the present, or a supernatural power of prediction on the part of a character who senses his future, these imaginary flashes signify the subjective speculation of the character's mind somewhat parallel to the subjective capacity for memory that the flashback often indicates. The imaginary course of events they predict is often contradicted by the actual narrative unfolding of events as the film's temporal unfolding catches up to what was previously the future of the narrative.

Diego's subjectivity is always manifest in the various temporally disjunct image sequences, though this subjectivity is indicated by various means. Some of these sequences are in fact flashback memories, as indicated either by a voice-over or due to the fact that they repeat images we have already seen in the narrative. The repeated images often center on women (as is the case of the erotic image memories of Nadine [Geneviève Bujold], as well as images of Marie [Ingrid Thulin] listening to him explain his life), but others recall his meetings with comrades such as Roberto. The past is indicated by voice-over in the case of the image of Madame Lopez, but here there is also a delay in providing the identification of this image as a flashback. The first time we see Madame Lopez open the door of an apartment in the foreground of a shot, while Juan is visible inside the apartment in depth, it is as part of a montage insert before we know this woman is Madame Lopez. From the image framing and her direct look into the camera, the spectator deduces that this anonymous woman is to be understood as opening the door to someone standing in the position the camera is occupying. However, we do not know when this event occurs (past, simultaneous present, or future), or who knocked at the door. This image when we first see it appears somewhat hypothetical in the same sense that many other image inserts represent things that could be taking place or will take place. However, after Diego tries to find Madame Lopez's apartment in a modern apartment complex only to end up knocking on a stranger's door, his voice-over recounts the fact that he was searching on the basis of a memory he had of finding Madame Lopez and therefore Juan, his comrade, the previous year at the same address. This is coupled with an image segment that repeats the image of Madame Lopez, this time allowing us to identify her and ascertain that this event occurred in the past, and that Diego was present outside the frame of the image, making this a subjective point of view. Similarly, after the death of another comrade, Ramon, an image showing him standing in front of his house is accompanied by a voice-over both remembering Ramon in the past and commenting on how Ramon will be remembered throughout the trip to Madrid that Carlos is making in Ramon's place.

It is also interesting to consider the image sequences that are the flashbacks, but which correspond formally to the flashback inserts. When Diego imagines the location of the apartment of his alias and the appearance of his alias' daughter whom he has only previously heard as a voice on the phone and never seen, the representation hesitates. The first time, eight different young women flash through "his mind" as indicated by the montage of various images of typical university-age parisiennes walking along the streets of the rue Mouffetard area near the address Diego knows belongs to his alias. The segment ends with a fluid movement in to the street sign for rue de l'estrapade followed by a movement out on the number 7, establishing the known address. The second sequence imagining Nadine and this site follows a cut from an unknown woman on Diego's train to this same woman taking up the part of Nadine near l'estrapade, followed by eleven montage images of other possible Nadines (some of which repeat) and again ending on the number 7, but this time with a camera movement in on it.

These speculative flashes, then, can not take for granted what the flashback, regularly, though perhaps somewhat misleadingly, assumes: the ability to accurately reproduce the appearance of things. Imaginary and potential future spaces are obviously less available to "visualization" than are the events of the past. The street and neighborhood are exact (Diego could be represented as familiar with this famous Parisian site). The appearance of Nadine is unknown and therefore oscillates between a number of possibilities. This directs us to a certain assumption inherent in the traditional use of the flashback, that memory is clear and accurate when it is not lying. Flashbacks traditionally give us a clear visual image of the past. One of the modernist impulses will be to throw this clarity of visualization of memory into question. When *La Guerre est finie* asks for a viewing that considers the problematics of voice within representation of an imaginary vision of the future (a question that the categorization of this film as one using flashforwards has largely ignored), it raises some of the same theoretical issues as the hypothetical flashbacks in *L'Année Derniere à Marienbad* raise concerning the problematics of vision into the past. The concrete visual reconstruction of a "real" narrative past can no longer be taken for granted. These processes of raising doubts about image memory and imagination ask for an investigation of the means of narration, voice, and "vision" in films, even as they present concrete options within narrative representation. Their play with reflexivity occurs within certain limits, and the terms of these limits are finally as important as the reflexivity. A tension develops between the boundaries imposed by the creation of a character mimetically linked to human beings and the power of an author to fabricate all elements of narrative, including character and temporality. The representation of vision of mental processes in film, per se, are called into question by these films, a question which is of course very important to the history and theory of the flashback.

In a sense, *Je t'aime, Je t'aime,* by way of its metaphor of time travel, "of reliving a moment in one's past," represents the opposite pole of memory representation. It treats memory as manifestly visual. Film clips come to embody the experimental subject's reinsertion into the past. Instead of calling into question the exactitude of visual memory, the film shows the time traveler in precise image sequences from his past. The past becomes like a giant film archive, composed of billions of shots covering every lived instance; to relive a moment of the past means to arbitrarily start the image sequence at a certain point in this mass of accumulated film footage. However, Resnais, himself, at the time of the film's release, rejected the term "retour en arrière" (flashback) to describe the complex reorganization of time sequence that occurs in the film. Instead, he commented:

> I had the impression of a sort of eternal present. The hero relives his past, but when he relives it we are with him, the film always takes place in the present. There are absolutely no flashbacks or anything like them. I hope to arrive at a kind of dramatic vision different from that of a chronological narrative. I want to say, like one of my heroes, "I am mixed up." I would like to achieve a dramatic unfolding that while being completely clear and comprehensible for the spectators, does not cut itself off from the roots I hope to have kept in surrealism and automatic writing.[30]

If the term "flashback" for Resnais holds connotations of viewing a character's subjective vision of his or her memory of the past (as implied in the above objection to the term) within the way we have been examining the flashback in this book, the term still seems relevant to evoke here, albeit problematically. It should be noted that this same relationship between memory, images, and time travel was established in Chris Marker's *La Jetée* (1962). *La Jetée*'s surging memory images are equally problematic as actual flashbacks. Marker's time traveler gains access to the past by means of a series of image associations he has of the time before the war; his ability to access the past will later be used to project him into the future so that he can gather the technology needed by his devastated culture. Are his images of the past truly flashbacks? They fall more closely into conceptual categories than into a narrative sequence (a peacetime morning, for example), but they could be fragments of a narrative that eludes us. The shot of the woman in bed, often remarked upon because it is the only shot in the film that shows movement, could be understood as a personal memory image of the experimental subject. Then the traveler is sent back to the time before the war, entering into a past that is not presented as his personal past at all, but a romance he is experiencing for the first time. However, this distinction collapses when he witnesses the death of his adult time-traveler self as a young boy on the "jetée," the airplane ramp, at Orly. Thus the flashback memory association is finally operative *après-coup* in a most startling and innovative way, one that supplements the flashback's association with memory and the unconscious.

Similarly, the sequences that follow the experiment in the "sphere" in *Je t'aime, Je t'aime* in which Ridder (Claude Rich) "relives a moment of his past," can be considered a particular type of flashback, one that relies on a sense of chronology more than Resnais admits, but one which develops a distinct sense of the interspersal of various temporal instances. Therefore it is useful to return to the metaphor introduced above that describes the way the film compares the past and present to an infinite film, subject to montage. This is particularly clear in the case of the "target" moment of the experiment as the fictional scientists have selected. They intend for Ridder to travel back in time to relive one minute that occurred in his life exactly a year before the date of the experiment, the 5th of September. This is the first "flashback" sequence, a minute on the beach in the south of France in which Ridder emerges from snorkeling to join Catrine on the beach during their vacation, their dialogue and actions presented in continuity. If the experiment were successful, Ridder would have emerged from the sphere after "seeing" or "being back at" this moment. However, the machinery fails, and Ridder goes spinning back through various instances in his life in a virtually arbitrary order. When Ridder tries to escape, he struggles to pull himself back to this moment on the beach at his point of exit. The film returns to the beach scene eight times, each time cutting into and away from the scene at slightly different points, sometimes stuttering and repeating its action. Each time the image remains identical in terms of camera angle; we just enter or leave it at a different moment. Time seems to be measured in film frames, the same way it is on an editing table. Repeatedly, the time in the sphere following the exit through the beach scene lacks the requisite duration to allow a lasting return from the archives of Ridder's memory. The symbolic element of this trajectory is obvious; Ridder is condemned to remember, to keep traveling back in time with no exit.

One of the effects of the repetition of the beach scene is comic, though the tension builds when the repeating clearly comes to indicate Ridder's imminent death, itself a repetition of his failed suicide attempt. His suicide transverses space and time, so that he appears dead of a gun shot wound, not in the solitude of his bedroom on the day he shot himself, August 5th, but on the lawn of the experiment site on September 5th. If this repetition asks for a psychoanalytic reading within the framework of the character's psychology, the disposition of the "arbitrary" sequences also begs for analysis of some sort of symbolic logic within the "unconscious" of not only the character, but the film itself. As it turns out, the events chosen in the period of Ridder's life from 1951 to 1967 can be grouped into overlapping thematic categories: 1) the boredom of work, 2) the affair with Catrine, 3) other women, 4) vacations and beaches, 5) dreams, 6) philosophy and games, 7) death. If Ridder can't stay at the scene of his vacation, if other moments pull him towards his death in repetition, it suggests not just a failure of the mechanics of the sphere time-travel device, but a representation of the force of the unconscious, pulling memory away from one instance to other overdetermined associations, associations sometimes ruled by guilt and desire, sometimes by similarity (other beaches, Septembers of other years, other 5ths of the month, other dialogues in which he uses animals allegorically, etc.). In analyzing the structure of the film, we can see that as different as the generic style might be, Ridder continues the journey of the film noir hero though now this journey moves through modernism. Ridder lends his body to a symbolic venture into the representation of the force of the unconscious, entering a sphere that is at once like a gigantic brain and like a womb, but whose operations leave the scientist baffled and lacking control. The allegory is richer than it might at first seem, for if in the process of the flashback the film careens further towards the complete rearrangement of narrative temporality than it has since Louis Delluc's *Le Silence,* this modernist impulse once again finds its inspiration in an attempt to mimetically represent memory. Modernism here gains its force by imagining its tropes to embody the functioning of the unconscious.

Jorge Semprun's script for *Stavisky* continues this work on image memory, here coupling the flashback segments with segments in which characters within the narrative directly address the spectator, offering commentary on the life of Stavisky. In retrospect, these segments could correspond to the statements of Stavisky's associates at the hearing investigating his scandalous business affairs, but they are interspersed in the narrative considerably in advance of the narrative exposition of the government's investigation. The direct address commentary serves to provide a psychological history for Stavisky, emblematized throughout the film by an abstract recurring symbol, a conical structure built of bricks. For those who are familiar with this structure the reference is a more concrete one; the relic is one of the artificial monuments of the Parc Monceau in Paris, whose landscape architecture is riddled with such fraudulent but amusing artifacts. This symbol both serves to remind us of Stavisky's childhood in the nouveau-riche 16th arrondissement of Paris near this park (presented explicitly in the first flashback) and as a symbolic commentary on the slim difference between fraudulent and legitimate artifacts or practice. Most of the great monuments of Paris are self-proclaimed artifacts; triumphal arches, obelisks, or statues of lions or women, these structures replace historical architectonic spaces with newly designed emblems of power which by the weight of their erection and symbolic self-importance establish themselves as the legitimate markers of history. The fake monuments of the Parc Monceau only exaggerated this traditional monumental construction of the modern city, in a manner parallel to the way Stavisky exaggerates the schemes of capital investment, profit making, and empire building that were considered legitimate, exaggerated them enough to clearly constitute fraud. Semprun's flashback structure lends itself to exegesis as psycho-history, presenting Sacha Alexander (Jean-Paul Belmondo) as the son of a Jewish businessman whose policies inverted his father's survival tactics in a France marked by anti-Semitism; the father counseled a retreat into anonymity and conformity, whereas Stavisky desired the attention of others.

In this context it is also interesting to examine the "false flashbacks," the segments toward the end of the film that seem to indicate past events and turn out to be tricks on the audience. One such false flashback is the product of a temporary disguise Stavisky adopts that reminds us of his appearance years earlier, but is in fact a sequence in linear temporality. The other concerns Stavisky's funeral, which at first might appear to be a flashback as it intervenes as an insert within a sequence that follows an ellipsis. However, the funeral is also recuperated later as itself being a flashforward, occurring not during the ellipsis, but after the sequence into which it is inserted; this becomes clear when we actually see Stavisky die at the very end of the film. The funeral, then, is an event "after the end of the film" so to speak, or to put it differently, the last event in the film's story.

Mon Oncle d'Amerique is a film titled to mark an absence and longing. Rather than referring to any actual uncle of any character within the narrative, this phrase refers to shared imaginations of the three main characters, their ability to imagine the possibility of escape that the existence of such an uncle might mean. This absence of a reference to an actual uncle suggests the search for some other raison d'etre for the title, which we might find by a kind of anagramic declension into "onerique" and "clef d'âme" ("dreamlike" and "key to the soul of spirit"), a move that is in keeping with the film's puzzle-like construction. The past figures doubly in this puzzle as both the past of the characters, their childhoods, and the cinematic past (represented by a series of inserts of three French film stars, Jean Gabin, Danielle Darrieux, and Jean Marais, whose film images are seen in montage with matches-on-action to the gestures of the film's characters in the present). Reflections on image cognition and image memory is one of the by-products of the cinematic references. These associative flashes are inscribed for the viewer in a manner that anticipates what the viewer's own associations might be between contemporary actors and actresses and their luminary ancestors. The flash associations are also linked in the narrative to the characters' love of these particular film stars.

One of the innovations of the returns to the pasts of the characters in this film is that in each case, the images of childhood precede the images of the adult character, but these first childhood images are nonetheless marked as flashbacks by the voice-over that accompanies them and the subsequent introduction of the adult period of the character's life as being the temporality which is dominant and primary. Throughout the film flashes to childhood or adolescence precede various sequences in the present adult lives of these characters, so that there is a continual circulation of temporal references, with some of the same free-associative quality that the scrambled time of *Je t'aime, Je t'aime* attains. This quality, in one sense presents all moments of time, past and present, as equally accessible as if they all existed side-by-side in a place that always remains in some sense available to reentry. Temporality, the constantly renewed realm of replacement is lent a spatial dimension of perpetual existence. This power to circulate and associate these different temporalities is divided between the character's voice and a voice of omniscience; the free association is ambiguously represented as both interior to the narrative itself and exterior to it, authorial.

The Resnais films from *Hiroshima, Mon Amour* through *Mon Oncle d'Amerique,* all concerned with flashbacks and memory, vary greatly in tone and also have distinct textual differences in their treatment of memory. The tonal differences range from the seriousness of *Hiroshima, Mon Amour* and *La Guerre est finie* to the more playful *Je t'aime, Je t'aime* and *Mon Oncle d'Amerique,* for example. Even the visual and conceptual jokes remain quite serious in their import, of course, but the difference is between the latter which foreground the ludic qualities of the text versus texts which do not reflect ironically on their representations of memory in the same way, but rather set out to mimetically inscribe memory processes. The consequences of this difference is an ambiguity in the ongoing treatment of eidetic memory and imagination, highlighting the problematic relationship within these fictions between the past as it could be remembered and the image representation of those memories. Sometimes these films revel in the power to mimetically produce a model of the memory process; sometimes they reflexively question their power to represent memory or self-consciously question the nature of image memory. All these possibilities are interwoven, allowing for absolute belief—we are seeing what memory looks like—but also contesting this belief. Despite the questioning, which is always there in some way in each film, audiences have had their own notions of memory affected by the process of memory imaging represented in these films. Resnais's image montage remains so graphically fluid, so stylistically designed in each of these films as to render this conception of image memory particularly enticing. We would like to believe perhaps that our own personal memories are marked by the same kind of elegant associative matching. Resnais's aesthetic supplement to the depiction of memory process is in a certain sense so far removed from the science of the matter that it instead reminds us of all the intermediary processes of encoded information. In Resnais's work the cinematic metaphor prevails. Memory is a shuffling of images, the past is filed in our minds as a collection of so many images of its having once been perceived.

Singling out Resnais's oeuvre in order to analyze the literary aspects of the reemergence of filmic modernism could give a false picture of these films as more particular to an author's style than they are to an aspect of modernism, but this is not at all the case. Resnais's films are not only similar to the earlier films discussed at the beginning of this chapter, they also are part of a larger movement. The reemergence of modernism is nourished in part by its concern with a relationship between narration and the unconscious on one hand and the ludic play of structure on the other, and Resnais's films serve as good examples of the interweaving of these forces. These forces coalesce to produce works that seek new elements of difference in both realms, distinguishing themselves in a pattern of variations from that which they take to be the norm. Their use of variation and repetition often becomes marked on some level as an obsession. If this obsession is sometimes located in a character, it can also be seen as permeating the text's structural metaphors for desire. Modernism in this sense is not simply a question of style, for no single style is indicative of modernism in this period. Modernism can be located on either side of the baroque/minimalist opposition, for example; the textual style of modernism is not singular, but varied. Modernism is rather a question of something we might call a textual strategy of difference, an inscription of Otherness. If it finds inspiration in various forms of modernist literature in Resnais's films, it is because this literature offers a strategic Otherness to the conventions of the film scenario historically.

This relationship between literature and film in the modernist flashback is highly complex, however, and can't be limited to an importation of the modernist logos to transform the filmic image. If anything it is a constant give and take between language and image, the filmic image seeking a transformative relationship to the literary voice in these modernist films. We have seen how the camera movements and graphic matches in Resnais's films, for example, work as supplements to the relationships suggested in the written scenarios, decentering configurations of narration, adding to them.

We can see how image structure works quite differently in modernist configuration with a literary source in Robert Bresson's *Une Femme Douce* (1969), which is adapted from the Dostoyevsky story. The story's mode of narration is arguably far less modernist than that of the film. For Dostoyevsky's form of narration Bresson substitutes a cinematic form that might be termed minimalist. The rigor of the filmic style, its pronounced structure, and its investigation of voice, silence, and image are all based on isolating and reducing signifiers, on accenting metonymic representation, on the leveling of emotional gestures to the significant detail rather than the large stroke. The film has a large number of flashback sequences that all return to the same scene in the present, that of the husband mourning the corpse of his wife

(Dominique Sanda). Paradoxically, each time we return to this scene, it is to a different fragment of it, a different angle on the corpse, a different graphic configuration. It is the formal quality of this structure and deliberate aspect of choice and variation of all elements that create the tone of obsession, in contrast to the kind of obsession indicated through the more expressionist style of *Wild Strawberries* and *Providence*. What remains structurally similar in the film is the function of the numerous flashbacks. They isolate fragments of the past, giving us a narration as a series of disjunct episodes. The flashbacks in *Une Femme Douce* are all temporally progressive, but even so, the repeated returns to the present emphasize the fragmented, elliptical aspect of this progression, and the shifts in tone.

Modernist films from this period display some of the elements of differentiation one might associate with a Hollywood genre. To reinvest a structure through variation is a common goal in each case, the difference being that the degree of reworking and the margins of difference are much more significant here. It is possible to see filmic modernism as possessing its own limited range of possibilities of variation that it will come (or has come) to exhaust. However, modernism has continued to provide intriguing reworkings of the kinds of filmic writing we have seen in the innovations of Bergman or Resnais, for example. If Bergman is still striving for a mimesis of the troubled psyche and if Resnais, along with his scriptwriters, is motivated by a more concrete contextualization of this troubled psyche as being produced by contemporary political situations, other modernist texts break with the unconscious as reality to be mimetically traced in fiction. The innovative reworking of modernism by these texts that disturb this mimesis of the unconscious and thus reframe their ideological discourse will be the discussion of the next section of this chapter.

Flashbacks and the Unconscious/Structural Obsessions

We will next look at films whose strategy opposes them to the psychological melodramas discussed in the last chapter, for rather than concealing the implicit psychoanalytical figuration of their filmwork and foregrounding an exploration of character psychology, these films directly engage character psychology as a structure through which to explore reflexively the psychoanalytic components of both film form and of social history. They use film form to represent the structure of the unconscious and do not rein that representation into the individual character, although the individual character is used as a point of departure and focus. Ultimately, the exploration of the unconscious escapes the level of the psychological realism within the structuration of character and becomes the project of film expression and structure itself.

One manner of representing the unconscious is the surrealist tradition, although often this tradition has chosen to be more paradoxical about the passage of time and the temporal moment assigned to an image than the use of a flashback device would allow. In Buñuel's *Un Chien Andalou* (1928), for example, an intertitle intervenes to announce "Ten years earlier" in the midst of a scene that is marked by the absence of any such temporal leap in reference. Temporal references are beside the point and appear to be unable to affect the course of the actions represented. The flashback seems impossible, the temporal indication in language superfluous; the title can be taken as joke that marks the film's time as purely imaginary and satirizes the clear temporal references in "normal" films. Or perhaps it indicates the constantly shifting temporality of the unconscious, a temporality without reference to the clocks and calendars of a real world. In marking the play of its images against the conventional temporal structure of filmic representation, *Un Chien Andalou* develops an alternative practice of representation.

The later forms of filmic surrealism are less absolute about this mockery of temporal reference. As a result, flashbacks find their place in such films alongside the dream imagery that juxtaposes the "impossible" next to the commonplace, the fantasy next to a fictional reality. The flashbacks introduce more psychoanalytic and historical sorts of explanations for the surreal juxtapositions found in the films.

An example is Buñuel's *Belle du Jour* (1967), where the flashbacks offer two incidents from the character's (Catherine Deneuve) childhood from which we might derive various explanations for both her fantasies and current sexual frigidity. This psychological and historical explanation for a certain state of mind is not the only way to interpret these images, or the film in general. Rather, ambiguous and multiple meanings are indicated from the very opening of the film. The first images are ones of the heroine's masochistic fantasies, though we take them due to the lack of any other indication as the film's first events. Only subsequently are they placed in context as one of many such fantasies that intrude into her mundane existence as a wife who feels no sexual desire for her husband and whose fantasies of being a prostitute are inspired by the sexual imagination of her husband's best friend, Husson (Michael Piccoli).

The first flashback occurs as Séverine has returned home to find that someone (possibly Husson) has sent her flowers. She breaks first the vase of flowers, then a bottle of perfume, and her self-questioning about these "failed actions" leads into a flashback memory of her as a young child being kissed by a plumber as her mother calls her off-screen.

The second flashback occurs in the context of the first visit to the brothel, on the steps before entering: Séverine has a flashback to a scene where she refuses the communion wafer from her priest who then repeats the question she posed aloud to herself preceding the first flashback. In the first instance her phrase is "Qu'est-ce que j'ai au'jourd'hui?.," in the second, "Séverine, Séverine, qu'est-ce que tu as?," which translates roughly as "What's come over me, today?" and "What's come over you?" (though the French uses an idiomatic expression of the verb "to have," carrying with it the covert meaning of possessing within the self something inappropriate). Yet these flashbacks do not tell us what Séverine "has."

The reasons for Séverine's behavior in both cases remain opaque: why does this young girl remain with the plumber instead of heeding her mother's call and why does she refuse the communion? Why do these events flash through her memory at these particular junctures in the present? These flashbacks differ from those of the expressionist film or the psychological melodrama in an adamant decision to avoid offering explanations all the while that they remain close to a psychological process and evoke possible causal and associative relationships through their placement in the film's structure. Nonetheless, the images of the psyche are manifest as curious and puzzling, the external manifestations of behavior are beyond the common sense of verisimilitude, and the mysteries manifest in the investment and repulsion of desire remain present as mysteries. Critics have sometimes rushed in to provide a superficial and dubious reading of the film that analyses Séverine's neuroses from these fragments as if that were the point. They miss this film's difference from a film like *The Locket* in that it contains within it an already decentered position for the spectator vis-à-vis the character's psyche. Never will the spectator be allowed the security of knowing what Séverine "has" instead of becoming implicated in it.

Surrealism leaves its traces on use of the flashback in a series of films by Carlos Saura, all of which explore a similar narrative structure: *El Jardin de las delicias* (1970), *La Prima Angélica* (1973), *Cría Cuervos* (1975), and *Dulca Horas* (1982). Saura orchestrates two periods of time in each film against each other. Each of the two periods represents a critical juncture in a personal family history and a political moment in the history of Spain. This interweaving allows for a particular form of psychohistory to be coupled with allegory. The films can be read on two distinct levels simultaneously, and these readings can also be meshed to create a theoretical reflection on narrative, history, and allegory. This obviously means a movement away from a purely surrealist gesture, instead incorporating elements of a surrealist sensibility of juxtaposition within these other narrative strategies.

The initial film of this series, *El Jardin de las delicias,* is a satire of a wealthy amnesiac whose family tries to restore his memory by retelling incidents from the past. Their motivation is mercenary, for their patriarch has forgotten the secrets of his financial holdings in Switzerland. The satire has a sharp political edge (an allegorical reading possibly constitutes the amnesiac as Franco), while the film humorously explores the unconscious associations of a mind thrown out of normal functioning, one that has become a stranger to its own class identity. One notes the difference in tone in the use of an amnesiac character and flashbacks than in more a traditional film. Here the entire situation is exaggerated for the purposes of allegory and satire.

Saura's *La Prima Angélica* almost surreptitiously introduces its first flashback with a change of angle on a shot of a car on the road between Barcelona and Segovia, introducing into the new shot a car and characters from twenty years earlier. However, the main character, Luis (José Luis López Vázquez) remains exactly the same in appearance across this cut to the past. This constancy of appearance has several curious and significant effects. One effect, which is strongest in this first cut to the past, but which operates residually at other moments even once the spectator knows the rules of this representational game, consists of suspending audience apprehension of the fact that we are in a flashback. Despite the obviousness of the shift, its referential markings are masked by this single constant sign contained within it. The audience hesitates between recognition of present and past, experiencing each transition with some uncertainty that highlights this narrative's similarity to the overlapping shape of time within the unconscious.

Another effect is the sense of irony and the uncanny produced by the incongruity of seeing an adult actant in the world of his childhood. He enters there not as outside observer to a scene in which his younger self is present (as in the film versions of *The Christmas Carol*), but as the displaced representation of his younger self. The sign system itself has been altered away from the semblance of the narrative-real towards an impossible subjectivity.

As we have shown, the flashback is traditionally often marked as a memory image in which the self in the present reexperiences the past. However, the traditional flashback disguises the potential problem of this "doubled" subjectivity by resolving this double figure into two separate and distinct representations. The self within the flashback representation is more like another person than it is like an internalized part of the focalizing self. By mobilizing the trope of adult-image substitution for the child actant in the flashback, this film marks this doubled subjectivity. It reminds us continually that the self who focalizes the memory is an adult. The substitution of the adult for the child in the image of the past thus marks the barrier of exteriorization of one's past self in such a memory. For the other characters, there is no problem; they are their younger selves in the flashback as they were observed and remembered in the past, for they are consistently the object of Luis's gaze and subject to his focalization. The self of Luis as a youngster, on the other hand, evades his subjective recall. His present self troubles his ability to project an image of his past self, and the film, in its innovative gesture, refuses to lend this character its powers of omniscience. Memory is imperfect and subject to displacements as this mark of incongruous age representation indicates.

A third effect of this adult figuration in the flashback is to surround the entire trip to Segovia and the return to the family, during which the flashbacks occur, with an aura of regression in the psychoanalytic sense.[31] Keeping Luis figured as an adult even when he is a child contaminates his image as adult, and we realize that his adult self displays many of the same reactions, fears, and fantasies as those depicted in the flashbacks. Luis is represented as an adult who behaves in a manner determined by early childhood. This may seem to be the opposite of the point stated above, but in fact it is another side of the same basic situation—two selves exist historically within Luis, but they cannot be totally distinguished one from the other. Luis is at once a child and an adult in his present life as an adult, just as his youth is now conditioned by the fact that it is the memory of this adult Luis.

The two temporal moments connected by the film's structure are the summer of the outbreak of the Civil War, 1936, and the contemporaneous moment in the late seventies when Franco is still in power, though signs of change and an erosion of dictatorial authority are beginning, after a long period of more absolute control and censorship.[32] The film's present in 1977 is conditioned by a desire for the vindication of the Republicans by the main character, symbolized by his efforts to disentomb the bones of his mother to rebury them in the familial gravesite that has been dominated by the Franquist side of the family. The political allegory finds its psycho-historical symbolism in an act of reburial that is rich in personal psychohistory.

As such, it is fascinating to examine this film in the light of the theoretical questions posed in chapter four concerning the manner in which the flashback is used to create a subjectivized and particular view of history. Here the film strategically interweaves the personal and the historical on both referential and symbolic levels, but does so in a manner that is decidedly anti-heroic and greatly departs from the type of structures of identification that we analyzed as the strategy of the Hollywood flashback films treating two historical periods discussed earlier. Instead of building a strong positive identification with the Republicans and their struggle, the film engages in a satire of the Franquists as it examines the vulnerability of a youth whose own immediate family identity is Republican. Luis is depicted as subject to the law of the patriarchal fascist movement at the moment of his awakening to desire in puberty. His subsequent rejection of this law is not so much heroic but troubled, so disturbing that he seems to have paid the symbolic price of a stunted sexual and emotional development. His flashback memories, then, are a means of displaying the period of psychological torment in 1936 that created this arrested development, that stunted symbolically the growth of the generation Luis represents within the allegory.

The ideological *parti pris* of such a film is far from direct. The critique of Franco's reign is coupled with an exploration of the psychoanalytic formation of the subject in childhood; rather than focusing on a critique of the political behavior or caricaturing the psychology of the powerful within the Franco regime, the film takes as its central concern the psychoanalytic frame constructed for the subject under such a regime at the level of an individual family and as concerns one subject, Luis, in particular.

This structure continues in *Cría Cuervos,* where the subject in question is female. The structure of this film has rarely been described accurately in reviews, indicating a certain misunderstanding of the film's project. The present moment from which the flashbacks are generated is represented by the direct address of the adult (Geraldine Chaplin), who speaks of her past as if to a therapist although none is figured in the film. She appears as an adult only four times. The sparsity of her interventions could lead one to assume the past as the central time frame for the film and her role as one of a partial meta-commentary; however, the sequences in the past are not linear progressions. They are instead fragments of past time rearranged as memory associations, even though the focalization of these memories is not always anchored in the adult explicitly. Thus without marking the process of flashing back and while leaving the present moment sketched in the most minimalist fashion, the film still marks the segments as being in a past, as being memories, and as being the kind of subjective memories that are fragmented and rearranged by the order of an unconscious associational patterning.

The film begins with a particularly perverse primal scene of Ana witnessing the death of her father, Anselmo, while he is making love to his best friend's wife; events continue in apparent linear progression through his funeral, after which time the adult Ana intervenes in the present for the first time. However, even within this linear opening there are two scenes of Ana with her mother that, we learn retrospectively (during the funeral sequence), are imaginary scenes whose elements are drawn from the past, since Ana's mother died before her father. From this point on, the film careens temporally through Ana's childhood, mixing moments before the death of her parents with the period following her father's death when she and her sister are in the charge of her Aunt Paulina and cared for by the maid Rosa.

As in *Cousin Angélica,* Ana's childhood is recounted primarily in terms of her initiation to the mysteries of sexuality and desire. The movement between distinct temporal instances is often linked by associations within this sexual puzzle. For example, a flashback scene with a greater anteriority (Anselmo is shown flirting with Rosa by pretending to touch her breasts through the pane of glass she is cleaning) occurs between two scenes of the adjustment by the girls to their orphan status. The scene following the flirtation insert is centered on a story Rosa tells Ana of a peasant girl who claimed her pregnancy was the result of a leaf falling down her breasts while she walked through the woods. The association that determines this montage is the mysterious role of breasts as sexual objects.

Later, after another intervention of the adult Ana, we see the scene just before Ana's mother's death, followed by an earlier scene where Ana's mother plays piano for her and another where the mother and Anselmo fight. The temporal jumps thus give us first the death, as it denies Ana her mother's love, then a scene which presents the desire for the mother's love before that death, then the father's mistreatment of the mother and the dismissal of her sexual desire. This inversion of temporal order emphasizes ambiguity and polysemy by disturbing causal logic in the arrangement of the elements. Is the mother's chronic illness merely a plea for attention? Does it result from sexual abandonment? Does the mother die because she loses the will to live due to her husband's mistreatment? Or is part of the father's mistreatment his denial of the mother's actual illness? The film's disjunct order and fragmented representation raise questions for which it refuses simple answers, leaving the discourse on desire and death entirely ambiguous and multiply suggestive.

Holocaust Flashbacks: Trauma and Repression

The violent resurgence in the present of images from the past that a peacetime existence has necessarily sought to repress is the image of memory offered by holocaust films. World War II in general, and the holocaust especially, has been the initiating reference for many modernist flashbacks. This group of films does not just follow the patterns of the films made by Hollywood that connect the War to the pre-war period discussed in chapter four; instead, many of these films seek an analogue in modernist editing for the way in which the memories of the past, particularly memories of the concentration camps, disturb the continuity of action in the present.

We have already seen how in *Hiroshima, Mon Amour* the memory of occupied France develops comparatively to the memory of the Hiroshima bombing, forever unimaginable and unattainable for a foreign visitor. The pain of surviving and remembering World War II is only displayed as the personal, European memory, while the mass, Japanese memory is only alluded to as beyond this, infinitely more difficult to "see." In the holocaust flashback films, the devastation of masses of humanity by the Nazis in the concentration camps, and the personal psychic damage inflicted on victims and survivors, are symbolically interwoven.

While the mass act is presented in its individual dimension as personal memory, the enormity of the holocaust magnifies the scope of events. The individual who suffered represents a shared experience of masses of victims, and this weight of a collective horror resonates through the remembered images of the camps. Modernism serves these films as a means of mitigating against the familiar melodramatic aspects of a horror personally experienced. If modernist techniques of narration are particularly common in these films with holocaust thematics, it is perhaps because the dislocation of modernist storytelling serves as analogy for the psychic damage.

Andrzej Munk's *Pasazerka (Passenger, 1962)* presents flashbacks to two contradictory versions of the interaction in Auschwitz of an SS guard, Liza (Aleksandra Slaska), and a political prisoner and member of the camp resistance, Marta (Anna Ciepielewska). The modernism inherent in these contradictory flashbacks is accentuated by the fact that the film was reassembled after being left unfinished due to the director's accidental death in 1961. The sequences of the present encounter on a cruise ship of the former German official and the Polish dissident are given only as stills in black and white, apparently all that remained of footage originally meant to be projected in continuity. The lack of movement and a different aspect ratio creates a striking visual contrast with the concentration camp scenes from the past. Further, a voice-over narration explaining the circumstances of the film's compilation opens a speculation on its form and meaning. This device of self-conscious narration is here grounded in production conditions of salvaging a story that became fragmented by an actual past (the time between writing, filming, and editing) as well as a fictional one (memories from 1960 of the events of the holocaust).

Some of the fragmentation could have been the design of the director and the novelist Zofia Posmusz, who worked with Munk on the adaptation of her book.[33] Preceding the first major flashback there is a series of flash images, themselves flashbacks to the camp, but outside of the chronology given in the two longer flashbacks. The first of these flash images shows prisoners naked inside a circle of uniformed guards. It remains extremely enigmatic and primarily symbolic until given a narrative explanation towards the end of the second major flashback, as part of a torturous ritual that Liza devises to dramatize the condemnation of prisoners to the gas chamber. This repeated image, as much symbol as event, keys the viewer that the flashbacks which follow should be seen in the context of this repressed material that surfaces unexplained at the outset, awaiting a working through of a dishonest remembering before it can resurface in context.

Liza's first major flashback to the camp provides a self-justifying, voice-over narration of how her management of the supply room of the camp and her treatment of inmate-workers like Marta was devoid of the horrors of the camp's atrocious purpose. The second flashback continues voice-over narration but adds synchronous dialogue. This counterpart to the subjective voice helps this more detailed exposé of Marta's role as camp resister undercut whatever truth value one might have assigned Liza's verbal denials. In addition, extra-textual knowledge of Auschwitz and attention to the images that are juxtaposed to Liza's justifications puncture her stance. As she claims she was only responsible for "things" the film shows her commanding the confiscation of Judaic religious objects. The plea of individual innocence when one is part of a larger crime is what such juxtapositions effectively attack.

The structure of the film urges a retrospective rereading of Liza's first flashback in light of the second. Liza's claim of innocence not only tries to mask her guilt, it serves as a cover for her obsession with this victim who represents someone who tries to resist her power. The second flashback juxtaposes the confession of "a weakness" for Marta on Liza's part to events such as Marta's attempt to smuggle out a Jewish baby and her role in passing information to the outside. It not only shows Liza to be guilty as a Nazi, but to be obsessively involved in the ultimate proof of her power, with seducing her victim into self-betrayal and betrayal of her cause, as well as obsessively denying her role both as persecutor and seducer. Liza wants to court, conquer, and degrade Marta.

Unlike *Rashomon, Passenger* does not suggest a philosophical inquiry into the relativity of subjectivity, but rather a critique of the self-serving framing and selectivity of memory that the guilty adopt towards their war criminality. Its view of the politics of the holocaust is focused on the individual psychology of the victimizers.

In a similar manner *The Pawnbroker* (1965) focuses on individual psychology, but in this case that of the victim-survivor. The anti-hero, Sol Nazerman (Rod Steiger), is a man haunted by images of his concentration camp past. These memories are intercut with an elaborate narrative in the present that traces Nazerman's life as a suburbanite who runs a pawnshop in Harlem.

Independently financed, the film was directed by Sidney Lumet from David Friedkin's and Morton Fine's adaptation of the 1961 Edward Lewis Wallant novel. Produced in the context of U.S. imports of "art films" using modernistic techniques, *The Pawnbroker* is a rare example of an American film allowing itself such formal explorations.

The novel already suggested this modernist treatment in its use of nine dream-flashbacks set off from the rest of the text with italics. The last of these, an idealized dream of life before the holocaust, even employs cinematic metaphors within the description of how it fades from Nazerman's dream-consciousness:

And then they stopped, every blade of grass froze, each of them was arrested in motion. David balanced impossibly on one short, sturdy leg, Ruth maintained her pose of reaching. All was silence; it was like a movie which has suddenly stopped while its projecting illumination continued. And he was paralyzed, too, forever out of reach of the dear faces, frozen a few feet short of all he had loved. And then it all began dimming; each face receded, the sunny afternoon turned to eternal twilight, dusk, evening, darkness.[34]

Though in the book this is the last of the dreams, in the film it becomes the first flashback and precedes the credits, a configuration which in itself is somewhat innovative, though such precredit sequences do characterize sixties' stylistics. It is the only flashback in the film marked as a dream by the shot which brings us back to the present, a zoom-in on Nazerman asleep on a lounge chair in his backyard, as well as by the cinematic tropes of slow motion throughout and the freeze frames that end it. Yet because this dream-coding is an isolated instance in the film, the audience is likely to interpret this as more of a pure memory, taking the slow motion to highlight the lyricism of the scene and taking the freeze images to denote not the dreamer's loss of his phantasy, but the arrival of some paralyzing force on the scene in the past, as members of Sol's family look up and off-screen in fear at what we imagine is the family's arrest. Further, this interpretation is reinforced by returns to this flashback later in the film.

If the dreamwork from the novel is rendered less suggestively as literal memory in the film, and if the flashbacks are embedded in a style of exaggerated realism, laced with the stereotypes and symbolism characteristic of the American "social comment" film, certain of the flashbacks gain greater force in their filmic embodiment. For example, Nazerman remembers an incident from the camp in which an escaped prisoner who has been traced down by the German guards and their dogs, is tortured and killed in front of the other prisoners. The memory is presented as flashback fragments, first as brief flash images that are associative edits from the date on the calendar that marks the anniversary of Nazerman's wife's death, and then from children on a Harlem playground. This associative montage sets up a metaphoric parallel between the concentration camp and urban poverty, but beyond this symbolism it is one of the more piercing depictions of memory flashes to be found anywhere in film. The staccato cross-cutting of past and present in images that both graphically match (the fence, the violent action) and contrast (night and day) builds to a visual power echoed elsewhere in the film by other memory inserts that punctuate Nazerman's actions. The holocaust survivor is portrayed as a man haunted by images that slice into his daily existence against his will and outside of his control.

Several more recent films rework these holocaust flashback connections. *Sophie's Choice,* directed by Alan Pakula in 1982 from William Styron's novel, essentially reworks *The Pawnbroker*'s use of flashbacks to a concentration camp past to explain an enigmatic character, though here the primary flashback is given in continuity as the illustration of Sophie's (Meryl Streep) verbal account of her past. *Malou* (1980) depicts a daughter's search for her mother's past in Nazi Germany, undertaken following her mother's death in Argentina. It employs frequent cuts between the present and the past linked by graphic matches depicting associative memory, like the first flashback in *Hiroshima, Mon Amour*. The flashbacks attempt to explain the mother's decline into alcoholism, offering a fragmented story of the entertainer-mother's conversion to Judaism to marry a rich Jew, the couple's clandestine escape to avoid incarceration, and the break up of their marriage once they arrive in South America. The act of investigation is presenting as cleansing and curing the daughter, substituting the search for her mother's history for her own psychoanalysis. Here the role of the holocaust is limited to that of an unexpected dislocation, with Jewishness and persecution acting as a nearly circumstantial element in a strange personal history.

While most of the holocaust flashback films treat the history of the holocaust as psychologically damaging to individuals who themselves have less than honorable responses to it, *Julia* (Fred Zinnemann, 1977) uniquely portrays its heroine as behaving honorably and struggling against fascism. *Julia* uses its flashbacks to reveal Lillian Hellman's reminiscences of her memory of her friend, Julia (based on Dr. Muriel Gardner) culminating in her discovery of Julia's involvement in the Austrian resistance. It makes interesting use of auditory flashbacks that precede the visual flashbacks as a means of linking the voice of Hellman (Jane Fonda) as narrator to the remembered voices, a device that emphasizes the film as illustration of a text in the process of being written.

It does seem logical that the holocaust should figure repeatedly as a cause of haunting memory or historical memory which needs to be recovered. What seems odd is how often the horror of the Nazi regime is condensed into a single persona or displaced onto people who were its victims. If condensation and displacement are the terms chosen here, it is for their psychoanalytical resonance; the history of the holocaust seems to overwhelm the fictional imagination, which seeks to discharge the drama of its effect in microcosm, in the idiosyncratic character psychologies invented for the likes of Liza, Sol Nazerman, and Malou.

The Politics of the Modernist Flashback

The patterns established by these holocaust flashback films are used in a number of other recent films set in different historical contexts. Whereas some forms of filmic modernism sought a certain abstraction from social and historical issues, i.e. the often isolated world of Ingmar Bergman's fictions, more recent films favor a specifically politically charged setting. Spatial and temporal reordering, metaphorical representation, complex narrative modalities are recently very likely to occur in films that reference historical confrontations or the most heated headlines of international news. We have already seen some examples of the function of this type of reference and ideological intervention in certain films of Alain Resnais and Carlos Saura. Unlike the innovation that characterizes their work, other politicized and historicized uses of flashbacks, particularly in the New German and Australian cinema, present what might be called a restricted modernism. Their flashback structures are borrowed from the flashback use in genres such as the trial narrative, the thriller, the detective story, and the domestic melodrama.

The journey of the European or American to a foreign country engaged in a political civil war is a particular subjective view that the flashback structures reinforce. *Circle of Deceit* (Volker Schlöndorff, 1981), for example, uses a simple frame story set in Germany to mark the journey of a reporter to Beirut in the midst of its civil war as the past, remembered and reexamined. The trope is central to marking the attitude of the film as critical of the West German press and the middle class as exemplified in its anti-hero. However, American critics tended to read the frame and the strategy of juxtaposition and understatement as equivalent to its main character's position, a mere self-indulgence of poetic angst.[35] This misreads aspects of the film's self-conscious use of this character-frame, but responds to a larger problem of the treatment of foreign conflicts primarily as they are seen by or as they affect one's own nationals. Further, the critique of the German press is strangely duplicated by the film's own narrative preoccupation with the sensational. Similarly, *Missing* (Constantine Costa-Gavras, 1981), uses its flashbacks to illustrate the detective work of the father and wife into the circumstances of the death of an American journalist, Charles Horman, who was a victim of the military coup that deposed Salvador Allende. Here the flashbacks primarily illustrate Horman's personal journal which not only provides a voice-over narration, but a Preston Sturges style "narratage" of the dialogue within the scenes occurring in the past. Later, a pair of flashbacks are used differently, to depict graphically the contradictory accounts of the arrest given by eyewitnesses. The discovered journal and the witnesses both function to provide clues to the mystery of Horman's disappearance, which ultimately is tied to an effort by the C.I.A. to disguise its role in the coup. The larger political questions are raised more clearly than in *Circle of Deceit,* but in both films the flashbacks reinforce a subjectivity outside the conflict as a means of presenting these wars as fictions of identification for the home audience.

Few modernist flashback films have been able to construct an alternative to such subjective identification that might pose the ideological issues more forcefully. *Die bleierne Zeit (Marianne and Juliane,* Margarethe Von Trotta, 1981), depicts the conflict between two sisters, one of whom, Marianne, has become a member of the red brigade, while the other, Juliane, is a feminist writer who objects to her sister's underground existence and violent tactics. The childhood memories of Juliane take us in flashback to the years 1945–1955 and are presented in an achronological order that emphasizes the subjectivity of recall and association. Yet they cannot escape being offered by the film as a psychological explanation of a terrorist personality and therefore raise theoretical questions about the overdetermined causality they suggest (the desire of the future terrorist to conform to an authoritarian father, until this snaps, as she comes to oppose the Vietnam War).[36] While feminism has suggested that personal life poses political issues, the oversimplification of individual psychology in a political biography is potentially abusive of the serious psychoanalytical and ideological concepts at stake.

Restricted modernism often investigates some aspects of the structures of conventional fiction while leaving others intact. In its ideological investigation of political circumstances, *Breaker Morant* (Bruce Beresford, 1980) uses a trial flashback form, but here the trial is a political court-martial that the film depicts as orchestrated by the British command against Australian soldiers as a means of appeasing the Boers and Germany as prelude to a peace treaty. Instead of simply illustrating the testimony, the flashbacks adopt an innovative form, ranging from preceding the testimony explanation, punctuating it with enigmatic flash frame images, developing rhythmic cross-cutting between present and past, day and night, bleeding voices from present to past, including personal reminiscences outside the courtroom by the three accused, and illustrating one of the Australian's alibis (apparently false) with the same mode of imagery as the incidents presented as true within the fiction. The structure of these interventions of the past provides the film with much of its originality, as it dares to risk a difficulty in audience comprehension to achieve its rhythmic montage and its sense of the past being pieced together from the fragments the Australian lawyer can assemble. While the film uses flashbacks to render cinematic the testimony of its theatrical source, as is conventional within the trial flashback genre, it does not restrict itself to visual illustration. Its modernist vision of the cinematic is as complex montage. This coincides with a questioning in the film of the ideologies governing the war in South Africa, the utilization of troops from colonies to support the British Empire, and the morality of a military chain of command in general. The film's Australian nationalist slant seems to not fully account for the possibility of an allegorical reading, one which would compare the tactics of these soldiers confronted with guerrilla warfare to the U.S. forces in the more recent Vietnam War. Seen as allegory or parallel tale, the film's heroic treatment of the Australian defendants is more suspect, and we can object to the way in which the focalization of the flashbacks as well as other narrative devices deflect our scrutiny from the issue of war crimes on the part of foot soldiers.

In these modernist flashbacks within highly politicized fictions, what is often at stake, then, is the extent to which the vision of the past serves a psychology of the individual in an appeal to a humanist tradition. If no critical strategy of the film can pose the ideology of the historical, political circumstance depicted *outside* a purely conventional notion of identification with heroic characters, then the modernism risks remaining but a stylistic decoration, one that merely varies the Hollywood's historical flashback. However, if the film can complicate the portrayal of the past beyond a fictive individual's psychology, then a far more radical intervention can be made.

Such an intervention is pursued in *Man of Marble* (1977) and *Man of Iron* (1981), Andrzej Wadja's pair of films depicting labor history in post-war Poland. *Man of Marble* frames the uncovering of a scandal surrounding one of the Stakhonovites, the workers idealized in fifties propaganda as a monumentalized example of worker productivity, by using the device of the investigation of a young filmmaker trying to make a documentary. It is therefore structurally indebted to *Citizen Kane,* even beginning as that film does with a newsreel, in this case a government film of the rise to fame of the worker, Birkut. This official version will later be filled out and contradicted by other films, interviews, and visits to sites such as the museum where Birkut's once-heralded statue is stored in disgrace; in the process, the hypocrisy of the propaganda mobilized by Poland's Stalinist-styled bureaucracy in the fifties, as well as its lingering influence, is exposed. The force of this film is directly linked to its use of the newsreels and clips from films which, while fabricated around a fictional character, are to be taken as copies of a propaganda style which is then contextually deconstructed. Like Dušan Makavejev's *Innocence Unprotected* (1970), which uses an actual Czechoslovakian silent film as its point of departure, the "found" footage (in *Man of Marble,* fabricated to resemble "found" footage), represents a closer link to the historical past than other sorts of flashbacks. It gives us a mode of seeing, a film style from the past, which speaks to an historical analysis perhaps more strongly than the events represented therein.

The end of *Man of Marble* sets the stage for *Man of Iron* to follow, for while the filmmaker ends her quest to find Birkut after learning of his death, she also encounters the willingness of his son, a Gdansk shipyard worker, to help her complete her film on his stakhonovite father. *Man of Iron* becomes a sequel in which flashbacks continue the process of historical analysis by supplying the now deceased father's reactions to the son's activity in Solidarity, filling in the years of the late sixties and early seventies, bridging the temporal gap between the fifties flashbacks of the first film and the present sequences in both films with sequences (fictional and fabricated documentary) which depict the student and worker movements of opposition. *Man of Iron* relies more heavily than *Man of Marble* on flashbacks depicting fictional relations set in history and makes less of the exploration of past modes of representation. It is more conventional as a result. Yet both films infuse the historical flashback with a certain urgency of historical representation lacking in most historical flashback films. The citing of history is given as the substance of a critical analysis rather than merely a "reality effect" or a background set against which a romance develops. In this directed focus on history Wadja's films approach the self-conscious historical flashback in Jean-Luc Godard's *Tout va bien* (1972), in which the lead characters discuss their relationship to the events of May '68 as part of an argument on the future of their relationship. In both cases, the films serve the thesis that individuals are subjects of a historical moment by making the historical circumstance loom larger than the fictional characterizations.

The films of Nagisa Oshima beginning in the late fifties offer an even more radical alternative within the impulse towards a modernist and ideological use of the flashback. *Night and Fog in Japan* (1960) is a direct look at the political self. Oshima's cinematic techniques, which characteristically use panning and reframing of the cinemascope image, intensify through his focus on the long take. The film is composed of forty-three shot-sequences. This minimalism and rigor, this extreme emphasis on the long take is coupled with an equally important emphasis on theatri-cality. Theatricality in *Night and Fog in Japan* includes the concept of a topical theater, one which can risk direct political reference and intervention. It is a theater that thrives on the tension between improvisational and scripted elements. The film's theatricality also includes restricted spatiality; the "action" is mainly statically located in a set of rooms in the present and past. Gesture, lighting, and spatial alignment color the dialogue exchanges. While verbal signifiers are, in a sense, highly privileged in a film displaying such theatricality, it is cinematic form that shapes the reception of these words.

The shot, its framing and changeability, is the index of this theatricality. The studied quality of Oshima's shots becomes even more pronounced. Camera move-ment creates a theatricality that is spatial and subject to reframing, a blocking of character interaction that is specifically visual and cinematic. The dialogue is not one's usual concept of film dialogue (immediate, action- and object-oriented, direct), but rather it contains many specific political references to factional debates between the Communist Party and other leftist groups and theoretical analyses. Despite this form of verbal debate, the camerawork remains graphically fascinating, creating a new form of cinematic theatricality.

The film is set in 1960, the year it was made and the time of the defeat of the protests against the security treaty. Nozawa, a journalist and former member of the Zengakuren (student protest organization), is marrying a young student Reiko, who was a participant in the most recent demonstrations. The reception is attended by his former comrades, many of whom have also become professionals somewhat distanced from political struggles, and Reiko's female friends. Also in attendance are an older liberal professor, Utakawa and his wife, and another married couple of the groom's generation, Nakayama and his wife Misaku. The attributes of these various characters and others are learned in the course of the ceremony and its disruption by two uninvited guests, Oota, who is actively being pursued by the police as a result of his participation in a political demonstration, and Takumi, who has taken the identity of a friend who died during an earlier political struggle and serves to initiate a ghostly haunting of the past. This haunting is accomplished by a series of flashbacks to two prior time periods; one series covers a period ten years earlier in which the Zengakuren participated in the first AMPO demonstrations, while the second series chronicles the recent protests of the renewal of the treaty upon its tenth year expiration. Also at issue is the history of the Zengakuren; in the fifties, student protest was dominated by Communist Party directives, despite much autonomous feeling and dissension by many students. By 1960 the Zengakuren again tried to assert autonomy, but internal conflicts, intensified by the failure of the protest to stop the treaty, hampered this effort. Since Nozawa represents the CP affiliation of the Zengakuren and Reiko those who tried to break with this affiliation, their marriage represents on an allegorical plane the reconciliation of factions on an institutional basis, without any resolution of the issues. The two intruders each insist that the unresolved issues of the past be remembered and faced. This insistence takes the form of recalling two figures from the past, Takao, a Zengakuren leader from the fifties who committed suicide after being accused by the CP faction of helping an informer escape, and Kitami, a friend of Reiko's who disappeared after she abandoned him at the hospital upon meeting Nozawa. These stories of these two figures illustrate the mistakes and callousness of the movement. In forcing Nozawa and Reiko and their guests to remember Takao and Kitami, Takumi and Oota recall how the personal betrayals are linked to political issues.

This linking of the personal and the political is an aspect of the film not often commented upon, but it has great significance, especially as a commentary on a leftist milieu that represses or takes for granted unconscious motivations. For example, the anti-Stalinist attacks on Nakayama are colored with residual jealousies, as earlier several of the men were attracted to Misako, who marries Nakayama, the leader and the most Stalinist of the group. Takao's suicide and Nozawa's marriage to Reiko are somewhat motivated by their loss of Misako. The doubling between the wedding of Nakayama and Misako in the flashback and that of Nozawa and Reiko in the present is a major key to the narrative structure, a parallel marked by a graphic match from one to the other. The film raises the issues of women's role in the political struggle on the one hand and the relationship of political struggle to desire on the other, weaving these through its other questions.

Night and Fog in Japan ends with the arrest of Oota, followed by a debate on response to this event by all present, followed by a droning denunciation of Oota's radicalism by Nakayama in favor of Communist Party fidelity. Visually, the film ends on the dark fog clouding the exterior, as if commenting on a voice-over to which no one any longer listens. This dark fog gains its full visual impact in reference to the tableau shots elsewhere in the film; a cinemascope frame filled with red flags against a night sky, another of torches, another a high angle shot on a pavement flowing with blood. This recall of images from across the film begs for a deciphering of the connections they draw between protest, repression, and political intrigues internal to the left.

Night and Fog in Japan echoes Kurosawa's *No Regrets for our Youth* in its flashback structure and concerns, but differs in its treatment of political involvement and memory. Oshima breaks with Kurosawa's humanism that salutes the courage of the righteous in the past and reinscribes that respect in another form in the present. If Oshima is concerned with presenting the issues which led to political involvement through retrospection, this is coupled with a harsh critique of political motivations and organizations. Memory sequences are sites of reexamination, and the angles on the past are not defensive or celebratory, but sharp and analytical. Even more negative is his ending on the fog of betrayal and uncertainty.

In Oshima's *Ceremonies* (1972), this critical invocation of a subjective recalling of the past submits the Japanese family during and following World War II to critical analysis.[37] The film pivots through a double trajectory not simply of past and present, but of conscious recall and unconscious acting out, reenaction. The flashback narrative structure can be understood as an exoskeleton for the film, a formal order of double, linear narrative progressions within two distinct temporalities. The present sequences narrate the journey of two cousins, Masuo and Ritsuko by train, ship, and then small boat to an island in the days following their grandfather's death in response to a telegram announcing the suicide of Terumichi, another cousin who is also Ritsuko's husband. Intercut with this voyage are five flashbacks referring to five separate historical moments (1947, 1952, 1956, 1961, and 1971), which track the troubled survival and then demise of the Sakurada family.

Described only in terms of this structure, the film appears more conventional than it is. Fitting it back too neatly into its skeletal frame, we might see all of the difficult disjunctures we encounter in the film as emblems of the main character's, Masuo's, disturbed psyche. The flashbacks would conform with the Hollywood dream or fantasy sequence, a vision whose motivation is explained as belonging to a character in a distorted mental state. Instead, we have a text which itself is constituted as a trope for the psyche and whose characters and narrative are offered up as elaborate ruses, falsely mirroring, motivating, deflecting, and activating textual figuration. The "acting-out" that dominates the flashback sequences sends the representation off into another register, that of the symbolic gesture.

The flashbacks do attempt to recover the traces of several enigmas concerning the Sakurada family's past, beginning with the disappearance of Masuo's younger brother as the family fled Manchuria in 1947. The flashback, instead of depicting the death itself (as a more conventional narrative might), presents the ritual the young Masuo performed with his dead brother as object of his acting-out. Once the family has returned to Japan, Masuo places his ear to the ground to listen for his brother's cries from the grave in a sequence whose camerawork and editing accentuate the surreal disjunction of this act. This mystery is joined by a whole series of questions concerning the family tree; its forms and branches are withheld by the narrative, but the suggestion of the grandfather's incestuous rapes of female family members is likewise the object of repeated figuration in equally symbolic terms. For example, the game of baseball that ends the flashback to 1947 is actually a symbolic configuration of the cousins and aunt to whom the voice-overs in the flashbacks are addressed. Masuo's address to Terumichi over the game image is only apparently disjunct in its concern about Masuo's father's marital intentions, why Setsuko could not comply with those intentions, and the unknown story of Terumichi's mother. The voice and baseball image come together to present Setsuko as the referee to the children's attempt to figure out sexuality in the older generation and in themselves.

Figural flourishes such as these transform the entire film, sending it outside the bounds of realism, but without lessening the historical overview that the flashbacks provide. The subject, Masuo, becomes a site, the locus of activities suspended between two temporalities. His past includes references to repatriation of Japanese colonizers in the wake of national defeat, the emergence of the peace movement, the Communist opposition, the revival of the right-wing in the fifties, and the achievement of a material prosperity by the sixties that cannot conceal the emptiness symbolized by the brideless wedding that is held to keep up appearances. When the past joins the present in 1971, it is as a journey with a dead end, to the isolated, uninhabited island, the island of the double of the lost brother, the island where the others, who might have provided love and who might have struggled against the existing order, have committed suicide.

In telling a story of patriarchal incestuous control within one Japanese family, the film references events that accompany the growth of the Zaibatsu, the big industrial concerns which are themselves modeled on the family. The film addresses the notion of historical processes. It explores the extraordinarily difficult theoretical problems of how the subject is formed in culture, exploring the affectivity of a political/social order on the psyche.

A Third World Perspective on History and Memory

If *Ceremonies* stands out in the manner it sharply and complexly raises issues of the subject in history, it may be that the contestatory element within contemporary Japanese cinema, incorporating both Western and Eastern traditions, has a special ability to open such questions, where other films might simply reiterate a more standard and obvious treatment of the historical flashback.[38] Certainly, many recent flashback films do reiterate classic flashback patterns, offering only a surface renewal of form by borrowing certain modernist styles without an innovation that addresses the philosophical principles of flashback subjectivity and historical positioning. *The Godfather II* (Frances Ford Coppola, 1975) and *Once Upon a Time in America* (Sergio Leone, 1984), for example, use their juxtapositions of disparate historical times to trace what is finally an oversimplified notion of the effects of events on the individual. As their description of how the unfulfilled hopes of dislocated immigrants were channeled into the illegal and excessive entrepreneurship of organized crime is a fairly linear concept, these films could have begun at the beginning of the century and progressed towards the corruption of the present.[39] Certainly, they would be less interesting in that format, as the shuffling of temporality permits intriguing juxtapositions, scrambles the suspense patterns in the various temporal moments to achieve a greater complication of the enigmas, and adds to the epic qualities of both films. Their myth-producing focus on the effect of events on individuals and families, like that of earlier gangster films, not presented in flashback, restores anti-heroic (anti-pathetic) characters to a heroic status. The critical eye of modernist flashback structure is at the very least mitigated and rendered uncertain.

There is then a recent trend in the flashback film that runs counter to many of the deconstructive and challenging aspects of modernism while assuming some of modernism's stylistics. *True Confessions* (Ulu Grosbard, 1981), *Looking for Mr. Goodbar* (Richard Brooks, 1978), *Ordinary People* (Robert Redford, 1980), *Dressed to Kill* (Brian De Palma, 1980), *Frances* (Graeme Clifford, 1982), *The Formula* (John Avildsen, 1980), *An Officer and a Gentleman* (Taylor Hackford, 1982) all use flashbacks with some modernist stylistic flair that finally serves simplistic psychology of character or standard suspense formulas that rework Hollywood melodrama without transforming it.

As I have already implied, an alternative to the "renewal of the same" that governs commercial filmmaking is sometimes linked to a position outside the Hollywood and European systems of production and expression. Cultural difference can be the source of a new vision of flashback narration. Flashback films that come from third world countries break through the mold of political flashback films and seem to provide a constructive alternative view of historical memory. Three such films are *Memorias del subdesarrollo* (*Memories of Underdevelopment*, Tomás Gutiérrez Alea, 1969, Cuba), *La Muralla Verde* (*The Green Wall*, Armando Robles-Godoy, 1970, Peru), and *Yawar mallku* (*Blood of the Condor*, Jorge Sanjines and the Grupo Ukamau, 1969, Bolivia). It is with discussion of their difference in utilizing the flashback to examine memory and history that this study will close.

Memory in *Memorias del subdesarrollo* is of two different sorts. One set of memories is refracted as the vision of an individual, Sergio Corrieri, who typifies his class, the bourgeoisie, or more specifically, that intellectual portion of the bourgeoisie which sustains a self-conscious attitude. Sergio's personal memories, of a discussion with his wife before she left Cuba for the United States (first presented as a diegetic auditory instance as the playing of a tape recorder, later given as a flashback), of an evening at a nightclub, of his Catholic education, of his first sexual encounter, of his first love affair with a German in exile from the Nazis, are presented ironically, due to his class type; spectators are invited to sustain an ideological distance from his past, rather than merely identify with it. In contrast to the personal past, the film is studded with newsreel footage of Cuba's public past, historical events dating from the end of the Batista regime through the aftermath of the 1961 Bay of Pigs invasion. Some of the newsreels are commented on in voice-over by Sergio, who describes his singular view of those events. Sergio as an intellectual writer is not unsympathetic to the compelling reasons for the revolution; he can remember the death that spread over Cuba during its past from which the bourgeoisie and foreign powers profited. However, as a member of the privileged class, the struggle to change conditions was alien to him, except, as he says at one point, as "revenge" on the members of his class whom he detested for their shallowness.

In the film's view, Cuba remains underdeveloped, living in the shadow of its past, so that the title also refers to the conditions of the present. It lives with an historical memory that comes at the film's end to fuel the country's resistance during the Cuban missile crisis, while the protagonist remains isolated, passive, outside. He functions as a device that allows the author of the novel from which the film was adapted, Edmundo Desnoes, and the film director, Alea, to self-critically examine their role as writers who remember historical events and create a slant on those events through fiction (each also makes brief appearances in the film and neither is simply the equivalent of Sergio, both are more engaged than he is).

Memorias del subdesarrollo makes a rare effort to frame its flashbacks to personal memory ironically, in contrast to a larger historical memory. The strategy is nearly the opposite of the American films from World War II which use individuals' memories of the past through a process of identification to build a patriotic sense of historical destiny and purpose. It also differs from the use of a self-conscious historical strategy discussed earlier as characteristic of *Man of Iron* and *Tout va bien,* for in those cases the framing and the purpose are at once more obvious and more directed ideologically. The flashbacks in *Memorias del subdesarrollo* are part of a strategy of ideological critique, but one that is complicated by an ambiguity and polysemy which persists in the rendering of subjectivity, similar to the tone adopted in the flashbacks in Costa-Gavras's *Z* (1969). Within the context of memories whose historical and political implications are great, memory remains infused with psychological nuances on a more personal level.

In contrast to this complicated irony of perspective, the flashbacks in *La Muralla Verde* and *Yawar mallku* more straightforwardly chronicle a past history that raises contestatory political issues. In *La Muralla Verde* the flashbacks chronicle the move of a bourgeois family to the interior region as part of a homesteading program.[40] The sequences in the present narrate the unfolding of a personal tragedy, as the young son is bitten by a poisonous snake and medical attention is delayed due to bureaucratic incompetence. The family's alienation from the culture in Lima and the boy's death after they try to resettle turns the film into a parable for the failure of a governmental resettlement program. The middle-class protagonists are presented as sympathetic idealists whose memories reveal how the government promoted resettlement yet failed to provide the infrastructure that could support their efforts. This sort of colonialization of the jungle is politically controversial in ways the film doesn't directly address; a more radical perspective on government policy would be that of the indians, which is what *Yawar mallku* offers in the Bolivian context.

The flashbacks in *Yawar mallku* are introduced as illustrating the narration of an indian woman, Paulina, to her city-dwelling brother. She tells of events that occurred in her village which resulted in her husband, Ignacio, being wounded by the police. The verbal frame has a stronger function here than in other films, not because the flashbacks fully subscribe to the restrictive point of view of their initiating narrator (they don't), but rather because this act of narration signals that the film is structured to evoke, indirectly, the indians' own experience and perspective as much as is possible in a fiction film written and directed by an outsider to this community. The film is made in the indians' language, Quecha, and has a largely indian cast. Further, its pattern of silences, detailed unfolding of indian rituals, cut-aways to objects, and temporal ellipses attempt a visual and auditory analogy for the indian perspective. It is attentive to detail in depicting the everyday life of the indians, their closeness to their environment and their ritual patterns of coping with problems, with ellipses used for chronicling their tense interaction with the foreigners, emphasizing just the significant events. Most importantly, the flashback structure withholds from the audience the cause of the indians' grief, placing the film's audience in a position parallel to the indian's own.

The flashbacks are preceded by elliptically edited opening segments that are temporally located just after the conclusion of an investigation by Paulina's husband of the causes of infertility in his village's women; Ignacio's drunkenness, a cleansing ritual of climbing the mountain, and the police arrest and slaughter all indicate that Ignacio had learned who was responsible and acted upon that knowledge ("They have been punished," he says), without revealing any details. This enigmatic beginning opens a space to be filled in by the flashbacks and provides a motivation for the indian woman to tell the story, emphasizing how her community pieced together the history of the Peace Corps' policy of forced sterilization (changed to "Progress Corps" in the film) and its devastating effect on its population, given the high child mortality rate. The flashbacks are intercut with sequences depicting the continued action of the film, the search for medical care for Ignacio. This pattern of temporal juxtaposition brings together the narrative of the foreigner's mistaken mission in the indians' villages with sequences showing the discrimination they face in La Paz. Inverted temporal order then directly serves the film's ideological intervention, framing perspectives, positioning the audience, and allowing for a comparative unfolding which expands upon the nature of the problems the indians face in Bolivia.

Still, these three examples of third world films that use flashbacks point more to a lack, to works still to be made, than to a fulfilled exploration of the meaning the flashback might have as a device to present memory and history in the modes of thinking of other cultures. In the films we have examined here, the Hollywood model imposes itself less than does a modernism which remains an uncertain alternative, not necessarily breaking with the implicit values it inscribes as a product of European culture.

Conclusion: The Future of the Flashback

I conclude my history of the flashback with a final, perhaps inevitable question: Is the flashback exhausted as a technique of filmic expression, or does it still have the potential for filmic innovation? One way of beginning to answer this question is by posing another one: Are there flashbacks in recent avant-garde films, films that relinquish customary patterns of narrative and indices of temporality and causality, however inverted, fragmented or transformed?

In avant-garde films, as we have seen, floating temporalities may loosen temporal placement to the point that one might have the evocation of memory or the past in a deliberately vague and poetic sense, without defining this past historically or as the memory of a character or the filmmaker. Too, the texture of the image or the use of long dissolves might evoke the qualities of past occurrence or memory without any definite sense that the images seen belong to a marked anterior time. Larry Gottheim's recent *Mnemosone, Mother of Muses* (1986), for instance, thematizes a floating space of uncertain memory as integral to the poetic function of filmic imaging; all of the images in the film unfold in their own indefinite time, each representing actions or sites that remain distinct from one another. Are these memory traces without the ordering structure of conscious recall or narrative association?

Evoking the muse of memory suggests that all film images are memories of their own inscription. In this sense much of the diaristic work of the avant-garde, the personal film, can be seen as researching a kind of unframed flashback structure, revising the immediacy of narrative or documentary film in favor of the memory album.

In other recent cases, avant-garde films frame a kind of flashback in their innovative use of found footage or home movie footage. These reedited traces of a past need not be framed by a narrative present to transmit the concepts of history and memory associated with the flashback.[41] Such are the found home movie images embedded in Abigail Child's *Covert Action* (1984) that apparently chronicle the amorous encounters of two men with various women at their vacation house; the historicity of these images is apparent in the women's clothing and hairstyles as well as the texture of the film stock. Here the "flashback" is outside of a narrative frame though it bears within it its own narrative elements and a notion of being of the past, a past not regained, but reframed in montage with other found footage in rapid fragmentation.

Voice also has the power to evoke the past without concretizing the narration of a past event in the image in the manner of the voice-over of Hollywood in the forties. In recent works, the dislocation of voice from the diegetic space of the image can create a complex play of tenses that never really posits a present in relation to a flashback, but still manifests distinct temporalities for both verbal and visual enunciations. Marguerite Duras's pair of films, *India Song* (1975) and *Son nom de Venise dans Calcutta desert* (1976) use the same sound track over two different image tracks: in the first case, images loosely pertaining to events discussed by the voices in their narration of the past, but not illustrating the events discussed; in the second case, images of the ruined mansion that was the site of the narrative and the images of the first film. The voices narrate through questions and answers, the past history is always a story, always itself in question, never simply able to be flashed on the screen as the embodiment of its own truth.

My examples would seem to indicate that future innovation with the flashback lies with avant-garde modes of expression that reconstruct narrative time and space so as to dissolve the definitive sense of a past the present can clearly access. Floating temporalities do not maintain the points of reference necessary to the flashback as a device. Still, in reviewing the project of modernism in this last chapter, I believe, too, that simultaneous with this sort of "borderline" narration there is much more work to be done on marked flashbacks in more direct narrative forms. Subjectivity is still so haltingly investigated, still so burdened with the limiting assumptions of classical narrative coding. I can imagine flashback films yet to be made that do not simply echo the brave transformations of the "new wave" but make of the act of remembering and retelling something as yet unexplored.

Notes

Chapter One: Definition and Theory of the Flashback

1.   c.f. *The Oxford Companion to Film*, ed. Liz-anne Bawden (New York and London: Oxford University Press, 1976), which offers the following definition: "Flashback, a narrative device in which chronological continuity is broken to show earlier events. In silent cinema direct storytelling was rarely complicated by the use of flashbacks, . . . The flashback was a frequent feature of Hollywood films of the thirties—action being preferable to description it replaced the verbal recollection of past events customary in the theatre, . . . Orson Welles's free-wheeling treatment of the past in *Citizen Kane* (1941) was hailed as a revolution in narrative cinema." (As we shall see this thumbnail history is wrong on the silents and on the thirties.) Also, Leslie Halliwell, *The Filmgoer's Companion*, Third Edition (New York: Hill and Wang, 1970), tells us "Flashback. A break in chronological narrative during which we are shown events of past time which bear on the present situation. The device is as old as the cinema: you could say that *Intolerance* was composed of four flashbacks. As applied to more commonplace yarns, however, with the flashback narrated by one of the story's leading characters, the convention soared into popularity in the 30s until by 1945 or so a film looked very dated indeed if it was not told in retrospect. In the 50s flashbacks fell into absolute disuse, but are now creeping back into fashion again." (As we shall see there are a fair number of 1950s flashbacks, American and, especially, in films of other countries, while the technique hardly "soared to popularity" in the thirties.) Ephraim Katz, *The Film Encyclopedia* (New York: Perigee, 1982) offers a more convincing definition and overview than the other sources, but ends with the statement, "Although generally a useful device in advancing a complicated plot, the multiple flashback can be absurdly confusing, as demonstrated by John Brahm's *The Locket* (1946) in which a flashback four layers deep makes Sheridan Gibney's script hopelessly difficult to follow." I find Katz's dismissal amusing; see chapter five of this book for the reasons why.

2.   Most introductory texts now include glossaries that define cinematic terms including "flashback," though often the discussion of the technique is limited within the text itself. David Bordwell and Kristin Thompson, *Film Art: An Introduction*, Second Edition (New York: Alfred Knopf, 1985) is an exception in that it provides several references to flashback use in different contexts as it discusses narrative form. A sophisticated definition and explanation of the flashback is offered in the entry by Marc Vernet in *Lectures du film* (Paris: Editions Albatros, 1976), pp. 96–98. A special issue of *Cinématographe* devoted to flashback (February 1984) offers several views of the use of the device, primarily journalistic. Most useful in this issue is the contribution by Jean Mitry. Mitry provides a short history of the early flashback, in which he makes the point that I further develop here, that the flashback occurred in early silents (pp. 9–11). See also footnote 36 below for a discussion of contemporary screenwriting manuals and chapter two for a discussion of early manuals.

3.   *A Supplement to the Oxford English Dictionary*, "Flash" entry (Oxford: Oxford University Press at the Clarendon Press, 1972), p. 1099.

4.   *A Supplement to the Oxford English Dictionary*, "Flashback" entry, p. 1099.

5.   M. H. Abrams, *A Glossary of Literary Terms* (New York: Holt Rinehart and Winston, 1971).

6.   Yuri Tynianov, "Plot and Story-line in the Cinema," *Russian Poetics in Translation*, 5 (1978), p. 20.

7.   Boris Tomashevsky, "Thematics," *Russian Formalist Criticism: Four Essays*, ed. Lee Lemon and

Marion Reis (Lincoln, Nebraska: University of Nebraska Press, 1965), pp. 78–85, and Victor Shklovsky, "On the Connection Between Devices of *Syuzhet* Construction to General Stylistic Devices," trans. Jane Knox, *20th Century Studies*, 7/8 (December 1972), p. 54.

8.   See David Bordwell and Kristin Thompson, *Film Art*, as well as books each has written individually, especially the following: Thompson, *Eisenstein's Ivan the Terrible: A Neoformalist analysis* (Princeton: Princeton University Press, 1981) and Bordwell, *Narration in the Fiction Film* (London: Methuen, 1985). The distinction between plot and story is also quite important to the structuralist narrative theory of Gérard Genette, a discussion of which follows in this chapter. In *Narration in the Fiction Film* Bordwell discusses the flashback in his chapter, "Narration and Time," pp. 74–98 with a fascinating analysis of Bertolucci's *The Spider's Strategem* and also in this chapter takes up the categories of frequency and duration developed by Genette. Neo-formalism earns its "neo" in that it infuses formalism with certain structuralist concepts and contemporary expansions.

9.   Abrams, *A Glossary of Literary Terms*.

10.   Keith Cohen, *Film and Fiction: Dynamics of an Exchange* (New Haven: Yale University Press, 1979).

11.   Sergei Eisenstein, "Dickens, Griffith and the Film Today," *Film Form*, trans. Jay Leyda (New York: Harcourt and Brace, 1969).

12.   See also the discussion of Zweig in chapter five in the context of the film adaptation of his novel, *Letter from an Unknown Woman;* Zweig is a writer sensitive to the psychoanalytic dimension of memory and it is particularly interesting that Eisenstein would cite his writing.

13.   Gérard Genette, "Poétique et l'histoire," *Figures III* (Paris: Editions du Seuil, 1972), p. 13–20.

14.   Genette, "Discours du récit," *Figures III*, pp. 71–121, trans. as *Narrative Discourse: An Essay in Method*, tr. Jane E. Lewin (Ithaca: Cornell University Press, 1980), pp. 33–85.

15.   In his "Après-propos" that closes *Figures III*, Genette recognizes this problem and suggests that he expects that posterity will not hold on to a large number of his terminological inventions and distinctions (p. 269).

16.   Critiques of the application of Genette's work to film narratives include Michèle Lagny, Marie-Claire Ropars and Pierre Sorlin, "Le Recit saisi par le film," *Hors Cadre*, no. 2 (1984), pp. 99–124; and Francis Jost, "Discours cinématographique, narration: deux façons d'envisager le problème de l'énonciation," *Théorie du film*, ed. Jean-Louis Leutreat and Jacques Aumont (Paris: Editions Albatros, 1980), pp. 121–31.

17.   Christian Metz, *Essais sur la signification au cinéma*, Vol. 1 (Paris: Klincksieck, 1968), p. 27, as quoted in "Discours du récit, p. 77 (my translation—note that Metz's original passage is slightly different from the way he is quoted by Genette and I have added the brackets at the beginning to indicate that Metz's "le récit est" is taken from the previous sentence of the original. I have translated this use of *récit* in its more general sense as equivalent to the American "narrative," while using "plot" to translate the more restricted meaning of *récit* in the next sentence).

18.   Gilles Deleuze, *Cinéma II: L'Image-Temps* (Paris: Editions de Minuit, 1985), pp. 66–75. As I will discuss later, Deleuze has relatively little to say about the flashback, with the exception of Joseph Mankiewicz's scripts and films. The flashback fails to fulfill the concept, taken from Henri Bergson, of "image-souvenir," an image which seeks "pure memory" rather than giving us the past, and, further, the concept of memory remains separate and more privileged than "image-souvenir." Deleuze is interested in what he calls the "nappes de temps," the sheets or layers of time and looks to the films of Welles and Resnais for examples of this layering. Yet he wants to separate Resnais's success from his play with flashback structures, seeing it rather in his work on all forms of the imaginary (p. 160). I find Deleuze stubbornly reductive in his view of the flashback as he insists that it loses validity by external justification (ie. fate in Marcel Carné's *Le Jour se lève*, 1939), and is not mixed with imagination, subjectivity, or

multiplicity except in unusual cases. This book argues that the technique is open to far more complex uses than Deleuze allows.

19. Marc Vernet, "Narrateur, personnage et spectateur dans le film de fiction à travers le film noir," unpublished Ph.D. dissertation, L'Ecole des Hautes Etudes, 1985. Vernet argues that differences in enunciation between film and literature circumscribe the applicability of a theory built on verbal textuality to the visual constructs of film.

20. Roland Barthes, *S/Z*, trans. Richard Miller (New York: Hill and Wang, 1974).

21. Among the writings of Jacques Derrida most relevant here are: *De la Grammatologie* (Paris: Editions de Minuit, 1967), *Ecriture et la différance* (Paris: Seuil, 1967), and *Glas* (Paris: Editions Denoël/ Gonthier, 1981). See also Marie-Claire Ropars, *Le Texte divisé* (Paris: Presses Universitaires de France, 1981) for an excellent discussion and practice of a Derridean analysis of films. I also mean to include the writing of Jean-François Lyotard and much of the writing of Julia Kristeva, among others, within a more general sense of what we might mean by deconstruction.

22. Pierre Macherey, *Pour une théorie de la production littéraire* (Paris: Maspero, 1970). See also the Marxist criticism of Fredric Jameson, Terry Eagleton, Raymond Williams, among others and the influence of Macherey on *Cahiers du cinéma* in the early seventies.

23. André Bazin, "Ontology of the Photographic Image," *What is Cinema?*, Vol. 1, trans. Hugh Grey (Berkeley, Los Angeles, and London: University of California Press, 1967), pp. 9–16.

24. Roland Barthes, *La Chambre Claire: Note sur la photographie* (Paris: Editions de l'étoile, Gallimard, Seuil, 1980).

25. Christian Metz, *Essais sur la signification au cinéma*, vol. 2 (Paris: Klinksieck, 1973) and *The Imaginary Signifier: Psychoanalysis and the Cinema*, trans. Celia Britton, Annwyl Williams, Ben Brewster, and Alfred Guzetti (Bloomington: Indiana University Press, 1977), pp. 42–57.

26. The history of negative reception to flashbacks is long. Even in the twenties, *New York Times* reviews implied that flashbacks were often tedious or tired. Since then flashbacks have often been advised against by scriptwriting manuals. Michel Chion's recent *Ecrire une Scénario* (Paris: Cahiers du cinéma, INA, 1985) who presents his own somewhat negative evaluation of the technique by arguing that Lewis Hermann already found flashbacks dated in his 1952 *A Practical Manual of Screenwriting for Theater and Television Films* (New York: Meridian, 1952). There was certainly a generalized disfavoring of the flashback in the sixties and seventies in Hollywood, which may have been partially responsible for the cutting of the flashback sequence from the distributed prints of Sergio Leone's *The Good the Bad and the Ugly* (1966); this example is one·in which spectator participation in the action is key to the film's functioning, and a second-level knowledge of structure would interfere with this direct affectivity.

27. The writings of Sigmund Freud on these issues include *Interpretation of Dreams, Beyond the Pleasure Principle*, "Notes on the Mystic Writing Pad," "The Uncanny," and "Jensen's *Gradiva*." This will be discussed in greater detail in chapters five and six.

28. The discussion in chapter six includes references to Alan Richardson, *Mental Imagery* (New York: Springer, 1969); Ulric Neisser, *Cognitive Psychology* (Englewood Cliffs, N.J.: Prentice-Hall, 1967); Peter E. Morris and Peter J. Hampson, *Imagery and Consciousness* (London: Academic Press, 1984), tracing the role of images in memory functioning.

Chapter Two: Flashbacks in American Silent Cinema

1. Bulletin ad, *The New York Dramatic Mirror*, Dec. 3, 1911.

2. Edward Wagenknecht claims in his book *The Movies in the Age of Innocence* (Norman, Oklahoma: University of Oklahoma Press, 1962), p. 89, that two of the Griffith adaptations of Tennyson's poem, *After Many Years* (1908) and *Enoch Arden* (1911) contain flashbacks (Griffith also made a third). Jean Mitry locates a flashback in Griffith's *Adventures of Dolly* (1908), in his article, "Les Origines du

flashback," *Cinématographe* (February 1984), but again this seems to be a cutaway mistaken for a flashback.

3. Jean-Louis Comolli, "Technique et idéologie," *Cahiers du cinéma*, no. 229 (May 1971), pp. 4–21; no. 230 (July 1971), pp. 51–57; no. 231 (August-September 1971); no. 233 (November 1971), pp. 39–45; nos. 234–35 (December 1971/January-February 1972), pp. 94–100; and no. 241 (September-October 1972), pp. 20–24.

4. My attempt to trace early flashback films that might be collected in archives to include in this analysis surveyed three types of sources: film histories and monographs, personal consultations with historians of early film history, and a systematic combing of *New York Times* reviews and the *American Film Index* on the Hollywood films of twenties (the latter process with the help of my students, Jim Fanning and Lisa Dickerson, at the State University of New York at Binghamton). In many cases, the advice of historians of early film history was very helpful in finding films (I am particularly grateful to Kristin Thompson for not only pointing out which early films she screened had flashbacks, but also which archive owned them). Written sources often neglect to mention flashbacks in films that contain them, and occasionally (see footnote 2, above) claim that another montage figure constitutes a flashback—thus indicating that a flashback exists in a film that has none. In many cases, I was able to view the films that from these sources were indicated to contain flashbacks at one of the following archives or in general distribution or at a special screening showing: the Library of Congress, the Film Archives of the University of Wisconsin at The State Historical Society in Madison, Wisconsin, The British Film Institute, and the UCLA film archives. In addition, regularly scheduled screenings at La Cinémathèque française, Paris and The Museum of Modern Art allowed me to see films as well. Occasionally reviews from the teens and twenties would give descriptions of flashbacks in films that were not available for screening at my four major archival sources during the research on this part of the book; I list those films in the appendix.

5. Ricciotto Canudo and Elie Faure were two early, eloquent proponents of the argument that cinema should be considered as an art, to be considered as a synthesis, and even a transcendent mixture of the aesthetic processes introduced by other art forms. See the writings of Ricciotto Canudo for the development of this argument of film as an art form, "L'art pour le septième art," *Cinéa,* 2 (13 May, 1921) and "Manifestes des sept arts," *Gazette des sept arts* (25 January, 1923). See also, Elie Faure, "La Danse et le cinéma" and "De la cinéplastique," essays originally published in 1922 and "Vocation du cinéma," originally published in 1937, collected in the book, *Fonction du cinéma* (Paris: Editions Gonthier, 1964).

6. Gérard Genette, "Discours du récit," *Figures III* (Paris: Editions du Seuil, 1972).

7. Sergei Eisenstein, "Dickens, Griffith and the Film Today," *Film Form,* trans. Jay Leyda (New York: Harcourt and Brace, 1969).

8. John Fell, *Film and the Narrative Tradition* (Norman, Oklahoma: University of Oklahoma Press, 1974). See also A. Nicholas Vardac, *Stage to Screen: Theatrical Method from Garrick to Griffith* (New York: B. Blom, 1968 [1949]) for a discussion of the interrelation between theater and film during this period.

9. Kemp R. Niver, *The First Twenty Years: A Segment of Film History* (Los Angeles: Locare Research Group, 1968) provides an overview of the paper print restoration of the holdings of the Library of Congress. In short summaries of selected films Niver mentions the various techniques used to insert an image within another image, though none of the images he discusses are flashbacks. See his discussion of Edwin S. Porter's *Uncle Josh at the Picture Show* (1902), p. 22; Porter's *Jack and the Beanstalk* (1902), p. 27; Méliès's *The Kingdom of the Fairies* (1903), p. 39; Méliès's *The Magic Lantern* (1903), p. 43.

10. See, however, the discussion of the flashback in Méliès's *Le Juif errant* (1903), later in this chapter.

11. André Gaudrault, ed., *Cinéma 1900–1906,* Vol. 2 (Brussels: FIAF, 1982), p. 53.

12. c.f. Edwin Bronner, *The Encyclopedia of the American Theatre, 1900–1975* (San Francisco:

A. S. Barnes and Co., 1980), p. 349: "A cleverly crafted courtroom melodrama, *On Trial* dramatized the prosecution and defense of a man charged with murder in the first degree. It was the first play to use the 'flashback' technique of the cinema, with the testimony of the witnesses visualized, with each flashback carrying the story forward. The play was hailed as 'a triumph of dramatic construction.' Another reviewer (Louis Sherwin, Globe) called it: 'The most striking novelty that has been seen for years. Undoubtedly it will bring about important changes in the technique of the theatre."

13. See Noël Burch, "Porter or Ambivalence," *Screen* (Winter 1978/79), pp. 91–105; André Gaudrault, "Narrativité et temporalité: Le Cinéma des premiers temps (1895–1908)," *Etudes Littéraires*, vol. 13, no. 1 (April 1980), pp. 109–39; and Tom Gunning, "The non-Continuous Style of Early Film 1900–1906" in *Cinéma 1900–1906*, Vol. 1, ed. Roger Holman (Brussels: FIAF, 1982).

14. Barry Salt, *Film Style and Technology: History and Analysis* (London: Starwood, 1983).

15. Salt, *Film Style*, p. 167. Salt's cited examples are for the most part those films held in the BFI collection. I am grateful to his book for indicating these titles, as I was able to screen these films at the BFI. Flashbacks are one of the least indexed items and one research difficulty was locating flashback films. At the same time, the BFI collection represents a very small fraction of filmic production, so that conclusions drawn from these films must use them as cautious examples, not a quantitatively sufficient representative historical sample.

16. David Bordwell, Janet Staiger, and Kristin Thompson, *The Classical Hollywood Cinema: Film Style and Mode of Production to 1960* (New York: Columbia University Press, 1985).

17. Ernest A. Dench, *Playwriting for the Cinema: Dealing with the Writing and Marketing of Scenarios* (London: Adam and Charles Black, 1914).

18. See *Cinéma 1900–1906*, Vol. 2 for a description of this film, that unfortunately was not among the Méliès prints I have been able to view.

19. Edward Azlant, *The Theory, History and Practice of Screenwriting*, unpublished Ph.D. dissertation, University of Wisconsin-Madison, 1980, p. 32. Epes Winthrop Sargent's *Technique of the Photoplay* was first published in *Moving Picture World* (July 22, 1911 and September 9, 1911) and then republished in book form (New York: Chalmers, 1912).

20. The first example is from the review of *Yellow Men and Gold* (Irvin Willat, 1922), May 29, 1922, *The New York Times*, while the second is from a review of *His Children's Children* (Sam Wood, 1923), Nov. 5, 1923, *The New York Times*.

21. Marguerite Bertsch, *How to Write for Moving Pictures: A Manual of Instruction and Information* (New York: George H. Doran Co., 1917), and Howard Dimick, *Modern Photoplay Writing* (Franklin, Ohio: James Knapp Reeve, 1922).

22. Hugo Münsterberg, *The Psychology of the Photoplay* (New York: D. Appleton and Co., 1916), reissued as *The Film: A Psychological Study: The Silent Photoplay in 1916* (New York: Dover, 1970). Page references in text are to the Dover edition.

23. Earlier flashbacks did not necessarily have such punctuation; a direct cut joined the present to the past. Note that in the scriptwriting manuals from the teens and twenties cited earlier the term "dissolve" was used to mean flashback, even though we now take this term to mean the actual simultaneous fade out of one image overlapping with a fade in on the other. The fact that the optical punctuatiuon could be used as a metonymic label for the flashback indicates that the punctuation was seen as obligatory.

24. For example, "The expedient of the cutback is resorted to a trifle too freely" noted *The New York Times'* reviewer of *Tarzan of the Apes* on January 28, 1918.

25. Curiously, *Orphans of the Storm* is cited in Dimick's *Modern Photoplay Writing* as his example of a film that properly dispenses with the flashback in order to "eliminate retrospect and enhance continuity. Thus in *Orphans of the Storm*, the violence by which the de Vaudreys rid themselves of a commoner and his child framed a kind of prologue to the story. The critical conditions lay in later

circumstances, such as the blindness of Louise and the innocence of Henriette, when added to the times or period. But the details precedent, which were organically related to the plot, had either to prelude the story or be consigned to retrospect. Mr. Griffith took the more dramatic alternative" (p. 200). While it is true that this sequence is part of the prologue, it and other parts of the prologue are repeatedly recalled in flashbacks, a point central to my analysis of the film.

26.   See the discussion in the next chapter of an early French film adaptation of *Les Misérables*.

27.   Unfortunately, I have not been able to see *Secrets*, despite inquiries at numerous archives and therefore base my comments solely on reviews that appeared at the time. This is also the case with *The Lady, The Woman on Trial, The Night Watch, Soul Fire, The Last Moment*, and *A Million Bid*, but these are the only films discussed in this book whose analysis is not based on my own viewings. Ordinarily I would not include films that I have not seen, as secondary, written descriptions are often not accurate and never adequate replacements of viewings as the basis of analysis. I made the exception in this case in consideration of the historical importance of these categories of films, as evidenced by the many review references made to biographical flashbacks in this period. Given the likelihood that copies of many of these films are no longer available, it became necessary to work in some cases from written descriptions. This circumstance restricted my comments to elements of the narrative that reviewers mention and therefore the discussion of these films is not as involved in actual image and intertitle montage as I would like it to be.

28.   See the discussion of Abel Gance's melodramas in the next chapter.

29.   Paul Fejos is indeed a curious figure as he came to the States to serve as a bacteriologist at the Rockefeller Institute. See the review of *The Last Moment* in *The New York Times*, March 12, 1928.

30.   See the discussion of G. W. Pabst's *The Love of Jeanne Ney* (1927), in the next chapter for a comparable treatment of a similar flashback narrative, which I take to be indicative of how the Kammerspiel film remains closer in its flashback use to Hollywood models than the German expressionist film.

Chapter Three: European and Japanese Experimentation with Flashbacks in Silent Films

1.   Lotte Eisner, *The Haunted Screen* (Berkeley and Los Angeles: University of California Press, 1969).

2.   This is the thesis discussed in recent work of Tom Gunning, "Early Development in Film Narrative: D. W. Griffith's First Films at Biograph (1908–1909)," unpublished Ph.D. dissertation, New York University, 1986; and André Gaudrault, "Narration et monstration au cinéma," *Hors Cadre*, Vol. 2 (1984), pp. 87–98. See also works cited in last chapter, Nöel Burch, "Porter or Ambivalence," *Screen* (Winter 1978/79), pp. 91–105. Also André Gaudrault, "Narrativité et temporalité: Le Cinéma des premiers temps (1895–1908)," *Etudes Littéraires,* vol. 13, no. 1 (April 1980), pp. 109–39; and Tom Gunning, "The Non-Continuous Style of Early Film 1900–1906" in *Cinéma 1900–1906*, Vol. 1, ed. Roger Holman (Brussels: FIAF, 1982).

3.   I am indebted to Aldo Bernardini and Paulo Cherchi Usai for pointing out the early development of flashbacks within Italian cinema at the Colloque de Cerisy on Film History, 1985, and encouraging my study of this question via the retrospective of Italian Cinema held at the Centre George Pompidou, that Bernardini co-coordinated with Jean Gili. See also *Le Cinéma italien 1905–1945*, ed. Bernardini and Gili (Paris: Editions du Centre Pompidou, 1986).

4.   See the discussion by Emanuelle Toulet of French criticism of Italian films of this period in her article, "Le Cinéma muet italien et la critique française," *Le Cinéma italien 1905–1945*, which indicates great initial exposure to and interest in the Italian work, until a more competitive and negative attitude faults the Italians for repeating the same formulas following 1916. Several other authors in this volume (Aldo Bernardini, Gian Piero Brunetta, and Claudio Camerini) suggest a potential precursor status of Italian films of this period, although the issue of flashbacks per se is taken up directly only in discussion

of *Nozze d'oro* (Luigi Massi, 1911): "the director utilized a very modern filmic language based on the flashback, well-served by skillful photography" (p. 192, my translation). Also, Barry Salt discusses *Nozze d'oro* in his discussion of the earliest examples of the flashback in silent cinema, in *Film Style and Technology: History and Analysis* (London: Starwood, 1983).

5. Henri Bergson, *Matière et mémoire*, 46th ed. (Paris: Presses Universitaire de France, 1946). *Matter and Memory*, trans. Nancy Margaret Paul and W. Scott Palmer (London: George Allen & Unwin, 1950).

6. For discussions of Bergson contemporaneous with the films discussed here see Harald Höffding, *La Philosophie de Bergson* (Paris, Felix Alcan, 1917); Albert Thibaudet, "Le Bergsonisme," 2 vols. (Paris: NRF, 1922); Quercy, "Sur une théorie bergsonienne de l'imagination," *Annales medico psychologique* (1925); de Chevalier and Boyer, "De l'image a l'hallucination," *Journal de psychologie* (April 15, 1926); and especially, Pierre Janet, *L'évolution de la mémoire et la notion de temps* (Paris: A. Cahine, 1928), particularly the sections entitled "Les variétés du récit," pp. 227–48, and "Les procédés de la narration," pp. 249–72. See also Jean-Paul Sartre's discussion of Bergson in *L'imagination* (Paris: PUF, 1936) which is critical of Bergson, precisely because Sartre believes Bergson retains too much of the idealist position found within associationist theories of the image that Bergson himself attacked. See also the more recent writing on Bergson by Gilles Deleuze; *Le Bergsonisme* (Paris: PUF, 1966), *Cinéma I: Image-Mouvement* (Paris: Editions de Minuit, 1983), and *Cinéma II: Image-Temps* (Paris: Editions de Minuit, 1985). In the two most recent volumes Deleuze draws on Bergson's theories to speak of the functioning of images and signs in cinema.

7. See Richard Abel's discussion of the film journals and ciné-clubs that formed what he calls "The Alternate Cinema Network" in his *French Cinema* (Princeton, New Jersey: Princeton University Press, 1985), pp. 241–75. Also Dr. Allendy's essay, "La valeur psychologique de l'image"—which Abel notes was given as one of a series of lectures at the Théatre du Vieux-Colombier in the winter 1925–26 and which has been preserved as a clipping from *l'Art cinématographique*, no. 1 (1926) in the collection of La Bibliothèque de l'arsenal, Paris—is strong evidence of this cross-fertilization between psychoanalysts' interested in the perception of images and their symbolism within the unconscious and the filmmakers of the avant-garde.

8. Marcel Proust, *Le Temps*, November 13, 1913, p. 4.

9. Étienne Burnet, "Proust et le Bergsonisme," *Essences* (Paris: Seheur, 1929), p. 171.

10. See, for example, Floris Delattre *Bergson et Proust: accords et differences* (Paris: Albin Michel, 1948), and Robert Champigny, "Proust, Bergson and other Philosophers," in *Proust: A Collection of Critical Essays*, ed. René Girard (Englewood Cliffs, New Jersey: Prentice-Hall, 1962), pp. 122–31.

11. Elie Faure, "De la cinéplastique," was first published in 1922 and appears in the posthumous volume, *Fonction du cinéma* (Paris: Editions Gonthier, 1953). The lines cited appear on pages 32 and 33 of this volume and the translation is mine.

12. Leon Moussinac, *Naisssance du cinéma* (Paris: Pavlovsky, 1925), p. 95, my translation.

13. Louis Delluc, *Photogénie* (Paris: Editions Bunoff, 1920), p. 125. Articles discussing "photogénie" included in this volume appeared as early as 1916. See also the prologue to Louis Delluc's *Drames du cinéma* (Paris: Editions du Monde nouveau, 1923).

14. "Impressionist" has now become a standard categorization of films of this period. Nearly all world film history books give some account of the characteristics of impressionist style (see, for example, David Cook, *A History of Narrative Film* [New York and London: Norton, 1981], drawing on the presentation of the impressionists in earlier French sources—such as the writings of the filmmakers themselves and film histories such as René Jeanne and Charles Ford, *Histoire encyclopédique du cinéma*, Vol. 1: *Le Cinéma français 1895–1929* (Paris: Robert Laffont, 1947); Georges Sadoul, *Le Cinéma français* (Paris: Flammarion, 1962); and Jean Mitry, *Histoire du cinéma*, Vols. 2 and 3 (Paris: Editions Universitaires, 1969 and 1973), amongst others. However, Jeanne, Ford, and Mitry use the term

"impressionist" only in passing, while Sadoul introduces his discussion with its qualified use. A thorough formalist study of techniques in impressionist film is presented in David Bordwell, *French Impressionist Cinema* (New York: Arno Press, 1980).

15. Abel is critical of the term in *French Cinema*, pp. 279–81 and cites other critical discussions of "impressionism" as a term. He notes that the way in which the filmmakers themselves used the terms was to refer to a realist style depicting the atmosphere of landscapes, as in French impressionist painting or as rhythmic montage reminiscent of impressionist music. Abel prefers the term "narrative avant-garde" to impressionism, for he finds that the subjective style of filmic impressionism is characteristic of only some of the avant-garde films. I find impressionism, with some qualification, a richer term than the one he substitutes—for in emphasizing the narrative aspect of these films, his substitute term emphasizes that aspect of the films that seems the least avant-garde: if they still use narrative, they refocus its presentation conceptually and that refocusing on temporality, subjectivity, spatial distortions, or permeability, etc., is what constitutes their difference as textual practice.

16. Delluc, *Drames du cinéma*.

17. Moussinac, *Naissance du cinéma*, p. 29, my translation.

18. Sadoul develops a broad picture of this shifting economic situation in *Le Cinéma français*, but as Abel notes in the conclusion of *French Cinema* (p. 529) more research needs to be done on the question of possible economic and technological factors in the demise of an alternative cinema.

19. Sandy Flitterman, *"La Maternelle,"* *Enclitic*, Vol. 5, nos. 5–6 (Fall 1981/Spring 1982).

20. See the entry on "Neurosis of Abandonment" (*l'abandonique*) in Jean Laplanche and J.-B. Pontalis, *The Language of Psychoanalysis* (New York and London: Norton, 1973), p. 270, in which they define the way in which this term was introduced by Swiss psychoanalysts Germaine Guex and Charles Odier. See also Germaine Guex, *La nevrose d'abandon* (Paris: Presses Universitaires de France, 1950).

21. Abel, *French Cinema*, pp. 429–30 and footnotes on p. 589.

22. See Siegfried Kracauer, *Theory of Film: The Redemption of Physical Reality* (London and Oxford: Oxford University Press, 1960), and André Bazin, *What is Cinema?*, trans. Hugh Grey, 2 vols. (Berkeley: University of California Press, 1967, 1971), both of which present a theory of cinematic realism derived from an ontological argument that the camera is an instrument whose ability to record a physical reality privileges this as the proper vocation of cinema. (Kracauer's *From Caligari to Hitler: A Psychological History of the German Film* (Princeton: Princeton University Press, 1947) rests on similar assumptions, and determines to show that the expressionist style built the foundation of a fascist ideology.

23. Kracauer, *From Caligari to Hitler*, p. 64.

24. Sigmund Freud, *The Interpretation of Dreams*, trans. James Strachey (New York: Bantam, 1969).

25. Sigmund Freud, "The Occurrence in Dreams of Material from Fairy Tales" (1913), *The Standard Edition of the Complete Psychological Works of Sigmund Freud*, vol. 12 (London: Hogarth Press, 1953), pp. 279–88, and *Interpretation of Dreams*.

26. Carl Schorske, *Fin-de-Siècle Vienna: Politics and Culture* (New York: Knopf, 1980).

27. Patrick Lacoste, "Chambre à part: Mystères d'une chose visuelle," *Nouvelle Revue de Psychanalyse*, n. 29 (Spring 1984), pp. 221–48.

28. Sigmund Freud, "Delusions and Dreams in Jensen's *Gradiva*" (1907), *The Standard Edition of the Complete Psychological Works of Sigmund Freud*, Vol. 9, pp. 3–98.

29. See Sigmund Freud, "The 'Uncanny' " (1919), *The Standard Edition of the Complete Psychological Works of Sigmund Freud*, Vol. 17, pp. 219–56.

30. Griffith's *True-Heart Susie* is discussed in chapter two. The flashback in Sjöström's *The Girl*

from the Stormy Cove is similar to the comic revelation flashback in *Little Meena's Romance* (1916), also discussed in chapter two.

31. Ulla Britta Lagerroth, quoted by Peter Christianson in his paper, "Levels of the Fantastic in Sjöström's *The Phantom Chariot*," delivered at the annual meeting of the Society for Cinema Studies, 1983.

32. Some of these imaging techniques and concern with memory and guilt will again resurface in the work of Ingmar Bergman, whose work with memory images will be discussed in chapter six.

33. See Noël Burch's discussion of this in his book, *To the Distant Observer: Form and Meaning in Japanese Cinema* (Berkeley and Los Angeles: University of California Press, 1979), p. 126. Burch suggests in footnote 4 that "Japanese authorities feel" that Kinugasa must have seen and been influenced by such films as *The Cabinet of Dr. Caligari* and *La Roue,* which according to these same (unnamed) sources were shown in Japan during the early twenties. Burch speculates that it is possible that Kinugasa felt he had not lived up to his European models and therefore did not show *Page of Madness* in Europe, but he also entertains the idea of an independent development of this aesthetic. In the body of his text, Burch later suggests that Kinugasa's film was in fact "slightly ahead of its time" (p. 128).

34. Robert Cohen, "A Japanese Romantic: Teinosuke Kinugasa," *Sight and Sound,* vol. 45 (Summer, 1976).

35. Joseph L. Anderson and Donald Richie, *The Japanese Film: Art and Industry* (Princeton: Princeton University Press, 1982), pp. 54–55. They also claim the film was a "big success" at its Tokyo opening at a theater in Shinjuku that normally showed foreign films.

Chapter Four: The Subjectivity of History in Hollywood Sound Films

1. Eisenstein's early films and theoretical statements are the most marked by this concept of the drama of mass action in which the collective replaces the individual hero as focus of the action. See Sergei Eisenstein, *Film Essays,* trans. Jay Leyda (New York: Praeger, 1970), especially the first three essays, "A Personal Statement," "The Method of Making Workers' Films," and "Soviet Cinema." However, Eisenstein's writing is not without its contradictions; consider his praise for John Ford's *Young Mr. Lincoln* (1939) in his essay bearing the same title from 1939 (pp. 139–49 in *Film Essays*), a film whose concentration on the individual's contribution to history would seem to fall under the category of a bourgeois representation of history as Eisenstein described it earlier in his career. And, of course, the later films, *Alexander Nevsky* (1938) and *Ivan the Terrible* (1944–46) represent a quite different narrative strategy than the earlier films. It is intriguing to note in this light that the only flashback in Eisenstein occurs in *Ivan the Terrible, Part II* where the focus on Ivan as the central character in this historical epic allows for a flashback to his youth, offered as a psychological explanation of Ivan's mistrust of the Boyards.

2. See the discussion of the historical formation of the individual as sovereign self in relationship to representation in Michel Foucault, *Les Mots et les choses* (Paris: Gallimard, 1966), translated as *The Order of Things* (New York: Vintage, 1970), and *The Archaeology of Knowledge,* trans. A. M. Sheridan Smith (New York: Pantheon, 1972). See also, Fredric Jameson, "Realism and Desire: Balzac and the Problem of the Subject," in *The Political Unconscious: Narrative as a Socially Symbolic Act* (Ithaca: Cornell University Press, 1981), pp. 151–84.

3. R. G. Collingwood, *The Idea of History* (Oxford: Oxford University Press, 1946), pp. 282–302.

4. Collingwood's method, that allows for speculative imagination in addressing the questions of historical explanation, brings history closer to the realm of letters and the human sciences than to the natural sciences. Its popularization may have something to do with the interest in the historical novel and film, the recreation and personalization of history as narrative. In the United States, this tendency was epitomized by the "You Are There" series of educational films shown to grade school history classes, in

which Walter Cronkite served as a newscaster who could propel the viewer back into a period of history that could be relived as drama.

5.   See Maurice Mandelbaum, *The Problem of Historical Knowledge: An Answer to Relativism* (New York: Liveright, 1938); *Theories of History,* ed. Patrick Gardiner (New York, Free Press, 1959); and Arthur Danto, "Laws and Explanations in History," *Philosophy of Science,* Vol. 23 (1956). Historical materialism, based on dialectical materialism and the writings of Karl Marx and Frederick Engels critiques a dualist method as idealism. Hannah Arendt offers an interesting counterpoint to traditional historical materialism in her essay, "The Concept of History," in *Between Past and Future: Six Exercises in Political Thought* (New York: Viking, 1961). See also, Paul Ricoeur, "History and Narrative," Part II of *Time and Narrative,* Vol. 1, trans. Kathleen Maclaughlin and David Pellauer (Chicago and London: University of Chicago Press, 1984), pp. 95–225.

6.   The manner in which these alternatives come to inform the flashback film are examined in chapter six.

7.   For an explanation of this process of identification see Stephen Heath, *Questions of Cinema* (Bloomington: Indiana University Press, 1981) and Christian Metz, *Le Signifier imaginaire* (Paris: L'Union générale d'Editions, 1977), translated as *The Imaginary Signifier,* trans. Celia Britton, Annwyl Williams, Ben Brewster, and Alfred Guzzetti (Bloomington: Indiana University Press, 1982).

8.   A use of intertitles as a kind of "voice-over" during flashback sequences did occur in some silent films, as noted in chapter two. When I say that voice-over becomes a major addition to sound flashback technique, I am referring to the complex and greatly nuanced intervention of voice that sound allows, a practice of auditory voice-over that we will consider in its stylistic appearance in films in this chapter and the ones that follow.

9.   Theories on the escapism of Hollywood production in the thirties have contended that the Depression caused the Hollywood studios to market their product as an entertaining antidote to the problems of the economic crisis. See, for example, Andrew Bergman, *We're in the Money: Depression America and Its Films* (New York: New York University Press, 1971); however, such generalizations do not account for the rise of the social problem film nor do they document their assumptions about causality. And all too often they assume that a production/exploitation strategy is a choice made by the audience. It is acknowledging the theoretical difficulties in seeking such a direct correspondence between the presence or absence of a certain type of film and economic and social causes that I do no more than suggest that films shied away from the exploration of flashback liaisons in the thirties.

10.   *Smilin' Through* (1922, Sydney A. Franklin), *New York Times* review, April 17, 1922.

11.   *Smilin' Through* (1932, again directed by Franklin), *New York Times* review, Mordant Hall, Oct. 15, 1932.

12.   Sigmund Freud, "The 'Uncanny' " (1919), *The Standard Edition of the Complete Psychological Works of Sigmund Freud,* Vol. 17, trans. and ed. James Strachey (London: Hogarth Press, 1953), pp. 219–56.

13.   Both of these versions, as well as the 1941 and 1961 versions of the film, tone down and transform the ethnicity of the characters in Fanny Hurst's novel where the heroine is from a family of working-class German immigrants while her married lover is a wealthy Jew involved in New York politics. As such, the social dimension of this liaison is diminished (more so in the 1932 version than in the 1926 version). Hollywood tends to tone down referential coding, leaving only the more innocuous elements of the stories it adapts; the film versions of *Back Street* retain a refusal to condemn the "other" woman in an extra-marital affair, but do so by emphasizing that she sacrifices herself to the man just like a wife, without the critical view of such role definitions one finds in the novel. The flashback serves to recapitulate these moments of sacrifice and therefore contributes greatly to this reframing of the narrative as a story of the sanctification of an illicit affair.

14.   See the discussion of *The Last Moment* in chapter two. A review by Mordant Hall of *Two Seconds*

in the *New York Times*, May 19, 1932, noted the similarity between the two films. "In its main idea it is very much like Dr. Paul Fejos's old film, *The Last Moment*, but the events in the tale are quite different."

15. Sturges's "narratage" is explained by Jesse Lasley in *Newsweek*, 26 Aug. 1933, p. 31.

16. The rise-to-fame film narrative told chronologically is particularly common in the thirties, both in the form of the historical biography and in musicals. Consider the plots of the Fred Astaire-Ginger Rogers musicals, for example, in which the fictions of *Top Hat* (Mark Sandrich, 1935) or *Swing Time* (George Stevens, 1936) establish the pattern which will be used in the fictionalized biography *The Story of Vernon and Irene Castle* (H. C. Potter, 1939). This upbeat tendency within the musical genre may also help explain the exceptionally optimistic flashback biography of George M. Cohan, Michael Curtiz's *Yankee Doodle Dandy* (1942), which is discussed at the end of this section. The biographies popular in the mid- and late thirties included fictionalized accounts of the lives of the famous, intended to be particularly edifying, such as William Dieterle's *The Story of Louis Pasteur* (1936) and Irving Pichel's *The Story of Alexander Graham Bell* (1939).

17. David Bordwell, "Citizen Kane," *Film Comment* (Summer, 1971).

18. This argument contradicts Bruce Kawin's argument about the flashbacks in *Citizen Kane* in his book *Mindscreen: Bergman, Godard and First-Person Film* (Princeton: Princeton University Press, 1978), pp. 23–44.

19. The shooting script of the film by Herman Mankiewicz and Orson Welles and the cutting continuity of the completed film are published in Pauline Kael, *The Citizen Kane Book* (Boston: Little, Brown and Co., 1971), pp. 87–434.

20. See Michael Renov, "Hollywood's Wartime Woman: A Study of Historical/Ideological Determination" (Ann Arbor: UMI Press, 1987). I am indebted to the author for first bringing to my attention several of the wartime flashback films discussed in this chapter.

21. See Heath, *Questions of Cinema*, and Annette Kuhn, *Women's Pictures: Feminism and Cinema* (London and New York: Routledge and Kegan Paul, 1982), for examples of theories that address the Hollywood film's strategies of containment.

22. See Mary Ann Doane's excellent and quite different analysis of desire in this film in her book, *The Desire to Desire: The Woman's Film of the 1940s* (Bloomington: Indiana University Press, 1987), pp. 97–104.

23. The focalization is more or less nominal in each case. Once inside the flashback, there is a deviation from the anti-heroine or anti-hero as central "voice" of the narration, as indicated in the earlier analyses.

24. Again, a certain caution must be exercised in calling a certain observed tendency an ideological imperative. It should be remembered that *The Hard Way* is also produced during World War II and it contains none of the upbeat moral charge we might associate with this period (see footnote 9 above).

25. See the discussion of the flashback before death as it appears in *The Last Moment* (chapter two) and *La Roue* (chapter three).

26. Sigmund Freud, *The Interpretation of Dreams*, trans. James Strachey (New York: Avon, 1965), pp. 56–64, 71–73, 256–60, 271–72, and 428–29.

27. Freud, *Interpretation of Dreams*, pp. 312–39.

28. Later, Margo's dresser (Thelma Ritter) will come to doubt Eve more vociferously than Margo, but in this introduction scene she joins the others in sympathizing with Eve and critiquing Margo's haughty attitude toward her fan. This scene is curiously summarized incorrectly by Gilles Deleuze in his analysis of the film in *Cinéma II: L'Image-Temps* (Paris: Editions de Minuet, 1985): "Mais, bien que la bifurcation ne puisse en principe être découverte qu'après coup, par flash-back, il y a un personnage qui a pu la pressentir, ou la saisir su le moment, . . . D'abord, l'habilleuse-secrétaire de l'actrice a compris

immédiatement la fourberie d'Eve, son caractère fourchu: au moment même où Eve faisait son récit mensonger, elle a tout entendu de la pièce a coté, hors champ, et rentre dans le champ pour regarder Eve intensément et manifester brièvement son doute" pp. 71–72. (But even though bifurcatiuon cannot in theory be discovered until after-the-fact, in flashback, there is a character who can sense it ahead of time or seize it right away, . . . first, the dresser of the actress understood immediately the deceit of Eve, her forked tongue: at the instant when Eve tells her lie, the dresser hears all from the side room, off screen, and enters the shot to scrutinize Eve intensely and briefly manifest her doubt; my translation). Further, Deleuze's discussion of Joseph Mankiewicz on pages 68–74, as "without doubt the greatest author of the flashback" for his use of the principle of bifurcation is at once too auteurist and too ahistorical (all of Mankiewicz's scripts and films are made to conform to the same principle, one that Deleuze implies other flashbacks don't achieve). Deleuze is led to his reading of Mankiewicz by way of Philippe Carcassone's article, "Coupez!," *Cinématographe*, n. 51 (October 1979), as he acknowledges in footnote 8, p. 70 and like Carcassone, he overestimates the break with linearity and circularity in these works, both in terms of its uniqueness and its extension. This is not to say that the play with point of view and voice in *All About Eve*, *A Letter to Three Wives* (1949), and *The Barefoot Contessa* is not intriguingly wrought, but no more so than Herman Mankiewicz's and Orson Welles's script for *Citizen Kane* which predates these films, or many other films I discuss in this book. Whatever bifurcations structure *Suddenly, Last Summer* (1959, an adaptation of the Tennessee Williams play), can hardly be credited to Mankiewicz alone. My objections to Deleuze's analysis of the flashback are not limited to these minor points; his application of Bergson to film temporarily is challenging and significant, but the short section on the flashback is disappointing, since with the exception of this problematic lauding of Joseph Mankiewicz and a one paragraph treatment of Marcel Carné's *Le Jour se lève* (1939), he doesn't pay much attention to the device, due to the "l'insuffisance du flash-back par rapport à l'image-souvenir" (the insufficiency of the flashback in relationship to the "memory image" in Bergson; my translation). He attempts to disassociate the rearrangement of filmic temporality in Resnais from the technique of the flashback to avoid contradicting his earlier negative view of the technique, whereas my own analysis of Resnais's work sees important inscriptions and variations on the flashback as central to his modernism.

29.   The original script from 1949 presented this conceit of the narrating corpse much more literally and elaborately. When Gillis's corpse is placed among the other recently deceased bodies at the Los Angeles County morgue, he finds them all exchanging accounts of their deaths. The original version is more maudlin than the tighter one that was finally filmed, but even the revision, brilliantly shot though it was, was criticized at the time of its release as "a device completely unworthy of Brackett and Wilder" in *The New York Times* review, Aug. 11, 1950, by Thomas M. Pryor.

30.   See Robert Aldrich's *The Legend of Lylah Clare* (1968) for a more contemporary flashback treatment of the decadence of Hollywood, one that is less partial and less compromised (as well as more exploitative of the perversity of the mythic scene). The intriguing aspect of the flashbacks in Aldrich's film is the superimposition of the present teller in the corner of the frame as a modernist adaptation of an early cinematic technique.

31.   Recall the discussion of this in chapter one.

32.   Bosley Crowther, *New York Times,* February 20, 1942.

Chapter Five: Flashbacks and the Psyche in Melodrama and Film Noir

1.   Elizabeth Strebel, "Jean Renoir and the Popular Front," *Feature Films as History,* ed. K. R. M. Short (Knoxville, Tennessee: University of Tennessee, 1981).

2.   Strebel, "Jean Renoir and the Popular Front."

3.   This intertitle was added at the insistence of the producers to aid viewers in following the flashback structure, according to the annotated script of *Le Jour se lève* published in *l'Avant-scène du cinéma,*

1965. It is absent from prints distributed in the United Kingdom. The English translation of the script by Dinah Brooke and Nicola Hayden is published as *Le Jour se lève* (New York: Simon and Schuster, 1970).

4. Bosley Crowther, review under the American release title *Daybreak, New York Times,* July 30, 1940.

5. Francis Ponge, *Le Parti pris des choses* (Paris: Editions Gallimard, 1944).

6. See the contemporaneous reviews of *Le Jour se lève* published in excerpted form in *L'Avant-scène du cinéma,* 1965.

7. See Diane Waldman, "Horror and Domesticity: The Modern Gothic Romance Film of the 1940's," unpublished Ph.D. dissertation, University of Wisconsin, 1981, for a discussion of the historical dimension of the popularity of explicit psychoanalytic narratives and her "At Last I can Tell Someone: Feminine Point of View and Subjectivity in the Gothic Romance Film of the 1940's," *Cinema Journal,* vol. 23 (1984), pp. 29–40.

8. For an historical overview of the home-front period and its relationship to film narrative see Dana Polan, *Power and Paranoia: History, Ideology and the American Cinema* (New York: Columbia University Press, 1986); Michael Renov, "Hollywood's Wartime Woman: A Study of Historical/Ideological Determination" (Ann Arbor: UMI Press, 1987); and Andrea Walsh, *Women's Film and Female Experience, 1940–50* (New York: Praeger, 1984).

9. Nicholas Abraham and Maria Torok, *Cryptonomie: Le Verbier de l'homme aux loups,* preceded by "Fors" by Jacques Derrida (Paris: Aubier-Flammarion, 1976).

10. Review of *The Locket, Time Magazine,* February 3, 1947.

11. Freud, *Interpretation of Dreams,* trans. James Strachey (New York: Avon, 1965), pp. 389–94. On page 389 he states, "Boxes, cases chests, cupboards and ovens represent the uterus and also hollow objects of all kinds. Rooms in dreams are usually women; if the various ways in and out of them are represented, this interpretation is scarcely open to doubt. In this connection interest in whether the room is open or locked is easily intelligible." The emphasis on the lock is intriguing for the locket as symbol.

12. See the discussion of equivocation in Roland Barthes, chapter one.

13. Abraham and Torok, *Cryptonomie.*

14. See Michael Renov, "*Leave Her to Heaven:* the Double Bind of the Post-war Woman," *Journal of the University Film and Video Association,* vol. 35 (1983), pp. 28–36.

15. See Stephen Heath's discussion of *Letter From an Unknown Woman* in his essay, "The Question Oshima," pp. 145–64 in *Questions of Cinema* (Bloomington, Indiana: Indiana University Press, 1981), in which he presents the film as a model of a Hollywoodian positioning of women in relationship to desire. Teresa de Lauretis cites Heath and takes up his argument in her book, *Alice Doesn't: Feminism, Semiotics, Cinema* (Bloomington: Indiana University Press, 1984).

16. See Heath and De Lauretis cited above. Heath's reading of *Letter From an Unknown Woman* is also Lacanian and in this respect my point is similar to his argument. However, I see in Zweig's work a literary presentation of psychoanalytical concepts that is far from naive; but rather is one of those examples of fictional narratives that describe principles which psychoanalysis comes to by other means. The irony of the writing of the letter is left out of Heath's account, as is the novelistic source.

17. Kristin Thompson, "The Duplicitous Text: An Analysis of *Stage Fright,*" *Film Reader,* no. 2 (Winter, 1976/77). See also Richard Abel, "*Stage Fright:* The Knowing Performance," *Film Criticism,* vol. 9, no. 2 (Winter 1984–85), pp. 41–50.

18. See my discussion of Barthes's notion of how details cited by a text produce an effect of reality in chapter one. In a more general sense, Christian Metz's discussion of the illusion of reality in cinema explains why cinematic expression elicits greater belief than narrative forms that don't reinforce their enunciation by mimicking perceptual reality.

19.   See Otto Rank, *The Don Juan Legend,* trans. David Winter (Princeton: Princeton University Press, 1975), pp. 58–59. An interesting, but less theoretical discussion of the double occurs in François de la Bretaeque, "La structure du double dans le mélodrame," *Les Cahiers de la Cinémathèque,* n. 28 (1979), pp. 104–09.

20.   See Francis Guerif, *Le Film noir américain* (Paris: Henri Veyrier, 1979); Foster Hirsh, *The Dark Side of the Screen: Film Noir* (New York: A. S. Barnes, 1981); Raymond Borde and Etienne Chaumeton, *Panorama du film noir américain* (Paris: Editions du Minuit, 1955); Amir Karimi, *Toward a Definition of American Film Noir (1941–49)* (New York: Arno Press, 1976).

21.   Sigmund Freud, *Beyond the Pleasure Principle* (New York: W. W. Norton, 1961).

22.   Freud, *Beyond the Pleasure Principle,* pp. 15–16.

23.   Jean Laplanche and J.-B. Pontalis, *The Language of Psychoanalysis* (New York and London: W. W. Norton, 1973).

24.   Karen Horney, *New Ways in Psychoanalysis* (New York: W. W. Norton, 1939).

25.   Karen Horney, *The Neurotic Personality in our Time* (New York: W. W. Norton, 1937).

26.   See Pierre Klossowski, "Nietzsche's Experience of the Eternal Return," Gilles Deleuze, "Active and Reactive," and "Nomad Thought," and Maurice Blanchot, "The Limits of Experience: Nihilism," in *The New Nietzsche,* ed. David Allison (New York: Dell, 1977).

27.   Robert Porfirio, "No Way Out: Existential Motifs in the Film Noir," *Sight and Sound,* Vol. 45 (Autumn 1976), pp. 212–17, discusses the relationship between existentialism and film noir, without making any claims for the influence of philosophical writings on Hollywood productions. Porfirio tends to be vague in his references to actual existential texts. As I indicate in the text, I find the suicidal compulsion evidenced in the film narratives the major point of contact between existential narratives, essay formulations of existential philosophy, and the film narratives; it would be interesting to pursue this intertextuality from a psychoanalytic perspective in greater detail.

28.   Stuart Kaminsky, "Literary Adaptation and Change: *The Killers,* Hemingway, Film Noir and the Terror of Daylight," *American Film Genres* (Dayton, Ohio: Pflaum Publishers, 1974), pp. 43–59.

29.   See, for example, Paul Willeman, *Tourneur* (London, BFI, 1976); Michael Walsh, "Out of the Past," *Enclitic,* double film issue, Vol. 5, no. 5–6 (Fall 1981/Spring 1982); Tania Modleski, "Film Theory's Detour," *Screen,* Vol. 23, no. 5 (1982), pp. 72–79.

30.   Marc Vernet first drew my interest to this film in a brilliant talk he gave on the function of names in *The Enforcer* for a seminar in Paris, 1974.

31.   For a more complete definition of disavowal and for references to Freud's use of the term see Laplanche and Pontalis, *The Language of Psychoanalysis,* pp. 118–21.

32.   Kristin Thompson, "Closure Within a Dream: Point of View in *Laura,*" *Film Reader,* no. 3 (1978), pp. 90–105.

Chapter Six: Disjunction in the Modernist Flashback

1.   For a theoretical discussion of this inversion see Scott Nygren, "Paper Screen: Video Art in Japan," *Journal of Film and Video,* Vol. 39, no. 1 (Winter 1987), pp. 26–34.

2.   Recently American film theory and criticism has reacted against this art cinema and its initial positive reception by certain American critics, partially in defense of the aesthetic merits of Hollywood films, partially to escape the elitism inherent in critically embracing a body of films foreign to American culture and virtually inaccessible to American audiences.

3.   I develop a notion of modernism as a reordering of codes and structures in the first chapter of my book, *Abstraction in Avant-Garde Cinema* (Ann Arbor: UMI Press, 1985).

4. See Wm. Theodore de Bary's forward to Ihara Saikaku, *Five Women who Loved Love* (Rutland, Vermont, and Tokyo: Tuttle, 1956), pp. 13–38.

5. Joseph L. Anderson and Donald Richie, *The Japanese Film: Art and Industry* (Princeton: Princeton University Press, 1982), pp. 163–65. Joan Mellen in *The Waves at Genji's Door: Japan through its Cinema* (New York: Pantheon, 1976), p. 46, discusses a scene which is not in the American print of the film: "Kurosawa shows her, as a child, painting airplanes and locomotives and involved with 'other mechanical things' unlike other girls—suggesting, quite prophetically that a non-sexist educational experience will produce a new kind of woman, one equal to men in every way." From Mellen's description is it possible that this scene is a flashback deleted from some prints and intriguing for its feminist implications. However, Mellen's interpretation of the film seems to force it into a far more radically reminiscent statement than is necessarily evident in the film text.

6. Oshima has remarked in interviews that *No Regrets for our Youth* was a film that inspired him, a favorable remark towards Japanese film history that is rare for this iconoclast.

7. See *Focus on Rashomon*, ed. Donald Richie (Englewood Cliffs, N.J.: Prentice Hall, 1972).

8. Faubion Bowers, *Japanese Theatre* (Rutland, Vermont and Tokyo: Tuttle, 1974), p. 17.

9. There is a British film directed by Anthony Asquith, *The Woman in Question* (1952), which uses five flashbacks to give five different perspectives on a murder. It is a film whose dark and dry sense of humor carries a Hitchcockian tradition to an extreme where the tongue-in-cheek suspense thriller almost defies such categorization. It can be seen as comparable to *Rashomon* in structure, and though its tone does not insist on the same philosophical analysis, there is no reason not to analyze the play of voice in this film just as seriously.

10. *Focus on Rashomon*, ed. Richie.

11. For another detailed examination of the flashbacks in *Ikiru* see Noël Burch, *To the Distant Observer* (Berkeley and Los Angeles: University of California Press, 1979), pp. 301–8. Curiously, Burch's evaluation of *Rashomon* is much lower, as he finds the flashback structure in it "insistently artificial" and "rudimentary," p. 297.

12. A key work is Ulric Neisser, *Cognitive Psychology* (Englewood Cliffs, N.J.: Prentice-Hall, 1967). Neisser divides his subject into three sections, "Visual Cognition," "Auditory Cognition," and the "Higher Mental Processes." More recently, Peter E. Morris and Peter J. Hampson summarize the research through the sixties and seventies on the differences and similarities of verbal and visual memory in *Imagery and Consciousness* (London: Academic Press, 1984), especially pp. 149–72.

13. See the discussion of Münsterberg in chapter two.

14. Neisser, *Cognitive Psychology*, p. 146.

15. Neisser, *Cognitive Psychology*, p. 8.

16. Alan Richardson, *Mental Imagery* (New York: Springer, 1969), pp. 29–42.

17. Richardson, *Mental Imagery*, p. 29.

18. Richardson, *Mental Imagery*, p. 29, cites Heinrich Klüver's citation of the dates of this historical research in "An Experimental Study of the Eidetic Type," *Genetic Psychology Monograph*, 1 (1926), pp. 70–230.

19. Richardson, *Mental Imagery*, p. 40. Much of the research cited by Richardson here took place in the twenties and thirties and while experimental methodology has changed since then, research on eidetic memory has been somewhat dormant until a revival in the sixties. Apparently, some of these findings have not been rigorously reinvestigated.

20. Richardson, *Mental Imagery*, p. 32, cites Erich Jaensch, *Eidetic Imagery* (London: Kegan Paul, 1930); D. M. Purdy, "Eidetic Imagery and Plasticity of Perception," *Journal of General Psychology*, 15

(1936), pp. 437–53; and G. W. Allport, "Eidetic Imagery," *British Journal of Psychology*, 15 (1924), pp. 99–110 on these phenomena.

21.   Heinrich Klüver, "Mescal Visions and Eidetic Vision," *American Journal of Psychology* (1926), and "Mescal: the Divine Plant and its Psychological Effects" (London: Kegan Paul, 1928), and Jaensch, *Eidetic Imagery*.

22.   R. R. Holt, "Imagery: The Return of the Ostracized," *American Psychologist*, no. 12 (1964), pp. 254–64.

23.   As cited in Neisser, *Cognitive Psychology*, pp. 167–70.

24.   Neisser provides a bibliography and an overview of the critiques, *Cognitive Psychology*, p. 169.

25.   Peter E. Morris, *Imagery and Consciousness*.

26.   Claire Clouzot, *La Cinéma depuis la nouvelle vague* (Paris: Fernand Nathan, Alliance Française, 1972).

27.   Godard uses flashbacks in *Le Mépris* (1963), Chabrol in *Violette Nozière* (1978), Truffaut in *L'Histoire de Adèle H.* (1975) and *La Chambre Verte* (1978).

28.   Marguerite Duras, *Hiroshima, mon amour* (New York, Grove Press, 1961), p. 7.

29.   As noted earlier, the structure used by scriptwriter David Mercer for Resnais's 1976 film, *Providence,* is essentially the same as that of Bergman's *Wild Strawberries*.

30.   Resnais is quoted in Robert Benayoun, *Alain Resnais: L'arpenteur de l'imaginaire* (Paris: Stock, 1980), p. 137. Of course, such authorial pronouncements are not necessarily the last word on filmic functioning.

31.   For an historical analysis of this figure of regression and for details of the film's reception in Spain, see Marcel Oms, *Carlos Saura* (Paris: Editions Edilig, 1981), pp. 55–58.

32.   Oms, *Carlos Saura*. The distribution of the film was subject to the mixed attitudes it itself described within its narrative. The film was subjected to post-production censorship after initial pre-production approval, but finally even this secondary censor was revoked and it was shown due to outside influences like the Jury prize at Cannes.

33.   Accounts of the film are sketchy on the actual conditions of the print and script at the time of compilation, assuming the voice-over as authority. See Annette Insdorf, *Indelible Shadows: Films and the Holocaust* (New York: Vintage, 1983), pp. 45–47.

34.   Edward Lewis Wallant, *The Pawnbroker* (New York: Harcourt Brace Jovanovich, 1961), p. 243.

35.   David Denby, "The Enemy Within," *New York Magazine*, March 8, 1982, says "*Circle of Deceit* offers powerful images of war, but no illumination of the conflict—just voyeurism and gloom." Stanley Kauffmann, "Landscapes of War," *The New Republic*, February 17, 1982, sarcastically states, "If you've been confused about the reasons for the horrible civil war in Lebanon, be easy . . . all the bloodshed and destruction have occurred so that Bruno Ganz could have a setting in which to plumb his soul."

36.   The ideology of the film has been discussed from quite different perspectives. See a reading that favors a feminist psychology in a sense doubling the view of the character Juliane, in E. Ann Kaplan, "Female Politics in the Symbolic Realm: Von Trotta's *Marianne and Juliane,*" *Women and Film: Both Sides of the Camera* (New York: Methuen, 1983), pp. 104–12, and "Discourses of Terrorism, Feminism and the Family in Von Trotta's *Marianne and Juliane,*" *Women in Literature,* Carol Fairbanks Meyer, ed. (Metuchen, NJ: Scarecrow Press, 1976). For a view that critiques the film's psychologizing of the political conflict, see Charlotte Delorme, "Zum Film '*Die bleierne Zeit*' von Margarethe Von Trotta, *Frauen und Film,* no. 31 (1982), p. 55. Ellen Seiter presented a paper at the Society for Cinema Studies Conference, 1984, in which she argued for a contextual reading of the film, tempering Kaplan's position with Delorme's German perspective.

37. Parts of this analysis were published in my article, "Rituals, Desire, Death in Oshima's *Ceremonies*," *Enclitic* Double Issue, 5:2/6:1 (Fall 1981/Spring 1982), pp. 181–89.

38. Another intriguing Japanese film that explores history through flashbacks is *Sandakin 8* (Kei Kumei, 1977). Here the flashbacks are more standard in form, but the story from the past is actively sought by a female historian who seeks to learn of the lives of Japanese women who served in brothels in the colonial outposts. This framing by an historian's investigation is similar to the journalist as frame device, but accents the question of historical method and imagination in relationship to oral history.

39. *The Godfather II* was produced as a sequel to *The Godfather* and instead of just continuing on with the second generation of the Corleone family in America, its flashback structure facilitates its "surrounding" the events in the first film, adding events that preceded the first film. *The Godfather II* was, in fact, reedited by Coppola into linear temporal sequence with *The Godfather* for television presentation after its theatrical release, so that the narrative of the history of the Corleone family began in Sicily, showed the future godfather's arrival as a young boy at Ellis Island, etc. If we can believe remarks made in *Time Magazine,* December 16, 1974, p. 74, before the film's original release, the flashback structure of Part II was a compromise, one that Coppola always hoped to straighten out by rearranging the two films in linear temporal order: "It took months to convince Francis Coppola to do another *Godfather* at all. He demanded that it be not a sequel but an extension of the original, which Coppola would embellish considerably. Now he dreams of some day cutting both features together into a single huge family epic."

40. Robles-Godoy used inverted temporal structures in his first film, *En La Selva no Hay Estrellas* (1966) and the subsequent *Espejismo* (1973), but these films have not had the U.S. distribution that *La Muralla Verde* has received. A polemical critique of Robles-Godoy's films is offered by Issac Leon Frias in his chapter on Peruvian film in *Les Cinémas de l'Amérique latine,* Guy Hennebelle and Alfonso Gumucio-Dagron, eds. (Paris: Lherminier, 1981), pp. 431; Frias accuses Robles-Godoy of an "unconvincing" use of spatio-temporal structures "inspired by the experiments of Resnais and other European auteurs" that is "pretentious and inadapted to the conditions of filmmaking in Peru." However, Robles-Godoy spent years homesteading in the manner depicted in the film, and I am willing to grant to his work a more direct attempt to seek spatio-temporal structures that express the dislocations and memories of his perspective as a Peruvian. The phrase "inadapted to the conditions of filmmaking in Peru" seems to indicate the author's imperative for a more direct form of political intervention and certain assumptions concerning the Peruvian audience.

41. See my article, "Childhood Memories and Household Events in the Feminist Avant-Garde," *Journal of Film and Video,* Vo. 38, nos. 3–4 (Summer-Fall 1986).

Bibliography

Abel, Richard. *French Cinema*. Princeton: Princeton University Press, 1985.

—— *"Stage Fright:* The Knowing Performance." *Film Criticism,* vol. 9, no. 2. Winter 1984–85, pp. 41–50.

Abraham, Nicholas and Maria Torok. *Cryptonomie: Le Verbier de l'homme aux loups,* preceded by "Fors" by Jacques Derrida. Paris: Aubier-Flammarion, 1976.

—— *L'Ecorce et le noyau.* Paris: Aubier-Flammarion, 1978.

Abrahms, M. H. *A Glossary of Literary Terms.* New York: Holt, Rinehart and Winston, 1971.

Allport, G. W. "Eidetic Imagery." *British Journal of Psychology,* 15, 1924, pp. 99–110.

Anderson, Joseph L. and Donald Richie. *The Japanese Film: Art and Industry.* Princeton: Princeton University Press, 1982.

Arendt, Hannah. "The Concept of History." *Between Past and Future: Six Exercises in Political Thought.* New York: Viking, 1961.

Azlant, Edward. *The Theory, History and Practice of Screenwriting.* unpublished Ph.D. dissertation, University of Wisconsin-Madison, 1980.

Bachelard, Gaston. *L'Intuition de l'instant.* Paris: Editions Gonthiers, 1972 [c. 1952].

Barthes, Roland. *S/Z.* trans. Richard Miller. New York: Hill and Wang, 1974.

—— *La Chambre Claire: Note sur la photographie.* Paris: Editions de l'étoile, Gallimard, Seuil, 1980.

Bazin, André. *Le Cinéma français de la libération à la nouvelle vague.* Paris: Editions de l'étoile, Gallimard, Seuil, 1980.

—— *What is Cinema?* trans. Hugh Grey. Berkeley: University of California Press, Vol. 1, 1967 and Vol. 2, 1971.

Benayoun, Robert. *Alain Resnais: L'arpenteur de l'imaginaire.* Paris: Stock, 1980.

Bergman, Andrew. *We're in the Money: Depression America and Its Films.* New York: New York University Press, 1971.

Bergson, Henri. *Matière et mémoire.* 46th ed. Paris: Presses Universitaire de France, 1946.

Bernardini, Aldo and Jean Gili, eds. *Le Cinéma italien 1905–1945.* Paris: Editions du Centre Pompidou, 1986.

Bertsch, Marguerite. *How to Write for Moving Pictures: A Manual of Instruction and Information.* New York: George H. Doran Co., 1917.

Blanchot, Maurice. "The Limits of Experience: Nihilism." *The New Nietzsche.* ed. David Allison. New York: Dell, 1977.

Bonitzer, Pascal. *Le Champ Aveugle: Essais sur le cinéma.* Paris: Cahiers du cinéma, Gallimard, 1982.

Borde, Raymond and Etienne Chaumeton. *Panorama du Film Noir Américain*. Paris: Editions du Minuit, 1955.

Borde, Raymond, Freddy Buache, and Francis Courtade. *Le Cinéma réaliste allmand*. Lyon: Serdoc, 1965.

Bordwell, David. "Citizen Kane." *Film Comment*. Summer, 1971.

——— *French Impressionist Cinema*. New York: Arno Press, 1980.

——— *Narration in the Fiction Film*. London: Methuen, 1985.

Bordwell, David and Kristin Thompson. *Film Art: An Introduction*. 2nd ed. New York: Alfred Knopf, 1985.

Bordwell, David, Janet Staiger, and Kristin Thompson. *The Classical Hollywood Cinema: Film Style and Mode of Production to 1960*. New York Columbia University Press, 1985.

Bowers, Faubion. *Japanese Theatre*. Rutland, Vermont, and Tokyo: Tuttle, 1974.

Bronner, Edwin. *The Encyclopedia of the American Theatre, 1900–1975*. San Francisco: A. S. Barnes and Co., 1980.

Branigan, Edward. *Point of View in the Cinema: A Theory of Narration and Subjectivity in Classical Film*. New York: Mouton, 1984.

Braudel, Fernand. *Ecrits sur l'histoire*. Paris: Flammarion, 1969.

Brée, Germaine. *Marcel Proust and the Deliverance from Time*. New York: Evergreen, 1955.

Burch, Noel. *Marcel l'Herbier*. Paris: Editions Seghers, 1973.

——— "Porter or Ambivalence." *Screen*, Winter 1978/79, pp. 91–105.

——— *To the Distant Observer: Form and Meaning in Japanese Cinema*. Berkeley and Los Angeles: University of California Press, 1979.

Canudo, Ricciotto. "L'art pour le septième art." *Cinéa*, 2, 13 May, 1921.

——— "Manifestes des sept arts." *Gazette des sept arts*, 25 Jan., 1923.

Champigny, Robert. "Proust, Bergson and other Philosophers," in *Proust: A Collection of Critical Essays*, ed. René Girard. Englewood Cliffs, New Jersey: Prentice Hall, 1962, pp. 122–31.

Chion, Michel. *Ecrire une Scénario*. Paris: Cahiers du cinéma, INA, 1985.

Christianson, Peter. "Levels of the Fantastic in Sjöström's *The Phantom Chariot*." paper delivered at the annual meeting of the Society for Cinema Studies, 1983.

Cinématographe, special issue devoted to the flashback, February 1984.

Clouzot, Claire. *Le Cinéma Français depuis la nouvelle vague*. Paris: Fernand Nathan, Alliance Française, 1972.

Cohen, Keith. *Film and Fiction: Dynamics of an Exchange*. New Haven: Yale University Press, 1979.

Cohen, Robert. "A Japanese Romantic: Teinosuke Kinugasa." *Sight and Sound*, vol. 45, Summer, 1976.

Cohn, Dorrit. *Transparent Minds: Narrative Modes for Presenting Consciousness in Fiction*. Princeton, New Jersey: Princeton University Press, 1981.

Collingwood, R. G. *The Idea of History*. Oxford: Oxford University Press, 1946.

Comolli, Jean-Louis. "Technique et idéologie." *Cahiers du cinéma*, no. 229, May 1971, pp. 4–21; no. 230, July 1971, pp. 51–57; no. 231, Aug.–Sept. 1971; no. 233, Nov. 1971, pp. 39–45; nos. 234–35, Dec. 1971, Jan.–Feb. 1972, pp. 94–100; and no. 241, Sept.–Oct. 1972, pp. 20–24.

Cook, David. *A History of Narrative Film*. New York and London: Norton, 1981.

Danto, Arthur. "Laws and Explanations in History." *Philosophy of Science*, vol. 23, 1956.

de Bary, Wm. Theodore. Forward to Ihara Saikaku. *Five Women who Loved Love*. Rutland, Vermont, and Tokyo: Tuttle, 1956, pp. 13–38.

de Chevalier and Boyer. "De l'image a l'hallucination." *Journal de psychologie*, 15 April 1926.

de la Bretaeque, François. "La structure du double dans le mélodrame." *Les Cahiers de la Cinémathèque*, no. 28, 1979, pp. 104–9.

de Lauretis, Teresa. *Alice Doesn't: Feminism, Semiotics, Cinema*. Bloomington: Indiana University Press, 1984.

Deleuze, Gilles. *Le Bergsonisme*. Paris: Presses Universitaires de France, 1966.

——— *Cinéma I: Image-Mouvement*. Paris: Editions de Minuit, 1983.

——— *Cinéma II: Image-Temps*. Paris: Editions de Minuit, 1985.

——— *Difference et répétition*. Paris: Presses Universitaires de France, 1969.

——— *Marcel Proust et les signes*. Paris: Presses Universitaires de France, 1970.

——— *Nietzsche et la philosophie*. Paris: Presses Universitaires de France, 1962. trans. of "Active and Reactive" and "Nomad Thought" in *The New Nietzsche*. ed. David Allison. New York: Dell, 1977.

Delluc, Louis. *Photogénie*. Paris: Editions Bunoff, 1920.

——— *Drames du cinéma*. Paris: Editions du Monde nouveau, 1923.

Delorme, Charlotte. "Zum Film '*Die bleirne Zeit*' von Margarethe Von Trotta. *Frauen und Film*, no. 31, 1982, p. 55.

Dench, Ernest A. *Playwriting for the Cinema: Dealing with the Writing and Marketing of Scenarios*. London: Adam and Charles Black, 1914.

Derrida, Jacques. *De la Grammatologie*. Paris: Editions de Minuit, 1967.

——— *Ecriture et la différance*. Paris: Seuil, 1967.

——— *Glas*. Paris: Editions Denoël/Gonthier, 1981.

Dimick, Howard. *Modern Photoplay Writing*. Franklin, Ohio: James Knapp Reeve, 1922.

Doane, Mary Ann. *The Desire to Desire: The Woman's Film of the 1940s*. Bloomington: Indiana University Press, 1987.

Douin, Jean-Luc, ed. *La nouvelle vague 25 ans âpres*. Paris: Les Editions du Cerf, 1983.

Duras, Marguerite. *Hiroshima, mon amour*. Paris: Gallimard. 1960. trans. New York: Grove Press, 1961.

——— *India Song*. Paris: Gallimard, 1960. trans. Barbara Bray. New York: Grove Press, 1976.

Eisenstein, Sergei. "Dickens, Griffith and the Film Today." *Film Form*. trans. Jay Leyda. New York: Harcourt and Brace, 1969.

——— *Film Essays*. trans. Jay Leyda. New York: Praeger, 1970.

Eisner, Lotte. *The Haunted Screen*. Berkeley and Los Angeles: University of California Press, 1969.

Eizykman, Claudine. *La Jouissance-cinéma*. Paris: Union générale d'éditions, 1976.

Faure, Elie. *Fonction du cinéma*. Paris: Editions Gonthier, 1964.

Fell, John. *Film and the Narrative Tradition*. Norman, Oklahoma: University of Oklahoma Press, 1974.

Flitterman, Sandy. "*La Maternelle*." *Enclitic*, vol. 5, nos. 5–6, Fall 1981/Spring 1982.

Foucault, Michel. *Les Mots et les choses*. Paris: Gallimard, 1966, trans. as *The Order of Things*. New York: Vintage, 1970.

——— *The Archaeology of Knowledge*. trans. A. M. Sheridan Smith. New York: Pantheon, 1972.

Freud, Sigmund. *Beyond the Pleasure Principle*. New York: W. W. Norton, 1961.

—— "Delusions and Dreams in Jensen's *Gradiva*" (1907). *The Standard Edition of the Complete Psychological Works of Sigmund Freud,* vol. 9. trans. and ed. James Strachey. London: Hogarth Press, 1953, pp. 3–98.

—— *The Interpretation of Dreams.* trans. James Strachey. New York: Avon, 1965 and Bantam, 1969.

—— "Notes on the Mystic Writing Pad." *The Standard Edition,* vol. 19, pp. 227–234.

—— "The Occurrence in Dreams of Material from Fairy Tales" (1913). *The Standard Edition,* vol. 12. pp. 279–88.

—— "The Uncanny" (1919). *The Standard Edition,* vol. 17. pp. 219–56.

Frias, Issac Leon. "Peruvian film." *Les Cinémas de l'Amérique latine.* eds. Guy Hennebelle and Alfonso Gumucio-Dagron. Paris: Lherminier, 1981.

Gardiner, Patrick, ed. *Theories of History.* New York: Fress Press, 1959.

Gaudrault, André, ed. *Cinéma 1900–1906.* Vol. 2. Brussels: FIAF, 1982.

Gaudrault, André. "Narrativité et Temporalité: Le Cinéma des premiers temps (1895–1908)." *Etudes Littéraires,* vol. 13, no. 1, April 1980, pp. 109–39.

—— "Narration et monstration au cinéma." *Hors Cadre,* vol. 2, 1984, pp. 87–98.

—— "Récit singulatif, récit itératif: Au bagne." *Les Premiers ans du cinéma français.* Perpignan: Institut Jean Vigo, 1985.

Genette, Gérard. *Figures I.* Paris: Editions du Seuil, 1966.

—— *Figures II.* Paris: Editions du Seuil, 1969.

—— *Figures III.* Paris: Editions du Seuil, 1972.

Girard, René, ed. *Proust: A Collection of Critical Essays.* Englewood Cliffs, New Jersey: Prentice-Hall, 1962.

Guerif, Francis. *Le Film Noir Americain.* Paris: Henri Veyrier, 1979.

Guex, Germaine. *La nevrose d'abandon.* Paris: Presses Universitaires de France, 1950.

Gunning, Tom. "The non-Continuous Style of Early Film 1900–1906." in *Cinéma 1900–1906,* Vol. 1. ed. Roger Holman. Brussels: FIAF, 1982.

—— "Early Development in Film Narrative: D. W. Griffith's First Films at Biograph (1908–1909)." unpublished Ph.D. dissertation, New York University, 1986.

Heath, Stephen. *Questions of Cinema.* Bloomington: Indiana University Press, 1981.

Hermann, Lewis. *A Practical Manual of Screenwriting for Theater and Television Films.* New York: Meridian, 1952.

Hirsh, Foster. *The Dark Side of the Screen: Film Noir.* New York: A. S. Barnes, 1981.

Höffding, Harald. *La Philosophie de Bergson.* Paris: Felix Alcan, 1917.

Holt, R. R. "Imagery: The Return of the Ostracized." *American Psychologist,* no. 12, 1964, pp. 254–64.

Horney, Karen. *New Ways in Psychoanalysis.* New York: W. W. Norton, 1939.

—— *The Neurotic Personality in our Time.* New York: W. W. Norton, 1937.

Insdorf, Annette. *Indelible Shadows: Films and the Holocaust.* New York: Vintage, 1983.

Jaensch, Erich. *Eidetic Imagery.* London: Kegan Paul, 1930.

Jameson, Fredric. *The Political Unconscious: Narrative as a Socially Symbolic Act.* Ithaca: Cornell University Press, 1981.

Janet, Pierre. "L'évolution de la mémoire et la notion de temps." Paris: A. Cahine, 1928.

Jeanne, René and Charles Ford. *Histoire encyclopédique du cinéma*. Vol. 1: *Le Cinéma français 1895–1929*. Paris: Robert Laffont, 1947.

Jost, Francis. "Discours cinématographique, narration: deux façons d'envisager le problème de l'énonciation." *Théorie du film*. ed. Jean-Louis Leutréat and Jacques Aumont. Paris: Editions Albatros, 1980, pp. 121–31.

Kael, Pauline. *The Citizen Kane Book*. Boston: Little, Brown and Co, 1971.

Kaplan, E. Ann. "The Search for the Mother/Land in Sanders-Brahm's *Germany Pale Mother*." In *German Film and Literature: Adaptations and Transformations*. ed. Eric Rentschler. New York and London: Methuen, 1986.

——— *Women and Film: Both Sides of the Camera*. New York: Methuen, 1983.

Karimi, Amir. *Toward a Definition of American Film Noir (1941–49)*. New York: Arno Press, 1976.

Kaminsky, Stuart. "Literary Adaptation and Change: *The Killers*, Hemingway, Film Noir and the Terror of Daylight." *American Film Genres*. Dayton, Ohio: Pflaum Publishers, 1974. pp. 43–59.

Kawin, Bruce. *Mindscreen: Bergman, Godard and First-Person Film*. Princeton: Princeton University Press, 1978.

——— *Telling it Again and Again: Repetition in Film and Literature*. Ithaca and London: Cornell University Press, 1972.

Klossowski, Pierre. "Nietzsche's Experience of the Eternal Return." In *The New Nietzsche*. ed. David Allison. New York: Dell, 1977.

Klüver, Heinrich. "An Experimental Study of the Eidetic Type." *Genetic Psychology Monograph*, 1, 1926, pp. 70–230.

——— "Mescal Visions and Eidetic Vision." *American Journal of Psychology*, 1926.

——— "Mescal: the Divine Plant and its Psychological Effects." London: Kegan Paul, 1928.

Kracauer, Siegfried. *From Caligari to Hitler: A Psychological History of the German Film*. Princeton: Princeton University Press, 1947.

——— *Theory of Film: The Redemption of Physical Reality*. London and Oxford: Oxford University Press, 1960.

Kuhn, Annette. *Women's Pictures: Feminism and Cinema*. London and New York: Routledge and Kegan Paul, 1982.

Lacoste, Patrick. "Chambre à part: Mystères d'une chose visuelle." *Nouvelle Revue de Psychanalyse*, no. 29, Spring 1984, pp. 221–48.

Laffay, Albert. *Logique du cinéma*. Paris: Masson, 1964.

Lanser, Susan Sniader. *The Narrative Act: Point of View in Prose Fiction*. Princeton: Princeton University Press, 1981.

Laplanche, Jean and J.-B. Pontalis. *The Language of Psychoanalysis*. New York and London: Norton, 1973.

Lagny, Michèle, Marie-Claire Ropars, and Pierre Sorlin. "Le récit saisi par le film." *Hors Cadre*, no. 2, 1984, pp. 99–124.

Macherey, Pierre. *Pour une théorie de la production littéraire*. Paris: Maspero, 1970.

Mandelbaum, Maurice. *The Problem of Historical Knowledge: An Answer to Relativism*. New York: Liveright, 1938.

Marion, Denis. *Ingmar Bergman*. Paris: Gallimard, 1979.

Mellen, Joan. *The Waves at Genji's Door: Japan through its Cinema*. New York: Pantheon, 1976.

Metz, Christian. *Essais sur la signification au cinéma*. Vol. 1. Paris: Klincksieck, 1968.

———— *Essais sur la signification au cinéma*. Vol. 2. Paris: Klinksieck, 1973.

———— *Langage et cinéma*. Paris: Librairie Larousse, 1971.

———— *Le Signifiant imaginaire*. Paris: Union générale d'éditions, 1977. trans. as *The Imaginary Signifier: Psychoanalysis and the Cinema*, trans. by Celia Britton, Annwyl Williams, Ben Brewster, and Alfred Guzetti. Bloomington: Indiana University Press, 1977.

Meyer, Carol Fairbanks, ed. *Women in Literature*. Metuchen, New Jersey: Scarecrow Press, 1976.

Mitry, Jean. *Esthéthique et psychologie du cinéma*. 2 vols. Paris: Editions Universitaires, 1963 and 1965.

———— *Histoire du cinéma*. Vol. 2 and Vol. 3. Paris: Editions Universitaires, 1969 and 1973.

Modleski, Tania. "Film Theory's Detour." *Screen*, vol. 23, no. 5, 1982, pp. 72–79.

Morris, Peter E. and Peter J. Hampson. *Imagery and Consciousness*. London: Academic Press, 1984.

Moussinac, Leon. *Naissance du cinéma*. Paris: Pavlovsky, 1925.

Münsterberg, Hugo. *The Psychology of the Photoplay*. New York: D. Appleton and Co., 1916. reissued as *The Film: A Psychological Study: The Silent Photoplay in 1916*. New York: Dover, 1970.

Neisser, Ulric. *Cognition and Reality: Principles and Implications of Cognitive Psychology*. San Francisco: Freeman, 1976.

———— *Cognitive Psychology*. Englewood Cliffs, New Jersey: Prentice-Hall, 1967.

Niver, Kemp R. *The First Twenty Years: A Segment of Film History*. Los Angeles: Locare Research Group, 1968.

Nygren, Scott. "Paper Screen: Video Art in Japan." *Journal of Film and Video*, vol. 39, no. 1, Winter, 1987, pp. 26–34.

Oms, Marcel. *Carlos Saura*. Paris: Editions Edilig, 1981.

Polan, Dana. *Power and Paranoia: History, Ideology and the American Cinema*. New York: Columbia University Press, 1986.

Ponge, Francis. *Le Parti pris des choses*. Paris: Editions Gallimard, 1944.

Porfirio, Robert. "No Way Out: Existential Motifs in the Film Noir." *Sight and Sound*, vol. 45, Autumn 1976, pp. 212–17.

Prédal, René. *Le Cinéma français contemporain*. Paris: Les Editions du Cerf, 1984.

Proust, Marcel. *A la Recherche du temps perdu*. Paris: Gallimard, 1954.

———— *La Temps*, November 13, 1913, p. 4.

Purdy, D. M. "Eidetic Imagery and Plasticity of Perception." *Journal of General Psychology*, 15, 1936, pp. 437–53.

Quercy. "Sur une théorie bergsonienne de l'imagination." *Annales medico psychologique*, 1925.

Rank, Otto. *The Don Juan Legend*. trans. David Winter. Princeton: Princeton University Press, 1975.

Renov, Michael. "Hollywood's Wartime Woman: A Study of Historical/Ideological Determination." Ann Arbor: UMI Press, 1987.

———— "*Leave Her to Heaven:* the Double Bind of the Post-war Woman." *Journal of the University Film and Video Association*, vol. 35, 1983, pp. 28–36.

Richardson, Alan. *Mental Imagery*. New York: Springer, 1969.

Richie, Donald, ed. *Focus on Rashomon*. Englewood Cliffs, New Jersey: Prentice-Hall, 1972.

Ricoeur, Paul. *Time and Narrative*, Vols. 1–3. trans. Kathleen Maclauglin and David Pellauer. Chicago and London: University of Chicago Press, 1984.

Ropars, Marie-Claire. *De la Littérature au cinéma*. Paris: Colin, 1970.

——— *Le Texte divisé*. Paris: Presses Universitaires de France, 1981.

Sadoul, Georges. *Chroniques du cinéma français*. Paris: Union générale d'éditions, 1979.

——— *Le Cinéma français*. Paris: Flammarion, 1962.

Salt, Barry. *Film Style and Technology: History and Analysis*. London: Starwood, 1983.

Sargent, Epes Winthrop. *Technique of the Photoplay*. New York: Chalmers, 1912.

Sartre, Jean-Paul. *L'imagination*. Paris: Presses Universitaires de France, 1936.

Schorske, Carl. *Fin-de-Siècle Vienna: Politics and Culture*. New York: Knopf, 1980.

Shklovsky, Victor. "On the Connection Between Devices of *Syuzhet* Construction to General Stylistic Devices." trans. Jane Knox. *20th Century Studies*, 7/8, December, 1972, p. 54.

Strebel, Elizabeth. "Jean Renoir and the Popular Front." *Feature Films as History*. ed. K. R. M. Short. Knoxville, Tennessee: University of Tennessee, 1981.

Thibaudet, Albert. "Le Bergsonisme," 2 vols. Paris: NRF, 1922.

Thompson, Kristin. "Closure Within a Dream: Point of View in *Laura*." *Film Reader*, no. 3, 1978, pp. 90–105.

——— "The Duplicitous Text: An Analysis of *Stage Fright*." *Film Reader*, no. 2, Winter, 1976/77.

——— *Ivan the Terrible: A Neoformalist analysis*. Princeton: Princeton University Press, 1981.

Tomashevsky, Boris. "Thematics." *Russian Formalist Criticism: Four Essays*. eds. Lee Lemon and Marion Reis. Lincoln, Nebraska: University of Nebraska Press, 1965, pp. 78–85.

Toulet, Emanuelle. "Le Cinéma muet italien et la critique française." *Le Cinéma italien 1905–1945*. ed. Aldo Bernardini and Jean Gili. Paris: Editions du Centre Pompidou, 1986.

Turim, Maureen. *Abstraction in Avant-Garde Cinema*. Ann Arbor: UMI Press, 1985.

——— "Childhood Memories and Household Events in the Feminist Avant-Garde." *Journal of Film and Video*, vol. 38, nos. 3–4, Summer-Fall, 1986.

——— "Fictive Psyches: The Psychological Melodrama in 40's Films." *Boundary II*, Spring/Fall, 1984.

——— "French Melodrama: Theory of a Specific History." *Theatre Journal*, vol. 39, no. 3, Oct. 1987, pp. 307–27.

——— "*Le Jour se lève:* Poetic Realism as Psychoanalytical and Ideological Operation." In *French Film in Context*, ed. Susan Hayward and Ginette Vincendeau. London: Routledge, forthcoming.

——— "Rituals, Desire, Death in Oshima's *Ceremonies*." *Enclitic*, 5:2/6:1, Fall 1981/Spring 1982, pp. 181–89.

Tynianov, Yuri. "Plot and Story-line in the Cinema." *Russian Poetics in Translation*, 5, 1978.

Vardac, A. Nicholas. *Stage to Screen: Theatrical Method from Garrick to Griffith*. 1949; New York: B. Blom, 1968.

Vernet, Marc. "Le Flashback," entry in *Lectures du Film*. ed. Jean Collet, Michel Marie, Daniel Percheron, and Marc Vernet. Paris: Editions Albatros, 1976, pp. 96–99.

——— "Narrateur, personnage et spectateur dans le film de fiction à travers le film noir." unpublished Ph.D. dissertation, L'Ecole des Hautes Etudes, 1985.

Waldmand, Diane. "Horror and Domesticity: The Modern Gothic Romance Film of the 1940's." unpublished Ph.D. dissertation, University of Wisconsin, 1981.

——— "At Last I can Tell Someone: Feminine Point of View and Subjectivity in the Gothic Romance Film of the 1940's." *Cinema Journal*, vol. 23, 1984, pp. 29–40.

Walsh, Andrea. *Women's Film and Female Experience, 1940–50*. New York: Praeger, 1984.

Walsh, Michael. "Out of the Past." *Enclitic*, vol. 5, nos. 5–6, Fall 1981/Spring 1982.

Wagenknecht, Edward. *Movies in the Age of Innocence*. Norman, Oklahoma: University of Oklahoma Press, 1962.

Wessles, Michael G. *Cognitive Psychology*. New York: Harper and Row, 1982.

Willeman, Paul. *Tourneur*. London: BFI, 1976.

Index